The CASSELL
Dictionary of Anecdotes

The CASSELL
Dictionary of Anecdotes

Nigel Rees

CASSELL

This edition first published in the UK 1999 by
Cassell
Wellington House
125 Strand
London WC2R 0BB

Distributed in the United States
by Sterling Publishing Co. Inc.
387 Park Avenue South,
New York, NY 10016–8810

British Library Cataloguing-in-Publication Data
A catalogue record for this book is available
from the British Library

ISBN 0-304-35195-4

Designed and typeset by Tim Higgins

Printed and bound in Great Britain
by MPG Books Ltd, Bodmin, Cornwall

They are the abstract and brief chronicles of the time. After your death you were better have a bad epitaph than their ill report while you live.

William Shakespeare, *Hamlet* (1600)

Fasionable fax and polite annygoats.

William Thackeray – attributed in G. W. E. Russell, *Collections and Recollections* (1898)

Among my earliest literary friends, two distinguished themselves by their anecdotical literature: James Petit Andrews, by his *Anecdotes, Ancient and Modern*, and William Seward, by his *Anecdotes of Distinguished Persons*. These volumes were favourably received, and to such a degree that a wit of that day, and who is still a wit as well as poet, considered that we were far gone in our 'Anecdotage'.

Isaac Disraeli, *Curiosities of Literature* (1839). The wit may have been De Quincey, who used the word in 1823.

When a man fell into his anecdotage it was a sign for him to retire from the world.

Mr Pinto, in Benjamin Disraeli's *Lothair* (1870)

Contents

Introduction

Just recently, when I was reading what was billed as an *anecdote* book, I discovered that it was what I would have described, rather, as a *joke* book. So there is a difference? Yes.

In fact, as part of my continuing efforts to define what we mean by an anecdote, I would say that what really constitutes an anecdote is *a joke involving actual people*. This definition has the benefit of implying several things: that an anecdote is a brief tale; that it is most probably a funny tale; and, above all, that it derives its point from the fact that it is about real people and real life. Indeed, it is usually a tale involving named people.

The fact that it is a 'tale' or a 'story' conveniently gets over the question of whether it is true or not. I doubt whether very many anecdotes are literally true at all, but they usually contain a grain of truth, and that is why they get told and re-told. Indeed, as I have argued before, even if an anecdote is totally without foundation, the very fact that it has entered circulation at all is significant. By attempting to say something about a particular person or about a type of person, it betrays a need so to do. This, in turn, tells us something about the way particular people are perceived.

In this book, if the 'story' does not involve real people, then it is not an anecdote.

Having said which, however, I am sure that there are quite a few examples in this collection of a joke or story being attached to actual people – indeed being attached, detached, and re-attached to actual people over the years. But, again, the fact that this has occurred, tells us at least something about those people.

It is my belief that an anecdote, being a 'brief chronicle', can often say more about a person than pages of biography or history. The fact that it may be about a small incident or act in that person's life relates to my view that it is often the trivia of life, rather than the major events, that can more readily evoke a personality or period.

There are one or two anecdotes from history – Canute and the waves, Drake playing bowls before the Armada, Henry II wondering out loud who will rid him of Thomas Becket – that are, in their way, significant historical incidents. But as with Alfred and the cakes, they are small enough encapsulations (vignettes, if you like) of more grandiose matters to be considered as anecdotes.

I must also address myself to the difference between anecdotes and quotations. Much of the material in this dictionary has come my way from guests on, and listeners to, my BBC Radio programme *Quote … Unquote* over the past quarter century. Latterly, the phrase 'quotes and anecdotes' has crept into the programme's billing. This is because, in presenting a quotation, a little story is often told about the circumstances in which it was said (or written), and a humorous context or pretext is given. In the opposite direction, when an anecdote is told, it is often the case that the climax of the story involves the speaking of a memorable group of words. So, what I am saying is, an anecdote should not just consist of a quotable line – however quotable that may be. The line should be uttered in a particular situation that makes it unusually significant or pertinent or especially amusing.

Inevitably, there will be cases where I have completely ignored the guidelines that I have laid down here. Sometimes the urge to relate a good story – or, indeed, joke – may have made me backslide. But do I need to apologize for that?

The point of an anecdote may be hard to pinpoint. It may reflect an aspect of human nature or just a particular person's quirk. The material in this dictionary has, however, been grouped under keyword headings according to what is thought to be the main point of each anecdote. Additionally, at the end of the dictionary there is a keyword index where anecdotes may be traced through other keywords, including names of participants.

Finally, I should like to give a big thank-you to all the friends and correspondents who have communicated anecdotes to me over the years. Whether or not their names also appear in the text of this dictionary, I should mention especially: Glyn Allen; Douglas J. Bolger; Jonathan Cecil; John Clarke; Bill Cotton; Noël Currer-Briggs; Patrick Daly; Charles G. Francis, IdeaBank®, New York; Timothy Halstead; Roger Hammond; the late Sir David Hunt; Antony Jay; Anthony Lejeune; Ivan Marinov; Peter Marriott; Michael and Valerie Grosvenor Myer; Raymond C. H. Morgan; the late Frank Muir; Sylvia Nash; Denis Norden; Peter L. Norman; John O'Byrne; John Patrick; Derek Parker; Brian A. Robinson; Derek Robinson; John Rushby-Smith; Dr Mario Sica; Robert O. Skovgard, *The Executive Speaker*®, Dayton, Ohio; Muriel Smith; J. R. Tardif; Alison Thorne; Michel Vercambre; Bill Watts; Ean Wood.

Nigel Rees
London, May 1999

The Dictionary

Abortion

1 One doctor consulted another because he wished to have the other doctor's opinion on the termination of a pregnancy. The circumstances were as follows. The father was syphilitic, and the mother tuberculous. Of the children that had already been born the first was blind, the second had died, the third was deaf and dumb, the fourth was tuberculous. 'What would you have done?' the first doctor asked his colleague. 'I would have ended the pregnancy,' replied the second. Said the first: 'Then you would have murdered Beethoven.'

A story told by Maurice Baring and quoted by Enid Bagnold in *The Times* (14 November 1962). Bagnold had been a neighbour of Baring's when he lived at Rottingdean in Sussex.

Absence

2 When Trevor Nunn was sole artistic director and chief executive of the Royal Shakespeare Company in Stratford-upon-Avon and in London, it seemed to be the case that he absented himself frequently to work in the commercial theatre (directing the musical *Cats* and the like). It was said that some RSC actors began to pine for their leader's presence. One of them even suggested that they should write to the TV show *Jim'll Fix It* and see if it's eponymous host, Jimmy Savile, could possibly arrange a meeting ...

Nunn is not very fond of this story. Indeed, he wrote at length to the *Independent* Magazine (26 June 1993) trying to establish the correct facts. According to his version, an actor 'friend' of his had, indeed, joked about making contact through the good offices of Jimmy Savile on an occasion when Nunn was absent from a company meeting. But – Nunn protested – this was during the period when he was *joint* artistic director of the RSC and entitled to work elsewhere for three months of each year.

Absent-mindedness

3 Archbishop Richard Chenevix Trench (1807–86) retired from the see of Dublin and spent his last two years in London. On returning to visit his successor Lord Plunkett, in Dublin, his memory lapsed and he forgot that he was no longer host, remarking to his wife: 'I'm afraid, my love, that we must put this cook down among our failures.'

Told in *The Monarch Book of Christian Wisdom*, ed. Robert Paterson (1997).

4 The utterly distinguished Justice Oliver Wendell Holmes Jr (1841–1935) once boarded a train in Washington DC but

soon found out that he had lost his ticket. The conductor recognized him and said, 'Don't worry about it, sir. I'm sure when you find it, you'll send it in.'

Justice Holmes replied: 'Young man, the question is not, Where is my ticket?, but rather, without it, how am I supposed to know where I am going?'

Source untraced. The story is also told about Ambassador Dwight Morrow and William Cecil, Bishop of Exeter (1863–1936) – of the latter in John Train, *True Remarkable Occurrences* (1978).

1 The portly novelist, poet and critic, G. K. Chesterton was noted for being disorganized and absent-minded. On one occasion, heading off by train to make a speech, he had to get out and send his wife a telegram saying, 'Am in Market Harborough. Where ought I to be?'

Often misquoted as 'Am in Wolverhampton'. Indeed, according to one biographer, Maisie Ward, in *Return to Chesterton* (1944), a hundred different places have been substituted for 'Market Harborough'. Chesterton's wife, Frances, on this occasion cabled the answer: 'Home' – because, as she explained, it was easier to get him home and start him off again than to reroute him. Yes, Market Harborough was the original, and is confirmed by Chesterton himself in his *Autobiography* (1936).

2 Michael Ramsey – later to become Archbishop of Canterbury – was, as a young man, on the staff of Boston Parish Church in Lincolnshire. On one occasion he went out of his lodgings without his door key. When he came back, he rang the doorbell, but his landlady was nervous of strangers and called out through the door, 'I'm sorry, Mr Ramsey is out.' Ramsey replied, 'I'll return later.'

Told in Owen Chadwick, *Michael Ramsey, A Life* (1991). Chadwick says of this story that 'there is excellent evidence of its truth'. Compare one of several *Punch* cartoons based on this kind of incident: G. L. Stampa's 'ABSENCE' (1 February 1899) has this caption: *Mr Brownrigg (an absent-minded old Gent)*: 'Let me see – does Mr Brownrigg live here?' *New servant (not recognizing her master)*: 'Yes, Sir; but he's not in at present.' Mr B.: 'Oh, well, never mind, I'll call again.'

Academics

3 One day in Oxford, two elderly dons were observed walking along the High Street engaged in weighty discourse. To this day, no one knows what the subject of it was, but as they passed by, one was overheard saying just two words: 'And ninthly …'

In my book *Eavesdroppings* (1981), I glee-fully printed this wonderful story as told by S. H. Jarvis of Bristol. I am sure Mr Jarvis did indeed hear such a thing, but I have subsequently discovered that the pedantic ninth point is a venerable institution. In Ronald Knox's *Juxta Salices* (1910), he includes a group of poems written while he was still at Eton. 'As no less than three of them wear the aspect of a positively last appearance [i.e. a promise not to write more], they have been called in the words of so many eminent preachers "ninthlies and lastlies".' Even before this, *The Oxford English Dictionary* (2nd edition) has Thomas B. Aldrich writing in *Prudence Palfrey* (1874) of 'The poor old parson's interminable ninthlies and finallies.'

Much the same, though marginally different: in 1745, Benjamin Franklin concluded his *Reasons for Preferring an Elderly Mistress* with: 'Eighth and lastly. They are so grateful!!' And the *OED2* takes such pedantry even further back, more loosely, finding a 'fifthly and lastly' dated 1681.

Ultimately, the origin for all this sort of thing must be the kind of legal nonsense talk parodied by Shakespeare's Dogberry in *Much*

Ado About Nothing (1598): 'Marry, sir, they have committed false report; moreover, they have spoken untruths; secondarily, they are slanders; sixthly and lastly, they have belied a lady; thirdly, they have verified unjust things; and to conclude, they are lying knaves.'

Whatever the origin, this is a story that will not go away. On BBC Radio *Quote ... Unquote* (24 April 1998), the Oxford philosopher Anthony Quinton told a version involving Dean Hastings Rashdall and his wife. As they circumnavigated the university Parks, the Dean was overheard saying, 'And seventeenthly, my dear ...'

1 When Sir Maurice Bowra was Warden of Wadham College, Oxford, he was interviewing a young man for a place at the college. He eventually came to the conclusion that the young man would not do. Helpfully, however, he let him down gently by advising the young man, 'I think you would be happier in a larger – or a smaller – college.'

Told by Sir Claus Moser (a later Warden of Wadham) in a speech at Oxford (28 June 1998).

Accents

2 The Morningside accent is one of the glories of Edinburgh: it is what the posh people use. And yet there are many recollections of a Morningside lady whose tones you could cut with a knife, remarking, 'People talk of an Edinburgh accent, but I've never heard it.'

Recalled by Dr Eric Anderson on BBC Radio *Quote ... Unquote* (9 July 1986). Robert Stephens recalled (24 March 1992) how his then wife Maggie Smith had been complimented on her Edinburgh accent when playing the title role in the film *The Prime of Miss Jean Brodie*. A woman speaking in pure Morningside said, 'But there is no Edinburgh accent ...'

Accidents

3 The novelist George Eliot (Mary Ann Evans) had a long unmarried relationship with George Henry Lewes that lasted until his death in 1878. Nevertheless, in 1880 she did actually wed John Walter Cross who was twenty years her junior. On a trip to Venice, this John Walter Cross fell, 'with an ignominious plop, from their hotel window into the Grand Canal beneath.' It is about the only fact anyone can remember about him.

Told in James Morris, *Venice* (1960). Morris returns to the incident for the closing words of his book: 'There's romance for you! There's the lust and dark wine of Venice! No wonder George Eliot's husband fell into the Grand Canal.'

Accomplishments

4 A strangely little-celebrated talent possessed by one or two distinguished individuals is the ability to pick out tunes by tapping their fingernails on their teeth. In 1947, Winston Churchill's daughter Sarah wrote to him commiserating over the death of his brother. She recalled her Uncle Jack's playing 'God Save the King' and 'The British Grenadiers' in this manner. She added that it seemed to her, as a child, 'the height of artistic achievement'.

There is a downside also. When I myself performed this feat as presenter of the BBC Radio *Today* programme in 1977, I received a cautionary tale from a correspondent: 'A great aunt of mine, very beautiful, was being courted by an eligible young man. One day when he called, instead of his usual formal greeting he tapped on his teeth and asked, "What am I playing?" "The fool, I should think!" my aunt replied. History does not record what happened to him, but my aunt never married ...'

One morning on the *Today* programme I was told that I would be doing an interview with a man from Wolverhampton who played tunes on his teeth. So what, I replied, surely everyone does that? You don't have to be an *ateethyonnado* to do it. We proceeded to have a learned discussion on the technicalities of playing tunes on your teeth. Can false teeth produce the requisite tone? Should one clean one's teeth before playing, as a courtesy to one's listeners? Could he read music, I asked my fellow musician, or did he play his teeth *by ear*?

We ended up playing a duet – he in Birmingham, and I in London – a version of the *William Tell* overture. Our performance was rapturously received, and I received many letters. But most curious of all, I received a request from a Canadian radio station to take part in a three-way broadcast: an interviewer in Montreal, myself in London, and my fellow *odontophone* in Birmingham. It occurred to me, as we launched into a performance of the *Marseillaise*: did Marconi, when he was inventing radio, say to himself, 'When I've got this thing together, people will be able to play duets on their teeth across the Atlantic?'

At that time, as you may have surmised, *Today* was in a terrible mess and a new format for the programme was introduced shortly after this incident. I remember a critic in *Time Out* writing that '*Today* is better in the new format. Less time for playing tunes on teeth.'

Achievements

1 Towards the end of his brilliant Hollywood career, the film director and writer Billy Wilder was summoned to a studio by the 'movie brat' who was now its head. 'Great to meet you at last, Billy. Hope you'll come on the team. Believe we can make you some very interesting offers ... Now, Billy, tell me – what have you done?' Wilder paused a

second and then said, with the utmost politeness: 'After you ...'

As told to me by Alexander Walker (1985).

Acronyms

2 The name of the German airline Lufthansa is not an acronym. As Luftwaffe means 'air force', so Lufthansa means 'air association'. This has not prevented the invention of a sentence that could give rise to such an acronym, viz.: 'Let Us F*** The Hostesses And Not Say Anything.'

I obtained this from a book that had been alluded to by Godfrey Smith in his *Sunday Times* column some time prior to 1983. Alas, I have quite forgotten what the book was. The acronym was broadcast on BBC Radio *Quote ... Unquote* (1983), using the word 'fondle'.

Acting and actors

3 A little boy said to his father, 'Dad, when I grow up I'm going to be an actor!'

The father replied: 'You have to do one or the other, you can't do both ...'

Story attributed to one Nicolas Slade and published in *The 'Quote ... Unquote' Newsletter* (July 1998).

4 Two old actors were reduced to thumbing a lift up the Thames on a barge which, as it happens, was carrying sewage. When they came to a lock, the lock-keeper asked the bargee what he had on board.

'A load of shit, and two actors,' he replied promptly.

'Ah,' murmured one of the actors, 'still not getting top billing ...'

As told by Martin Jarvis (1994).

5 Somebody once asked W. S. Gilbert

whether he had been to see the great Sir Henry Irving who was appearing on the London stage at that time in *Faust*. He had not. 'I go to the pantomime,' replied Gilbert, 'only at Christmas.'

Told in Leslie Ayre, *The Gilbert and Sullivan Companion* (1972).

1 The great Sarah Bernhardt was one of the first actors whose aversion to performing with animals or children was made apparent. When asked to appear on the music-hall stage in a scene from *L'Aiglon*, she declined, saying: 'Between monkeys, not.'

Recounted in Michael Billington, *Peggy Ashcroft* (1988).

2 Katharine Hepburn, sighing with relief after she had completed filming *A Bill of Divorcement* with John Barrymore in 1932, said, 'Thank goodness I don't have to act with you any more.' Barrymore replied: 'I didn't know you ever had, darling.'

Told in Leslie Halliwell, *The Filmgoer's Book of Quotes* (1973).

3 In the 1930s and 1940s, the actor-manager Anew McMaster would travel with his company around Ireland by train. One Sunday, when the train stopped at an isolated rural station, McMaster lowered the window and revealed his extravagant hat and other thespian garb, to a porter on the platform. McMaster inquired, 'What country, friend, is this?' Being an educated Irish railway employee, the porter recognized Viola's opening line from *Twelfth Night* and promptly gave Shakespeare's own reply: 'This is Illyria ... lady.'

Told by Ian McKellen on BBC Radio *Quote ... Unquote* (15 June 1977).

4 It is said that the American playwright and screenwriter George S. Kaufman effectively put an end – with a single remark – to the career of an actor with the interesting name of Guido Nadzo. He said: 'Guido Nadzo is nadzo guido.'

Told in Scott Meredith, *George S. Kaufman and the Algonquin Round Table* (1977).

5 Charles Bickford was an American film actor who played a standard villain in Westerns for many a year. One day a director handed him his lines for the scene they were about to shoot, but Bickford stuffed the script into his pocket without looking at it.

'Aren't you going to study your lines?' the director inquired, somewhat huffily.

'I know what they are,' replied Bickford, 'I turn to the gang and say, "We'll head 'em off at Eagle Pass."'

Astonished at this display of mind-reading, the director asked for an explanation. 'Listen, buddy,' said Bickford. 'For fifteen years I've been heading 'em off at Eagle Pass, and this is no time to change.'

As told by C.A. Lejeune in 'Head 'em off at Eagle Pass' in *Good Housekeeping* Magazine (in about 1954).

6 Wallace Ford was an English actor who went to Hollywood in the early 1930s and ended up playing character parts. After a number of 'semi-leads', Ford was condemned to a succession of supporting roles in Hollywood films and decided that his gravestone epitaph should read, 'At last – I get top billing.' This inscription was duly put on his grave. Then along came a graffiti artist who chalked above it, 'Clark Gable and Myrna Loy supported by ...'

Told by Terence Frisby on BBC Radio *Quote*

... *Unquote* (26 June 1979). Ford's suggested epitaph is mentioned in Leslie Halliwell, *The Filmgoer's Book of Quotes* (1973).

1   W. Somerset Maugham paid a visit to the set of the 1941 remake of the film *Dr Jekyll and Mr Hyde* with Spencer Tracy playing the title roles. He inquired at one point: 'Which is he playing now?'

Told in Leslie Halliwell, *The Filmgoer's Book of Quotes* (1978 edn). The point of this story is that Tracy did not use any shock make-up, other than a pair of false teeth, to show the transformation from Dr Jekyll to Mr Hyde. The effect was rather subtle – obviously as far as Maugham was concerned. The matter is discussed in John Sutherland, *Can Jane Eyre Be Happy?* (1997).

2   Spencer Tracy once gave this piece of advice to the young Burt Reynolds who had said he wanted to be an actor: 'That's OK, son. Just take care they never *catch* you at it.'

Variously told. Richard Griffiths (to whom it had been told by Lee Marvin) gave this version on BBC Radio *Quote* ... *Unquote* (10 November 1998): 'Don't ever let the camera find you not thinking.'

3   On the disastrous first night of Sir John Gielgud's *Othello* at Stratford – in which the scenery fell down and an actor cut his hand – the play had taken 4½ hours with some scenes still to go. Ian Bannen, who was playing Iago, attempted to reduce the running time of the tragedy by announcing, 'Rodrigo's dead, my lord' when Rodrigo still had two scenes to go. Gielgud replied, 'Dead, sayst thou?' Bannen as Iago replied, 'Well, not dead. Just not very well, my lord.'

Told in Melvyn Bragg, *Rich: The Life of Richard Burton* (1988). The production was in 1961.

4   During rehearsals for Peter Brook's production of Seneca's *Oedipus* at the National Theatre in 1968, the cast was required to go through many days of primal screaming and other aids to great drama. The actors were then required to prepare an improvisation based on the most terrifying thing they could imagine. Sir John Gielgud did not comply, so he said, because there was nothing he could think of. But then he spoke up: 'Actually, there is something that is absolutely terrifying ... we open in ten days.'

Told by Myfanwy Talog on BBC Radio *Quote* ... *Unquote* (16 July 1983). In a Channel 4 programme screened in January 1993, Sir John appeared to ascribe the threat 'We open next week' in this sort of context to Dame Edith Evans.

5   When he was making the film *Marathon Man* with Dustin Hoffman, Laurence Olivier was aghast at one of the techniques used by the young actor. In order to make himself look the way the script required, as though he had gone two nights without sleep, Hoffman actually went for two nights without sleep. In consequence, he was in a terrible state and barely able to stand up to face the camera. Olivier put it to him, 'Dear boy, why not try acting?'

A much-told story. Another version was published in *The Times* (17 May 1982): 'Dear boy, you look absolutely awful. Why don't you try acting? It's so much easier.' *Marathon Man* was released in 1976.

6   With his booming voice and flamboyant persona, the English actor and director, Simon Callow, doesn't have to climb very far in order to go over the top. At least, however, he is aware of this. 'There was the time,' he recalls, 'when I went out in my fedora and a

rather big coat to hail a taxi. The taxi-driver said to me, "Where to?" and I said, "The National Theatre". He gave me a look and he said, "Where else?" And I *suppose* I understood what he meant . . . '

From an interview in the *Independent on Sunday* (23 February 1992).

1 When Deborah Warner directed a production of Shakespeare's *Richard II* at the Royal National Theatre, with stunning originality she cast Fiona Shaw (that is to say, a woman) in the title role. Some of the senior male members of the cast did not think too highly of Ms Warner's methods and took to referring to the show in irreverent pantomime terms: 'Ten miles from Pomfret and still no sign of Dick.'

Told in the *Guardian* (23 April 1995). Apropos the unusual casting, it was also reported about the same time that Paul Scofield (allegedly) had wondered why the nonagenarian Joan Hickson had not been cast as John of Gaunt.

Adultery

2 Randolph Churchill, Winston's journalist son, was notorious for his loud and drunken behaviour at parties, but this brazenness appears to have extended to other contexts as well. On one occasion, in bed with someone else's wife, he rang up the woman's husband. 'Guess who I'm in bed with!' he barked at the man. '... Doris!'

(Or some such name). Told to me by Sir Osbert Lancaster when recording an obituary of Churchill for the BBC in 1968 (though not, I should add, actually included in the obituary). On re-reading my diary entry for 6 June 1968 I see that what Sir Osbert really told me was that he himself had once gone into a room and found Randolph in bed with a blonde. 'He reached for the telephone and rang up Lord Castlerosse and said, "Guess where I am! In bed with Doris!"' Doris was, I gather, Lady Castlerosse . . .

3 Back in 1976, when Jimmy Carter, the peanut farmer from Plains, Georgia, started to run for the presidency, Americans had little or no idea who he was. Indeed, when he appeared in the celebrity guest spot on TV's *What's My Line?*, he had absolutely no difficulty in beating the panel. They had never heard of him. In no time at all, he became very recognizable indeed. During what, in later years, would no doubt have been called the 'defining moment' of his campaign for the presidency, Carter gave an interview to *Playboy* in which he said: 'I've looked on a lot of women with lust. I've committed adultery in my heart many times. God recognizes I will do this and forgives me.' The American electorate, perceiving a useful working relationship with the Almighty, voted Carter in to the White House.

From his interview with *Playboy* (November 1976).

Advertising

4 One of the great pioneers and practitioners of advertising was J. Walter Thompson. Travelling one blustery day on 'the El' (the elevated railway in Chicago), Commodore Thompson found himself next to a shabby, grubby, burly fellow, carrying a large sandwich board. The board touted a local restaurant on the front, and on the back a good place to get a haircut. Finally, the man spoke to Thompson: 'Hi, I'm just going to work. I'm in advertising, you know. What do you do?'

Shifting in his seat, the Commodore

replied that he, too, was in advertising. With a conspiratorial smile, the board-man leaned toward the Commodore, nudged him with his elbow, and said, 'Ain't it hell when the wind blows?'

Source untraced.

1 The man sitting next to Philip K. Wrigley on a flight to Chicago asked the multi-millionaire why he continued to advertise his chewing gum when it was far and away the most successful product in the field. Wrigley replied: 'For the same reason that the pilot keeps this plane's engines running even though we're already 30,000 feet in the air.'

Source untraced.

2 Joking and the serious business of devising advertising campaigns do not really go together. Shirley Polykoff, the noted American advertising executive, says that she once jokingly suggested to a corset manufacturer that 'HER CUP RUNNETH OVER' would make an excellent slogan for his product. Unfortunately, he loved it and – so Polykoff adds – 'it took an hour to unsell him'.

Told in Shirley Polykoff, *Does She ... Or Doesn't She?* (1975).

3 According to Jerry Della Femina, the American advertising executive, every-body at the agency was sitting around and scratching their heads over how they could most effectively promote Panasonic, the Japanese electronics account. Finally, Della Femina decided he would suggest a line to loosen them up. It was: 'From Those Wonderful Folks Who Gave You Pearl Harbor ...' As he says, this suggestion was followed by complete silence.

Recounted in Jerry Della Femina, *From Those Wonderful Folks Who Gave You Pearl Harbor* (1970).

4 The following conversation was over-heard between a man and a woman in a northern English supermarket: *He:* 'I say, what was the name of the tea bags them monkeys talked about on the telly?' *She:* 'PG Tips.' He: 'I think we should get some – they spoke very highly of them.'

As contributed by Mrs Joan Scott of Burton, Carnforth, Lancashire, to BBC Radio *Quote ... Unquote* (19 June 1980). John A. Thornton of London SW11 sent another version in 1992: 'I overheard a very English old lady in a smart chemist's shop in St James's, when offered the choice of two tooth-brushes, say, "I will take that one; they speak very well of them in the advertisements."'
And then I noticed in David Ogilvy's introduction to *Confessions of an Advertising Man* (1963): 'My father used to say of a product that it was "very well spoken of in the advertisements". I spend my life speaking well of products in advertisements.' In fact, this sort of remark has become an oft-quoted example of amused comment on advertising influence. Recently I discovered this caption to a cartoon in the *Punch Almanack* for 1911: two women are being served in a chemist's shop and one, called 'Sweet Simplicity' is say-ing: 'And I'll have a bottle of that Dentifrine – I must try some of that. All the advertisements speak so well of it.'

5 Peter Marsh was a flamboyant presence on the British advertising scene in the early 1980s, appearing to win for the agency Allen, Brady and Marsh some of the most high-profile accounts. When the agency was pitching for the British Rail account, representatives of the client were summoned to Marsh's office for a meeting. They were appalled at what they found. The reception area had paper peeling off its walls, there were broken springs sticking out of the

seats, and none of the ashtrays had been emptied. When the BR people approached the receptionist, she did not remove the cigarette from her mouth and continued to hold an involved personal conversation over the phone. After about twenty minutes of this – and amid mounting exasperation – the BR executives were just preparing to walk out, when in came Peter Marsh. Gesturing about the reception area, he beamed: 'There you are. You think we've got an image problem? Don't you see this is just how people see British Rail?'

The agency won the account.

Told to me in March 1981 by a Guinness PR. (Marsh's agency also had the Guinness account for a while.)

1 A woman answered a box number in a newspaper offering a bedsit that sounded much, much better than the one she had. Two days later, her landlady came in with the letter in her hand. She said, 'I see you are thinking of moving ...'

Told to me by the woman involved in about 1982.

Advice

2 Dr Samuel Johnson recalled some harsh but sensible advice once given him by his college tutor. It is of value to anyone who has to put pen to paper. 'Read over your compositions,' he said, 'and where ever you meet with a passage which you think is particularly fine, strike it out.'

In James Boswell, *The Life of Samuel Johnson*, for 30 April 1773 (1791). This has survived in the modern sayings 'kill your darlings' and 'throw away your babies', advice often given to aspiring journalists (and in use by the 1960s). 'In writing, you must kill all your darlings' is ascribed to William Faulkner in William Goldman, *Adventures in the Screen Trade* (1983).

3 Joseph Grimaldi (born in 1779) was known as the 'King of the Clowns' and changed the face of English pantomime. But he had a tough life. Indeed. On one occasion, he went to see his doctor complaining of depression. The doctor advised him to get out and about a bit more. 'Tell you what,' he said, 'a very good thing would be if you went to Sadler's Wells and saw Grimaldi the clown.'

'Ah, yes,' said the man, 'but I am Grimaldi the clown.'

Told by Peter Jones on BBC Radio *Quote ... Unquote* (21 August 1980). A version is also told in *Roy Hudd's Book of Music-Hall, Variety and Showbiz Anecdotes* (1993). T. Pettigrew, *Medical Portrait Gallery* (1840) has it that the doctor involved was John Abernethy, the British physician, surgeon and teacher (1764–1831).

4 Orson Welles, as a small boy, was introduced to Houdini, who taught him to do a simple trick with a red handkerchief and then counselled him, 'Never perform any trick until you have practised it a thousand times.' Welles went away and duly practised the handkerchief trick the requisite thousand times. When Welles next met Houdini, a manufacturer of magic called Carl Bremer was showing him a new vanishing lamp trick. Welles was utterly shocked when he heard Houdini say, 'Fine, Carl, I'll put it in the act tonight.'

Told by Frank Brady in *Citizen Welles* (1989).

5 After a long life spent doing public duties, King George V summed up his experience in this piece of advice: 'Never miss an opportunity to relieve

yourself; never miss a chance to sit down and rest your feet.'

His son, the Duke of Windsor, was later to ascribe this remark to 'an old courtier', but it seems likely that it was said by George V himself. A correspondent who wished to remain anonymous told me in 1981 that a naval officer of her acquaintance who was about to accompany Prince George, Duke of Kent, on a cruise, was asked by George V to make sure that the Prince was properly dressed before going ashore. He also advised: 'Always take an opportunity to relieve yourselves.' Another correspondent suggests that it was an equerry's first advice to the new King George V; yet another that Edward VII was the first to say this when he was Prince of Wales. On the other hand, more than a century earlier, the Duke of Wellington had advised: 'Always make water when you can.'

Compare also the remark of Samuel Freeman, who served in the US Supreme Court from 1862 to 1890. He advised: 'Never walk when you can ride, never sit when you can lie down.' Winston Churchill is reported by Sir David Hunt to have said: 'Never stand when you can sit and never sit when you can lie down.'

1 More useful advice – from a very old man. The Reverend H. J. Bidder, aged 86, sat silently, with a crumpled face, all through dinner and then promulgated the following: '(1) Never drink claret in an east wind. (2) Take your pleasures singly, one by one. (3) Never sit on a hard chair after drinking port.'

Recalled in *Geoffrey Madan's Notebooks* (ed. Gere & Sparrow, 1981). Madan died in 1947.

2 Sir John Gielgud was approached by another actor in order to get some advice on playing the role of King Lear. Lear, famously, has to carry the body of his dead daughter, Cordelia, around for some considerable time, so Gielgud's considered advice was: 'Get a small Cordelia.'

Told by Sir Ian McKellen on BBC Radio *Quote ... Unquote* (10 April 1998).

3 Jean Trumpington recalls that her grandmother gave her an excellent piece of advice a very long time ago: 'If you are ever attacked in the street or mugged always shout "Fire!" Never shout "Help!" People adore fires and will always come rushing. Nobody will come if you shout "Help!"'

Told by Baroness Trumpington on BBC Radio *Quote ... Unquote* (10 June 1997).

4 When she was asked by a young actress how to set about speaking her lines, Edith Evans advised: 'Say everything as if it were improper.'

Told by Rula Lenska on BBC Radio *Quote ... Unquote* (24 July 1980). In Donald Sinden, *A Touch of the Memoirs* (1982), he has it thus: 'If she could not think what to do with a line, she spoke it as if it was obscene. One has only to think of her delivery of "A handbag!" in *The Importance of Being Earnest* to know what she meant.'

5 Josephine Hull, the American actress, once advised: 'Shakespeare is so tiring. You never get a chance to sit down unless you're a king.'

Told in *Time* Magazine (16 November 1953). Compare what a part-time actress (Judy Holliday) says in *The Solid Gold Cadillac* (US film, 1956): 'Do you like Shakespeare?... Take my advice, don't play it. It's so tiring. They never let you sit down unless you're a king.'

6 The actor Jim Broadbent was appearing in a film with Mia Farrow in Ireland when he learned that he had been selected by Woody Allen to play in one of *his* films. As this was at the height of the public blood-letting between Allen and Farrow over their family arrangements, Broadbent waited until the film

deal was confirmed before mentioning it to Farrow: 'I went along to Mia's trailer and knocked and said, "Mia, I've got some rather bizarre news: Woody Allen has asked me to be in his next film."'

"Oh, my, that is bizarre news," replied Mia. "Congratulations! He's a great director. Just don't have babies by him …"'

Jim Broadbent adds that this was advice he heeded.

Told by Broadbent on BBC Radio *Quote … Unquote* (10 June 1997).

Age and ageing

1 The distinguished actress had been so impressed by the flattering work of this particular photographer that she engaged him again to take her picture. 'Oh dear,' she remarked, looking at the new prints when they were finished, 'you make me look a lot older than last time.' The photographer was the quintessence of tact. Said he: 'Ah yes, but I was much younger in those days.'

Who were the original participants? Possibly Marlene Dietrich and the cinematographer Hal Mohr. When they were working together on the film *Rancho Notorious* (US, 1952), Dietrich asked why she wasn't looking as good on the film as when the same cinematographer had shot her in *Destry Rides Again* thirteen years before. Mohr replied that he was, of course, by now thirteen years older. This version is quoted in Leslie Halliwell, *The Filmgoer's Book of Quotes* (1973). Also told as having been an exchange between Joe Ruttenberg and Greer Garson.

2 Robert Helpmann went to see a matinée performance of *Hamlet* by a touring company and noticed that the lady playing Queen Gertrude 'should have played it a few years earlier'. He was heard to say, 'I hope they cut that

line about "Go not to thy uncle's bed" because, frankly, she'd never make it.'

Told by Robin Bailey on BBC Radio *Quote … Unquote* (27 July 1985).

3 The English politician Reginald Maudling had held a number of the principal offices of state under previous Conservative leaders until Margaret Thatcher came along and kicked him out of the Shadow Cabinet. When he was replaced by a man four years his senior, he said: 'There comes a time in every man's life when he must make way for an older man.'

Reported in the *Guardian* (20 November 1976). He also said: 'I have never been sacked before. I was appointed by Winston Churchill and I am now being dismissed by Margaret Thatcher. Life goes on. The world changes.'

4 Anita Brookner, an art historian, was a woman of 'a certain age' when she achieved public recognition by winning the Booker Prize for Fiction with her novel *Hotel du Lac* in 1984. Irritated by speculation over her precise years and, in particular, by the 'increasing churlishness' of *The Times* in alluding to her age and that of Erica Jong – an age which she withheld from publications like *Who's Who* – she eventually penned a letter to *The Times* (5 November 1984) saying, 'I am 46, and have been for some time past.'

Brookner had already used this idea in *Hotel du Lac*: 'She was a handsome woman of forty-five and would remain so for many years.' Compare No. 99 in the original *Joe Miller's Jests* (1739): 'A Lady's Age happening to be questioned, she affirmed, she was but Forty, and call'd upon a Gentleman that was in Company for his Opinion; Cousin, said she, do you believe I am in the Right, when I say I am but Forty? I ought not to dispute it, Madam, reply'd he, for I have heard you say so these ten Years.'

1 Walter Matuschanskayasky, better known as the film actor Walter Matthau, was at a party with his wife, Carol. He wandered off and, in due course, she spotted him chatting to a woman who was somewhat 'mutton dressed as lamb'. Carol even heard Walter ask this apparition, 'How old are you?' At which point, Carol butted in and said, 'Why don't you saw off her legs and count the rings?'

Told by George Axelrod on BBC Radio *Quote... Unquote* (11 September 1979). Also told by Truman Capote in *Answered Prayers* (1986).

Alimony

2 The ex-wife of the American director, Raoul Walsh, used to attend all his films to make certain that he was still working and that, therefore, his alimony payments would keep on coming. Accordingly, whenever he could, Walsh always used to insert the same line of dialogue especially for her – 'I'm going to get out of here faster than I left my first wife' – even if it had no relevance to the plot.

Recounted in the *Independent* (12 January 1989).

Alterations

3 The American *National Inquirer* once produced a 27-page guide by its owner (Generoso Pope Jr) containing instructions to reporters. One was, 'Do not alter quotations. Don't think you can write them better than other people. For example, if someone says "Never in the field of human conflict was so much owed by so many to so few", don't change it to "The RAF did a grand job ..."'

Told by Shelley Rohde on BBC Radio *Quote... Unquote* (6 October 1984).

Ambition

4 Field Marshal Montgomery was the foremost self-publicist of his age and by no conceivable stretch of the imagination in any way short on ambition. Winston Churchill said to King George VI, 'I'm worried about Monty – I think he's after my job.' And the King said, 'Thank God! I thought he was after mine.'

This version was told in the *Observer* (30 August 1992). Richard Collier, in *The Freedom Road 1944–1945* (1984) has it that it was Alan Brooke, Chief of the Imperial General Staff, who had this exchange with the King. Writing a footnote to a 'London Letter' in the *Partisan Review* (17 April 1944), George Orwell gave it as 'a sample of the kind of story now told about Montgomery', but names General Eisenhower as the provoker of the King's response. Orwell goes on: 'Other similar stories are told of Eisenhower or Montgomery interchangeably. For example: "Three doctors who had just died arrived at the gates of Heaven. The first two, a physician and a surgeon, were refused admittance. The third described himself as a psychiatrist. 'Come in!' said St Peter immediately [to this last]. 'We should like your professional advice. God has been behaving in a very peculiar way lately. He thinks He's General Eisenhower (or Montgomery)."'

5 Jonathan Cecil, the English actor, is the son of the writer and academic Lord David Cecil. When asked what he was going to be when he grew up, Jonathan replied: 'I'm going to be neurotic like daddy.'

Told by Kingsley Amis in his *Memoirs* (1991). Amis ponders the question of whether it wasn't said rather by Hugh Cecil, Jonathan's younger brother. According to Ned Sherrin, *Theatrical Anecdotes* (1991), Jonathan appeared as a fairy in a New College production of *A Midsummer Night's Dream* and was interviewed by a reporter from *The Oxford Mail* who also asked what he wanted to be when he grew up. The reply: 'An aesthete, like Daddy.'

I recall being told the 'neurotic' version at New College, Oxford, in about 1963. Both father and son had strong connections with the college. In 1997, Jonathan confirmed to me that he had probably said the 'aesthete' version on some occasion, but would have said 'like my father', never 'like daddy'. Also, he simply would not have described his father as neurotic, 'because he wasn't'.

1 Marilyn Monroe was once asked if all the haggling over money and contracts in the movie business ever got her down. 'I'm not worried about the money,' she replied, 'I just want to be wonderful ...'

Told in John Robert Colombo, *Wit and Wisdom of the Moviemakers* (1979).

Anecdotes

2 In his book *Roughing It* (1872), Mark Twain tells of his ramblings all over the American West during the previous decade. In Chapter 20, he is sitting with a driver, having crossed the Great American Desert, and the driver produces an anecdote about Horace Greeley, the politician and editor, who is chiefly celebrated now for having coined the saying 'Go west, young man' (which in fact he didn't, but that is not important here). 'I can tell you a most laughable thing indeed, if you would like to listen to it,' says the driver. 'Horace Greeley went over this road once. When he was leaving Carson City he told the driver, Hank Monk, that he had an engagement to lecture at Placerville and was very anxious to go through quick. Hank Monk cracked his whip and started off at an awful pace. The coach bounced up and down in such a terrific way that it jolted the buttons all off of Horace's coat, and finally shot his head clean through the roof of the stage, and then he yelled at Hank Monk and begged him to go easier – said he wasn't in as much of a hurry as he was awhile ago. But Hank Monk said, "Keep your seat, Horace, and I'll get you there on time" – and you bet he did, too, what was left of him!'

Amusing enough as such anecdotes go. The only trouble is that a day or two afterwards they pick up a Denver man who tells Twain exactly the same story. And then a cavalry sergeant at Fort Bridger, who does the same. And then, after a stop at Salt Lake City, a Mormon preacher recounts the anecdote. And then a dying man also embarks on it with the words, 'Horace Greeley ...'

At this point Twain leaps in. 'Suffering preacher, proceed at your peril,' he says. 'You see in me the melancholy wreck of a once stalwart and magnificent manhood. What has brought me to this? That thing which you are about to tell. Gradually but surely, that tiresome old anecdote has sapped my strength, undermined my constitution, withered my life. Pity my helplessness. Spare me only just this once, and tell me about young George Washington and his little hatchet for a change ...'

Twain then exaggerates wildly and claims to have had to listen to the anecdote 481 or 482 times. He says he has seen it in print in nine different foreign languages. 'I now learn with regret that it is going to be set to music.' He concludes: 'I do not think that such things are right.'

1 I once had to interview Kirk Douglas at very short notice, so I had not had a chance to read through the cuttings and background material before it was time for me to be shown up to his room at the Dorchester Hotel in London. I asked him questions off the top of my head, and he answered them thoughtfully and with many vivid anecdotes.

At the end, Douglas showed me to the door and bade me farewell. As I padded off down the corridor, I couldn't help hearing him say to his publicity person, 'That was a really good interview, wasn't it? Such a good interviewer.'

Was it possible that he had not closed the door before making the remark so that I was bound to hear it? Just another sign of his great professionalism, rather. When I eventually did get to go through the cuttings of his previous interviews, I discovered that every single one of his observations and anecdotes had been conveyed to other interviewers before me – in some cases many years previously.

The interview took place on 17 July 1975.

2 The Irish broadcaster Eamonn Andrews, originally a radio boxing commentator, made a considerable name for himself in Britain despite a lack of ease with anything approaching thought. He sweatily hosted many editions of the British TV version of *This Is Your Life* and presided uneasily over *The Eamonn Andrews Show*, an early chat show in the 1960s. Now it came to pass that a journalist was once writing a profile of Andrews but encountered a dearth of anecdotal material. Accordingly, he phoned up a researcher on *This Is Your Life* and asked if there were any nice anecdotes about Eamonn.

'Er, no,' replied the researcher. 'You see, I don't think Eamonn would want to be involved in anything as risqué as an anecdote.'

A version of this story appears in Ned Sherrin, *Cutting Edge* (1984).

Aplomb

3 Lord Uxbridge, later to become 1st Marquess of Anglesey, was a cavalry officer at the Battle of Waterloo in which he was savagely wounded. 'By God! I've lost my leg!' he exclaimed to the passing Duke of Wellington, who replied, 'Have you, by God?' and rode on. The partly severed leg was amputated and buried in a garden in the village of Waterloo. Anglesey consequently acquired the nickname 'One-Leg'.

Told in Elizabeth Longford, *Wellington: The Years of the Sword*, Chap. 23 (1969).

4 Radio newsreaders have two keys which they can operate while on the air. The cough key cuts out the microphone so that the throat can be cleared. The other key enables contact to be made with the control cubicle through the otherwise soundproof glass.

At the height of the Soviet invasion of Czechoslovakia in August 1968, I recall watching Ronald Fletcher read the ten o'clock news on BBC Radio 4. At the conclusion of a lengthy report containing any number of impossible Czech names, all pronounced with dazzling confidence and nary a stumble, Fletcher pressed down both keys and remarked to those in the control cubicle, 'How about that then?'

My memory of the occasion.

1 Recovery with aplomb, overheard at a party in Vancouver: one man said: 'All the students at Simon Fraser are either football players or old bags.' The other replied: 'My wife goes to Simon Fraser!' And the first saved himself by saying, 'Oh, really? What position does she play?'

Contributed by Mr H. Tucker of York to BBC Radio *Quote... Unquote* (26 May 1982). In *The Best of 606 Aggie Jokes* (1988), this reappears with the initial line, '... football players or fast women'.

Apologies

2 Randolph Churchill, famous for his drunken and boorish behaviour at social events, once wrote apologetically to a hostess whose dinner party he had ruined with one of his displays of drunken rudeness. He said: 'I should never be allowed out in private.'

Recounted in Brian Roberts, *Randolph* (1984). Writing a letter to his father (16 October 1952), Churchill called this a 'mot' he had coined about himself. Malcolm Muggeridge (so it is said) pushed forward the boundaries of obituaries in *The Times* when he wrote of Randolph (7 June 1968): 'At social gatherings he was liable to engage in heated and noisy arguments which could ruin a dinner party, and made him the dread of hostesses on both sides of the Atlantic. The tendency was exacerbated by an always generous, and occasionally excessive alcoholic intake.'

3 Arturo Toscanini was rehearsing his orchestra one day and decided to take it out on the Second Clarinet. He bawled him out as the clarinettist had never been bawled out before. Reaching a crescendo of vituperation, Toscanini ordered him out of the rehearsal. Pausing only to collect his instrument and other belongings, the musician said out loud: 'Silly old fart!' Toscanini screamed: 'This is no time to apologize!'

Told by John Julius Norwich on BBC Radio *Quote... Unquote* (12 April 1994). A version with 'Nuts to you!' as the disputed phrase appears in Laning Humphrey, *The Humor of Music and Other Oddities in the Art* (1971).

Appearances

4 In June 1855, when the poet Tennyson entered the Sheldonian Theatre in Oxford to receive an honorary degree of doctor of civil laws, his long hair was in disorder, dishevelled and unkempt. A voice cried out to him from the gallery, 'Did your mother call you early, dear?'

Recounted by Julian Charles Young in *A Memoir of Charles Mayne Young* (1871) based on his son's diary note (8 November 1863). The allusion is to Tennyson's poem 'The May Queen' (1832): 'You must wake and call me early, call me early, mother dear; / Tomorrow'll be the happiest time of all the glad New-year; / Of all the glad New-year, mother, the maddest merriest day; / For I'm to be Queen o' the May, mother, I'm to be Queen o' the May.'

5 The verdict on Clark Gable's first screen test was 'Ears too big', and comments on the size thereof did not cease when he soon after managed to break into films. Howard Hughes said, 'His ears made him look like a taxicab with both doors open', and Milton Berle described them as 'the best ears of our lives'.

Sources include: Charles Higham and Joel Greenberg, *Celluloid Muse* (1969), and Leslie Halliwell, *The Filmgoer's Book of Quotes* (1973).

6 James Agate writing in his diary for 25 September 1935 (published in *Ego*) tells of lunching at the Ivy with Curt

Dehn, his lawyer, who asked the name of the man lunching opposite. 'I said, "John Gielgud." Dehn said, "It's a rum sort of head. The profile's Roman Emperor, but the rest is still at Eton.'"

Thus the process of describing Gielgud began. My favourite attempt, much later, was by Anthony Shaffer, the playwright. 'Of course,' he said, 'he's a camel.'

The Shaffer comment is from my diary (19 November 1974).

1 Watching the 1953 Coronation on TV, Noël Coward was asked who the man was riding in a carriage with the portly Queen of Tonga. 'Her lunch,' he replied.

In fact, it was the Sultan of Kelantan. This famous story made an early appearance in Dick Richards, *The Wit of Noël Coward* (1968). It is often told differently and may well be apocryphal. About the only thing to be said for certain is that Coward did spend most of Coronation Day watching TV – he says so in his diaries. According to Ned Sherrin, *Theatrical Anecdotes* (1991), Coward always denied the story, 'not least because she [Queen Salote] was a personal friend and would have been very upset'. Sherrin suggests that Emlyn Williams was the perpetrator and, curiously, casts Emperor Haile Selassie in the role of 'the lunch' (he did not even attend the Coronation).

In *his* diary entry for Coronation Day, James Lees-Milne has the Coward story and wrongly identifies the man as Queen Salote's husband. The passage is included in the published diaries, *A Mingled Measure* (1994), but seems probably to have been inserted at a later date. In *The Sayings of Noël Coward* (1997), Philip Hoare reveals that 'Coward disowned the line, ceding credit to David Niven.'

2 In 1956, the critic Kenneth Tynan went to interview the aged theatre designer, Edward Gordon Craig, at his home in the south of France. Almost at once,

Craig said, 'You have the right face for a critic. You have the look of a blooming martyr.'

Reported by Tynan in the *Observer* (29 July 1956). Subsequently, Sir Alec Guinness admitted that he had drawn on Tynan's cadaverousness when creating the make-up for his part in the film *The Ladykillers* (1955).

3 The irascible TV personality Gilbert Harding was invited to the official opening of the BBC Television Centre in 1960 and observed the Director-General, Hugh Greene, talking in a group with two of his predecessors, Sir William Haley and Sir Ian Jacob. 'Ah,' said Harding, 'either the Holy Trinity or Pip, Squeak and Wilfred.' Then he added: 'The latter, I fear.'

Told in Paul Ferris, *Sir Huge* (1990). Pip, Squeak and Wilfred were, respectively, a penguin, a dog and a rabbit who appeared in a *Daily Mirror* comic strip from 1919 to 1946.

4 Fred Russell, ventriloquist father of Val Parnell, when very old and almost blind liked to attend the rehearsal of his son's *Sunday Night at the London Palladium*. On one occasion after he had watched Winifred Atwell rehearsing her performance, Russell exclaimed about his son: 'He gets some extraordinary acts, he does. I've just seen a gorilla playing the piano.' Indeed, he could be forgiven for thinking so. The artistes used to rehearse in their street coats and Atwell had been wearing a big hairy overcoat.

Told to me by Roy Hudd (June 1984).

5 Coral Browne was taking part in a New York production of *Tamburlaine*, directed by Tyrone Guthrie. Alec Guinness, who had been invited to the first dress rehearsal, records that Coral 'looked magnificent and was gloriously dressed in some barbaric style, but

perhaps there was a tidge too much hair in her wig.' At one point, Guthrie asked her if she was happy with the wig. 'If you really f***ing want to know,' she answered, 'I feel as if I am looking out of a yak's asshole.'

Told in Alec Guinness, *My Name Escapes Me* (1996).

1   The Earl of Home renounced his peerage in order to become Conservative Prime Minister with the name of Sir Alec Douglas-Home. His looks more or less guaranteed that this otherwise amiable man would be a disaster on television. He recalled the following exchange with a make-up woman as she plied her trade prior to a prime ministerial broadcast:
    'Can't you make me look better than I do on television? I look rather scraggy, like a ghost.'
    'No.'
    'Why not?'
    'Because you have a head like a skull.'
    'Doesn't everyone have a head like a skull?'
    'No.'

Told in Lord Home, *Where the Wind Blows* (1976).

2   Kenneth Williams, the comic actor, was taking part in a Christmas radio show in which a group of comedians challenged the more obviously intelligent participants of the *Brain of Britain* quiz. Williams wailed out loud: 'I don't want to look like a fool.' The chairman, Robert Robinson, commented: 'Nature has already seen to that.'

Told by Williams on BBC Radio *Quote... Unquote* (12 June 1980).

3   The poet W. H. Auden famously said of his cracked face that it looked 'like a

wedding-cake left out in the rain'. Another unknown commentator imagined that if a fly walked over the face, 'it would break its leg'. Neither of these compares with what the artist David Hockney is reported to have said after Auden had sat for him: 'I kept thinking, if his face looks like this, what must his balls look like?'

Told by Alan Bennett in the *London Review of Books* (1985).

Approbation

4   Alan Ayckbourn, talking of the odd things that bereaved people do and say (apropos his play *Absent Friends*), recalled what one member of the audience had said coming out of a play of his at Scarborough: 'Oh, Mr Ayckbourn, I haven't laughed so much since my father died!'

Told to me by Ayckbourn (in my diary for 17 May 1974). Incidentally, 'I haven't laughed so much since my husband died' is also said to have been 'a compliment from a woman to Victor Borge' – according to Frank S. Pepper, *Handbook of 20th Century Quotations* (1984).

Architectural criticism

5   The Reverend C. L. Dodgson (Lewis Carroll) took a marked dislike to the Gilbert Scott belfry that was erected at his college, Christ Church, Oxford, in the 1870s. He commented: 'The advantage of having been born in the reign of Queen Anne, and of having died in that or the subsequent reign, has never been so painfully apparent as it is now.'

From 'The New Belfry of Christ Church, Oxford, A Monograph by D.C.L.' (1872), reprinted in *The Complete Works of Lewis Carroll* (1939).

1 Worcester College, Oxford, although very pleasant within and having a delightful garden with pond, is rather austere when viewed from Beaumont Street – not least because of the large clock over the entrance gate. 'Oh, I though that was the railway station,' a certain undergraduate is supposed to have remarked.

According to Dacre Balsdon's *Oxford Life* (1957), this remark was made by a 'bright young man' in a 'novel'. Which one, I know not. I first heard this remark in the more sophisticated form, *'C'est magnifique, mais ce n'est pas la gare'* in about 1961. Frank Loxley told me (1996) that during his time at Cambridge (1947–51) he used to hear the joke-phrase applied to the 'hideous Water-house Tree Court' at Caius College. 'As this monstrosity was erected in 1870 and Marshal Bosquet made his famous remark about the Charge of the Light Brigade in 1854, it seems likely that this joke was already current in the nineteenth century.'

Whatever the origin, I remembered the jest in 1975 when I was devising what later became the radio programme *Quote ... Un-quote*. I knew that a quotations quiz required some kind of twist, and so I put in the pro-posal that the participants would not only have to identify quotations but also invent them for specific situations. The example I gave was, 'What would Napoleon have said if he had arrived at Euston instead of Waterloo?' Suggested answer, *'C'est magnifique, mais ce n'est pas la gare ...'* The series was accepted by the then Controller of Radio 4 – Clare Lawson Dick – who thought it was a very witty idea. I then dropped the idea because, when it came to it, the participants were less inspired. When asked what Edward Heath might have said to Lord Nelson, one suggestion was 'Hello sailor ...!'

2 The American architect Stanford White was murdered in 1906 on the opening night of a new roof-garden theatre at Madison Square Garden, of which he had been the designer. He was shot by Harry K. Thaw, a millionaire industri-alist, because of White's 'exotic house-keeping' with a 22-year-old girl, Evelyn Nesbit, who was Thaw's wife. Thaw got away with the murder by pleading temporary insanity, and was put in an asylum. After several weeks, his friends freed him and spirited him out of the country to Europe. And the rule was that if you went for six weeks without committing another psychotic act, you clearly weren't mad.

Thaw came to England, and when he was being shown the sights of London he was in a carriage going past the Albert Memorial. He said, 'And what was that?' They said, 'The Albert Memorial', And he shouted, 'I shot the wrong architect!'

Told by Richard Griffiths on BBC Radio *Quote ... Unquote* (10 November 1998).

Art criticism

3 Edith Cavell was the English nurse shot by the Germans for helping Allied pris-oners to escape during the First World War. She was instantly hailed as a martyr and in 1920 a statue of her was erected outside the National Portrait Gallery in London (where it stands to this day). The artist James Pryde was watching the unveiling of the statue and evidently considered it a poor likeness. As the drapes fell away, he remarked, 'My God, they've shot the wrong person!'

Told in a letter from Derek Hudson of Hindhead, quoted on BBC Radio *Quote ... Unquote* (6 July 1977).

4 When Sir Alfred Munnings was President of the Royal Academy in April 1949, one of the guests at the annual dinner was Winston Churchill,

who had just been admitted to the Academy. Munnings supposedly ruffled the politician's feathers by saying in his speech: 'Seated on my left is the greatest Englishman of all time. I said to him just now: "What would you do if you saw Picasso walking ahead of you down Piccadilly?" – and he replied: "I would kick him up the arse, Alfred."'

Thus a report in *The Times* Diary (29 March 1983). Alas, the BBC recording of the event fails to confirm that Munnings ever said this. Not a born speaker, to put it mildly, what Munnings actually mumbled was: 'Once he said to me, "Alfred, if you met Picasso coming down the street, would you join with me in kicking his something-something?" I said, "Yes, sir, I would!"'

The Times report also suggested that, 'as the laughter died, Munnings yelled at the top of his voice: "Blunt, Blunt [i.e. Sir Anthony Blunt, the art connoisseur later unmasked as a traitor] – you're the one who says he prefers Picasso to Sir Joshua Reynolds!"' If Munnings did yell this, he was very quiet about it because the barb is not audible on the recording.

1 On his 80th birthday in November 1954, both Houses of Parliament presented Sir Winston Churchill with a portrait painted by Graham Sutherland. He did not like it, but accepted the portrait with a gracefully double-edged compliment: 'The portrait is a remarkable example of modern art. It certainly combines force and candour. These are qualities which no active member of either House can do without or should fear to meet.'

Lady Churchill's dislike of the portrait took a more practical form: she had it destroyed.

Another of Churchill's remarks on the same portrait was, 'I look as if I was having a difficult stool' – quoted in *The Lyttelton Hart-Davis Letters* (for 20 November 1955). Other

versions of this criticism are: 'How do they paint one today? Sitting on a lavatory!' (said to Charles Doughty, secretary of the committee which organized the tribute), and 'Here sits an old man on his stool, pressing and pressing.'

2 In 1956, the Soviet leader Nikita Khrushchev paid an eventful visit to Britain in the company of Marshal Bulganin, with whom at that time he nominally shared power ('B and K'). At Oxford, Khrushchev visited New College chapel and – famously disliking modern art – viewed the Jacob Epstein statue of the risen Lazarus with marked distaste. Next morning, back in London, at Claridge's, he declared that he had not slept well. 'I had nightmares from that terrible statue at Oxford,' he said.

Reported in Sir William Hayter, *A Double Life* (1974). Hayter, as British ambassador to Moscow, accompanied Khrushchev on his visit to New College (of which Hayter himself became Warden in 1958). Khrushchev's initial derogatory remarks about the statue were overheard by a journalist and printed. Sculptor Epstein fired off a telegram to Hayter: 'Tell your guest to keep off art criticism, which he does not understand, and stick to his own business, which is murder.'

Ashes of the deceased

3 One old woman is reported to have said to another, 'Yes, I had him cremated and his ashes made into an eggtimer.'

The other asked, 'Why an eggtimer?'

And the first replied: 'Well, he never did any work while he was alive, so he might as well do some now he's dead.'

A traditional exchange. In J. B. Priestley's *English Journey* (1934), he recounts attending a lunch club in Manchester where commercial travellers told stories. He repeats one: 'A weaver up Blackburn way had just lost her husband. "Where yer going to bury 'im?" a neighbour asked her. "Ah'm not going to bury 'im," she replied. "Ah'm going to 'ave 'im creamated," she replied. The neighbour was impressed. "But whatever will yer do wi' th'ashes?" she inquired. "Ah'll tell yer what Ah'm going to do wi' th'ashes," said the widow. "Ah'm going to 'ave 'em put into an eggtimer. Th'owd devil wouldn't ever work when 'e wer alive, so 'e can start doing a bit now 'e's deead.'"

Priestley comments: 'That still seems to me a very good story, even though I am no longer under the influence of beer and Bury Black Puddings. It is a fair sample of Lancashire's grimly ironic humour.'

Alan Bennett used the story in his 'English Way of Death' sketch in the Broadway version of *Beyond the Fringe* (1963).

1 I once knew of some people called Sands. They lived overlooking the seaside, and Mr Sands decreed in his will that when he died he was to be cremated and his ashes scattered over the, er, sands. And so it turned out, though not quite in the way he expected.

Shortly after the cremation, a small group of his relatives was seen trooping down to the shore carrying the casket containing his ashes. After they had stood in silent prayer for a minute or so, the lid was removed. At that very moment, a gust of wind whipped the ashes out of the casket and blew them all over the family.

But Mr Sands had had his wish – even if his ashes were scattered over the Sands rather than over the, er, sands.

I heard this story from my parents in the early 1970s.

2 Then there was the (unidentified) actor who put in his will that he wanted to be cremated and ten per cent of his ashes thrown in his agent's face.

Told by Larry Adler on BBC Radio *Quote...Unquote* (25 January 1976).

Assumptions

3 One elderly person was overheard saying to another: 'If anything should happen to either of us, you may take it that I'm definitely going to live in Bournemouth.'

This version of an old story appeared in *Pass the Port Again* (1980). In my *Eavesdroppings* (1981), I called it 'traditional' and gave it as said on a park bench: 'When one of us passes on, I shall move south to live with my daughter.' There is nothing new, etc.: in *Samuel Butler's Notebooks* (which covered the years 1874–1902) there appears the entry: 'Warburg's old friend ... said to Warburg one day, talking about his wife, who was ill, "If God were to take one or other of us, I should go and live in Paris."'

Athletic pursuits

4 The Welsh-born politician Roy Jenkins – now Lord Jenkins – is still best known popularly for his love of claret and for a curious screwing gesture of the right hand he makes while speaking. However, he has not neglected the pursuit of physical fitness. In 1986 it was revealed that he was an inveterate jogger round the streets of Kensington, although one witness (his biographer, John Campbell) did tell me that Jenkins had once been observed jogging *with a walking stick* in his hand. Later, in a TV profile, Michael Cockerell said that when Jenkins was the President of the European Commission in Brussels he had even been spied jogging *with a cigar* in hand. Even more bizarrely, perhaps for security reasons, he had taken to jogging round and across and in a fixed pattern over a tennis court. How very peculiar.

Michael Cockerell's TV film was shown in May 1996.

Audiences

1 Oscar Wilde was once asked by a friend how his latest play had gone. 'It was a great success,' he replied, 'but the audience was a total failure.'

According to Edmund Fuller, *Thesaurus of Anecdotes* (1942), the play was *Lady Windermere's Fan* (1892).

2 Driven to fury by the coughing of members of a theatre audience, John Barrymore picked up a large sea bass and threw it in their direction, saying: 'Busy yourselves with that, you damned walruses, while the rest of us proceed with the play.'

Told in Bennett Cerf, *Try and Stop Me* (1944). Cerf has it that the incident occurred when Barrymore was playing Fedor in *The Living Corpse*, a version of Tolstoy's *Redemption*, in 1918. Quite why he should have had a sea bass so readily to hand is not clear.

3 In the days of silent films, two elderly women were in an Edinburgh picture house watching a thriller. As the explanatory titles came up on the screen, one of the women was reading them aloud to her companion. When the situation reached its climax, came the subtitle, and then the voice: 'The thick plottens,' it said.

Told to me by Mrs Dora Thomas of Edinburgh, in 1979.

4 When Sybil Thorndike was playing Jocasta in *Oedipus Rex*, the actress Mrs Patrick Campbell, who was by then an elderly woman and in a wheelchair, came to watch. She was put in a stage box for a matinée, and in due course Thorndike came on, making a tremendous entrance, with an extraordinary wailing noise. Whereupon Mrs Patrick Campbell, who was now fast asleep, woke up and said very loudly, 'There's somebody in the room!'

Told by Bryan Forbes on BBC Radio *Quote ... Unquote* (1 May 1998). This cannot have been Laurence Olivier's production in 1945, as Campbell had died in 1940.

5 Apropos costume drama, Lee Shubert, the American impresario, is said to have averred that, 'Audiences don't like plays where people write letters with feathers.'

Also ascribed to Max Gordon, Broadway producer, by Arthur Miller – in Ned Sherrin, *Theatrical Anecdotes* (1991). On the other hand, it has also been attributed, regarding film costume epics, to a Missouri cinema owner of the mid-1930s – by Robin Bailey on BBC Radio *Quote ... Unquote* (27 July 1985). Simon Rose, *Classic Film Guide* (1995) gives the remark to a Kansas City cinema owner in the wake of the 1933 success of *The Private Life of Henry VIII*. He apparently told a Hollywood rep that his audiences would not put up with any more pictures 'in which men wrote with feathers'.

6 Eric Morecambe, the likeable English comedian, was teamed with an excellent foil in Ernie Wise. The annual *Morecambe and Wise Christmas Show*, especially on BBC TV, was part of what people now think Christmas used to be like. In their long apprenticeship, when Eric and Ernie were appearing for the third time at the Glasgow Empire – a notorious graveyard of English comic talent – they walked off stage to complete silence. The stage doorkeeper confided in them: 'Aye, lads, they're beginning to like you.'

Recalled in Roger Wilmut, *Kindly Leave the Stage* (1985).

7 Des O'Connor, at one time chiefly famous from jokes made about his singing style by Morecambe and Wise,

also braved the old Glasgow Empire in his early days. He recalls that the audiences were indeed hostile, especially to any entertainer coming from south of the border – ice-cream cones and shipyard rivets were said to have rained down on hapless comedians. The slowhand clap, cries of 'Away and catch yer train', 'Och, go bile your heed', were among the methods used to wear down newcomers. On one occasion, the young O'Connor, who is nothing if not an all-round entertainer, was finding it extremely difficult to get any response from the audience. He sang, he danced, he told jokes, and then started working his way through a whole bandstand of instruments. As he reached for a trumpet, a voice arose drily from the audience, and asked, 'Och, is there no end to this man's talent?'

From Des O'Connor's own reminiscences, recorded for the BBC in 1985, and as recounted by Arnold Brown (1990).

1 The English comedian Bernie Winters, originally half of a double act with his brother, Mike, also had a Glasgow Empire tale to tell. The comedians were once playing there in front of an awesome Scots audience. Mike began by playing the clarinet and then was joined by Bernie. A voice in the audience exclaimed: 'My God, there's two of them!'

Told by Ernie Wise in the *Independent* (6 May 1991).

2 The great musical-hall and variety comedian Billy Bennett was on a variety bill preceding the West Indian entertainer 'Hutch'. Bennett found the audience hard work that night. As he came off the stage at the end of his act, Hutch asked him what the audience was like. Bennett snorted: 'Not worth blacking up for.'

Hence the expression 'not worth blacking up for!' to describe anything that is not worth the trouble – but especially an audience that is not worth performing in front of. Told in *Roy Hudd's Book of Music-Hall, Variety and Showbiz Anecdotes* (1993). The story has also been given as though involving Robb Wilton and the Deep River Boys when their act had been cut at the London Palladium (by Leslie Thomas on BBC Radio *Quote . . . Unquote*, 26 January 1982).

3 The biographer Robert Lacey was in a Bristol cinema with his wife Sandi, watching the Ken Russell film of D. H. Lawrence's *Women in Love*. At the conclusion of the memorable scene in which Alan Bates and Oliver Reed wrestle with each other totally naked and then lie exhausted on the carpet, a woman in the audience was heard to comment: 'Nice carpet!'

Told by Robert Lacey on BBC Radio *Quote ... Unquote* (19 February 1979).

4 The Scottish actor Nicol Williamson soon lost patience with a group of noisy young Americans in the audience at a performance of *Macbeth*. He got off his throne, walked down to the footlights and calmly said, in iambic pentameters:

If you don't shut your mouths a friend
  of mine
Will pass amongst you with a baseball
  bat.

Whereupon he adjusted his crown and continued in complete silence.

Told by Sheila Hancock in *Ramblings of an Actress* (1987).

5 It is said that the pianist Alfred Brendel once stunned an expectorating concert

audience at a pianissimo point by announcing, 'I can hear you, but you can't hear me,' – thus ensuring absolute silence for the remainder.

As told in the *Observer* (20 May 1991).

Australians

1 A traveller arriving at an Australian airport was confronted by an immigration officer requiring to know, 'Do you have a criminal record?' The traveller told him he hadn't – 'I didn't realize it was still compulsory.'

This – 'the oldest and hoariest Australian joke in existence' – has sometimes been credited to Henry Blofeld, the English cricket commentator, according to *The Times* Diary (13 January 1990).

Autograph-hunting

2 John Hancock, from Boston, was one of the (if not the) first to sign the Declaration of Independence in 1776. His signature is quite the largest on the document and he is variously reported to have made it that way 'so the King of England could read it without spectacles' or with 'There! I guess King George [or John Bull] will be able to read that!'

Hence, 'John Hancock' is an American nickname for a signature or autograph. The second version above is in Herbert S. Allan, *John Hancock, Patriot in Purple* (1953).

3 On a train journey in the American Mid-West, the medical missionary and organist Albert Schweitzer was spotted by two women who asked, 'Oh, Mr *Einstein*, may we have your autograph?' Schweitzer was not put out by this request and agreed that he and Albert Einstein did have the same sort of hair, so it was an understandable mistake.

Then he said, 'Would you like me to give you Einstein's autograph?' The women nodded and so, taking out his pen, he wrote, 'Albert Einstein, by way of his friend, Albert Schweitzer.'

Told by T. D. Williams in *Reader's Digest* (September 1980).

4 The writers Tennessee Williams and Truman Capote were sitting talking together in a café one day when an over-excited female fan came bustling up and invited Mr Capote to sign one of her breasts. Before Capote could oblige, her furious husband rushed up, whipped out his penis and insisted that the diminutive writer sign that instead. Replied he: 'Well, I don't think I could manage to put my whole signature on that – but I could initial it.'

Recounted in the *Observer* (3 July 1994).

5 The comic Spike Milligan had great admiration for Evelyn Waugh. Whether this was reciprocated in any way must be in doubt. Once when passing White's Club in St James's, Milligan saw Waugh coming out and hastened over to ask for his autograph. Waugh duly scribbled on a bit of paper and handed the result to Milligan, who thanked him and went home. When he looked at what Waugh had written on the paper, it said, 'Go away.'

Told by Milligan on BBC Radio *Quote ... Unquote* (24 December 1977).

6 Peter Sellers once received a fan letter that read: 'Dear Mr Sellers, I have been a keen follower of yours for many years now, and should be most grateful if you would kindly send me a *singed* photograph of yourself.' Unable to ignore this unfortunate spelling mistake, Sellers took a photograph and burned it round

the edges using a cigarette lighter. A few weeks later, another letter arrived from the fan thanking him for the photograph, but adding, 'I wonder if I could trouble you for another as this one is *signed* all round the edge.'

As told many times by Sellers (for example in *The Listener*, 2 October 1969).

1 When Eric Morecambe had a heart attack in Leeds, it was 'like a Brian Rix farce', he said afterwards. He lay helpless in his Jensen sports car in the deserted streets at about one o'clock in the morning, and the only living human being around was 'this man who'd been in the Territorial Army'. Eric recalled: 'I asked him if he could drive and he drove my £7,000 motor car like a tank, for miles.' Then this man had to wake someone up at the hospital before admittance could be gained. Finally, as

they wheeled Eric into intensive care, the comedian heard the man whisper in his ear: 'Can I have your autograph before you go? . . .'

This version is largely as told to John Mortimer for *In Character* (1983). It had earlier appeared in a book called *Eric & Ernie* (1973).

2 One of Arthur Marshall's anecdotes concerned the occasion when he was coming out of the BBC Television Centre and was accosted by a woman seeking his autograph. The woman (inevitably) explained that she wanted it not for herself but for her daughter. However, when Marshall handed back the book, duly inscribed, the woman was visibly put out. 'Oh,' she said with disappointment all over her face, 'I thought you were Arthur Negus.'

Recalled in the *Guardian* (28 January 1989).

B

Babes and sucklings

1 The children of Lord Lytton, a famous diplomat, organized a charade. The scene displayed a Crusader knight returning from the wars to his ancestral castle. At the castle gate he was welcomed by his beautiful and rejoicing wife, to whom, after tender salutations, he recounted his triumphs on the tented fields and the number of paynim whom he had slain. 'And I too, my lord,' replied his wife, pointing with conscious pride to a long row of dolls of various sizes – 'and I too, my lord, have not been idle.'

According to G. W. E. Russell, *Collections and Recollections* (1898) – describing an event 'some twenty years ago.'

2 The American baseball player 'Shoeless Joe' Jackson had been accused with others of the Chicago White Sox of deliberately losing the 1919 World Series at the behest of gamblers. As he came out of a grand jury session in 1920 about corruption in that Series, he was approached by a small boy who asked, 'It ain't so, Joe, is it?' He replied, 'Yes, kid, I'm afraid it is.' Over the years, the words rearranged themselves into the more euphonious order of 'Say it ain't so, Joe!' Jackson denied that the exchange had ever taken place – using any set of words.

Told in *Bartlett's Familiar Quotations* (1980 edn).

3 A view promoting the superior imagination-stirring qualities of radio as a creative medium is sometimes said to have originated in a letter to *Radio Times* in the 1920s. It quoted a child who had said, when comparing the radio version of a story with that seen on the stage, 'The pictures are better.'

If this letter ever was published it has not been traced. It was the early 1960s rather than the 1920s that were evoked when Trevor Hill, former North of England head of BBC radio's *Children's Hour*, was invited to comment on the origin of the phrase in 1996. He wrote: 'What I do know is that in January 1960, Dorothea Brooking produced a splendid visual adaptation of Frances Hodgson Burnett's *The Secret Garden* for BBC Children's Television; and then, in the Spring of 1962, radio also did a version as the Sunday serial and I most definitely received a letter from a young listener who came either from Bolton or Bingley telling me how much she was enjoying David Davis's production. She thought the television was good – but liked the radio version, "because the scenery is better". Now she *may* have got that phrase from a parent; there is no knowing.' Consider these citations: 'By way of illustration a young lad was quoted as saying he preferred radio to television – because the scenery is better.

A proof of the power of imagination!' – Prayer Book Society *Newsletter* (August 1995). '"I like the wireless better than the theatre," one London child wrote in a now legendary letter, "because the scenery is better"' – Derek Parker, *Radio: The Great Years* (1977). In a Joyce Grenfell letter of 22 September 1962, which is included in the book *An Invisible Friendship* (1981): 'Do you ever listen [to the radio]? I do. I like it best. As a child I know says: "I see it much better on radio than on TV."' Note how Grenfell personalizes the anecdote. She had been on the Pilkington Committee, which presented its report on broadcasting a month or two before that letter was written – perhaps she had collected the story in the course of her duties.

1 After Russell Harty had played host to Johnny Weissmuller, the former Olympic athlete and film Tarzan, on his London Weekend Television chat show, the two were coming out of the studios when they were confronted by a posse of small boys waving autograph books. Seeing Harty and the actor – who was 6ft 11in (or something) and broad of shoulder – one little kid asked, 'Hey, which one of you two guys is Tarzan?'

Told by Harty in the book *Russell Harty Plus* (1974).

2 A conversation between two small boys. The three-year-old remarked, 'We had custard for lunch today.' The four-year-old asked him if it was 'Bird's Custard?' 'No,' replied the three-year-old. 'People's.'

Reported by Mary Shippey of Worthing, West Sussex, and broadcast on BBC Radio *Quote … Unquote* (7 April 1992).

Backstage remarks

3 Going backstage after a particularly disastrous opening night, the English writer and caricaturist Sir Max Beerbohm is supposed to have reassured the leading lady with the compliment: 'My dear, good is not the word.'

Ascribed to Beerbohm on BBC Radio *Quote … Unquote* (14 August 1979), but later also to George Bernard Shaw.

4 A squelch that *might* have been well-meant came from Beatrice Lillie when she dashed into a colleague's dressing room after a first night and exclaimed: 'Darling, I don't care what anybody says – I thought you were marvellous.'

Told in a letter from Tony Hepworth of Heaton, Bradford, on BBC Radio *Quote … Unquote* (12 June 1980).

5 The actor Ernest Thesiger was overcome by the usual embarrassment over what to say when going backstage after a performance to greet fellow thespians. He settled for, 'You couldn't have been better.'

Told by Peter Jones on BBC Radio *Quote … Unquote* (17 September 1983).

Ballet dancers

6 An Englishman sat unmoved all through Anna Pavlova's 'Dying Swan' dance until, near the end, a feather detached itself from her costume and fell to the ground. He said but one word: 'Moulting'.

Reported by Arnold Bennett and recounted in *The Lyttelton Hart-Davis Letters* (for 28 March 1957).

7 In the 1930s, conducting for the Camargo Society, Sir Thomas Beecham took the 'Dance of the Cygnets' from *Swan Lake* at about four times the normal speed. Said he, 'That made the buggers hop!'

Recounted by Sarah Woodcock in *Images of Show Business*, ed. James Fowler (1982).

The version in Charles Read, *Thomas Beecham* (untraced) apparently has the work in question as the Polovtsian Dances from *Prince Igor* during a Diaghilev ballet season.

1 It is unforgivable, of course, to go on about what male ballet dancers carry around in their tights, but there was one reluctant ballet-goer who could never resist commenting: 'Ah, I see he's brought his sandwiches with him.'

Told to me by a *Quote ... Unquote* listener (*c.* 1983).

Beauty

2 A seven-year-old girl was watching her mother put on some face cream and asked, 'Mummy, is that the cream they show on the television that makes you beautiful?' When mummy told her it was, she commented, after a thoughtful pause, 'It doesn't work very well, does it?'

Told in *Pass the Port* (1976). Arthur Marshall told a version on BBC Radio *Quote ... Unquote* (5 June 1980) in which the child asked about its mother's make-up, 'When is it supposed to start working?' A *Punch* joke originally, in all probability.

Bedding and beds

3 In the days of rampant lust in stately homes, Lord Charles Beresford (1846–1919) went prowling down the corridors one night, tiptoed into one particular bedroom, and jumped into the vast bed, crowing 'Cock-a-doodle-doo!' When the lamp was lit, after a good deal of confusion, he found himself between the Bishop of Chester and his wife.

Recounted in Anita Leslie, *Edwardians in Love* (1972). She adds: 'The situation seemed very difficult to explain and he left the house before breakfast next morning.'

4 During his summer holidays in the 1930s, the poet W. H. Auden believed in keeping himself warm. He liked to have a fire blazing in the sitting room if at all possible. On his bed, he would have two thick blankets and an eiderdown, with both his and Christopher Isherwood's overcoats on the top.

At any time of year, if the bedclothes were too light, Auden would use anything he could lay his hands on to provide sufficient weight for his slumbers. Staying with one family, he put the bedroom carpet on his bed. Staying with another, he took down the bedroom curtains and used these as extra blankets. Another time it was the stair carpet. Once he was discovered in the morning sleeping beneath (among other things) a large framed painting.

Recalled in Charles Osborne, *W. H. Auden* (1980) and Humphrey Carpenter, *W. H. Auden* (1981).

5 Overheard outside the junior section of a public library. Two little girls were talking and one remarked, 'Yes, we've moved into a house now, so me and my brother have got a bedroom each.' Then she added, thoughtfully: 'But Mummy and Daddy still have to share.'

I repeated this from a *Quote ... Unquote* listener (10 July 1980) but I fear it had whiskers on it even then. With the tag, 'Mum still has to sleep with dad', it also appeared in *Pass the Port Again* (1980).

Behaviour

6 A useful instruction given by a small hostess to a notoriously disruptive guest at a children's Christmas party: 'If you can't behave nicely ... don't behave at all.'

Contributed by Margaret R. Jackson of Chipping Camden to BBC Radio

Quote ... Unquote (17 March 1994). In fact, this probably derives from a cartoon caption that first appeared in *Punch* (24 April 1897) and then again below a cartoon by George Belcher (27 April 1932) with the text: *Indignant Young Lady*. 'If you can't behave properly, you'd better not behave at all.'

Belief

1 The Queen demonstrated formidable tact when asked by a small Commonwealth person during a Christmas broadcast whether she believed in Father Christmas. She was ready for it, and replied simply: 'I like to believe in Father Christmas.'

From the soundtrack of the broadcast (25 December 1989).

Betting

2 An actor with whom she was rehearsing caught Coral Browne's fancy. Informed by a colleague that she was *most* unlikely to get anywhere with that particular man, she bet the colleague a pound that she would. Next morning, the colleague who had accepted the bet asked her, loudly and meaningfully, in the presence of the other actor, 'Well, dear, do you owe me anything?' Browne replied, disappointedly: 'Seven and six.'

Told to me by Roger Hammond in 1983.

Bible study

3 Although he once joked that he would like as an epitaph, 'On the whole I'd rather be in Philadelphia', the nearest to a memorable deathbed utterance W. C. Fields produced before his demise on Christmas Day 1946 was when the actor Thomas Mitchell, to his amazement, found the comedian thumbing through the Bible. When Mitchell asked him what he was doing, Fields answered, 'Looking for loopholes.'

Reported in *The Daily Mirror Old Codger's Little Black Book* (1977). Fields's actual last words were: 'Goddamn the whole friggin' world and everyone in it but you, Carlotta' (a reference to his mistress) – Robert Lewis Taylor, *W. C. Fields: His Follies and Fortunes* (1950).

4 There can be few who have not heard of the little boy who called his teddy bear 'Gladly' because of the line in the hymn that goes (for childish ears, at least): 'Gladly, my cross-eyed bear ...'

Known by the 1960s, certainly. John Hopkins used the phrase as the title of one part of his TV drama *Talking to a Stranger* in 1966. Other childish mishearings on religious themes include 'Blessed art thou, a monk swimming', 'Harold be Thy name', 'Suffered under bunch of spiders', 'Hail, Mary, blessed art thou swimming' and my own 'Holy Golf ball'.

Birth

5 One of the numerous legends associated with St Nicholas, patron saint of Greece and Russia, and popularly known as 'Santa Claus', concerns his birth. It is said that he leapt from his mother's womb and cried out, 'God be glorified!'

In Benjamin Britten's cantata *St Nicholas* (1948), which has a libretto by Eric Crozier, he can be heard saying it.

6 When the American painter James McNeill Whistler was asked why he had been born in such an unfashionable place as Lowell, Massachusetts, he replied: 'The explanation is quite simple. I wished to be near my mother.'

Told in *Medical Quotations* (1989). A similar

line was attributed to the British comedian Max Wall in his obituary in the *Guardian* (23 May 1990): 'I was born there because I wanted to be near my parents.' Note how the idea behind both these versions ended up as the caption to a cartoon in *Punch* (14 August 1935): 'What made them build the station such a long way from the town?' 'They 'ad to, M'm, so as to be near the railway.' Compare also William Powell's line to Myrna Loy in the film *Manhattan Melodrama* (US, 1934): 'I was born at home because I wanted to be near my mother ...'

1 A certain actor was not going to be put out when he heard someone state that 'actors have to be *born*'. He said, 'I looked up my birth certificate and I found I was all right.'

Told on BBC Radio *Quote ... Unquote* (1988). However, this would appear to be a re-working of: 'It occurred to me that I would like to be a poet. The chief qualification, I understand, is that you must be born. Well, I hunted up my birth certificate, and found that I was all right on that score' – Saki (H. H. Munro), 'Reginald's Rubaiyat', *Reginald* (1904).

2 Martin Amis, the English author, had such early success that some people were tempted to believe that his being the son of another novelist, Kingsley Amis, had probably been no hindrance. In the late 1970s, there was a *New Statesman* competition in which readers were asked to provide improbable titles for new books by famous authors. One suggestion was '*My Struggle* by Martin Amis.'

Recalled in the *Observer* (4 July 1993).

Bishops

3 Press comment on the relationship between King Edward VIII and Wallis Simpson finally burst through following some exceedingly innocuous remarks made on 1 December 1936 by Alfred Blunt, the Bishop of Bradford. Speaking at a diocesan conference, he was dealing with a suggestion that the forthcoming Coronation should be secularized and addressing criticism that the King was not a regular church-goer. Said he, 'The benefit of the King's Coronation depends under God upon ... the faith, prayer and self-dedication of the King himself ... We hope that he is aware of this need. Some of us wish that he gave more positive signs of such awareness.' The *Yorkshire Post* linked the Bishop's words to rumours then in circulation. Dr Blunt claimed subsequently that his address had been written six weeks earlier, without knowledge of the rumours, and added: 'I studiously took care to say nothing of the King's private life, because I know nothing about it.'

Told in Frances Donaldson, *Edward VIII* (1974).

4 The diarist Chips Channon once recorded that he visited Wells Cathedral and then lunched at the Palace with the Bishop of Bath and Wells. Inevitably, there was much talk of Barchester, and the Bishop said, to everybody's consternation, 'There is nothing I like better than to lie on my bed for an hour with my favourite Trollope.'

Chips Channon's diary (for 4 April 1943).

5 A bishop told Winston Churchill that his palace had no less than forty bedrooms in it. Churchill commented: 'Oh dear – and only Thirty-Nine Articles to put in them.'

Letter from Martin Hawkins of London SW2 on BBC Radio *Quote ... Unquote* (21 August 1979).

Bitchery

1 Edith Sitwell delivered this magisterial
rebuke to the one-time popular novelist
Ethel Mannin (and subsequently re-
applied it to various other targets): 'I do
not want Miss Mannin's feelings to be
hurt by the fact that I have never heard
of her ... At the moment I am de-
barred from the pleasure of putting her
in her place by the fact that she has
not got one.'

Told in John Pearson, *Façades* (1978), based
on a report in the *Yorkshire Evening News*
(8 August 1930). By 13 March 1940, James
Agate appears to have been re-ascribing this
(in his *Ego 4*): 'About an American woman
novelist [Mannin was English] who had
been rude to her in print, Lady Oxford [i.e.
Margot Asquith] is reported to have said,
"I would put Miss B. in her place if she had
a place."'

2 When asked about the apparent
absence of Eleanor Roosevelt from a
White House reception she was
supposed to be hosting, Groucho
Marx informed another guest: 'She's
upstairs filing her teeth.'

Source untraced. In my book *Say No More!*
(1987).

3 Elsa Lanchester reputedly said of her
fellow actress Maureen O'Hara: 'She
looked as though butter wouldn't melt
in her mouth. Or anywhere else.'

The source for this appears to be *News
Summaries* (30 January 1950).

4 Bette Davis said of a certain starlet
who was accustomed to putting herself
about a bit: 'I see – she's the original
good time that was had by all.'

Told in Leslie Halliwell, *The Filmgoer's Book
of Quotes* (1973).

5 Beatrice Lillie, the Canadian-born
actress, was married to a Sir Robert
Peel, and did not let people lightly
forget it. Miss Lillie, on tour in
Chicago, was in a beauty salon with
other members of her company. She
overheard another client who had been
kept waiting, complaining of 'All these
theatricals ...' Miss Lillie discovered
that the complainer was Mrs Armour,
wife of the Chicago meat-packing
tycoon. On leaving the salon, she said
to the receptionist – and in the hearing
of Mrs Armour – 'You may tell the
butcher's wife that Lady Peel has
finished.'

Told in L. and M. Cowan, *The Wit of
Women* (1969).

6 Laurence Olivier could be embarrass-
ingly frank about his sexual performance. In particular, he worried about
the smallness of his equipment. His
second wife, Vivien Leigh, didn't help
by being something of a nympho-
maniac. After the first performance of
Uncle Vanya, the Olivier production
that opened the Chichester Festival
Theatre in 1962, he was unhappy with
the way it had gone. In his dressing
room afterwards he confessed that it
had gone off at 'half-cock'. 'Better half-
cock,' rejoined Vivien Leigh, 'than no
cock at all.'

I first heard this from an actor friend in 1983.
If this really occurred at Chichester, Olivier
and Leigh had already been divorced since
1960 and Olivier was by this time married to
Joan Plowright (who was appearing with him
in *Uncle Vanya*).

7 When her husband, Harold Pinter, left
her for Lady Antonia Fraser, the actress
Vivien Merchant was devastated. In a
newspaper interview she came up with
this classic example of the higher bitch-
ery: 'He didn't need to take a change

of shoes. He can always wear hers. She has very big feet, you know.'

Told in the *Observer* (21 December 1975).

1 After leaving Johannesburg on a flight to London, a rather smug and self-opinionated woman travelling in the first-class section beckoned the stewardess to come to her. 'Tell me,' she said, grandly, 'What's the domestic situation in England these days?' Replied the stewardess: 'I don't think you will have any trouble finding a job, madam.'

Told in a letter from A. J. Humphreys of Hampton, Middlesex, on BBC Radio *Quote ... Unquote* (9 November 1982).

Blame

2 This is a story about four people: Everybody, Somebody, Anybody and Nobody. There was an important job to be done, and Everybody was asked to do it. Everybody was sure Somebody would do it. Anybody could have done it, but Nobody did it. Somebody got angry about that because it was Everybody's job. Everybody thought Anybody could do it. Nobody realized Everybody wouldn't do it. In the end, Everybody blamed Somebody when actually Nobody asked Anybody.

This story appeared in a letter to the editor (headed 'Successful Administration is Invisible – Poor Administration Is All Too Apparent') in the *Financial Times* (9 July 1988). Probably an example of 'office graffiti' and its original source never likely to be known.

Blessings

3 When Winston Churchill, having led the British people to victory in the war against Germany, was nevertheless ejected from office in the 1945 General Election, his wife told him it might be a

'blessing in disguise'. He repied: 'At the moment, it seems quite effectively disguised.'

Told in his *The Second World War*, Vol. 6 (1954). Despite this comment, Churchill seems to have come round to something like his wife's point of view. On 5 September 1945 he wrote to her from an Italian holiday: 'This is the first time for very many years that I have been completely out of the world ... Others having to face the hideous problems of the aftermath ... It may all indeed be "a blessing in disguise".'

Bluffing

4 The 5th Earl of Berkeley (1745–1810) always declared that it was no disgrace to be overcome by superior numbers, but that he would never surrender to a single highwayman. Then, when he was crossing Hounslow Heath one night, on his way from Berkeley Castle to London, he was duly stopped by a man on horseback. Putting his head through the window, the man said, 'I believe you are Lord Berkeley?' 'I am.' 'I believe you have always boasted that you would never surrender to a single highwayman?' 'I have.' 'Well,' said the man, presenting his pistol, 'I am a single highwayman, and I say, "Your money or your life".' 'You cowardly dog,' said Lord Berkeley, 'do you think I can't see your confederate skulking behind you?' The highwayman, who really was all alone, looked hurriedly round, and Lord Berkeley shot him through the head.

Told in G. W. E. Russell, *Collections and Recollections*, Chap. 1 (1898). Russell adds that he told this story to Lady Caroline Maxse (1803–86), who was born at Berkeley, and asked if it were true. 'Yes,' she replied, 'and I am proud to say that I am that man's daughter.'

Books and book-selling

1 William Lisle Bowles, poet and Vicar of Bremhill, was an eccentric. He engraved his own poems on the tombstones of parishioners, and on one occasion presented a friend with a copy of the Bible inscribed 'with the author's compliments'.

Told in S.C. Hall, *A Book of Memories* (1871), where the recipient was Hall's wife. Also in Terence de Vere White, *Tom Moore* (1977), where it is added that, 'Tuning his sheep bells in to thirds and fifths, he dressed as a druid and appeared at Stonehenge on the fourth of June. His absent-mindedness exceeded even [Thomas] Moore's.' On the other hand, Vanessa Letts in *New York* (1991) states that the author Theodore Dreiser once entered the Gotham Book Mart in that city 'and inscribed all the books as well as the Bible "with the compliments of the author".'

2 Lady Dorothy Nevill, so Sir Edmund Gosse tells, preserved her library by pasting in each volume the legend: 'This book has been stolen from Lady Dorothy Nevill.'

Told in *The Week-End Book* (1955).

3 When Alexander Woollcott was asked to sign a first edition of his book *Shouts and Murmurs*, he inquired rhetorically, 'What is rarer than a Woollcott first edition?' the humorist, writer and critic Franklin Pierce Adams produced the answer: 'A Woollcott second edition.'

Told in R. E. Drennan, *Wit's End* (1973). Also told of other people. In *The Treasury of Humorous Quotations*, ed. Evan Esar and Nicolas Bentley (1951), Adams is simply quoted as saying of a 'certain author' that, 'A first edition of his work is a rarity but a second is rarer still.' As is often the case, Oscar Wilde seems to have got there first: 'While the first editions of most classical authors are those coveted by the bibliophiles, it is the second editions of my books that are the true

rarities, and even the British Museum has not been able to secure copies of most of them.' – in Hesketh Pearson, *The Life of Oscar Wilde*, Chap. 14 (1946).

4 At a book-signing in Sydney, Australia, Monica Dickens asked the buyer of one of her books, 'May I dedicate it to someone?' 'Emma Chisit,' replied the woman. 'And is Chisit spelled with one "s" or two?' inquired Dickens. Then the light dawned: 'Thirty-two dollars,' she replied.

Told in *The Sydney Morning Herald* (30 November 1964) and recalled in Afferbeck Lauder, *Let's Talk Strine* (1965).

5 In 1962, Richard M. Nixon was signing copies of his book *Six Crises* in a bookshop in California. When he asked one purchaser to whom he should dedicate the book, the customer said, 'You've just met your seventh crisis, Mr Nixon. My name is Stanislaus Wojechzlechki!'

Told in *Reader's Digest* (November 1962).

6 When Edward Heath, the Prime Minister, fell from power in 1974 and was also subsequently ousted from the leadership of the Conservative Party, he sought to console himself by writing and promoting three books about his non-political interests: *Sailing – A Course of My Life* (1975), *Music – A Joy for Life* (1976), and *Travels – People and Places in My Life* (1977). He vigorously toured the country selling these works, even using a special train in the process. So many copies did he autograph in the course of selling them that it became a truism in publishing that the really rare edition of a Heath book was one that he had not managed to sign.

My recollection of the events.

1 As every author and publisher knows, it is no easy task getting people to buy books. Just what an uphill task it is can best be illustrated by the overheard conversation between two old biddies in a store in the run-up to Christmas. They were both obviously on the look-out for Christmas presents for their respective spouses. One said, 'What can I get Harold for Christmas? I don't know what to get him.' The other suggested, 'Why not get him a book?' 'No,' replied the other, 'He's got a book.'

Contributed by Miss E. Kissan, Bournemouth, to BBC Radio *Quote ... Unquote* (14 August 1980). Compare this exchange from the film *Charlie Chan Carries On* (US, 1931) – a Chicago gangster sneeringly says of his wife, 'I suppose she'll buy a book now.' Says she, on hearing this: 'No, I've already got one.'

Book titles

2 There is a story told about J. M. Barrie's advice to a young writer who did not know what title to give his first work. 'Are there any trumpets in it?' Barrie asked, and got the answer 'No'. 'Are there any drums in it?' he asked. 'No.' 'Then why not call it *Without Drums or Trumpets*?'

Untraced, but when I heard Ludovic Kennedy tell the story about Barrie in 1991, the title suggested was, rather, *No Horses, No Trumpets*. A similar story is told about the French playwright, Tristan Bernard (1866–1947) in Cornelia Otis Skinner's *Elegant Wits and Grand Horizontals* (1962). Somebody did take the advice: the Dutch author Jeroen Brouwers published a novel entitled *Zonder trommels en trompetten* [Without Drums and Trumpets] (1973); and the English translation of Alec Le Vernoy's Second World War memoir was entitled *No Drums, No Trumpets* (1983).

3 Since the early 1980s, *The Bookseller*

journal has reported annually on the Diagram Prize for the Oddest Title at the Frankfurt Book Fair. Publishers really do allow the most extraordinary things to go on title pages. Winners over the years have included: *The Joy of Chickens* by Dennis Nolan; *I Can Taste and Smell* by Peter Curry; *Entrepreneur: Career Management in House Prostitution*; *Proceedings of the Second International Workshop on Nude Mice*; *Eat Your House* by Frederic Hobbs (an eco guide to self-sufficiency); and *Entertaining with Insects*.

I cannot remember now – from a lifetime's reading – whether books with the titles *Biggles Pulls It Off* and *Noddy's Magic Rubber* were ever really published. However, *Views of Gentlemen's Seats* is mentioned in Sir Walter Scott's Journals and *Men and Horses I Have Known* was glimpsed by me in a bookcase at Blenheim Palace. I have also been told about *Instructions for the Best Positions on the Pianoforte* by Col. Peter Hawker. *Twice Round the World with the Holy Ghost* is mentioned in the published edition of Evelyn Waugh's letters.

4 Another problem for authors (and publishers and booksellers) is that few potential purchasers of books know what they are looking for. And even if they do, they probably don't know the name of the author, the title, or the name of the publisher with total accuracy. A bookseller in Leicester told me that a woman once came into his shop and said, 'Have you got a copy of Thomas Hardy's *Tess of the Dormobiles*?'

I think I acquired this anecdote during a visit to speak at a literary lunch organized by the *Leicester Mercury* in October 1980.

Boots

5 When asked what title he would give to any further volume of his autobiography, the jazz musician Humphrey

Lyttelton said that his father had long ago chosen the right one for him: *My God, What Boots!* Wearing, as he does, size 13 shoes, Lyttelton would find these words in the index of the hymnal containing 'My God, What Boots It To Repent'.

Told by Humph on BBC Radio *Quote ... Unquote* (24 August 1985).

1 Michael Bentine was playing Lorenzo in a Robert Atkins production of *The Merchant of Venice*, but Atkins decided that he looked too small. 'You've got to wear lifts,' Bentine was told, and accordingly wedges of cork, 2½ inches thick, were put in his boots. The result was that he came on stage with his body thrown forward as though walking in a high wind. Said Atkins, 'Michael, you're supposed to come from Venice, not from bloody Pisa!'

Told by Bentine on BBC Radio *Quote ... Unquote* (17 October 1989). Oddly, Kitty Black in *Upper Circle* (1984), telling the same story, casts Bentine as Demetrius – in *A Midsummer Night's Dream* – and has Atkins say, 'You're supposed to come from Verona, my boy. Not bloody Pisa.' Meanwhile Ned Sherrin, in *Theatrical Anecdotes* (1991), has it involving the *Dream*, Athens, and Pisa. I'll stick to Bentine's own version.

Bores and boring

2 The Reverend Sydney Smith's daughter describes in her memoir of him his re-action to the one-time reigning bore of Edinburgh, whose favourite subject was the North Pole: 'It mattered not how far south you began, you found yourself transported to the north pole before you could take breath; no one escaped him.' Francis Jeffrey (Lord Jeffrey), the critic, avoided this bore whenever possible, but one day the 'arch-tormentor'

met him in a narrow lane and immediately began on his favourite subject. Jeffrey brushed past him, saying, 'Damn the North Pole!'

Sydney Smith encountered the bore himself shortly after this incident. The bore was boiling with indignation at Jeffrey's contempt for the North Pole. 'Oh, my dear fellow,' Smith soothed. 'No one minds what Jeffrey says, you know; he is a privileged person; he respects nothing, absolutely nothing. Why, you will scarcely believe it, but it is not more than a week ago that I heard him speak disrespectfully of the Equator!'

Told in Lady Holland, *Memoir of the Rev. Sydney Smith* (1855).

3 Even worse are bores who know they are, and who keep asking, 'Am I boring you?' Even if you said yes, and you won't, it wouldn't help. The poet Browning was once cornered by an admirer who kept on at him for a whole evening. What had he meant by writing this line and who had he intended by such and such a character? Eventually, with considerable grace, Browning insisted, 'But, my dear fellow, this is too bad. *I* am *monopolizing* you,' and was freed from his embrace.

G. W. E. Russell, *Collections and Recollections*, Chap. 13 (1898). Russell indicates that he was present at the dinner when this move was made.

4 Sir Lewis Morris, a sort of poet, once bored Oscar Wilde with complaints that his books were boycotted by the press. He also believed that he should have become Poet Laureate after the death of Tennyson. After giving several instances of unfair treatment, he said: 'There's a conspiracy against me, a

conspiracy of silence! But what can one do? What should I do?' Replied Wilde: 'Join it.'

Told by Frank Harris in *Oscar Wilde, His Life and Confessions*, Chap. 20 (1930), and before that in Walter Jerrold, *A Book of Famous Wits* (1912).

1 Someone was telling Lord 'Linky' Quickswood a long and involved story when he broke off and said, 'I do hope I'm not boring you.' Quickswood replied: 'Not yet ...'

Told by John Julius Norwich on BBC Radio *Quote ... Unquote* (12 April 1994).

2 An elderly scientist was droning on to Mrs Patrick Campbell about ants – 'They are wonderful little creatures. They have their own police force and their own army.' Mrs Pat could bear it no longer. She leaned forward and, with an expression said to be 'of the utmost interest and in a voice like damson-coloured velvet', said: 'No navy, I suppose?'

Recounted in Margot Peters, *Mrs Pat* (1984). James Agate in *Ego 7* (for 11 February 1944) has it from someone called Bobby Andrews.

3 In the Ivy Restaurant, Sir John Gielgud was having lunch with a friend of his when another man came up and talked and talked and talked. When at last he went away, Gielgud turned to his friend and said, 'Oh god, that man's so boring. The only more boring man in the world is Eddie Knoblock.'

Edward Knoblock was his guest. Then he added: 'Not you, of course, dear boy. I mean the other Edward Knoblock.'

Told by Julian Mitchell on BBC Radio *Quote ... Unquote* (2 March 1982 and 10 April 1998). Also told in John Mortimer, *In Character* (1983).

4 Directing Nicol Williamson in *Richard III*, Trevor Nunn was taking infinite trouble over how to kill off the young princes in the tower. Williamson, exasperated at how long all this was taking, cried out: 'Why don't you take them into the wings and bore them to death?'

Told by Sheila Hancock on BBC Radio *Quote ... Unquote* (17 October 1989).

Breasts and breast-feeding

5 'On the bus the other day a woman with a baby sat opposite, the baby bawled, and the woman at once began to unlace herself, exposing a large red udder, which she swung into the baby's face. The infant, however, continued to cry and the woman said, "Come on, there's a good boy – if you don't, I shall give it to the gentleman opposite."'

This passage comes from *The Journal of a Disappointed Man* by W. N. P. Barbellion, first published in 1919. I included it in my *Eavesdroppings* (1981), but subsequently discovered that – like so much else – this much-quoted remark probably began life as a *Punch* cartoon caption. In the edition of 11 May 1904 (Vol. 126), 'THE UNPROTECTED MALE' shows a man in an omnibus being addressed thus: *'Mother (after vainly offering a bottle to refractory infant)* "'ERE, TIKE IT, WILL YER! IF YER DON'T 'URRY UP, I'LL GIVE IT TO THE GENTLEMAN OPPOSITE!"'

6 Norma Sykes of Blackpool (born about 1938) is one of the most fondly remembered British TV appearers of the 1950s. She was called 'Sabrina' after the recent Hollywood film *Sabrina Fair*. At the age of 17, she appeared with Arthur Askey in *Before Your Very Eyes* and simply stood there, not saying anything, in a tight-fitting sequinned dress, showing off her 41-18-36 figure. Subsequently, she went to live in

Hollywood, and little more was heard of her. After the TV studio where she made her appearances, she earned the nickname of 'the Hunchfront of Lime Grove'.

Detail from the *Sunday Express* (13 January 1985).

1 In about 1967, an exercise group in an undergraduate girl's dorm at the University of Michigan used a certain chant when doing a standard arm and shoulder exercise, known informally as the 'Sweater Filler'. The chant, in full, was:

> I must, I must, I must
> I must increase my bust
> I'd better, I'd better, I'd better
> I'd better fill out this sweater.

Note that it is 'increase' here rather than 'improve'. I have also heard of a 'develop' version. Told by Jennifer I. Brand of the University of Nebraska in *The 'Quote ... Unquote' Newsletter* (April 1999). Others remember similar versions from the mid-1950s. A suggestion that the chant made an appearance in *The Raquel Welch Total Beauty and Fitness Program* (1984) proved, sadly, to be unfounded. A possible origin is indicated in a reminiscence by the actress Jane Birkin of her short-lived marriage to the film composer, John Barry: 'I met John when we did a rather jolly musical called *Passion Flower Hotel* ... He got me to sing a song called "I must, I must improve my bust".' That would have been in 1964. The musical, written with Trevor Peacock, was a disastrous flop. But was it the start of the chant or merely a picking up of something that was around already? We should, we should, we should be told. I am also told the chant appears in the Rosalind Erskine novel *The Passion Flower Hotel* (1975), which may be related to the musical.

Breeding

2 When Alfred E. Smith, the American politician, was Governor of New York,

he was told by the Mayor of Boston, 'Of course, up in Boston, we think breeding is everything!' Smith replied: 'Well, down here in New York, we think it's quite fun, too, but we don't think it's everything.'

Told by Margaret R. Jackson of Chipping Campden (1994).

Britishness

3 In the 'phoney war' period of 1939–40, the Germans tried to sow discord among the Western Allies by organizing propaganda broadcasts. The French were told that the British had sent only six divisions, and that the eighty French divisions would have to bear the brunt of the fighting. The British, as usual, would fight 'to the last Frenchman.'

Told in Anthony Rhodes, Propaganda: *The Art of Persuasion in World War II* (1976).

4 At the Commonwealth Parliamentary Conference in 1986, a Mr Hall representing the Turks and Caicos Islands had the delegates applauding and banging on the tables by saying, 'There was an Englishman and an Indian ... And the Englishman was boasting that the sun really never did set on the British Empire. At which the Indian replied, "No, because God would never trust an Englishman in the dark."'

Reported in *The Guardian* (2 October 1986), which correctly identified this as an 'old chestnut'. The original description of the British Empire as one 'upon which the sun never sets' – i.e. one that, at its apogee, was so widespread that the sun was always shining on some part of it – was coined by John Wilson (Christopher North), who wrote in *Noctes Ambrosianae*, No. 20 (April 1829) of: 'His Majesty's dominions, on which the sun never sets'.

The earliest appearance of the joke

rejoinder I have come across is ascribed to 'Duncan Spaeth' (is this John Duncan Spaeth, the US educator?) in Nancy McPhee, *The Book of Insults* (1978) in the form: 'I know why the sun never sets on the British Empire: God wouldn't trust an Englishman in the dark.' During a visit to New York City by Prince Charles in June 1981, an Irish Republican placard was photographed bearing the words, 'The Sun Never Sets on the British Empire Because God Doesn't Trust the British in the Dark.'

Broccoli

1 President George Bush was a junk-food junky. It was said that he crunched chocolate bars over his breakfast and was addicted to pork scratchings. One of the few policies he stood firm on concerned broccoli. 'It tastes like a medicine,' he declared, and banned it from his official plane, Air Force One. When this caused ructions among broccoli growers (who unloaded a 10-ton juggernaut on the White House steps), he warned, 'Wait till the country hears how I feel about cauliflower.'

He followed this up by declaring his distaste for carrots also. He denounced them as 'orange broccoli'.

Reported in the *Independent on Sunday* (25 March 1990).

Bureaucracy

2 In his early days as a natural history broadcaster, David Attenborough was filming in Paraguay for a programme called *Zoo Quest*. In the course of his work, he was advised locally that it would be much cheaper to buy a couple of horses rather than to *hire* them. Besides, the horses were inexpensive, and could be set free when they were no longer required. On his return to London, Attenborough was faced with a formidable, desk-bound BBC administrator who had discovered the purchase among all the paperwork. 'The horses are clearly BBC property,' she insisted. 'So where are they?' Attenborough forestalled much further paperwork by saying conclusively, 'Madam, we ate them.'

Told by Leonard Miall in a broadcast talk 'In at the Start' (1982). Also told in Paul Ferris, *Sir Huge* (1990).

3 In the 1950s, Frank Muir was enjoying a hugely successful scriptwriting partnership with Denis Norden. They wrote *Breakfast with Braden, Take It From Here,* and much else. On one occasion, the BBC bureaucracy paid them twice for the same script. When this was discovered, the BBC asked for the overpayment to be returned. Naturally reluctant to do any such thing, Muir and Norden concocted a reply which stated that 'Messrs Muir and Norden regret that they have no machinery for the return of cheques.' Apparently, this satisfied the BBC bureaucracy.

Recounted in Ned Sherrin, *Cutting Edge* (1984). As I discovered for myself when I was also paid twice by the BBC for a whole series of programmes, the bureaucracy has become a little wiser since then. Any overpayment is now merely deducted from future payments. I like the cheek of the Muir and Norden message, however. It is reminiscent of the way things are done in the army. If you break something, it is very important to retain the broken pieces. All the bureaucracy is interested in is that a mistake can be 'accounted for'. In *A Kentish Lad* (1997), Muir finally gave his version of the story: the BBC Accounts Department had requested repayment of an advance given for a project called *Ça c'est Paris* that was cancelled. The writers' response was, 'We regret that we have no machinery for returning money.' Muir added, 'The BBC

Accounts Department was perfectly happy with this.'

1 In 1963, the British Army was mopping up after an uprising in Borneo. The Commanding Officer of the 1st Battalion (Royal) Green Jackets was later asked to account to the financial authorities for his hiring of twenty longboats. His reply was: 'Regret no short boats available.' Apparently he heard no more about it.

Told in *Bugle and Kukri*, Vol. 2 of the story of the 10th Princess Mary's Own Gurkha Rifles (1984).

Buses

2 Lord Curzon, viceroy and politician, is said to have commented on his first trip by bus: 'This omnibus business is not what it is reported to be. I hailed one at the bottom of Whitehall and told the man to take me to Carlton House Terrace. But the fellow flatly refused.'

This is among the 'Curzonia' included in *The Oxford Book of Political Anecdotes* (1986), though it is not quite clear what the original source was. Compare the story told about Sir Herbert Beerbohm Tree, the actor, which must have occurred at the same sort of period. Antony Jay tells me that his father (who was an actor) used to say that Tree hailed a taxicab and told the driver to take him home. 'Where's that?' the driver asked, understandably. To which Tree replied: 'Why should I tell you where my beautiful house is?'

As always, the origin of the tale could lie in *Punch*. On 10 April 1901, there was a cartoon by Everard Hopkins with this caption:

A GIRLISH IGNORANCE
Lady Hildegarde, who is studying the habits of the democracy, determines to travel by Omnibus. Lady Hildegarde: "CONDUCTOR, TELL THE DRIVER TO GO TO NO. 104, BERKELEY SQUARE, AND THEN HOME!"

Business acumen

3 After many years as a film producer and cinema owner, Sydney Bernstein applied for one of the first commercial television franchises in Britain. He was successful in winning the Northern region (which at first included Lancashire and Yorkshire) and set up a company called Granada TV. Some time later he explained to the Manchester Publicity Association why he had chosen to pitch for the North rather than London or the Midlands: 'It was brought about by two maps: a population map of Great Britain and a rainfall map. Any sensible person, after studying these two maps for a few minutes, would realize that if commercial TV is going to be a success anywhere in the world, it would be in the industrial North of England.'

Recalled in Caroline Moorhead, *Sydney Bernstein* (1984).

C

Camp

1 Coral Browne did not think much of a gay actor who was looking for a part for himself in Shakespeare's *King Lear*. Taking the text from him and flipping through the pages she eventually pointed to a stage direction in Act V and said: 'Here you are, dear, how about "A Camp, near Dover"?'

Told to me by Roger Hammond in 1983. Sometimes the actor in question is said to have been her first husband, Philip Pearman (d. 1964), and that she said it to him when they were lying in bed and she was learning her lines as Regan.

Casuistry

2 Sese Seko Kuku Ngbendu Wa Za Banga Mobuto (1930–97) was the President of Zaïre and generally regarded as a bad lot. By his sayings ye shall know him. He once said, 'All journalists are spies – I know, I have been one.' He also said, 'The people of Zaïre are not thieves. It merely happens that they move things, or borrow them.'

Told in *The Sunday Times* (28 May 1978).

Cats

3 A friend of Dorothy Parker, the American writer and wit, was upset at having to part with his cat but could not think how to get rid of it. 'Have you tried curiosity?' she suggested.

Told in *The Sayings of Dorothy Parker*, ed. S.T. Brownlow (1992).

Champagne

4 Noël Coward was once asked why he had champagne for breakfast. His reply was, 'Doesn't everyone?'

Contributed by J. Petty of Bradford to BBC Radio *Quote … Unquote* (29 June 1977)

Changes

5 Robert Runcie, a former Archbishop of Canterbury, asked a friend who was a rabbi what changes he thought there had been in the role of the Archbishop. The friend told a story. There was once a troublesome cat who made a great deal of noise chasing the lady cats in the neighbourhood, disturbing everyone's peace and quiet. Eventually, the owner had it neutered. When friends asked, 'Did it work?' he answered, 'Well, he's still making a lot of noise; but it is now only in an advisory capacity.'

Told in an address to bishops attending the Lambeth Conference (16 July 1998).

Charges

6 When a Fortnum and Mason salesgirl

insisted on fetching her threepence change, Edith Evans said: 'Keep the change, my dear, I trod on a grape as I came in.'

Related in Bryan Forbes, *Ned's Girl* (1977).

1 Arthur Rigby Jr was a character actor, best remembered as the desk-sergeant for many years in TV's *Dixon of Dock Green*. As a young man, Rigby was once staying in theatrical digs and found that the landlady's daughter not only made eyes at him but also ended up in his bed from the Monday night to Sunday morning. The landlady made absolutely no mention of a situation of which she must have been aware – except that when Rigby got his bill on Sunday morning it included 'Ten shillings for extra vegetables', a charge he otherwise had not incurred.

Told by Rigby's nephew, the actor William Franklyn, on BBC Radio *Quote … Unquote* (24 August 1985).

Charity

2 Outside the theatre one night, the American actress Tallulah Bankhead encountered a group from the Salvation Army, tambourines as always well to the fore. She promptly dropped a $50 dollar bill into one of the tambourines, saying, 'Don't bother to thank me. I know what a perfectly ghastly season it has been for you Spanish dancers.'

Recounted in Dorothy Herrmann, *With Malice Towards All* (1980).

Cheek and chutzpah

3 The playwright Richard Brinsley Sheridan had a son called Tom who was a spendthrift. After they had had an argument over some matter, Sheridan

told his son that he was cutting him out of his will – all except for a nominal shilling. 'You don't happen to have it about you now, do you?' asked the young man.

Told in Leon A. Harris, *The Fine Art of Political Wit* (1966).

4 The classic definition of chutzpah describes the behaviour of the young man had who killed his parents and then threw himself on the mercy of the court on the grounds that he was an orphan.

So given in Leo Rosten, *The Joys of Yiddish* (1968). Compare this from the film *Destry Rides Again* (US, 1939): the Deputy Sheriff (James Stewart) talks about a boy who killed his parents with a crowbar. At the trial, the judge asked the boy if he had anything to say for himself, and the boy replied, 'Well, I just hope that you have some regard for the feelins of a poor orphan.'

5 Marie Lloyd, the great English music-hall entertainer, was once, according to the story, forbidden by a watch committee (local guardians of morals) to sing the words, 'She sits among the cabbages and peas.' So she substituted, 'She sits among the cabbages and leeks.'

Told, for example, by John Trevelyan, the British film censor (*TV Times*, 23 April–9 May 1981). There is doubt as to whether any such song exists beyond the confines of this story. There was a song written in 1929, called 'Mucking About the Garden', but that was after Lloyd had died. It was written by Leslie Sarony, the British entertainer (1897–1985), using the *nom de plume* 'Q. Cumber' or 'Q. Kumber'. Unfortunately, I have been unable to find the sheet music (published by Lawrence Wright) to see if it really does contain the immortal line, 'She sits among the cabbages and peas / Watching her onions grow', as has been suggested. The only recording I have heard of the song, by George Buck, does not contain the couplet. I suspect that the recording by Sarony himself with Tommy

Handley and Jack Payne (on Columbia 5555), which I have not heard, does not have it either.

1 Orson Welles, the American film actor and director, obtained his first professional stage engagement in Dublin by sending a note to Micheál MacLiammóir and Hilton Edwards at the Gate Theatre. It stated, 'Orson Welles, star of the New York Theater Guild, would consider appearing in one of your productions and hopes you will see him for an appointment.' He was 16 years old at the time.

Recalled in Frank Brady, *Citizen Welles* (1989).

2 At the age of 22, Peter Sellers, confident of his ability to do convincing impressions but unable to get replies to his requests for work at the BBC, rang up the producer Roy Spears and pretended to be Kenneth Horne, by then an established radio star. 'Dickie Murdoch and I were at a cabaret the other night,' he said, 'and we saw an amazing young fellow called Peter Sellers. And he was very good. Just thought I'd give you a little tip.' Shortly after this, Sellers revealed who he was. Spears was won over by his cheek, booked him for a programme called *Showtime* (in 1948), and launched him on his career as a comedy actor.

As told by Sellers in a Parkinson interview, BBC TV (1974), included in a tribute LP *Peter Sellers: The Parkinson Interview* (released in about 1981).

Choice

3 Sir Herbert Beerbohm Tree (1853–1917), the actor-manager, went to the Post Office and said he wanted to buy a stamp. When he was shown a whole sheet of them, he pointed at one in the middle and said, 'I'll have that one.'

Told in Hesketh Pearson, *Beerbohm Tree* (1956).

Christmas

4 Samuel Butler recorded this in one of his notebooks: 'The little Strangs say the "good words", as they call them, before going to bed, aloud and at their father's knee, or rather in the pit of his stomach. One of them was lately heard to say "Forgive us our Christmasses, as we forgive them that Christmas against us."'

Samuel Butler's *Notebooks* were compiled between 1874 and 1902 and have been published.

5 Two women were looking into a card-shop window at Christmas where they read such greetings as, 'From my dog to your dog' and even 'From my budgie to your budgie'. Another woman was also looking in the window and was heard to say, on seeing a Nativity scene, 'Look at that – they bring religion into everything nowadays.'

Traditional. Compare what Richard H. Davies of London E13 contributed to BBC Radio *Quote ... Unquote* (25 December 1979): he recalled a Christmas 'a year or two ago' when he was on top of a bus outside Selfridges store in London where giant Christmas cards depicting biblical scenes were being used as the background to a window display. Mr Davies heard one woman passenger remark to another: 'Look, Mavis, now they're even dragging religion into Christmas.'

6 The great comedian once inserted a small paragraph in *Variety* stating: 'W. C. Fields wishes a Happy Christmas to all his friends but one.' The

consternation that ensued boggled all imagination.

Told in a letter from C.R.W. (1993).

1 A former British Ambassador to France was asked by *Paris Match* what he would like for Christmas if he could have absolutely anything he wanted. The Ambassador at first demurred and said no, no, he couldn't possibly, but eventually made his choice. The next issue of *Paris Match* duly carried its feature 'What the world would like for Christmas' in which Mikhail Gorbachev said he wanted an end to the arms race, Ronald Reagan opted for peace on earth, and so on. Finally there was the request of the British ambassador: 'A small box of crystallized fruits, please.'

This tale made an appearance late in its life in Lynn Barber's column in the *Independent on Sunday* (29 December 1991). I was well familiar with it, as Jonathan James-Moore, later to become the BBC's Head of Light Entertainment (Radio), used it invariably as his warm-up joke in the early 1980s. The earliest version of it I have found occurs in *Pass the Port* (1976), but also in Geoffrey Moorhouse, *The Diplomats* (1977), where it is told as the result of a Washington radio station telephoning various ambassadors in December 1948. In this version, the British ambassador, Sir Oliver Franks, was the one who said, 'I'd quite like a box of crystallized fruits.'

Claims

2 In 1977, the novelist Georges Simenon made an astonishing claim: 'I have made love to 10,000 women.' In an interview with the Zurich newspaper *Die Tat*, he explained: 'I contend that you know a woman only after you have slept with her. I wanted to know women – I wanted to learn the truth.'

When he was asked if he was sure of the figure, Simenon said he had gone back and checked. In Fenton Bresler's 1983 biography, Simenon's wife was quoted as saying, 'We've worked it out and the true figure is no more than twelve hundred.' Most of these were prostitutes.

The original version of the claim appeared in an interview conducted by Federico Fellini in *L'Express* (21 February 1977): 'I have made love to 10,000 women since I was 13½. It wasn't in any way a vice. I've no sexual vices. But I needed to communicate.'

Clarity

3 The English playwright Sir Arthur Wing Pinero (1855–1934) used to say that the only way to get anything across to an English theatre audience was for a character to say, 'I am going to hit this man on the head', then 'I'm hitting this man on the head', and finally 'I have hit this man on the head'. The audience might then just about realize what was going on.

Recounted in *The Lyttelton Hart-Davis Letters* (for 5 May 1957). Compare Hilaire Belloc's description of his lecturing method, as told to and reported by Hesketh Pearson in *Lives of the Wits* (1962): 'First I tell them what I am going to tell them; then I tell them; and then I tell them what I've told them.'

4 In the revival of his play *Hay Fever* that Noël Coward directed at the National Theatre in 1964, Edith Evans always said one line wrong in rehearsal. 'On a clear day you can see Marlow' was invariably changed by her to 'On a very clear day ... ' Coward would not let her get away with it. Said he: 'Edith, dear, the line is "On a clear day you can see Marlow." On a very clear day you

can see Marlowe and Beaumont *and* Fletcher as well ...'

The earliest showing of this story would appear to be in Dick Richards, *The Wit of Noël Coward* (1968).

Clergy

1 Jonathan Swift, much before he became Dean of St Patrick's in Dublin, was minister of three obscure church livings in County Meath (1701–9). At Laracor, his Sunday services seldom drew more than a dozen people, and his Wednesday and Friday prayer meetings could only rely on the presence of one person – the clerk and bell-ringer, Roger Cox. At the very first of these, where normally he would have begun with the Morning Prayer invocation, 'Dearly beloved brethren ...', Swift noticed that there was just this one man in the congregation, so he began: 'Dearly beloved Roger, the Scripture moveth you and me in sundry places ...'

Told in Stephen Gwynn, *The Life and Friendships of Dean Swift* (1933). Swift's biographer, Lord Orrery, first told the tale in 1751.

2 An Anglican bishop contemplating a gathering of clergymen from his diocese remarked, 'The see gives up its dead.'

Alluding to Revelation 20:13, 'The sea shall give up its dead.' Ascribed on BBC Radio *Quote ... Unquote* (15 September 1984) by the Reverend Roger Royle to Henry Montgomery-Campbell, Bishop of London (1956–61). In a letter broadcast on *Quote ... Unquote* in 1985, Professor Maurice Hugh-Jones ascribed the remark to 'a Bishop of Lichfield'.

3 At a revivalist meeting in Northern Ireland, the Reverend Dr Ian Paisley was holding forth on an eschatological theme in his customary loud tones: 'And when the day of judgement comes, there will be a great wailing and gnashing of teeth ...' At this point he was interrupted by a little old lady at the front, who said, 'This is all very well, but what about those poor old folks like me that don't have any teeth?' Paisley thundered back, 'Teeth will be provided!'

Told by 1996.

Clichés

4 In the early 1940s, Winston Churchill was asked to look over a draft of one of Anthony Eden's vague speeches on the post-war world. He did so and sent it back to the Foreign Minister with this curt note: 'I have read your speech and find that you have used every cliché known to the English language except "Please adjust your dress before leaving".'

Told by Allan A. Michie in *Reader's Digest* (August 1943). The version 'As far as I can see, you have used every cliché except "God is love" and "Please adjust your dress before leaving"' is quoted in Maurice Edelman, *The Mirror: A Political History* (1966), together with Churchill's actual comment: 'This offensive story is wholly devoid of foundation.' Apparently, in 1941, Churchill took the unusual course of writing to Cecil King of the *Daily Mirror* about the matter. The columnist Cassandra had used the story, though labelling it apocryphal and saying it had been taken from *Life* Magazine.

Clothes

5 The Duke of Cumberland was walking along Piccadilly when he saw the Duke of Gloucester (his first cousin and popularly known as 'Silly Billy') coming out of Gloucester House. 'Duke of Gloucester, Duke of Gloucester, stop

a minute. I was want to speak to you,' roared Cumberland. 'Who's your tailor?' 'Stultz' replied Gloucester. 'Thank you. I only wanted to know, because whoever he is, he ought to be avoided like the pestilence.'

Told by Sir Charles Wyke, who was with Cumberland at the time, to G. W. E. Russell, who included it in *Collections and Recollections*, Chap. 19 (1898).

1 King Edward VII had an obsessive interest in correct attire. On one occasion when a courtier unwisely appeared in a loud check suit, the King said: 'Goin' rattin', 'arris?'

Told by Miles Kington on BBC Radio *Quote … Unquote* (25 June 1986). Another version is that the offending Lord Harris appeared at Ascot in a brown bowler hat.

2 The Italian dictator Benito Mussolini is said to have styled his dress on that of Laurel and Hardy, his favourite film stars, whose 'sartorial distinctiveness he regarded as the embodiment of transatlantic chic'. He only changed his habit when told that Laurel and Hardy were more widely perceived as figures of fun, not as models of sophistication.

Thus according to A. N. Wilson, *Hilaire Belloc* (1984), who acknowledges D. Mack Smith, *Mussolini* (1981). However, Mack Smith merely says that Mussolini stopped dressing in this way because of Laurel and Hardy, not that he imitated their sartorial style.

3 Victor Mature was chiefly known for playing romantic and he-man roles in films. On being told that his clothes looked unusually rumpled on one occasion – 'as though he had slept in them' – Mature replied: 'Don't be ridiculous. I pay someone to do that for me.'

Told by William Franklyn on BBC Radio *Quote … Unquote* (20 July 1985).

4 The debonair actor Michael Denison (1915–98) was once favoured with a review in the *Tailor and Cutter* pointing out that he had an 'inadequate central vent'.

Told by Frank Keating on BBC Radio *Quote … Unquote* (6 December 1986).

5 A story that Arthur Marshall liked to tell against himself was about the occasion he turned up for a recording of TV's *Call My Bluff* wearing an unusually prominent suit. Fellow panellist Frank Muir sized him up and down, ran his fingers along the lapels, and pronounced: 'Why pay more, Arthur, why pay more?'

Recalled by Marshall on BBC Radio *Quote … Unquote* (14 August 1980).

6 Norman St John Stevas was a flamboyant member of Margaret Thatcher's first administration. When she asked him why he needed to leave a Cabinet meeting ahead of her in order to dress for some official function they were both attending, St John Stevas said, 'Yes, Margaret, but it takes me much longer to change than it does you.'

Told on BBC Radio *Quote … Unquote* (10 August 1985).

7 The broadcaster and TV executive Huw Wheldon was at a University of London convocation in the early 1980s, resplendent in a crimson robe topped by a huge black velvet hat. Asked what it was, he replied: 'Doctor of Music at the University of Lausanne. I borrowed it from the BBC's costume department.'

Recounted in Paul Ferris, *Sir Huge* (1990).

Coldness

1 V. M. Molotov (1890–1986) was the
Soviet Foreign Minister at the outbreak
of the Second World War and a man of
cold aspect. A British diplomat once
compared him to 'a refrigerator when
the light has gone out'.

Told in *Time* Magazine (24 November 1986).
In *The Second World War*, Vol. 1, Chap. 20
(1948), Winston Churchill wrote of 'his smile
of Siberian winter' but also of an 'affable
demeanour [that made him] the perfect agent
of Soviet policy in a deadly world'.

Compliments, back-handed or unusual

2 The first electric domestic vacuum-
cleaner was so big it was put on a horse-
drawn carriage and an 800-foot hose
was run into the place being cleaned.
King Edward VII remarked to its
inventor, Hubert Booth: 'Your appara-
tus is extremely impressive.'

Told on Channel 4 TV, *The Secret Life of
the Vacuum Cleaner* (1989).

3 The writer Somerset Maugham told of
the compliment he received on numerous occasions over a twenty-year
period from Edmund Gosse, the literary critic. Maugham's first book, *Liza
of Lambeth*, appeared in 1897 and he
went on to great success with other
novels, short stories and plays.
Gosse always greeted him 'in his unctu-
ous way', by saying: 'Oh, my dear
Maugham, I liked your *Liza of Lambeth*
so much. How wise you are never to
have written anything else.'

Told in *A Writer's Notebook* (1949).

4 Sir Thomas Beecham was conducting
the rehearsal of an opera in which the
presence of a horse was required. Verdi's

Aïda is thought to have been the one in
question. The horse came on and did
what horses usually tend to do in such
circumstances. Beecham stopped the
orchestra, leaned down over them like
a great condor and said: 'You see,
gentlemen, not only a great performer
but a critic, too.'

Told by Brian Sewell, the art critic, on BBC
Radio *Quote ... Unquote* (12 April 1994),
having heard it recalled by David Mellor who
was presenting him with the 'Critic of the
Year' award.

5 The English dramatic critic James
Agate considered that Lilian Braithwaite was 'the wittiest woman in
London' but, rather curiously, decided
to say to her (when he found her sitting
alone in the Savoy Grill on one occasion), 'My dear Lilian, I have long
wanted to tell you that in my opinion
you are the second most beautiful
woman in London.' If Braithwaite was
curious to know the identity of her
superior, Agate was going to award
the first place to 'a beauty of antique
and challengeless fame'. But she
was not curious and replied: 'Thank
you so much. I shall cherish that,
coming from our second-best dramatic
critic.'

Recounted by Agate in *Ego* (1935).

6 A passer-by said to the mother of a girl:
'Oh, what a pretty little girl! Is your
husband good-looking?'

Contributed to BBC Radio *Quote ... Unquote* (13 July 1985) by Mrs Miki Jakeman, a
medical missionary, who recalled that it was
said with regard to her when she was three
years old. A cartoon entitled 'A Doubtful
Compliment' in *Punch* (3 August 1904),
however, makes the same put-down to a *man*
regarding his children: *Lady*: 'ARE THESE
YOUR CHILDREN? WHAT DARLINGS! AND –

ER – WHAT A VERY PRETTY WOMAN
YOUR WIFE *MUST* BE!'

1 The jazz musician Bobby Hackett
was noted for never having a bad word
to say about anybody. Of Hitler he
remarked, 'Well, he was the best in
the field.'

Told in *Jazz Anecdotes*, ed. Bill Crow (1991).

2 During a dinner party, the conversation
turned to the Soviet Union, the excesses
of Stalinism, and the cruelties of the
KGB. Edith Evans was having none of
this. Drawing up her voice to full
throttle, she declared: 'The Russians
have always been very nice to *me*!'

Told by Peter Nichols on BBC Radio
Quote … Unquote (17 November 1998).

3 The actress Fenella Fielding was
approached by a woman in Edinburgh
who said to her, 'You look exactly like
Fenella Fielding – only you're much
prettier than she is!'

Told by Fenella on BBC Radio *Quote …
Unquote* (24 June 1997).

4 Many years ago, Peter Jones was taking
part in a play with John Gielgud for
the first time. As they were introduced,
Peter noticed a glint of recognition in
Gielgud's eye, and they shook hands
very warmly. Said Gielgud, 'No, we've
never actually met – but I've seen
you … in the street.'

Told on BBC Radio *Quote … Unquote*
(2 March 1982).

Conceit

5 There is a celebrated anecdote of an
actor who bored his listener to tears
with a relentless monologue about his
latest performance in a play. Then,
contritely, he broke off. 'But I'm talking

all about myself,' he apologized win-
ningly. 'Let's talk about *you*. How did
you like me in the part?'

As told by Godfrey Smith in *The Sunday
Times* (31 July 1983). W. G. McNay of
Strathaven, Lanarkshire, told me that this was,
in fact, the caption to a *Punch* cartoon by
D. L. Ghilchik who flourished in that journal
in the 1920s/30s. Indeed, it appears on page
200 of Vol. ix ('Mr Punch's Theatricals') in
The New Punch Library (*c*. 1933). The actual
wording is: 'CELEBRITY (after lengthy
monopoly of the conversation) "But enough
about me; let's talk about yourself. Tell
me – what do you think of my part in the
new play?"'

Conception

6 Invited by Sir Thomas Beecham to sing
in Handel's *Messiah*, a singer confessed
that she was not familiar with the ora-
torio. But she accepted the offer and set
to learning the part. Meeting her some
time later, Beecham inquired how she
was getting on. 'Oh, I've been working
very hard at it,' she replied. 'The score
goes with me everywhere … to work,
to meals, up to bed at night …'

'Then,' Beecham concluded, 'I trust
we may look forward to an immaculate
conception …?'

Told in *Beecham Stories* (ed. Atkins and
Newman, 1978).

7 The writer and politician A. P. Herbert
had a daughter called Crystal. She
was called this because she was either
conceived or born on the night that
the Crystal Palace burned down (on
30 November 1936).

Told by Malcolm Muggeridge on BBC Radio
Quote … Unquote (24 December 1977) but,
understandably, I have had difficulty in con-
firming this story. In fact, it is completely
untrue, as Crystal was old enough to become
the first wife of the poet John Pudney in

1934. But, presumably, Muggeridge must have been thinking of *somebody* about whom this story is told.

1 In the early 1960s, Edith Summerskill, the doctor and politician, took part in an Oxford Union debate on contraception or abortion. Her opening words were, 'Mr President, I cannot conceive …' She never got any further.

I think I was told this in about 1963, at the Oxford Union. (It wasn't true, of course – she had a lovely daughter.)

2 The 6th Marquess of Bath and his second wife, Virginia, were desperate to have a child and were reminded that nearby was the Cerne Abbas giant, an ancient fertility symbol carved in the chalk on the Wiltshire Downs. According to which story you believe, they either made love on the tip of the giant's substantial member, or merely sat on it. Either way, it worked. The result was Lady Silvy Thynne – whose second name is Cerne.

Sources for this story include: *Harpers & Queen* Magazine (June 1992).

Conclusions

3 When it came to Abraham Lincoln's turn to give his summation as the defence attorney, he said: 'My learned opponent has given you all the facts but has drawn all the wrong conclusions.' As it turned out he won the case. On the way out of court, the prosecutor stopped Lincoln and asked, 'How did you do it, Abe?'

'Well,' Abe said, 'During the recess I wandered into a bar, sat with the jurors, and told them a story about a farmer who was mending a fence when his ten-year-old son came running, crying, "Dad, Sis is up in the hay loft with a hired hand and he is pulling down his pants and she is pulling up her skirts and I think they are going to pee over the hay."'

According to Lincoln, the farmer said to his son, 'You got all the facts straight, but you have drawn the wrong conclusion.'

Told to me by Charles G. Francis (December 1992).

Consumption, conspicuous

4 On one occasion, Robert Maxwell, the Czech-born publisher, politician, tycoon and crook, received an unexpected invitation to a posh do in New York. He sent a courier back to London on Concorde to collect his tails.

Told in Tom Bower, *Maxwell, The Outsider* (1988).

Conversations

5 How careful Benjamin Disraeli was, in the great days of his political struggles, to flatter every one who came within his reach. To the same effect is the story that when he was accosted by any one who claimed acquaintance but whose face he had forgotten he always used to enquire, in a tone of affectionate solicitude, 'And how is the old complaint?'

As told in G. W. E. Russell, *Collections and Recollections*, Chap. 24 (1898).

6 Seeking to make conversation with Mrs Abraham Lincoln after her husband had unfortunately been shot while at the theatre, someone asked: 'Apart from that, Mrs Lincoln, how did you enjoy the play?'

Probably the world's first sick joke – or perhaps 'sickish' would be more precise. I wonder when it first arose? Oddly enough, *The Oxford English Dictionary* (2nd edition) mentions it twice with 1959 datings. Under the word 'cruellie' (a cruel joke) it quotes from the *News Chronicle* (6 July 1959): 'The famous American "cruellie" joke – example: "But what did you think of the play, Mrs Lincoln?" – is on the way out.' And defining 'sick humour, joke etc.', it quotes from *Punch* (2 September 1959): 'The prototype of sick jokes is one that goes "But apart from that, Mrs Lincoln, how did you enjoy the play?"'

'Sick humour' – with this name – appears to have been first identified in the 1950s. I have a hunch that the joke does not date from any earlier decade.

As for variations on this conversational gambit in similar circumstances: somewhere or other I have heard that on the evening in 1963 when news of President Kennedy's assassination reached London, the British Academy of Film and Television Arts was holding a dinner or awards ceremony of some kind. At this gathering, Bernard Braden, the Canadian-born broadcaster, is said to have wondered (publicly or privately, I don't know) how long it would be before people started joking, 'Apart from that, Mrs Kennedy, did you manage to do much shopping?'

1 It is interesting to be reminded that, from the word go, the telephone was used in a peremptory manner. Three days after receiving the patent on his invention, Alexander Graham Bell called out, 'Mr Watson, come here: I want you.' These were the first intelligible words transmitted by telephone (10 March 1876). Bell had just spilled acid on his clothes and was calling to his assistant, Thomas A. Watson, for help.

Told in John J. Carty, *The Smithsonian Report for 1922.*

2 At the end of the First World War, General Nivelle, hero of Verdun, made a tour of the United States. When he reached Los Angeles, a big public reception was held so that he could meet members of the movie colony. Among those invited were Charlie Chaplin and Will Rogers. Chaplin was oddly nervous about meeting the great war hero and confided in Rogers that he had absolutely no idea how he would start up a conversation. Advised Rogers, 'Well, you might ask him if he was in the war, and which side he was on ...'

Told in Irvin S. Cobb, *A Laugh a Day Keeps the Doctor Away* (1921). A version turns up later in an exchange in the caption to a *Punch* cartoon (4 July 1934): (Two bored people) 'My grandfather fought in the Zulu War' 'On which side?'

3 During a papal audience, Randolph Churchill produced an enthralling piece of small talk. To the Pope he said: 'I expect you know my friend, Evelyn Waugh, who, like you, your holiness, is a Roman Catholic.'

Told in *The Penguin Dictionary of Modern Quotations* (1971).

4 Dorothy Reynolds, the actress, was sitting on top of a No. 29 bus which had stopped outside the old Wood Green Town Hall on its way to Palmers Green in about 1938–39. She overheard a cockney factory girl conversing with her friend: 'So I sez to 'im "Oh", and 'e sez "Oh, it's 'Oh', is it?" and I sez, "Yes, it is 'Oh'."'

'This was a story often repeated over the years with varying intonations by my friend Dorothy Reynolds' – stated Mrs G. H. Alston of Lewes in a letter to me in January 1980. Peter Jones had quoted it on *Quote ... Unquote* in the summer of 1979, mentioning the same source. However, I now have rather more information as to its origins. A cartoon by Frank Reynolds in *Punch* (30 March 1921) shows a woman talking to two others and saying: 'Yes, 'e come up to me an' I sez, "Oh!" – an' 'e sez, "Oh, it's 'Oh,' is it?" – an' I sez "Yes, it *is* 'Oh!"'

1 The North Country broadcaster Wilfred Pickles spent most of the 'quiz' programme *Have a Go* chatting to the contestants. Faced with spinsters of any age from 19 to 90, he would ask, 'Are yer courtin'?' He would fish for laughs from all contestants with the question, 'Have you ever had any embarrassing moments?' One reply he received was from a woman who had been out with a very shy young man. Getting desperate for conversation with him she had said, 'If there's one thing I can't stand, it's people who sit on you and use you as a convenience.'

Probably from one of the Pickles books of reminiscence, such as *Wilfred Pickles Invites You To Have Another Go* (1978).

2 During the taping of his world-exclusive interviews with ex-President Nixon in 1977, David Frost was disconcerted to be on the receiving end of some Nixonian small talk. After a weekend break, Nixon welcomed Frost back on a Monday morning with, 'Well, did you do any fornicating this weekend?'

Told in David Frost, *They Gave Me A Sword* (1978).

3 Peter Cook was the inspirer of a generation of comic writers and performers. But it was his conversation in private that is remembered by all who knew him. Attempting to start up a dinner-party conversation, Cook asked the person seated next to him, 'What are you doing at the moment?' The person replied, 'Writing a book.' To which Cook rejoined, '... Neither am I.'

The story was told by Richard Ingrams on BBC Radio *Quote ... Unquote* (25 August 1984), though I gather that Cook later said he did not claim originality.

4 One of the great failures in Peter Cook's life was when he did an extremely short-lived stint as a chat-show host on BBC2 in February 1971. It had the warning title *Where Do I Sit?* and was cancelled after three editions. As he told it, the show was also voted by readers of the *Sun* newspaper as the 'worst programme of the year – or possibly the worst television programme ever'. One of the guests wheeled in before the somewhat nervous host was Kirk Douglas. Cook had spent some time thinking up questions for him and had decided to begin, with great originality, by asking, 'How are you?' Unfortunately, this did not come out right, but as, 'Who are you?' Evidently, Douglas was rather thrown by this and was lost for words. As Cook also told it, 'He had to consult the autocue.'

Recounted by Peter Cook on BBC Radio *Quote ... Unquote* (19 June 1979).

Correct form

5 A woman was overheard at an Eton College event saying: '... And as he'd had a long run down, he asked for the bathroom. When he was shown into it, he suddenly looked and there was his hostess in the bath. He couldn't think what was the correct thing to say, so he said, "You *are* looking well."'

C. D'O. Gowan of Ulverston contributed this snippet of conversation to BBC Radio *Quote ... Unquote* in 1980. In that same year, it also appeared in *Pass the Port Again*, told by Sir Peter Mursell about a plumber intruding upon 'my wife'. Mr Gowan said he picked it up when he was a housemaster at Eton and he and his wife were walking round Agar's Plough there on 4 June. But what should the man have said? That same year, I decided to consult Douglas Sutherland, author of the *English Gentleman* series of books. He advised that the correct reply in that situation was: 'I beg your pardon, *sir!*'

This sounded much better, and I subsequently found confirmation that it was the correct response when reading a 1932 novel, *Charming Manners* by John Michaelhouse (a pen name of the Reverend Joseph McCulloch). In the story, a group of Oxford undergraduates happen upon half-a-dozen naked nymphs dancing in the sunlight on the banks of the River Cherwell. 'We all collapsed in the punt at once, there being no chance of saying, "Sorry, gentlemen" in the approved style.'

In François Truffaut's film *Baisers Volés* (1968), the character played by Delphine Seyrig says that she was taught the difference between tact and politeness – if a man surprises a naked lady in the bathrooom, politeness is to say 'Sorry', tact is to say, 'Sorry, *sir.*'

The boot is on the other foot, so to speak, in a glancing comment from E. M. Forster's *A Room with a View* (1908): 'Mr Beebe [the clergyman] was not able to tell the ladies of his adventure at Modena, where the chambermaid burst in upon him in his bath, exclaiming cheerfully, *"Fa niente, sono vecchia"* [It doesn't matter, I'm an old woman].'

1 The newspaperman Frank Giles's wife was Lady Katharine Sackville who, being the daughter of an earl, retained her title though married to a plain 'Mr'. On a visit to Rome they received an invitation from the British ambassador which was incorrectly made out to 'Mr and Mrs Frank Giles'. Giles thought he ought to point out the error, rang the British Embassy and said, 'She's not exactly *Mrs* Giles, you see.' 'Oh, never mind,' said an embassy official, 'bring her along anyway. We're not at all stuffy here.'

A version of this appeared in the *Los Angeles Times* (15 December 1981).

2 When an intruder called Michael Fagan made his way into the Queen's bedroom at Buckingham Palace in 1982,

Her Majesty, by all accounts, behaved with exemplary coolness. On the other hand, when Elizabeth Andrews, a royal chambermaid, turned up, she exclaimed – with a beguiling blend of shock and courtesy: 'Bloody hell, *Ma'am*, what's he doing here?'

Told in the *Daily Mail* (July 1982).

Corrections

3 During a *Panorama* programme, the presenter Richard Dimbleby said 'RSPCA' when he meant 'NSPCC'. Many viewers phoned in to point out his error. At the end of the programme he said: 'The more intelligent among you will have realized what I meant. Goodnight.'

Told in my book *Say No More!* (1987).

4 When addressing guests at a reception in Jakarta, the capital of Indonesia, in 1985, Margaret Thatcher said, 'We are all impressed by the way that President Suharto and his cabinet are handling the problems of Malaysia.' Her husband, Denis, whispered, 'Indonesia, dear, not Malaysia.' The Prime Minister corrected herself and then said a little frostily to her husband, 'Thank you, dear.'

Reported in *The Times* (11 April 1985).

Courtesy

5 An actress, not noted for her good looks, met Oscar Wilde in the French capital and said to him: 'Mr Wilde, you are looking at the ugliest woman in Paris.' Courteously he replied, 'In the world, madam.'

Told on *Quote ... Unquote* (5 April 1978). Long before this, in Frank Harris, *Oscar Wilde, His Life and Confessions*, Chap. 20

(1930) is this version: 'Mdlle. Marie Anne de Bovet … was a writer of talent and knew English uncommonly well; but in spite of masses of fair hair and vivacious eyes she was certainly very plain. As soon as she heard I was in Paris, she asked me to present Oscar Wilde to her. He had no objection, and so I made a meeting between them. When he caught sight of her, he stopped short: seeing his astonishment, she cried to him in her quick, abrupt way: *"N'est-ce pas, M. Wilde, que je suis la femme la plus laide de France?"* (Come, confess, Mr Wilde, that I am the ugliest woman in France.) Bowing low, Oscar replied with smiling courtesy: *"Du monde, Madame, du monde."* (In the world, madame, in the world.) No one could help laughing; the retort was irresistible. He should have said: *"Au monde, madame, au monde,"* but the meaning was clear.'

Credits

1   The 1929 film of *The Taming of the Shrew* with Douglas Fairbanks and Mary Pickford is supposed to have displayed the on-screen credit: 'With additional dialogue by William Shakespeare'.

Not quite. What it does say is 'with additional dialogue by Sam Taylor', which is fair enough. See *Halliwell's Film Guide* (1987) for the in-accurate version. Compare the film *My Own Private Idaho* (1992), which does have the credit 'With additional dialogue by William Shakespeare' – legitimately, as it is a re-telling of the Prince Hal/Falstaff story using some of the dialogue from *Henry IV*.

Crimes and misdemeanours

2   Sir Hubert Parry, composer of such solemn High Victorian seriousness as 'Blest Pair of Sirens' and, of course, the alternative national anthem, 'Jerusalem', was also the first person to be fined for speeding in a motor car.

Source untraced.

3   In 1944, the much-fêted composer and entertainer Ivor Novello was imprisoned for two months (halved on appeal) for infringing wartime regula-tions that restricted the use of petrol for non-essential purposes. This should surely give pause for reflection to those who still campaign for a posthumous knighthood to be given to their hero.

Recounted in W. MacQueen Pope, *Ivor* (1951).

Cross purposes

4   During the Second World War, prior to the Allied landings in North Africa, the American General Mark Clark was landed secretly on the coast of Algeria to make contact with friendly French officials and pro-Allied conspirators. He narrowly escaped being captured by the Vichy French police. Unfortunately, there was a mix-up as to which beach Clark should land on, with the result that the reception committee consisted solely of a man who inquired whether the General would like to meet his pretty sister. The interpreter gave such a strong negative that the man got the wrong idea and said, hastily, 'My brother then?' At which point the General (who had not been following the conversation) said, 'Ask him if he can get us the harbour master.' The man replied, 'My brother will come cheaper.'

Told to me by T. A. Dyer (1992), who pointed out that a similar sequence of mis-understandings occurs between Heracles and Dionysus at the beginning of Aristophanes' *The Frogs*. And so it does.

Crowds

5   When the French footballer Eric Cantona came to England in the 1980s

to play for Leeds United, it was not long before crowds began to chant the slogan 'Ooh, ah, Cantona!' with the accent falling correctly upon the last syllable. Then, controversially, Cantona transferred to Manchester United. Rivalry between the two teams went back many years. The Leeds supporters were most upset by the transfer of their idol at what they considered to be a knockdown price – none more so than the supporter who had just named his newborn son 'Eric'. In due course, towards the end of his time at Manchester, Cantona received a lengthy suspension from football for an incident involving a supporter after Cantona had been sent off by the referee. On the next occasion on which Leeds played Manchester United, with a degree of subtlety of the type not normally associated with football crowds, it is said Leeds supporters, frustrated by the way in which Manchester fans had adopted the chant of 'Ooh, ah, Cantona!, took it for their own use again as, *'Où est Cantona?'*

Told to me by a Leeds fan (1998). It is now thought that the original chant actually began with the Irish footballer Paul McGrath, who played with Aston Villa for many years. (It neatly showed how the name 'McGrath' should be pronounced, incidentally). The story goes that when Nelson Mandela visited Dublin in October 1993, there was a certain resemblance remarked between these two heroes, whereupon the crowds called out: 'Ooh, ah, Paul McGrath's Da!'

Whatever its origins among the supporters, Cantona attempted to make the chant very much his own. No sooner had a record entitled 'Ooh, ah, Cantona' by 13Drums reached No. 11 in the British charts in 1996, than it was reported that the footballer had attempted to register the chant as a trademark.

D

Deafness

1 When Winston Churchill was a very old man, he paid one of his infrequent visits to the House of Commons, of which he was still a member. An MP, observing him, remarked, 'After all, they say he's potty.' Muttered Churchill, 'They say he can't hear either.'

Told in William Manchester, *The Last Lion* (1983).

Deaths

2 Francis Bacon, the philosopher and politician, was, at the last, a martyr to scientific experiment. One day as he was travelling in a coach towards Highgate with snow upon the ground, the thought occurred to him that snow might be as good a preservative for meat as salt was at that time considered to be. Accordingly, he and his companion, Dr Witherborne, alighted from the coach at the bottom of Highgate Hill and purchased a chicken from an old woman. She was asked to take out the entrails, and then the two experimenters stuffed the cavity with snow. Unfortunately, the snow so chilled Bacon that he immediately fell extremely ill. It was no help that he was put into a damp bed. He died two or three days later.

Told by John Aubrey in *Brief Lives* (c. 1693).

3 It was once put about that the Czech composer Antonín Dvořák (1841–1904) had died as the result of a chill caught while trainspotting. While this was not quite the case, it does draw attention to one of his enthusiasms. In fact, he caught a chill while paying his customary visit to the main-line engine-sheds in some unseasonably wintry weather.

Told in Gervase Hughes, *Dvořák: His Life and Music* (1967).

4 When a reporter from the *Evening Sun* tracked down the American writer and humorist Mark Twain, who was on a visit to London, regarding reports that he was dead or dying, Twain told him: 'Say the report is exaggerated.' Another reporter arrived, from the *New York World*, and Twain saw that he was clutching a telegram with the instruction: 'If Mark Twain dying send five hundred words. If dead send a thousand.' On this, he is said to have remarked: 'You don't need as much as that. Just say the report of my death has been grossly exaggerated.'

This last is Twain's own version of the incident and appears in A. B. Paine, *Mark Twain: A Biography* (1912). The first version is from *Mark Twain in Eruption* (1922). Frequently over-quoted and paraphrased ever since, this has become the inevitable remark to invoke when someone's death has been wrongly reported (most usually one's own). It is also now employed in the sense of, 'You thought I was finished, but look at me now' (for example, by George Bush in February 1988 regarding the decline in his political fortunes). Variations include: 'Reports of my death have been greatly exaggerated' or 'are premature'. A headline from the *Independent* (13 November 1993): 'Reports of Queen Mother's death exaggerated Down Under'.

1 While appearing in Montreal, the escapologist Houdini was visited in his dressing room by three students from McGill University. Although over fifty years old, Houdini was still very proud of his physique and invited one of the young men to punch him in the stomach. Alas, the blow came before he had had time to brace himself. His appendix was ruptured and he died within a fortnight.

Recounted in Roy Busby, *British Music Hall: A Who's Who 1840–1923* (1976).

2 For much of his life, the poet A. C. Benson was a schoolmaster. When he was a housemaster at Eton, a murder was committed in the College and one of the boys killed. On being told this rather unfortunate news, Benson posed the inevitable question in a somewhat unusual way. He inquired: 'What dangerous clown has done this?'

Told by Steve Race on BBC Radio *Quote ... Unquote* (17 January 1987). Kenneth Tynan in a 1948 review in *A View of the English Stage* gives this as an 'Alexander Woollcott story' of merely 'a schoolmaster', who, coming upon a mutilated torso in the Lower Third dormitory, remarked: 'Some dangerous clown has been here.'

Humphrey Lyttelton's father, George, apparently resolves the question of which schoolmaster it was in *The Lyttelton Hart-Davis Letters* (for 23 February 1956): 'Woollcott records in one of his books his

high appreciation when my colleague [at Eton] Booker was summoned one Sunday afternoon to his kitchen where his cook had been murdered, and on seeing the body, asked "What dangerous clown has done this?"' In fact, Woollcott tells the story in *Selections* (1945), but it does not involve Benson after all.

3 In the 1930s, Margot Asquith was still delivering her opinions on all and sundry and at full volume. Her wrath fell upon Lord Dawson, King George V's doctor. Said she: 'My dear old friend King George V always told me he would never have died but for that vile doctor, Lord Dawson of Penn.'

This remark was made by Lady Asquith several times in her old age, but especially to Lord David Cecil (and recorded first by Mark Bonham-Carter in his introduction to *The Autobiography of Margot Asquith*, 1962 edition). It turns out to be not so preposterous as might first have been thought. In December 1986, Dawson's biographer suggested in *History Today* that the doctor had in fact hastened the King's departure with lethal injections of morphine and cocaine at the request of Queen Mary and the future Edward VIII. Dawson's notes revealed that the death was induced at 11 p.m. not only to ease the pain but also to enable the news to make the morning papers, 'rather than the less appropriate evening journals'. *The Times* was advised that important news was coming and to hold back publication. So Dawson of Penn *might* have had a hand in the King's death, though quite how George V communicated his view of the matter to Margot Asquith is not known.

4 A young newspaper reporter in the North of England found himself ushered into a front parlour and shown the body of a recently deceased man. Unable to think of anything suitable to say to the bereaved wife, he remarked, 'Looks well, doesn't he?' Replied she,

'He ought to be. He only came back from Blackpool on Monday.'

Sometimes told by – or about – the broadcaster Robert Robinson. In Chapter 12 of Robinson's detective novel *Landscape With Dead Dons* (1956), he himself puts this experience in the mouth of a character called Bum: 'Corpses always turned me up – even when I was doing Bereaved Households on the old Maida Vale *Intelligencer* ... I remember once I was drinking tea in one of these front rooms with a middle-aged lady who'd just lost her husband, and she asked me if I'd like to have a look at him ... Over we went to the coffin ... Well, you don't really know what to say, do you, so I said, "He looks well, doesn't he?" and she said, "He ought to. We only came back from Brighton last week."'

In Lillian Ross, *Picture* (1952) the story is told with the punchline, 'Why not? he just got back from Palm Springs!' However, there is an even older version. In Irvin S. Cobb's *A Laugh a Day Keeps the Doctor Away* (1921), story number 254 tells of 'two sympathic friends' calling at a house of mourning in the Bronx. The bereft husband of the late Mrs Levinsky sat alongside the casket. 'Doesn't she look wonderful?' said one of them. The widower replied, 'Why shouldn't she look wonderful? Didn't she spend the whole winter in Palm Beach?'

1 An English couple were on holiday in Spain with the wife's grandmother. Shortly before they were due to drive back across France, the grandmother died. Knowing there would be a lot of red tape and fuss at border control points – and realizing that they could be back home in England after fifteen hours of steady driving – the couple decided to hide the old lady's body in a carpet, fix it on the roof rack of their car, and take a chance.

But first they agreed to stop for lunch before crossing the border into France. When they finished their meal and walked out of the restaurant, they discovered that their car had been stolen.

This is one of the most famous of 'urban myths'. Paul Smith in *The Book of Nasty Legends* (1983) records that it has been popular throughout Europe and North America since the Second World War. Alfred Hitchcock used the theme in 'The Diplomatic Corpse' (part of the TV *Alfred Hitchcock Presents* series, 1955–61), and it is related over dinner in Roger Peyrefitte's novel *La Fin des Ambassades* (1953).

Tom Burnam in *More Misinformation* (1980) calls it 'The Dead Grandma in the Station Wagon' story, and notes that Robert H. Woodward, writing in the American *Northwest Folklore* (Summer 1965), points to a possible origin in *The Grapes of Wrath* (1939), John Steinbeck's novel in which the Joads do carry the body of Grandma Joad about with them after she dies.

A very early record of the tale occurs in James Lees-Milne's diary entry for 15 December 1942 (published in his *Ancestral Voices*, 1975): 'I dined at the Ritz with ... Morogh Bernard [who] told a true story about a Belgian friend of his who, with a rich aunt, escaped in a closed car when the Germans invaded Belgium. The aunt, who was very delicate, died in the car. The niece could not stop to bury her for obvious reasons ... so the niece put her aunt on the roof of the car wrapped in some valuable rugs. At last she was able to stop at a café, and get out for a meal ...' You can guess the rest.

2 A friend said to the American film director, Clarence Brown, 'What do you want with all that money? You can't take it with you.' 'You can't?' replied Brown. 'Then I'm not going.'

Told by Gottfried Reinhardt in Lillian Ross, *Picture* (1952). In Irving A. Fein, *Jack Benny, An Intimate Biography* (1976), Eddie 'Rochester' Anderson is quoted as saying of Benny's trademark meanness: 'Is Mr Benny tight? Well, a little snug, perhaps ... If he can't take it with him, he ain't gonna go.' The remark has also been ascribed to

Bob Hope about Bing Crosby (BBC Radio *Quote ... Unquote*, 27 October 1998).

1 A. E. Matthews, the actor, lived until he was in his nineties, so most people's recollections of him are of an extremely doddery old man. He once said: 'I always wait for *The Times* each morning. I look at the obituary column, and if I'm not in it, I go to work.'

Told in Leslie Halliwell, *The Filmgoer's Book of Quotes* (1973). Matthews's own obituary appeared in *The Times* on 26 July 1960. Several people have used the line subsequently. In the *Observer* (16 August 1987), William Douglas-Home, the playwright, was quoted as saying: 'Every morning I read the obits in *The Times*. If I'm not there, I carry on.'

2 A barrister who worked as legal adviser to a businessman whom he despised was rung up by the businessman's wife to inform him that her husband had died suddenly. 'The funeral's on Wednesday,' she said. 'Are you coming?' 'No,' said the barrister, 'I believe you.'

Told by George Mikes on BBC Radio *Quote ... Unquote* (14 August 1979).

3 Two actors met in the Haymarket, London, and one said to the other, 'Where have you been?' 'I've been away ... but I've been away so long some people think I'm dead.' 'Oh, surely not,' said the first, 'not if they look closely enough.'

Told by Sir Anthony Quayle on BBC Radio *Quote ... Unquote* (13 July 1985).

4 The death of a political leader *can* be kept quiet. The amazingly protracted demise of General Franco led to a pointed story that told of someone asking Prince Juan Carlos of Spain, the

heir-in-waiting, whether he wanted the good news or the bad news. 'Tell me the good news,' he said. 'Franco is dead,' came the reply. 'What's the bad news?' asked Juan Carlos. 'You will have to tell him.'

Told in Jerrold M. Post and Robert S. Robins, *When Illness Strikes the Leader* (1993).

5 Overheard at a hospital, an elderly man saying: 'I'm not afraid to die ... dying isn't so bad ... the trouble is that you're so bloody stiff the next day.'

Contributed by Jack Jennings of Hampton Bishop, Hereford, to BBC Radio *Quote ... Unquote* (11 September 1979). Compare this exchange from Richard Brinsley Sheridan's short farce called *St Patrick's Day* (1775):

Justice Credulous: I don't like death.
Mrs Bridget Credulous: Psha! there is nothing in it: a moment, and it is over.
Justice Credulous: Ay, but it leaves a numbness behind that lasts a plaguey long time.

6 The delightful American novelist and writer Gore Vidal had a running feud with the rather less than delightful (and diminutive) Truman Capote. While he was alive, Vidal said, 'He should be heard, not read.' When Capote died, Vidal commented: 'Good career move.'

Sources: *The Observer* (26 April 1981) and Ned Sherrin, *Theatrical Anecdotes* (1991). Capote died in 1984. Compare *Time* Magazine (8 April 1985), in which was reported the graffito: 'Elvis is dead' under which had been written, 'Good career move.'

Dedications

7 The Duke of Wellington once refused the dedication of a song, informing a certain Mrs Norton that he had been obliged to make a rule of refusing such dedications, 'because, in his situation as

Chancellor of the University of Oxford, he had been *much exposed to authors'*.

Recounted in G. W. E. Russell, *Collections and Recollections*, Chap. 2 (1898).

1 Queen Victoria so much enjoyed *Alice's Adventures In Wonderland* that she let it be known that she would very much appreciate the next work from the author's pen being dedicated to her. She probably enjoyed considerably less the Reverend C. L. Dodgson's (Lewis Carroll's) *Syllabus of Plane Algebraical Geometry* when he sent it loyally to her.

Told in Leslie Robert Missen, *Quotable Anecdotes* (1966). Alexander Woollcott in his introduction to *The Complete Works of Lewis Carroll* (1939) gives the follow-up work in question as *An Elemetary Treatise on Determinants*. However, it is known that Dodgson/Carroll emphatically denied this story, whichever book was involved. Florence Becker Lennon wrote in *The Life of Lewis Carroll* (1945/1962): 'That famous untrue story about Carroll and Queen Victoria ... that the Queen after reading *Alice In Wonderland*, asked for his other works and received a packet of abstruse mathematical pamphlets ... Carroll specifically controverts it in the Advertisement to *Symbolic Logic* [which was in 1896].'

2 Clara Bow (1905–65), the American film actress known as the 'It Girl' after appearing in the film *It* (1928), wrote these words on a photograph that she gave to her fiancé, Harry Richman: 'To my gorgeous lover, Harry. I'll trade all my It for your that.'

Told in Bob Chieger, *Was It Good for You, Too?* (1983).

3 The dedication that appears in Jan Morris's book *The Oxford Book of Oxford* (1978) is: 'DEDICATED GRATEFULLY TO THE WARDEN AND FELLOWS OF ST ANTONY'S COLLEGE OXFORD. EXCEPT ONE.'

Delay

4 The actor and playwright Peter Ustinov did a screen test for the part of Nero in the film *Quo Vadis* and then the production was delayed for a year. The new producer of the film sent him a cable saying that he thought Ustinov was a little young for the part. Ustinov sent him a cable saying that if the film was delayed another year, he would be too old for it. MGM then sent him a cable saying, 'Historical research has proved you correct.'

Told by Ustinov on BBC Radio *Quote ... Unquote* (17 March 1992).

Desires

5 When Harold Macmillan was Prime Minister in October 1957, he wrote to Michael Fraser, head of the Conservative Research Department, in the following terms: 'Dear Michael, I am always hearing about the Middle Classes. What is it they really want? Can you put it down on a sheet of note paper and I will see whether we can give it to them.'

Told in the *Daily Telegraph* obituary of Lord Fraser of Kilmorack (5 July 1996).

6 When Groucho Marx was in his seventies, he commented on the Indian summer he was enjoying professionally. 'I'm going to Iowa for an award,' he said. 'Then I'm appearing at Carnegie Hall. It's sold out. Then I'm sailing to France to be honoured by the French government.' He then paused, and added: 'I'd give it all up for one erection.'

As told in the *Independent* (23 January 1999).

Dictation

1 The Irish novelist James Joyce dictated parts of his novel *Finnegan's Wake* to an amanuensis – later to become an extremely well-known writer himself, Samuel Beckett. During one of their sessions together, there came a knock on the door. 'Come in,' Joyce called out. Beckett wrote the words down. Later, when the work was read back to him, he asked Beckett, 'What's that "Come in"?' 'That's what you said,' said Beckett. 'Well then, let it stand,' said Joyce.

Recounted in Richard Ellman, *James Joyce* (1959).

Diet

2 Having taken it into his head not to eat vegetables, Beau Brummell, the Regency fop, was asked by a lady if he had ever eaten any vegetables in his life. This is what he replied: 'Yes, madam, I once ate a pea.'

Told in Daniel George, *A Book of Anecdotes* (1958) and, much earlier, in Charles Dickens, *Bleak House*, Chap. 12 (1852–53).

Difficulties

3 Winston Churchill had no time for people who raised difficulties. Just get working on the solution, he advised. On 30 May 1942, he issued a typed minute to Lord Louis Mountbatten, Chief of Combined Operations, describing his ideas for the Mulberry Harbours project. Handwritten at the bottom was this: 'They *must* float up and down with the tide. The anchor problem must be mastered. The ships must have a side-flap cut in them and a drawbridge long enough to overreach the moorings of the piers. Let me have

the best solution worked out. Don't argue the matter. The difficulties will argue for themselves. W.S.C.'

A facsimile of the minute is contained in Churchill's *The Second World War*, Vol. 5 (1952). At the Musée du Débarquement at Arromanches-les-Bains, there is an enlarged photocopy of this passage displayed on the wall.

Dining and dinners

4 Humphrey, Duke of Gloucester, was a politician of the early fifteenth century whose hospitality became a by-word. Every man of fashion, who was otherwise unprovided for, was welcome to 'dine with Duke Humphrey'. When, however, Humphrey died – and all these men of fashion found themselves going hungry – the meaning of the expression was completely reversed. 'To dine with Duke Humphrey' then came to mean that you were going without your dinner.

Told in Thomas Fuller, *The History of the Worthies of England* (1662). A similar expression would appear to be 'going to dine with Saint Giles and the Earl of Murray', meaning 'dining alone', because the Earl is buried in St Giles Cathedral, Edinburgh. Source: Penny Vincenzi on BBC Radio *Quote . . . Unquote* (18 April 1995). Unverified.

Diplomacy

5 Sir Henry Wotton was England's envoy to Venice in the reign of King James I. His punning view of the diplomat's calling very nearly cost him his job. As Izaak Walton recounted in his *Reliquiae Wottonianae* (1651), Wotton had managed to offend a Roman Catholic controversialist called Gasper Scioppius. In 1611 Scioppius produced a book called *Ecclesiasticus*, which abused James I and related an anecdote

concerning the envoy. Scoppius wrote how, on his way out to Italy in 1604, Wotton had stayed at Augsburg, where a merchant, Christoper Fleckmore, invited him to inscribe his name in an album. Wotton wrote: *'Legatus est vir bonus peregre missus ad mentiendum Reipublicae causa'* – 'which he would have been content should have been thus Englished: An ambassador is an honest man, sent to lie abroad for the good of his country.' Scoppius, on the basis of this joke, accused James I of sending a confessed liar to represent him abroad. According to the *Dictionary of National Biography*, 'Wotton's chances of preferment were ruined by the king's discovery of the contemptuous definition of an ambassador's function ... James invited explanations of the indiscreet jest. Wotton told the king that the affair was "a merriment", but he was warned to take it seriously, and he deemed it prudent to prepare two apologies.' James said that one of these 'sufficiently commuted for a greater offence', but the joke had done its damage, and, although Wotton was later to be given further diplomatic work and become Provost of Eton, he continued to suffer for it.

1 During the filming of Alfred Hitchcock's *Lifeboat*, released in 1944, the director of photography complained to him about a difficulty he was having with the star, Tallulah Bankhead: 'Because of the confines of the lifeboat, I have to have my camera down low and we're shooting up a lot. Well, er, Miss Bankhead doesn't wear any panties. She has nothing on underneath. What am I going to do? I can see everything, and it's there on the film.'
Hitchcock paused before replying, and then said: 'Well ... I don't know whether this is a problem for wardrobe, make-up, or hairdressing.'

Told in *Cary Grant: A Portrait in his own Words and by those who Knew him Best* (1991).

2 As US delegate to the United Nations, in a debate on the Middle East question, Warren Austin (1877–1962) exhorted warring Jews and Arabs to 'sit down and settle their differences like Christians'.

Told in Fadiman and Van Doren, *The American Treasury* (1955).

3 When he was due to give a recital with the Russian-born cellist Rostropovich, the violinist Yehudi Menuhin was annoyed to be informed by the Soviet authorities that Rostropovich was 'unwell' and would be unable to take part. Suspecting that this was unlikely to be the truth, he rang Rostropovich and confirmed that the authorities were merely being their customary obstructive selves. So he sent a telegram to the then Soviet President, Leonid Brezhnev, saying that if Rostropovich was not allowed to attend, he would call a news conference and announce that the Soviets had told a lie about Rostropovich's health and that he was perfectly capable of performing. Rostropovich was allowed to perform.

Told by Menuhin in May 1991.

4 During her successful General Election campaign in 1979, Margaret Thatcher undertook various photo opportunities to emphasize how in touch she was with ordinary people. On one occasion, she was photographed standing on the back platform of a bus. As this was taking some time, she said, 'I'm beginning to feel like a clippie ...' And then,

observers recall, you could see the realization in her eyes that she might have said something patronizing, so she added, '… who are all doing a *wonderful* job.'

Recounted by Graeme Garden on BBC Radio *Quote … Unquote* (4 September 1979).

Directions

1 A motorist asked a country yokel for directions as to how to get to Salisbury. The yokel had a go at describing the way, but then stopped in confusion. 'You know,' he said, 'if I was going to Salisbury, I wouldn't start from here at all …'

Also told of an Irish countryman. This must derive from the caption to a cartoon by George Belcher in *Punch* (31 March 1926): '*Motorist:* Can you direct me to Puddleford? *Native:* Well, sir, by rights, to get there I reckon yew didn't ought to start from yere at arl.'

Disapproval

2 Sir John Reith, the first Director-General of the BBC, set lofty aims, but also created an atmosphere of bureaucracy and pomposity that lasted until very recently. One of Reith's tasks was to announce the most famous of all pre-war broadcasts – the speech made after his abdication by the former King Edward VIII in 1936. 'This is Windsor Castle,' Reith announced. 'His Royal Highness the Prince Edward …' He was then heard (by some listeners) to leave the room and slam the door, thus indicating disapproval of what was to follow. In fact, all he had done as he slipped out of the chair to make way for the ex-King was to give 'an almighty kick to the table leg'.

Recounted by Reith in *Into the Wind* (1949).

Discomfort

3 Once when he was interviewing a man for a job on the Paris *Herald*, James Gordon Bennett Jr began to wriggle around on his chair. Then he found the cause of the trouble: a wad of thousand-franc banknotes was in his back pocket. He threw them in the fire. The surprised young interviewee leapt up from his chair and saved the notes from the flames. Bennett was not having any of that. He threw the money back into the fire.

Told in David Frost and Michael Deakin, *Who Wants To Be A Millionaire?* (1983).

Discovery

4 A Spanish courtier, jealous of Christopher Columbus's success, pointed out that if he had not discovered the New World someone else would have done so. Columbus did not reply to this taunt directly but asked the other people present if they could make an egg stand on its end. When they failed to accomplish the task, Columbus broke the end of the egg and stood it on its end in that way. The moral was plain: once he had shown the way, anyone could do it.

Told by Benzoni in his *Historia delo Mondo Nuevo* and quoted in Daniel George, *A Book of Anecdotes* (1956). Hence the allusions to 'Columbus's egg'. From Margery Allingham's novel, *Death of a Ghost* (1934): "Ah," said Mr Potter, "remember Columbus and the egg. They could all make it stand up after he'd shown them how to crack it at one end. The secret was simple, you see, but Columbus thought of it first."'

It is said that when Columbus started out from Spain, he did not know where he was going; when he got there, he did not know where he was; and when he got back, he didn't know where he had been (author unidentified in *H. L. Mencken's Dictionary of Quotations*, 1942). It is also added that the chief thing was, the whole trip was done on someone else's money.

Dislike

1 Andrew Lloyd Webber, the composer, is said to have asked Alan Jay Lerner, the lyricist, 'Why do people always take an *instant* dislike to me?' Lerner replied, 'Saves time.'

By the time it appeared in the *Independent on Sunday* (15 December 1991), this was an old story. Lerner (if it was really he who punched the line) died in 1986. However, as is the way with these things, a wandering slur may simply have been imposed upon Lloyd Webber. The earliest version involving Lloyd Webber and Lerner appears to have been that reported in the *San Francisco Chronicle* (27 November 1990). The earliest newspaper mention I have found of the format involved a Sheffield Wednesday football manager and player (the *Independent*, 12 January 1989). From June 1992, the joke was several times made against George Galloway, a Scottish Labour MP. Compare the exchange from the film *They Drive By Night* (US 1940): 'Do you believe in love at first sight?' asks George Raft. 'Well,' Ann Sheridan replies, 'it saves a lot of time.'

Distinguishing marks

2 Rupert Brooke, the glamorous English poet who died of blood poisoning during the First World War, had prehensile toes and could pick up a tennis ball with his foot. How useful this must have been, when the need arose to fish them out of Grantchester mere. He could also seize a matchbox with one foot and strike a match upon it with the other.

This interesting information was provided by Arthur Marshall as a Useful Fact for setting conversational balls rolling, in an article

'Master Beeton' included in *Sunny Side Up* (1987).

Double-entendres

3 Dr Samuel Johnson was not without a sense of humour, though Boswell does describe one occasion when a joke seriously passed him by. Johnson had started the whole thing off by saying, 'The woman had a bottom of good sense.' Boswell comments: 'The word *bottom* thus introduced, was so ludicrous when contrasted with his gravity, that most of us could not forbear tittering and laughing.' Johnson did not take kindly to this and demanded, 'Where's the merriment? ... I say the *woman* was *fundamentally* sensible.' Then, Boswell adds, 'We all sat composed as at a funeral.'

Told in James Boswell, *Life of Johnson*, for 20 April 1781 (1791).

4 Gerald Berners's paternal grandmother, Lady Bourchier, was very fond of birds, and encouraged robins, tits, nuthatches and sparrows to come to her windows and be fed. She claimed to have tamed a pair of blue tits to come and eat out of her hand, though nobody had ever seen them do this. However, one day, the boy Berners did catch a glimpse of them and he remembered causing a mild sensation by rushing into the drawing-room where several members of the family were sitting, and crying out excitedly, 'I say! I've just seen Grandmother's tits!'

An early citing of this double-entendre – it must have been about 1890 – and recorded by Lord Berners in *First Childhood* (1934). Compare the BBC announcer's utterance (quoted by 1982, and ancient even then): 'In winter bullfinches are best fed on bacon rinds and great tits like coconuts.'

1 When Robert Atkins founded the Regent's Park Open Air Theatre, London, in 1933, with Sydney Carroll, the acting arena was made of lush turf imported from south London. On one occasion, Carroll stepped forward during the curtain calls – with the cast ranged behind him – and proudly informed the audience: 'Every sod on this stage comes from Richmond.'

Told by Michael Coveney in the *Observer* (21 July 1991).

2 The comedian Kenneth Horne got into trouble on *Beyond Our Ken* (BBC radio, early 1960s) when he said that there was nothing he liked more of a cold winter's evening than to curl up on the hearthrug with Enid Blyton. The writer's husband evidently created a great fuss, threatened to sue, and the joke was excised from the repeat broadcasts.

Told to me in 1963 by Eric Merriman, who had written the offending line.

3 The sainted Iris, wife of Sir William Hayter, Warden of New College, Oxford, said something memorable to a group of irreverent freshmen (of which I was one) in February 1964. In the Warden's Lodgings is a valuable Quatrain Chest. Carved on the top is a depiction of the only battle the Belgians have ever won, or some such feature. Iris Hayter, who was very keen that all of us freshmen should view such college treasures, piped up: 'Now then, has everybody seen my chest?'

Dramatic criticism

4 A frequently employed critical witticism derives its modern popularity from the use made of the words by Tallulah Bankhead to Alexander Woollcott about the play *Aglavaine and Selysette* by Maurice Maeterlinck on 3 January 1922. She said: 'There's less in this than meets the eye.'

Told in Woollcott, *Shouts and Murmurs* (1922). However, long before this, James Boswell, in his journal, attributed a version to Richard Burke, son of Edmund (1 May 1783): 'I suppose here less is meant than meets the ear.'

5 Lady Diana Cooper told Noël Coward that she had not laughed once at his comedy *The Young Idea* when it was presented in London in 1922. 'How strange,' he replied. 'When I saw you acting in *The Glorious Adventure* [a film about the Great Fire of London], I laughed all the time!'

This exchange is quoted in *The Noël Coward Diaries* (footnote to entry of 13 March 1946). It appears to be the original of an anecdote that takes several forms. Here it is as told to me by another actress in 1979: 'Diana Wynyard said to Coward, "I saw your *Private Lives* the other night. Not very funny." He replied: "I saw your Lady Macbeth the other night – very funny!"'

Compare the story recounted in *Sheridaniana, or Anecdotes of the Life of Richard Brinsley Sheridan* (1826): the playwright Richard Cumberland took his children to see Sheridan's *The School for Scandal* and kept reprimanding them when they laughed at it – 'You should not laugh, my angels; there is nothing to laugh at.' When Sheridan was informed of this long afterwards, he commented: 'It was very ungrateful in Cumberland to have been displeased with his poor children for laughing at my comedy; for I went the other night to see his tragedy, and laughed at it from beginning to end.'

6 Lilian Baylis, manager of the Old Vic theatre, could be quite sharp on the question of dramatic criticism. Of critics she complained: 'They form too quick an impression of work it has

taken my dear producer and his boys and girls a whole week to prepare.' But she could also be quite withering herself. Of some poor unfortunate ingénue who had turned up in a production of *King Lear*, she remarked: 'Quite a sweet little Goneril, don't you think?'

Told in a show about Baylis's work, at the Old Vic (March 1976).

1 One of Eric Maschwitz's early successes was the play *Goodnight Vienna* in 1929. Three years later it was turned into a musical film. After a substantial run in London's West End, the play went on a tour of the then provincial circuit, gradually making its way to less and less glamorous venues. One night as he was driving back home through the London suburbs, Maschwitz spied that his show was playing at the Hippodrome in Lewisham. Interested to find out what business was like, he popped into the foyer and consulted a dinner-jacketed man he took to be the manager. Without revealing who he was, Maschwitz asked, 'And is *Goodnight Vienna* going down well in Lewisham?' Came the sour reply: 'I'd say, about as well as *Goodnight Lewisham* would go down in Vienna ...'

Another version is told in Peter Black, *The Biggest Aspidistra in the World* (1972) involving the Theatre Royal, Huddersfield. On the other hand, *Roy Hudd's Book of Music-Hall, Variety and Showbiz Anecdotes* (1993) has an agent phoning the man who booked the attractions for Walthamstow Palace. The agent, desperate to fill in vacant weeks for the tour of a musical comedy he was representing, asked, 'How do you think *Goodnight Vienna* would go in Walthamstow?' Replied the booker, 'About as well as *Goodnight Walthamstow* would go in Vienna!'

The only trouble about all these versions is that they concern themselves with a *stage*

production of *Goodnight Vienna*. In fact, it seems to have started life as a radio programme in 1932 and went straight to film in the same year. Only somewhat later did a stage version become a standby of amateur operatic societies. Perhaps Maschwitz was presented with the classic critical upsumming when he asked about the *film* at some suburban cinema?

2 An overheard remark from the Oberammergau Passion play in 1934: in those days, the play lasted from 8 a.m. to 6 p.m., with a two-hour break for lunch. At about 4.30 p.m., an American member of the audience announced so that all could hear, 'Let's go, I've had enough!' Her companion replied: 'I'd like to stay and see how it finishes.'

Told to me by Peggy Gardner of Swansea (1980). Compare, however, the story about Oscar Wilde recounted by Joyce Hawkins for *The Oxford Book of Literary Anecdotes* (1975): in a *viva voce* examination at Oxford, Wilde was required to translate from a Greek version of the New Testament. When the examiners were satisfied they told him he could stop, but Wilde went on, explaining, 'I want to see how it ends.'

3 Alfred Lunt and Lynn Fontanne, the great American husband and wife partnership, were appearing together in a play that had run for a long time. Like so many actors and actresses after a long run, their performances were, to say the least, a bit jaded. The producer called in and watched the Lunts do their stuff, then went and sent a telegram to them, saying: 'I am standing at the back of the stalls. I'd like you to join me.'

Told by George Jean Nathan, drama critic of *Esquire* in his monthly feature 'First Nights and Passing Judgements', in about 1937.

4 A comedy by Kenneth Horne with the title *Yes and No* featuring Steve

Geray and Magda Kun opened at the Ambassadors Theatre, London, in the autumn of 1938. It occasioned the shortest theatrical notice of all time. The journalist Hannen Swaffer wrote: '*Yes and No* (Ambassadors) – No!'

Told in a letter from Bill Galley of London WC1 to the *Sunday Telegraph* (24 March 1970). On BBC Radio *Quote... Unquote* (6 April 1993), Tony Hawks ascribed something similar to Dorothy Parker about the André Charlot musical show *Yes!*, which was presented in London in 1923. Her one word crit. was 'No!' – but I suspect this has been foisted upon her.

1 The American theatre director Guthrie McClintic recalled what an audience member said about his production of *Romeo and Juliet*. When the Capulets' tomb was revealed, he overheard one old lady say to another: 'I knew it! When the curtain went up on this show I knew it would have a bad end.'

Related in Guthrie McClintic, *Me and Kit* (1955).

2 The critic Kenneth Tynan was initially an actor, though not a very good one. Beverley Baxter, reviewing 'The Worst Hamlet I Have Ever Seen' in a 1951 edition of the *Evening Standard*, said of Tynan's performance as the Player King: 'He would not get a chance in the village hall unless he were related to the vicar. His performance was quite dreadful.' However, Tynan very shortly afterwards replaced Baxter as the paper's drama critic.

Recounted in Kathleen Tynan, *The Life of Kenneth Tynan* (1987).

3 At the pre-London opening of his *Quadrille* (1952) in Brighton, Noël Coward asked a local inhabitant, the TV personality Gilbert Harding,

'What did you think of my show?' Harding confessed, 'I'm afraid I slept through it.' Noël Coward: 'Don't worry about that, dear fellow, I've slept through so many of yours.'

Told in Wallace Reyburn, *Gilbert Harding* (1978).

4 Of the musical *Camelot* on Broadway, in December 1960, Coward said: 'It's like *Parsifal* without the jokes.'

Or 'It's about as long as *Parsifal*, and not as funny', in Dick Richards, *The Wit of Noël Coward* (1968). In *The Noël Coward Diaries* (entry for 16 December 1960) he merely relates how he took Marlene Dietrich to the first night and found the show 'disappointing ... music and lyrics uninspired and story uninteresting'.

5 In 1962, after Coward had been to see Lionel Bart's musical *Blitz!* – which was all about London in the Second World War and chiefly notable for the elaborate moving scenery by Sean Kenny – he commented: 'Just as long as the real thing and twice as noisy'.

Told in Sheridan Morley, *Spread a Little Happiness* (1987).

6 As the English actor Francis Matthews explains, 'Walter Plinge' is the name actors traditionally take in addition to their own when they are 'doubling', or playing two parts in a play. There was a lot of that in Matthews's early days in repertory theatre. But he remembers with mixed feelings a review he received in one local paper when he was playing two parts in a play: 'Francis Matthews was woefully inadequate in his part, but Walter Plinge gave a beautiful performance ...'

Told on BBC Radio *Quote... Unquote* (20 April 1993).

1 A play was in progress which was dying the death. Suddenly from the stalls a man stood up and asked, 'Is there a doctor in the house?' When a medical gentleman duly made his presence known, the first man said, 'Oh, doctor, isn't this a terrible play?'

A story told many times by Ralph Richardson – as in a TV interview (1982) and in *Pass the Port Again* (1980). It did not involve him, though Sheridan Morley has Richardson saying it himself to the audience of 'a truly terrible little thriller towards the end of his career' at the Savoy Theatre, London (*High Life*, September 1993).

2 In his days as a theatre critic, Bernard Levin once reviewed a play in a very particular way. He wrote that on the previous evening at the such-and-such theatre, the curtain rose to display a rather pleasant drawing room. The carpet was light green, he said, and the curtains at the window were darker. Then he described all the furniture. This went on for a whole column. He did not mention the actors. He did not even mention the play. He concluded by mentioning that just to the right of the French window was a well-stocked drinks cabinet and added: 'I wish I had spent the entire evening in it.'

Told by Roy Hudd on BBC Radio *Quote ... Unquote* (19 April 1994). The review was probably in the *Daily Express* in the early 1960s.

3 In a long and successful career as a theatre director, Peter Dews had ample opportunities to collect overheard reactions to his productions. After *Vivat! Vivat Regina!*, which he directed at Chichester and which ends with the execution of Mary Queen of Scots, he overheard a woman in the audience say: 'Do you know, it's extraordinary –

exactly the same thing happened to Monica.'

In a letter to me dated 10 January 1980, Dews called this anecdote, 'absolutely true. I heard it with my own ears.' Ned Sherrin, *Theatrical Anecdotes* (1991) mistakenly puts it after Dews's 1969 production of *Antony and Cleopatra* at Chichester. Robert Stephens used to recount a similar reaction of an Edinburgh lady to Lady Macbeth – 'Does she not remind you of Mrs McAndrew? She had something of the same problem ...' (BBC Radio *Quote ... Unquote*, 24 March 1992).

4 Patrick Garland, the director (and former actor), says the most withering theatrical indictment he has ever heard was of a well-meant but rather pretentious play at Brighton. He saw it at a matinée and as the curtain came down to rather desultory applause, the woman in front of him turned to her neighbour and said, 'Well, Emily, all I can say is, I hope the dogs haven't been sick in the car.'

Told by Patrick Garland on BBC Radio *Quote ... Unquote* (11 September 1979). Alan Bennett alluded to it in a book review in the *London Review of Books* in 1978. This overheard remark has also been ascribed to the actor and director Sir John Clements at the Chichester Festival Theatre. Sheridan Morley always tells the story as though it was said after the Peter O'Toole *Macbeth*, which was not until 1980.

5 When the singer Marianne Faithfull made an unexpectedly convincing acting debut at the Royal Court Theatre, London, in Chekhov's *The Three Sisters*, a disappointed member of the audience was overheard saying: 'If she's not awful soon, I'm leaving.'

Told by Terence Frisby on BBC Radio *Quote ... Unquote* (12 June 1979). On the other hand, this may be a borrowing from a story which concerns Elizabeth Taylor's appearance at a fund-raising poetry reading in New York. Here, Bea Lillie, sitting in front of Emlyn Williams, whispered to her companion, 'If she doesn't get bad pretty soon, people are going to start leaving ...' – quoted in Melvyn Bragg, *Rich: The Life of Richard Burton* (1988).

1 Ian McKellen, the actor with a very imitable North Country voice (once described as 'like munching biscuits'), played Hamlet at the Cambridge Theatre, London, in 1971. The production was reviewed by Harold Hobson, theatre critic of *The Sunday Times*, but it was on the radio rather than in the newspaper that he delivered his cruellest judgement. 'The best thing about Ian McKellen's Hamlet,' he said, 'is the curtain call.'

Recalled by McKellen on BBC Radio *Quote ... Unquote* (3 July 1979).

2 Michael Billington, the theatre critic of the *Guardian* for many years, went to review a revival of the musical *Godspell* at the Young Vic in 1981. He wrote: 'Heralded by a sprinkling of glitter-dust and much laying on of microphones, *Godspell* is back in London at the Young Vic. For those who missed it the first time, this is your golden opportunity: you can miss it again.'

Recounted in Diana Rigg, *No Turn Unstoned* (1982).

3 According to the story, Pia Zadora is said to have played the title role in *The Diary of Anne Frank* – the stage dramatization of the actual plight of a Dutch Jewish family hiding from the Germans in the Second World War. So unimpressed with her performance was one audience that when the Nazi stormtroopers arrived to search for Anne, a cry was heard from the auditorium: 'She's in the attic ...!'

Told, for example, by Irene Thomas on BBC Radio *Quote ... Unquote* (10 January 1987). Ned Sherrin, *Theatrical Anecdotes* (1991) says: 'I asked Ms Zadora about this on breakfast television and she said she was happy to put the record straight. She had never acted off-Broadway and never played Anne Frank.'

4 The Irish author Hugh Leonard went to see *Beyond Reasonable Doubt*, the first play by the novelist and politician, Jeffrey Archer, when it was put on in Dublin in 1988. He did not like it. When told that Archer had actually written the play very quickly – on a Friday, in fact – Leonard asked, 'What I would like to know is, what time on Friday?'

Source untraced. However, *Today* (2 September 1988) quoted Leonard on whether Archer had a future in this field: 'He doesn't even have a past.'

Drinking and drunkenness

5 The playwright Richard Brinsley Sheridan was frequently pickled, but his sense of humour did not entirely lose its bite in the process. Picked up in the street once and asked to identify himself, he did not admit to 'Sheridan' – he was a Member of Parliament after all – but announced: 'Gentlemen ... my name is Wil-ber-force.' Anti-slavery campaigner William Wilberforce was, of course, a by-word for sobriety and rectitude.

Told in Hesketh Pearson, *Lives of the Wits* (1962).

6 On the day the Japanese attacked Pearl Harbor, John Barrymore was visiting W. C. Fields at his home in Hollywood. When the news came in, Fields picked up the phone and ordered forty cases of gin from his liquor dealer. 'Are you sure that is going to be enough?' asked

Barrymore. 'Yes,' replied Fields, 'I think it's going to be a short war.'

Told by Charles G. Francis (1994).

1 Mrs Ronald Greville, chatelaine of the stately home, Polesden Lacey, had a 'house steward' who was prone to drink and lachrymosity. He was frequently intoxicated during her grand dinner parties and, on one occasion, Mrs Greville was forced to write him a note on the little silver pad she carried with her. It said: 'YOU ARE DRUNK. LEAVE THE ROOM IMMEDIATELY.'

Accordingly, the man swayed across the room and handed the note to one of Mrs Greville's guests.

Told by James Lees-Milne in his diary entry for 4 November 1942 (reprinted in *Ancestral Voices*, 1975 – where the guest is identified as Sir John Simon).

2 One Saturday, the actor playing the lead in Shakespeare's *Richard III* had taken rather too much drink with a fellow cast member prior to the evening performance. This fact communicated itself to the audience when the lead came on swaying like a ship at sea. Someone shouted, 'Get off – you're drunk!' At which the actor, steadying himself, replied: 'Who, me? Drunk? Just wait till you see Buckingham!'

Related by Sir Cedric Hardwicke in *A Victorian in Orbit* (1961). Sometimes told as though involving Wilfred Lawson, a noted tippler, though he does not appear to have played either part.

3 The impressively sized Liverpool MP, Bessie Braddock, once accused Winston Churchill of being drunk. He replied: 'And you, madam, are ugly. But I shall be sober in the morning.'

Heaven knows how this story entered the anecdote lists – or whether there is the slightest drop of truth in it. It appeared in Sykes and Sproat, *The Wit of Sir Winston* (1965), without naming Braddock. She was named in Leslie Frewin, *Immortal Jester* (1973). Compare this earlier exchange from the film *It's a Gift* (US, 1934): a swindling real estate agent says to W. C. Fields, 'You're drunk!' 'Yeah, and you're crazy,' replies Fields. 'I'll be sober tomorrow, but you'll be crazy the rest of your life.'

4 According to an (oddly) much-told tale, Philip Toynbee, the critic, was commissioned to write an article about the formidable novelist, Ivy Compton-Burnett, and was invited to have dinner with her. So apprehensive was he that he tanked up substantially before arrival and then accepted everything of an alcoholic nature that was offered to him. Up to the fish course, that is, when he passed out, face down on his half-finished plate.

When he finally awoke, many hours later, Toynbee's face was still in the fish, Miss Compton-Burnett and another guest had stolen away, and it was all too apparent that they had continued their substantial meal right to the end with Toynbee in this humiliating position.

Told by Paul Bailey on BBC Radio *Quote ... Unquote* (13 August 1983). A full-dress version can be found in Kingsley Amis, *Memoirs* (1991).

5 Wallace 'Bill' Greenslade (1913–61), a portly BBC radio newsreader and announcer, was noted for unbending sufficiently to introduce many editions of *The Goon Show*. One night, however, he appeared somewhat tiddly when reading the rather more solemn nine o'clock news on the BBC Home Service. There were the expected

complaints. After a dignified pause, a 'BBC spokesman' commented wisely, 'All of us have our off-days, and this was one of Mr Greenslade's.'

From my own memory of newspaper reports at the time – mid-1950s. In Jack de Manio's *To Auntie With Love* (1967), a 'BBC spokesman' is quoted as having said, on a similar occasion about another, 'News-readers never get drunk, but they are sometimes very upset.'

1 During his time as Foreign Secretary (1966–68), the English Labour politician George Brown rather bibulously teetered across the room to one of the guests at a reception, sank on his knees and cried out, 'Lovely creature in scarlet, dance with me! You *lovely* creature in scarlet ...' And the guest turned and said, 'I'm the Apostolic Delegate and I don't think you're in any condition to dance with me.'

This is the version told by Kenneth Williams on BBC Radio *Quote ... Unquote* (1979), though without naming Brown. He added, 'It must be true because I read it in *The Sunday Times*. I checked with Alan Brien about it.' Earlier it had appeared in *Pass the Port* (1976), safely consigned to 'a South American country', the politician unnamed, and the put-down: 'First, you are drunk, secondly the music is the National Anthem, and finally, I am the Cardinal Archbishop.'

In Peter Paterson's biography, *Tired and Emotional: The Life of Lord George-Brown* (1993), the story is set in Brazil, Brown is named, the creature is in crimson, and the put-down is administered by the Cardinal Archbishop of Lima (who was on a visit from Peru). Paterson, although hearing from a 'distinguished former member of the Foreign Office' who claimed to have been present at the reception was, unfortunately, unable to prove the veracity of this story. In fact, Brown never seems to have visited Brazil. Another

version of the tale has it occurring at a state function in Vienna and the put-down administered by the Cardinal Archbishop thereof.

In *The Kenneth Williams Diaries* (1993), it was further revealed that Williams had acquired the story from a friend, the actor Gordon Jackson, in December 1970 in the form of a newspaper cutting from *The Sunday Times* detailing some of Brown's eccentricities.

2 Michael Vermeulen, publisher of the magazine *GQ*, who died at the age of 38, liked a drink, to put it mildly. 'You know what I call a three-martini lunch?' he is said to have asked a friend. 'Dinner.'

Told at the time of his death in the *Independent* (2 September 1995).

Drugs

3 The actress Tallulah Bankhead may – or may not – have known the ancient motto 'Know thyself'. Whatever the case, she once addressed the question of whether cocaine was habit-forming. 'Of course not,' she wrote. 'I ought to know. I've been using it for years.'

In her autobiography *Tallulah* (1952). Compare: 'Typhoid is a terrible disease; it can kill you or damage your brain. I know what I'm talking about, I've had typhoid.' – Comte Maurice de MacMahon, quoted by Walter Redfern in *Clichés* (1989).

4 President Bill Clinton was a Rhodes Scholar at Oxford towards the end of the Swinging Sixties. In 1992, while seeking the Democratic nomination, he appeared on TV with a rival candidate, Jerry Brown. The two men were asked if they had ever violated state, federal, or international laws. Clinton admitted that while at Oxford between 1968

and 1970 he had used marijuana 'a time or two – and I didn't like it'. He also added, 'I didn't inhale – and I didn't try it again.'

Report in *The Times* (30 March 1992).

Dyslexics

1 When the word 'dyslexic' became popular for people with reading difficulties or 'word blindness', the actress Susan Hampshire, suffering from it herself, became one of those most often quoted in public on the topic. Others who had worked with her and had never noticed her having any trouble were unkindly wont to remark: 'I knew Susan Hampshire before she was dyslexic.'

Source conveniently forgotten, about 1982.

E

Ease, putting at

1 There are few things more embarrassing than being the only person to arrive not wearing evening dress at a function where everyone else is, and vice versa. When Noël Coward arrived in full fig at a function at which nobody else was similarly attired, he began his speech by saying, 'Now I don't want any of you to feel the slightest bit embarrassed ...'

The version of this incident in Cole Lesley, *The Life of Noël Coward* (1976) places it in about 1918 when Coward was invited to a meeting of the Tomorrow Club, which was made up of literary lions of the day: 'Not knowing the form, Noël arrived at his first meeting with the Tomorrow Club in evening dress, to find everybody in day clothes. He paused only a moment in the doorway as the eminent heads turned towards him, "Now I don't want anybody to feel embarrassed," he said.'

2 The future Poet Laureate, John Betjeman, married Penelope, the daughter of Field Marshal Lord Chetwynd, in 1933. Being only 27, Betjeman was a little doubtful as to how he should address his future father-in-law. Chetwynd soon put him at his ease. 'Well, Betjeman,' he said, 'if you're going to marry my daughter you needn't go on calling me "sir". Call me "Field Marshal".'

Recounted in the *Observer* (8 February 1959).

Effort

3 We sometimes wonder if there are any limits to a man's laziness. One said, 'I'm thinking of going to Australia. The news says that someone's discovered a diamond mine in the Outback where they sit all over the ground. All you have to do is bend down and pick them up.'

The other guy looked at his friend and said, 'Bend down?'

Included in *The Dumb Men Joke Book* (Volume II, 1994) by Nan Tucket. Compare this from Arthur Marx, *Son of Groucho* (1973): 'One day Father called [George S. Kaufman] long distance and filled him full of glowing tales about the fantastic salaries Hollywood movie writers were pulling down every week ... "George," pleaded Father, hoping to persuade him with his fine choice of cliché, "the streets are paved with gold." There was a moment's pause, and then Kaufman said, "You mean, you have to bend over and pick it up?"'

Elements

4 It is very important to know your element. There was once a Secretary of State for Air who was himself a qualified pilot. He went down to Southampton to see and try out a new flying

boat. He went up in it and after a bit he asked the pilot if he might take over the controls. This, of course, was agreed. They approached an airfield and the Minister circled round it and lost height steadily until the young man could bear it no longer. He said, 'Sir, this is a flying boat, you know.' The Minister gave him a very old-fashioned look and circled the airfield again. He then moved off and brought the flying boat down carefully on Southampton Water. As he turned to go, the young man, feeling that he might have blotted his copybook, said, 'I hope, sir, you didn't mind my saying that: you know I thought you might have forgotten this was a flying boat.' The Minister looked at him and said, 'My boy, cabinet ministers don't make elementary mistakes like that.' He then turned, said goodbye, opened the door and stepped out into six feet of water.

Told by General Sir Brian Robertson, chairman of the British Transport Commission at the annual dinner of the Municipal Passenger Transport Association (Inc) at Southend in 1954.

Elephants

1 In 1935, Rodgers and Hart, Hecht and MacArthur wrote one of their less successful shows, *Jumbo*, which involved the use on stage of practically an entire circus. At one point, a sheriff is repossessing the circus and Jimmy Durante, the American comedian noted for his big nose, comes on with a full-grown real-life elephant. The sheriff asks him, 'Hey, where are you going with that elephant?' Durante replies with sublime serenity, 'What elephant?'

The line was revived in the film *Jumbo* (US,

1962), with the line specifically credited to Charles Lederer.

Elocution

2 When Maggie Smith was playing Desdemona to Laurence Olivier's *Othello* at the National Theatre in 1963, Olivier made the mistake of criticizing her vowel sounds. She waited until he was blacked up for the role and carefully enunciated to him, 'How now, brown cow.'

Recounted in the *Independent on Sunday* (28 February 1993).

Encouragement

3 As an 18-year-old, just out of RADA, Richard Attenborough went to audition for the part of the young stoker in Coward's film *In Which We Serve*. Extremely nervous, he was instantly gratified when the Master arrived with his entourage and announced, 'You won't know me, but I'm Noël Coward. You, of course, are Richard Attenborough.' Attenborough later commented, 'I felt ten feet tall and immensely grateful.'

Recounted by Attenborough in *The Sunday Telegraph* (22 August 1965).

Enemies

4 One of the choicest so-called proverbs is this one: 'If you wait by the river long enough, the body of your enemy will float by.'

It was described by Julian Critchley MP as a *Spanish* proverb when he quoted it to Sir Edward Heath concerning the ousting of Margaret Thatcher in November 1990 (recalled in the *Observer*, 27 June 1993). Heath replied with a broad grin, 'Rejoice, rejoice' (echoing Thatcher's own exultation at one point in the Falklands War). In a

TV interview (September 1998), Heath told Michael Cockerell that he had also communicated similarly with his office: 'I said it three times – rejoice, rejoice, rejoice. She'd only said it twice.'

Englishness

1 In the early years of the century, the French actress Sarah Bernhardt was playing in Manchester, and was being taken for a drive in the countryside by a friend when they came across a noisy and vigorous football match in progress. Being a wet day, all the players were covered in mud. Bernhardt, swathed from head to foot in white furs, stood on her seat and watched the contest with eager interest. When it was over she sat down and sank back into her cushions, exclaiming, 'I adore this cricket; it's so utterly English!'

Recounted in the *Manchester Guardian* (13 July 1937) about an incident that occurred 'some thirty years ago'.

Entertainment

2 Christopher Stone is often described as the first 'disc jockey' – though that term had not, of course, been coined when, on 1 (or 7?) July 1927, he introduced a programme of gramophone records for the BBC. Others – including Compton Mackenzie in 1924 – may actually have done the job before him, but Stone was the first person to be perceived as what later came to be dignified with the term 'record presenter'.

Extraordinary though it may seem, Stone's popularity was such that George Black, the impresario, actually presented him on stage at the London Palladium in August 1933. And what was his act? He came on and said, 'I'm now going to play you a very nice record.

I hope you enjoy it.' He would then put a record on and sit there, listening to it, along with the audience.

Recounted by Alfred Black in Roger Wilmut, *Kindly Leave the Stage!* (1985).

Environmentalists

3 I once heard about a very environmentally minded couple who did all the right energy-saving things, grew their own vegetables, and recycled everything in sight. So successful were they that they had sufficient cash in hand to enable them to run a second car.

Early 1980s.

Epitaphs

4 'In Memoriam' notices in the Calcutta *Statesman* in the 1930s usually ended with a quotation and also a note in brackets to say who had inserted the notice. One such notice ended: '"Safe in the Arms of Jesus" (inserted by her loving husband)'.

Letter from K. W. Bevan of Milnthorpe contributed to BBC Radio *Quote ... Unquote* (1982).

5 The American humorist and drama critic Robert Benchley suggested the perfect epitaph for an actress of a certain type: 'She sleeps alone at last.'

Told in Edmund Fuller, *2500 Anecdotes for All Occasions* (1943).

6 In about 1950, it is said that the following notice appeared in a newspaper's Deaths column:

> The angel's trumpet sounded,
> St Peter called out 'Come',
> The pearly gates swung open,
> And in walked Mum.

'This must have appeared at least 30 years ago ... I remember a correspondence about it in the Live Letters column of the *Daily Mirror*, where some readers condemned its tastelessness, and others praised its simple sentiment' – letter from Margaret Holt, Manchester (1981). In *Ego 7* (for 6 March 1944), James Agate staked an earlier claim: 'The members [of the Column Club] were delighted with something I bagged out of the obituary notices in an august paper a few days ago:

> "The silver trumpets sounded loud,
> The angels shouted 'Come!'
> Opened wide the Golden Gate,
> And in walked Mum!"'

1 In their Classified Ads offices, many provincial newspapers keep a volume of standard tributes for the bereaved to consult. Presumably it was one such stock verse that gave rise to this interesting rhyme:

> Down the lanes of memory
> The lights are never dim
> Until the stars forget to shine
> We shall remember her.

Told by Alan Bennett as from 'a Lancashire newspaper' on BBC Radio *Quote ... Unquote* (26 January 1982). He had earlier included the lines in 'The English Way of Death' in *Beyond the Fringe* (Broadway version, 1964).

2 In the southern United States, a hypochondriac is said to have asked for the following words to be placed on his tomb: 'I told you I was sick.'

Remembered on BBC Radio *Quote ... Unquote* (22 December 1981). In January 1994, it was reported that the dying wish of Keith Woodward of Shrivenham, Wiltshire, had been to have a tombstone bearing the line 'I told them I was ill'. However, parish councillors ordered the message to be removed.

3 It is said that the following epitaph appears at the bottom of a tombstone in Tasmania: 'Lord she is thin.' The 'e' is on the back of the stone, the monumental mason not having left himself enough room to carve it on the front.

Is there a source for this much-told tale?

Euphemisms

4 When a man asked to be excused to go to the men's room, Dorothy Parker gently explained: 'He really needs to telephone, but he's too embarrassed to say so.'

Told in John Keats, *You Might as Well Live* (1970). Cole Lesley, in his *Life of Noël Coward* (1976), tells it like this, and describes it as a Coward favourite: 'She produced a personable young man, of which she seemed to have a supply, to fill in a last-minute cancellation at a literary dinner-party. Faced with such distinguished guests, through nerves he knocked back too many martinis and was drunk by the time he got to a table, from which he soon got up, loudly announced, "I wanna piss," and staggered from the room. "He's very shy," said Mrs Parker. "Actually he only wants to telephone."'

Excuses and explanations

5 Poets who take their inspiration from dreams must take care not to be interrupted while they are setting down their lines, is the advice to be gained from Samuel Taylor Coleridge's experience when writing what turned out to be 'Kubla Khan'. In 1797, he was staying in Somerset, had taken opium, and had fallen asleep. Two or three hundred lines came to him in his sleep and, when he awoke, he 'instantly and eagerly' wrote down as many lines as he could remember. Unfortunately, he was interrupted by 'a person on business from Porlock', so the task was never completed. Hence, the expression

'person from Porlock' to describe any kind of distraction, but especially from literary or other creative work.

Told in Coleridge's introductory note to 'Kubla Khan' (1816).

1 Gérard de Nerval, the French poet, had a penchant for taking his pet lobster for a walk in the gardens of the Palais Royal, Paris, on a long blue leash (or pink, in some versions). When he was asked why he liked to do this, he replied: 'Well, you see, he doesn't bark and he knows the secrets of the sea.'

Théophile Gautier, *Portraits et Souvenirs Littéraires* (1875), has a more elaborate version of the explanation, which translates as: 'Why should a lobster be any more ridiculous than a dog? Or any other animal that one chooses to take for a walk? I have a liking for lobsters; they are peaceful, serious creatures; they know the secrets of the sea; they don't bark, and they don't gnaw upon one's *monadic* privacy like dogs do. And Goethe had an aversion to dogs, and he wasn't mad.' An unanswerable explanation, surely?

2 After a hard day in Downing Street dealing with various international issues, Lord Salisbury changed into ceremonial dress and hurried to a levee at Buckingham Palace. King Edward VII took one look at his Prime Minister and pointed out that whereas the upper part of his body was clothed correctly in diplomatic uniform, his trousers were those of the Hertfordshire Yeomanry. Lord Salisbury excused himself with what has become a classic diplomatic formula: he had left his home, Hatfield House, at an early hour that morning, he explained, and since then his mind had been 'exclusively occupied with less important matters ...'

Told in Leonard Miall, broadcast talk 'In At

the Start' (No.2), BBC Radio 3 (1982). Miall had it from Maurice Farquharson, the BBC's Head of Secretariat (1953–63).

3 A man once demonstrated an 'indestructible' watch to Robert Benchley and Dorothy Parker in a speakeasy. He hit the watch repeatedly, dropped it and stamped on it. Curiously enough, the watch then stopped working. 'Maybe you wound it too tight,' the pair suggested.

Told in *The Sayings of Dorothy Parker*, ed. S. T. Brownlow (1992).

4 At the time Dorothy Parker joined the *New Yorker*, money at the magazine was tight. So much so that when Harold Ross, the editor, asked Parker why she hadn't come in to write a piece, she replied, 'Someone else was using the pencil.'

Told in *The Sayings of Dorothy Parker*, ed. S. T. Brownlow (1992).

5 Chico Marx was a noted womanizer. When his wife caught him kissing a chorus girl, he explained, creatively: 'But, you see, I wasn't kissing her. I was whispering in her mouth.'

Told in Groucho Marx and Richard J. Anobile, *The Marx Brothers Scrapbook* (1974).

6 Henry Montgomery-Campbell, when Bishop of Guildford (1949–56), was presiding over a retreat house called Farnham Castle. One of the clergymen became bored with the retreating and nipped out to do some shopping in Farnham town. As he departed he bumped into the Bishop and felt he owed him some explanation. 'My Lord,' said he, 'the Holy Spirit has moved me to go down to the town and do some shopping ...' Replied the

bishop: 'Then I feel bound to tell you that at least one of you is wrong ... it's early closing.'

This appeared in *Pass the Port Again* (1980), though without the Bishop's name. Told by the Reverend Roger Royle – including the Bishop's name – on BBC Radio *Quote ... Unquote* (20 October 1984).

1   Laurence Olivier's then five-year-old daughter Tamsin asked Noël Coward what two dogs were doing together. Coward produced a masterpiece of creative explanation: 'The doggie in front has suddenly gone blind, and the other one has very kindly offered to push her all the way to St Dunstan's.'

Told by Kenneth Tynan in the *Observer* (1 April 1973), but with 'push him all the way to St Dunstan's', interestingly. Tynan probably took this version from David Niven, *The Moon's a Balloon*, Chap. 17 (1971).

2   It is a tradition of the theatre that the last line of a play is not spoken during rehearsals – in fact, not until the first public performance. Otherwise, bad luck will result. Consequently, there is scope for forgetting the line or for the end of the play never really being rehearsed. When Sheila Hancock was playing in rep at the Bromley New Theatre, she was not only the female lead but also the assistant stage manager. Hence, it was not until the first performance that anybody faced the problem of how she was to release herself from a clinch with her lover on-stage left and exit off-stage right to lower the curtain. Resourceful as ever, she unclinched herself and said, 'Excuse me, I must go and clean my teeth.'

As told by Hancock in *Ramblings of an Actress* (1987).

3   In her old age and before obtaining a Disabled Driver's disc, Lady Diana Cooper used to park on double yellow lines and leave (eccentric but usually successful) notes to parking wardens, like these: 'Dear Warden – Taken sad child to cinemar – please forgive'; 'Dear Warden – Only a minute. Horribly old (80) and frightfully lame. Beware of the DOG [in reality a chihuahua]'; 'Disabled as you see – lunching on guard – Diana Cooper, Sir Martin Charteris's AUNT!' [this was outside St James's Palace]; 'Dearest Warden – Front tooth broken off: look like an 81-year-old Pirate, so at dentist 19a. Very old, very lame – no metres [meters]. Have mercy!'

Her son, John Julius Norwich, collected some of these notes and published them as part of the 1979 selection in *Christmas Crackers* (1980). Another version of the first of the above appeared in *The Lyttelton Hart-Davis Letters* (Vol. 6). Rupert Hart-Davis in a letter dated 11 November 1961 says he borrowed Lady Diana's Mini and found a piece of paper under the windscreen-wiper stating, 'HAVE MERCY. AM TAKING SAD CHILD TO CINEMA.'

4   During the first series of *Quote ... Unquote*, the reader Ronald Fletcher was, unusually for him, making very heavy weather of the script and fluffing heavily. At one point, he made a complete balls-up. What was astonishing was his explanation. 'You must excuse me,' he said, 'My wife has got the flu.'

This was during the recording on 10 February 1976.

5   The archetypal limp excuse for late-arriving railway trains – and now a part of British folklore – is: 'It was the wrong kind of snow.'

In the *Independent* (16 February 1991), this was ascribed to Terry Worrall, British Rail's director of operations. He had been attempting to explain why snow had disrupted services, even though a 'big chill' had been correctly forecast. In an interview with the BBC Radio *Today* programme on 11 February (presumably after he had made the original remark), he said, 'We have had a particular problem with this type of snow ... it has ... been very dry and powdery and it has actually penetrated all the protection that we have on our traction motors, beneath our multiple units, and on some of our locomotives.'

The other most often quoted excuse for disruption on British railways is '[there were] leaves on the line'. In the autumn, damp falling leaves have been known to form a layer on the rails and thus hinder the safe passage of wheels over them. The excuse was cited as though it was already an established one in the *Guardian* (22 December 1984).

1 The buffet car steward on an Inter-City express announced: 'For the benefit [*sic*] of the passengers, only cold meat and salad will be on the menu for dinner tonight. This is due to the buffet car being the wrong way round ...'

Contributed by David L. Coggins of Blackburn, Lancashire to BBC Radio *Quote ... Unquote* (10 January 1987).

2 The playwright Harold Pinter is a great cricket-lover (indeed, he once said that cricket was greater than sex). More recently he wrote a 'poem' about the great batsman, Sir Len Hutton, which consisted in its entirety of three lines:

> I saw Hutton in his prime.
> Another time,
> Another time ...

Pinter circulated this work among his friends, but as reaction was slow in coming he asked one of them, his fellow playwright, Simon Gray, what he thought of it. Gray hedged, and then said, 'I'm afraid I haven't finished it yet.'

Told in the *Observer* (8 March 1992). Anthony Powell has a slightly different version of the poem in his (published) diary for 2 June 1989. All Pinter anecdotes tend to be apocryphal and have the effect of bringing down his wrath upon the perpetrator and the teller. For example, a story current in 1999 was that Pinter had enlisted Tom Stoppard's support to have the Comedy Theatre in London renamed the Pinter Theatre. Stoppard is said to have replied: 'Why don't you change your name to Harold Comedy?' Pinter told the *Independent* (8 February 1999): 'It's totally without foundation. Sure, I had five plays put on there since 1990, and Bill Kenwright [a producer] made a joke and said, "Why don't they call it the Pinter Theatre?" But now I find myself landed with this extraordinary reputation ... There's an illness in the press in this country.' The interviewer, John Walsh, suggested that it had more to do with the journalistic habit 'of hoarding up apocryphal stories, like squirrels storing acorns'.

Expenditure

3 The lyricist Alan Jay Lerner and the composer Frederick Loewe were at the height of their powers and of their money-making capacity. They had written the musicals *My Fair Lady*, *Gigi*, *Camelot*, among others. One day in London they walked into a Mayfair motor-car showroom and both ordered Rolls-Royce convertibles. When Lerner reached for his cheque book, Loewe took out his own and said, 'I'll get this – you paid for lunch!'

It is true that both men did once order Rolls-Royce convertibles from a showroom in London in a transaction that took a mere five minutes to complete. As Lerner describes in his memoir *The Street Where I Live* (1978): 'The story of the two Rolls-Royces made the rounds and, as usual, became distorted. One day I picked up a newspaper where it was reported that we had bought two Rolls-Royces in five minutes, and that when I reached for my chequebook, Fritz took out his and said, "I'll get this. You paid for lunch"!'

The anecdote, distorted or not, has since come uncoupled from Lerner and Loewe. From the *Independent* (15 February 1992): 'One Lloyd's story tells how, after a particularly good lunch, [Bill] Brown and a brother found themselves outside a BMW car showroom. After his brother expressed admiration for a particular model, Mr Brown said, so the story goes: "I'll get that for you. You paid for lunch."'

Robert Lacey, the biographer, told an identical story about two Arabs and a Rolls-Royce on BBC Radio *Quote ... Unquote* in February 1979.

Michael Grosvenor Myer told *The 'Quote ... Unquote' Newsletter* (January 1993): 'Can't give you chapter and verse, but distinctly remember in my youth, certainly no later than the 50s, a version as one of those page-foot fillers in *Reader's Digest*, concerning two Texas oilmen in a Cadillac showroom.' Sounds quite likely.

Expenses

1 The radio reporter and journalist René Cutforth was something of a master at claiming expenses. On many occasions he claimed for expensive lunches with a certain General —— from the Polish Embassy in London. A diligent BBC accountant was suspicious about this and looked up the general in the Diplomatic List. There was no such person as General —— at the Polish Embassy. Accordingly, Cutforth was challenged over the veracity of his expenses claim. He was unfazed. 'I am very shocked,' he said. 'The man is clearly an impostor and I shall have nothing more to do with him.'

Told by Martyn Lewis at a lunch in Cardiff (1991).

Eyesight

2 The Queen was reading one of her speeches in Australia during 1977. She somewhat puzzled her audience by saying, 'In the 25th reign of my year ...' Shortly afterwards she started wearing spectacles.

Reported in BBC Radio *Quote ... Unquote* (24 December 1977).

Facts

1 The American entrepreneur Howard Hughes, when in Hollywood, was producing a mighty historical film. A lowly assistant pointed out that there were several historical errors in the script for one scene, and volunteered to go and check them out in the library. Hughes told him to forget it: 'Never check an interesting fact!'

Recalled in Peter Hay, *Harrap's Book of Business Anecdotes* (1988).

Failure

2 One of the great show-business stories is about the two pros – and it is always assumed they were comedians – who bumped into each other in the street. One asked the other how he was doing. 'Marvellous!' the man replied. 'I've just finished a sensational series on TV – top of the ratings every week!'

'Ah, yes,' replied the other pro, 'I'm afraid I didn't hear about that.'

'And on top of that, I made a record which went straight to the top of the charts.'

'I didn't hear about that either, I'm afraid,' said the other pro.

'Yes, and I also wrote my autobiography which is top of the best-sellers' list.'

'I didn't hear about that,' was the reply.

'Oh yes, and I just did two weeks at the Palladium – sold out every night.'

'Didn't hear about that.'

'The only disappointment was, I did a charity concert at Chingford and died a death ...'

'Ah, yes,' said the other pro, brightening, 'I heard about *that!*'

This version was told by Bill Cotton when Head of Light Entertainment group, BBC Television, at a BBC Lunchtime Lecture on 11 January 1977. The moral he drew from it was that, 'in terms of failure, news spreads fast and people have long memories'.

Fallibility

3 Largely working alone on his great *Dictionary* (published in 1755), Dr Samuel Johnson committed one or two errors. In the first edition he wrongly defined the word 'pastern' as 'the knee of a horse'. In fact, in a horse, it is rather the equivalent of the ankle in humans. It was corrected in later editions, but when a woman asked how Johnson had come to make this mistake, he splendidly forbore to give an elaborate defence. He simply put it down to: 'Ignorance, Madam, pure ignorance.'

Told in James Boswell, *Life of Johnson*, for 1755 (1791).

Fame

1 At the height of his fame, the radio broadcaster Jack de Manio was modelled, holding a microphone, for display in Madame Tussaud's famous waxworks in London. By the early 1980s, however, he had not quite suffered the usual Tussaud indignity of being melted down and turned into somebody else. Rather he stood anonymously in the reception hall, *sans* microphone, unidentified and, by most people, unrecognized.

My own observation in about 1983. The usual indignity did, however, befall the 1950s TV personality Gilbert Harding. Within three years of his death in 1960, the model of Harding displayed in the Brighton waxworks was melted down and turned into Christine Keeler – the concluding fact in Wallace Reyburn, *Gilbert Harding: A Candid Portrayal* (1978).

2 At the height of his fame, Kenneth Williams went into a bank in Great Portland Street, London, to draw out some cash – this was in the days before cash-dispensing machines. A bank employee gushed all over him and said he had seen all his films, heard all his broadcasts, was a great fan. 'So, what can I do for you, Mr Williams?' 'I want to draw £50.' 'Oh, yes,' said the bank clerk, 'and have you any identification ...'

Told to me by Kenneth Williams in about 1971. Of course this was preposterous, but Kennie created a great scene rather than simply saying, 'Fancy that.'

3 At the height of his fame, the broadcaster Russell Harty went into a branch of Marks and Spencer in London and bought six pairs of underpants (or, as he characteristically put it, 'those things you wear underneath what you wear over them'). When he got to the checkout desk, he overheard a woman who had been following him 'like a kind of pilot fish' through the store, saying to her friend: 'Fancy him buying underpants ...'

Told by Harty on BBC Radio *Quote ... Unquote* (19 June 1980).

4 Richard Whiteley's was the first face to appear on Channel 4 in 1982, and he has been host of the 'words and numbers game' *Countdown* ever since. Earlier, however, he was chiefly associated with Yorkshire Television's local *Calendar* programme for many years from its inception in 1968. Hosting a live afternoon chat show called *Calendar Tuesday* in October 1977, Whiteley was interviewing a man called Brian Plummer, who had written a couple of books about ferreting. Plummer was holding two ferrets and Whiteley one. Whiteley's (probably because it was nervous) proceeded to sink its teeth right into his finger and did not leave off for half a minute. Plummer said, 'Don't worry, she's only playing with you!' – and, indeed, if the ferret had meant business it could have gone right through to the bone. Even so, Whiteley's pain was excruciating and only ended when Plummer unloaded the two ferrets he was holding and applied appropriate pressure to the tender parts of Whiteley's errant ferret.

The tape of the incident having now been seen by almost everybody in the television-watching world has meant that wherever he goes Whiteley is known as 'the Ferret Man' and people call out 'Where's your ferret?' As he ruefully concedes, when he goes, the newspaper placards will not say, 'Perceptive TV Interviewer Dies' or 'First Man on Channel 4 Dies'; they will say, simply, 'Ferret Man Dies'.

Recounted to me by Richard Whiteley in August 1993.

Familiarity

1 Shortly after being made a Dame of the British Empire, Edith Evans was appearing on the stage and heard herself addressed by a call-boy with the words, 'Ten minutes, Miss Evans.' She exclaimed: 'Miss Evans! It'll be Edie next!'

Told by Terry Wogan on BBC Radio *Quote . . . Unquote* (29 May 1980). Ned Sherrin in *Theatrical Anecdotes* (1991) locates this specifically at Riverside Studios, when a stagehand said helpfully, 'This way, dear.' Evans said: 'Dear? They'll be calling me "Edie" next.'

Fans

2 Every letter written to *Blue Peter*, BBC Television's long-running children's show, receives an individual reply. The reason for this, according to Biddy Baxter, the programme's editor from 1962 to 1988, was because of Enid Blyton, the hugely successful children's author. As a six-year-old, Baxter had written Blyton two fan letters. The first letter, a hymn of praise, received a wonderful reply from Blyton – 'very chatty and with her own address on the top – I felt she was writing to me. But, being a typical child, I wrote again three days later. I got back exactly the same letter. I remembered for ever how awful I felt that day.'

Recounted in *Kingsgate*, Durham University's alumni magazine (September 1992).

3 Broadcaster Russell Harty received what he took to be a fan letter from a woman TV viewer who wrote: 'My parrot Joey gets a small erection every time you appear and I think you are getting better.'

Told by Harty in *Russell Harty Plus* (1974).

Farting

4 The Earl of Oxford, making a bow to Queen Elizabeth I, happened to let out a fart, about which he was so ashamed that he went into exile for seven years. On his return, the Queen welcomed him home with the words, 'My lord, we have forgot the fart.'

Told by John Aubrey in *Brief Lives* (c. 1693). Coincidentally, I am sure, there is a parallel story in the *Arabian Nights' Entertainment*: 'How Abu Hasan Brake Wind' tells of the poor chap who had too much to eat and drink at his wedding-banquet and 'let fly a fart, great and terrible' in front of the guests and before he was able to make it to the bridal chamber. He instantly exiled himself embarrassedly for ten years. On his return, he overheard a girl asking her mother about her birth date. The mother replied: 'Thou wast born, O my daughter, on the very night when Abu Hasan farted.' At this he said to himself, 'Verily thy fart hath become a date, which shall last for ever and ever' and went off into exile until he died.

5 Just before she died in 1728, the Comtesse de Vercellis broke wind. 'Good!' she commented, turning over. 'A woman who can fart is not dead.'

Told in Jean-Jacques Rousseau, *The Confessions*, Bk 2, 1728–1731 (1781). Rousseau had been in her service for a short while early in his life.

6 My diary for 14 May 1968 records: 'To Pinewood [to cover the filming of *Carry on Up the Khyber* for the radio

show *Movie-Go-Round*]. Talked first to Kenneth Williams [who] told one story which, alas, is not transmittable. He was playing a love scene with Joan Sims and broke wind. When shooting was stopped, he protested that Rudolph Valentino had done just the same thing in his time, so what was the matter? Gerald Thomas, the director, pointed out that in those days films were silent ...'

Williams had himself recorded the story on 3 May 1968 (presumably the day it had happened), as was revealed on publication of *The Kenneth Williams Diaries* (1993). It can only have been 'untransmittable' on dear old *Movie-Go-Round*, as it soon became a familiar part of Kennie's TV chat-show patter.

1 In June 1973, General Yakubu Gowon, at that time President of Nigeria, came to London on a state visit. Welcomed by Queen Elizabeth II at Victoria Station, he had barely sat down in a carriage for the short drive to Buckingham Palace, when one of the Royal horses gave vent to an ear-splitting, tail-lifting fart. The Queen was very put out by this, as well she might be, and turned to President Gowon, saying, 'Oh, I do apologize ... not a very good start to your visit!' 'Oh, please don't apologize,' said Gowon. 'Besides, I thought it was one of the horses ...'

I believe I first read this in *Private Eye* in the 1970s. In *Of Kings and Cabbages* (1984), Peter Coats has the exchange between King Edward VII and his nephew, the Kaiser.

2 Famously prone to farting, even before he was an old man, the actor Rex Harrison, in his later years, became equally famous for ill-advised attempts to disguise what he had done. Evidently, when he broke wind on stage, there was no mistaking the fact. It was

about as inaudible as a stage whisper. Fellow cast members would instantly begin to titter and eventually ended up crying with uncontrollable laughter as Harrison indulged in increasingly hammy stage coughing – which only served further to identify himself as the culprit. The ultimate indignity, caused by this unwise course of action, was that a substantial portion of Harrison's obituary in the *Independent* was devoted to this unfortunate failing.

Told in the *Independent* (3 June 1990).

Feelings

3 Interviewed around midnight on the night of the General Election night in 1964, Harold Wilson, the victor, was asked, 'Do you feel like a prime minister now?' He replied, 'Quite frankly, I feel like a drink.'

Told in the *Observer* Magazine (5 April 1992).

4 When Thurgood Marshall was retiring as a justice of the US Supreme Court, a journalist asked him the clichéd question, 'How do you feel?' He replied: 'With my hands.'

Told in *Texas Lawyer* (6 January 1992).

Fence-sitting

5 A critic – possibly a Welsh church leader – said of Randall Davidson, Archbishop of Canterbury from 1903 to 1928, that he became used to 'sitting on the fence with both ears to the ground'.

Told in *The Monarch Book of Christian Wisdom*, ed. Robert Paterson (1997). This criticism resurfaced in connection with Robert Runcie, a later Archbishop of Canterbury. In the *Observer* (8 September 1996), George Austin, an archdeacon, wrote that 'Runcie was once described in the General Synod by the then Bishop of Leicester as a man who enjoyed "sitting on the fence with both ears to the ground". It helped him to accommodate both sides in every argument, but in the long term had the effect of destroying trust in his own statements.' However, it may simply be an established expression ever in search of someone to be attached to. 'A politician is an animal who can sit on a fence and yet keep both ears to the ground' is from Anonymous in *H. L. Mencken's Dictionary of Quotations* (1942).

Fighting spirit

1   Early in his first term, President Reagan was the victim of an assassination attempt. A bullet missed his heart by inches, but the experience triggered off in him an almost manic series of jokes and quips. To surgeons as he entered the operating theatre, he said, 'Who's minding the store?' and 'Please tell me you're all Republicans.' Lying in intensive care with tubes in his mouth, he mumbled, 'Will I be fit for ranch work after this?' When aides told him, 'Sir, you'll be happy to know that the Government is running normally,' he shot back, 'What makes you think I'd be happy about that?'

He also rattled off a series of quotations. To his wife, Nancy, he explained, 'Honey, I forgot to duck' – the explanation Jack Dempsey gave to *his* wife after losing the world heavyweight boxing championship to Gene Tunney in 1926. In a written note coming out of anaesthesia he paraphrased W. C. Fields with, 'All in all, I'd rather be in Philadelphia.' In another note he recalled Winston Churchill's observation, 'There's no more exhilarating feeling than being shot at without result.'

The written notes continued: 'Send me to L.A. where I can see the air I'm breathing' and 'If I had this much attention in Hollywood, I'd have stayed there.' Complimented by a doctor for being a good patient, he said, 'I have to be. My father-in-law is a doctor.' To an attentive nurse, he said, 'Does Nancy know about us?' and to another nurse who told him to 'keep up the good work' of his recovery, he said, 'You mean this may happen several more times?'

Reported in the *Daily Mail* (31 March / 1 April 1981) and *Time* Magazine (13 April 1981).

In 1985, Ronald Reagan was described as conducting 'government by anecdote', apparently feeling more at home in the show-business mode than in historical tradition. He certainly had the heat-seeking approach to anecdotes of the true chat-show host. The fact that, on occasions, these anecdotes proved to be devoid of any foundation in fact would hardly bother him. They were true as far as he was concerned.

Film criticism

2   Frank Hauser, writing film criticism in the *New Statesman*, once commented that watching Bette Davis in the film *Another Man's Poison* (1951) was 'like reading Ethel M. Dell by flashes of lightning'.

Told in Leslie Halliwell, *The Filmgoer's Book of Quotes* (1978 edn). Compare the poet Samuel Coleridge's comment on actor Edmund Kean, in *Table Talk* (1835): 'To see him act is like reading Shakespeare by flashes of lightning.'

3   Of the 1955 film *I Am a Camera*, a certain critic is said to have written: 'Me no Leica.'

Told in Leslie Halliwell, *The Filmgoer's Book of Quotes* (1973) and ascribed to C(aroline) A. Lejeune in *The Penguin Dictionary of Modern Quotations* (1980 ed.). Also attributed to

George Jean Nathan, Walter Kerr and Kenneth Tynan. A very long time ago I was asked the identity of the critic who had opined 'No Leica' of either the play or film *I Am a Camera*. Frederic Raphael had stated confidently in a book review that it was George Jean Nathan. Well, I can now confirm that Caroline Lejeune, inclined to pithy dismissals though she was, did not use it in her review of the film. On the other hand, the *Sunday Dispatch* review of the film did quote, 'No Leica, snarled a New York critic', which may take us back to George Jean Nathan, who, being a drama critic, must have been talking about the play.

1 A film critic is said to have reviewed the 1959 remake of *Ben-Hur* with the words, 'Loved Ben, hated Hur.'

Told in Leslie Halliwell, *The Filmgoer's Book of Quotes* (1973).

2 The film *Exodus*, based on a novel by Leon Uris about the early years of the state of Israel, lasts very nearly four hours. The story has it that the American satirist Mort Sahl was invited by Otto Preminger, the director, to a preview but after three hours had ground by, he stood up and implored, 'Otto – let my people go!'

No doubt apocryphal, but that is how Sahl himself tells it in a comedy routine on the LP *The New Frontier* (1961).

3 *The Sound of Music* became famous as a film to which a certain type of cinema-goer returned time and time again. There were people who had seen it hundreds if not thousands of times. At one showing, an old lady was overheard saying to another: 'Isn't this the bit we like?'

Told by John Wells on BBC Radio *Where Were You In '62?* (1985).

4 A Jewish woman from North London told her friend: 'I've just been to

Dr Zhivago and, do you know, it cost me £5.50!' Replied the other: '£5.50! That's outrageous. What is he, some sort of specialist?'

Told by Kenneth Williams on TV-am *Good Morning Britain* (19 January 1985). In *The Diaries of Kenneth Williams* for 31 July 1978 (1993) he has another version in which Golda Meir, the Prime Minister of Israel, goes to a cinema box office and was told it would cost '1.50 to see *Dr Zhivago*' and she expostulates, 'What is he? Some sort of specialist?'

5 In 1969, when the film of *The Battle of Britain* was completed, a special showing was arranged in a Royal Air Force mess overseas at which some of those present had participated in the actual battle. As they headed for the bar at the end of the film, one of these pilots was heard to mutter: 'Not as good as the play.'

Told to me by T. R. H. Lyons of Buckfastleigh, Devon (1980).

6 Charlton Heston directed and took a title role in the 1972 film of Shakespeare's *Antony and Cleopatra*. It was generally considered to be a flop. One of the tabloids headlined its thumbs-down review: 'The Biggest Asp Disaster in the World'.

Recounted by Richard Boston on BBC Radio *Quote ... Unquote* (4 January 1976).

7 When I was dining at Le Grand Véfour restaurant in London, there was such a deathly hush that I was able to listen to a conversation between two fairly mature colonial types, both well travelled, seated nearby. He apparently lived in Guernsey; she had a hard voice like that of Lady Barnett. He admitted he had been to see the film *Last Tango in Paris* (then just released), and she

pressed him to explain what Brando got up to in the famous 'butter' sequence. I wondered whether he was going to explain it to the whole restaurant. 'Well, they got very excited about the butter,' he suggested diplomatically. 'But why?' she pressed on. 'Did he *throw* it at her?'

From my diary (26 April 1973).

1 After falling asleep during an in-flight movie, impresario Lew Grade asked his wife: 'Who made that terrible film?' She replied: 'You did.'

Confirmed by Grade as having happened. The film may have been *The Return of the Pink Panther* (1974). Quoted in the *Guardian* (23 April 1995).

2 The notoriously expensive and largely unsuccessful film *Heaven's Gate* lasted four hours when it was first released in 1980. At the end of a New York screening of this original version, a spectator was heard to remark to his companion: 'If we'd gone on Concorde, we'd be in Paris now.'

Recounted by Dick Vosburgh on BBC Radio *Quote... Unquote* (25 December 1980).

First words

3 In the early days of television, the floor managers became fed up with having to give hand signals to performers such as Jasmine Bligh, the first female announcer. This was because they thought the signals were coarse and rather tiresome (in radio, such cues had always been given by the flashing of a green light). So, at the BBC's studios at Alexandra Palace, they rigged up a little engine which they tried out, slipping it round Jasmine Bligh's ankle, out of shot. The idea was that when they

pressed a button in the control gallery, it would provide a little pulse that would cue the performer. The first time they used it, Ian Atkins was directing. 'Cue, Jasmine!' he said. They pressed the little button, and she said, 'AAARGH! Good evening.'

Recounted by Sir Huw Wheldon on BBC Radio *Quote... Unquote* (10 August 1985).

4 The first two climbers to reach the summit of Mount Everest, the world's highest mountain, were Edmund Hillary and the Sherpa, Tenzing Norgay. They were members of the British-led expedition of 1953. In his autobiography *Nothing Venture, Nothing Win* (1975), Hillary described what happened when they came down from the summit: 'George [Lowe] met us with a mug of soup just above camp, and seeing his stalwart frame and cheerful face reminded me how fond I was of him. My comment was not specially prepared for public consumption but for George ... "Well, we knocked the bastard off!" I told him and he nodded with pleasure ... "Thought you must have!"'

Flattery

5 The playwright Richard Brinsley Sheridan is said to have asked a young lady: 'Won't you come into the garden? I would like my roses to see you.'

Attributed in *The Perfect Hostess* (1980).

6 A French government clerk in the 1840s found himself having to complete the passport details for a particularly beautiful woman. Instead of writing in her height, colour of eyes, shade of her hair, or mentioning any

other distinguishing marks, the clerk simply put: 'More like an angel than a woman.' Whether this flattered the lady or not, it apparently enabled her to pass freely over several European frontiers.

Told by E. J. Priestley of Shrewsbury in *The Times* (July 1981).

1 When a beautiful young lady cried out to the Reverend Sydney Smith in the garden that he would 'never bring this pea to perfection', he replied: 'Then allow me to bring perfection to the pea.'

Told in T. H. White, *The Age of Scandal* (1950).

2 Mrs Claude Bettington recalled a very pretty compliment that she had once paid, as a little girl, to her uncle, the notoriously weak Poet Laureate, Alfred Austin. He had said to her in all seriousness one day, 'My child, have you ever noticed how many great men are called *Alfred* – Alfred the Great, Alfred Tennyson?' As a dutiful niece, she added, 'And you, Uncle Alf.'

Told in *All That I Have Met* (1929). Mrs Bettington goes on: 'No one could fathom why he was made Poet Laureate, since his only claim to fame was his exquisite prose. I therefore asked a niece of Lord Salisbury point blank, "Why on earth did your uncle give the laureateship to Uncle Alfred?" She answered, "Because it was absolutely the only honour Mr Austin would accept from the Government for his long years of service to the Conservative cause."'

3 A very young candidate for the Royal Navy was being examined by a selection board made up of admirals. One of them asked the lad, 'Now mention three great admirals.' The candidate replied: 'Drake, Nelson, and – I beg

your pardon, Sir, I didn't quite catch your name?'

In fact, the caption to a cartoon by an unknown hand in *Punch* (24 June 1914).

Fleas

4 A child in class, when asked to draw a picture of the Holy Family, produced a picture in which Mary and the baby sat on a recognizably donkeyish steed, led by Joseph. On the ground nearby lay a black blob. 'What is that?' asked the teacher. 'The flea,' answered the artist. 'What flea, dear?' asked the puzzled teacher. 'The one the Angel told Joseph to take.' Eventually, puzzled but not liking to challenge an imaginative child, the teacher checked out her Bible. And there it was in Matthew 2:13: '... The angel of the Lord saying, Arise, and take the young child and his mother, and flee into Egypt ...'

Told to me in a letter from Robina S. Dexter of Liverpool (April 1992). She had had the story from her mother, a kindergarten teacher.

Food criticism

5 King Alfred the Great was at one time leading a hazardous life among the woods and swamps of the county of Somerset. He was destitute, except for what he could get openly or by stealing from the heathens or even Christians who had submitted to heathen rule. As it says in the *Life of St Neot*, he lay in hiding with a certain cowherd and, one day, the cowherd's wife decided to bake some loaves, as the king was sitting by the hearth, seeing to his bow and arrows. When the woman discovered that the loaves were burning at the fire,

she upbraided Alfred for not keeping an eye on them. The woman added that he would, after all, be perfectly happy to eat the 'cakes' when they were eventually ready.

The story of King Alfred and the cakes first appeared in print in Matthew Parker's edition of *De Rebus Gestis Aelfredi* by Asser (a close associate of Alfred, whose *Life* was written in 893 before the King died). However, Parker had himself taken in the material from *The Annals of St Neots*, and this had nothing to do with what Asser had written. The text of this *Life of St Neot* has not survived. Robert Birley in a lecture on *The Undergrowth of History* (1955) reviewed the various tellings of the story but doubted whether the incident ever really took place.

1 Queen Victoria described in her journal the occasion when she and the Prince Consort, holidaying at Balmoral, descended upon an unsuspecting inn: 'It was only when we arrived [at the inn of Dalwhinnie] that one of the maids recognized me ... We had a very good-sized bed-room. Albert had a dressing-room of equal size ... But unfortunately there was hardly anything to eat, and there was only tea, and two miserable starved Highland chickens, without any potatoes! No pudding, and no fun! ... It was not a nice supper.'

In *Queen Victoria in her Letters and Journals*, for 8 October 1861 (1984).

2 'If the soup had been as warm as the wine, and the wine as old as the fish, and the fish as young as the maid, and the maid as willing as the hostess, it would have been a very good meal.'

Untraced restaurant criticism dating from the Austro-Hungarian Empire – at least, according to Clement Freud, who quoted it on BBC Radio *Quote ... Unquote* (15 January 1979).

3 Oscar Wilde was once offered a dreadful watercress sandwich. He said to the waiter, 'Tell the cook of this restaurant with the compliments of Mr Oscar Wilde that these are the very worst sandwiches in the world, and that, when I ask for a watercress sandwich, I do not mean a loaf with a field in the middle of it ...'

Recounted in a Max Beerbohm letter to Reggie Turner (15 April 1893). Quoted in *The Lyttelton Hart-Davis Letters* (for 3 June 1956).

4 Georges Feydeau, the French writer of farces, ordered lobster at Maxim's, one of those restaurants where your dinner is seen floating before you in a tank before it is cooked. When his choice was served, Feydeau noticed that the lobster only had one claw. The waiter was summoned and offered the explanation that it must have been in a fight. 'I want you to take this one back,' murmured Feydeau, 'and bring me the winner.'

Recalled in Peter Hay, *Harrap's Book of Business Anecdotes* (1988).

5 When Sir Edwin Lutyens's son Robert was attempting to write a book about the architect, they met for lunch at the Garrick Club in London so that Sir Edwin could make known his views on the project and its author. When the matter was broached, however, Sir Edwin, embarrassed, merely exclaimed, 'Oh, my!' Then, as the fish was served, he looked at his son over the two pairs of spectacles he was wearing and commented: 'The piece of cod passeth all understanding.'

Recounted in Robert Lutyens, *Sir Edwin Lutyens* (1942).

Football

1 Brian Clough, at the end of his career as a footballer, became a loquacious club manager. After watching his Nottingham Forest team defeat Queen's Park Rangers 5–2 in the Littlewoods Cup, Clough rushed on to the pitch to eject spectators from it. In full view of television cameras, he proceeded to clout offenders and clip them round the ear. An anonymous wit described this procedure as a case of 'the shit hitting the fan'.

The incident occurred in January 1989. Clough was banned for the rest of the season from watching his team from the touch lines.

Foot-in-mouths

2 A newly elected mayor was replying to a speech congratulating him on his elevation. He promised that during his year of office, he would lay aside all his political prepossessions and be, 'like Caesar's wife, all things to all men'.

Told by G. W. E. Russell in *Collections and Recollections* (1898).

3 In the early days of British radio, a leading churchman was conducting a live religious service, conscious that he had to modulate his voice to make it more acceptable for a studio than for a church. After he had concluded the broadcast with the Grace, he commented to the producer, 'I don't think that was too loud, do you?' Unfortunately, part of this came over the air as, '... the fellowship of the Holy Ghost, be with us all evermore ... I don't think'!

Told to me by the Reverend Vernon Sproxton in about 1955.

4 In the House of Commons, during the Second World War, the Conservative politician Irene Ward asked the Minister of Supply why Wrens were having to wait for their uniforms. The Minister replied that there were problems in providing uniforms for the Navy, and that sailors had been given priority over Wrens. To which Ward is supposed to have responded: 'How long is the Minister prepared to hold up the skirts of Wrens for the convenience of His Majesty's sailors?'

Told in Richard Needham, *The Honourable Member* (1983).

5 From 1928 to 1949, Don Carney ('Uncle Don') was the host of a popular children's show on radio station WOR, broadcasting over a large part of the United States. He spent his life trying to deny that he had ever let slip one of the most famous clangers of all when, thinking he was off the air, he had said, 'I guess that'll hold the little bastards ...'

I have also seen this attributed, without any justification, to Derek McCulloch, 'Uncle Mac' of BBC *Children's Hour* (as by the *Daily Star*, 24 April 1985).

6 Jack de Manio, who famously presented the BBC breakfast-time *Today* programme from 1958 to 1971, graduated to this post from being a not very successful radio announcer. Trailing a forthcoming programme on the BBC Home Service, de Manio unfortunately mispronounced the name 'Niger' and told a rather shocked Britain (not to mention parts of Africa that happened to be tuned in) that, 'After the news at nine o'clock, you may like to know that there will be a talk by Sir John MacPherson on "The Land of the Nigger" ...'

In *To Auntie With Love* (1967), de Manio

devotes considerable space to describing all the ramifications, personal and international, of this wonderful boob. It occurred on 29 January 1956.

1 A number of years ago, to say the least, an audience of tittering sixth-formers (myself included) believed it had stumbled upon a prime example of the Freudian slip. We were attending what was known as a Film Appreciation Lecture in the Philharmonic Hall, Liverpool. The speaker was a distinguished film director whose name fortunately I have forgotten, and he was introducing one of his distinguished films. In a throwaway line, he informed us he had just been with Dirk Bogarde in the South of France or somewhere, 'And we've been disgusting together ... er ... discussing ... oh God!'

I fear the name of the film director may be coming back to me. I think it was Roy (Ward) Baker, introducing a showing of his film *Morning Departure* (1950). He subsequently directed Bogarde in *The Singer Not the Song* (1960), which would fit the time scale.

2 At the end of a play, actor Michael Redgrave was about to commit suicide and was left alone on stage with a retainer. He was supposed to utter the line, 'Bring me a pint of port and a pistol.' What came out was, 'Bring me a pint of piss and a portal.' The retainer bravely sought to undo the damage by inquiring, 'A pint of piss, my lord?' 'Aye,' replied Redgrave, curtly: 'And a portal.'

Recounted in Melvyn Bragg, *Rich: The Life of Richard Burton* (1988).

3 In a studio discussion at ITN that was being directed by Diana Edwards-Jones, both interviewer and interviewee had earpieces (perhaps they were being joined by a third party from another location). Something was wrong, however, and this meant that Edwards-Jones's instructions to the interviewer were also heard by the interviewee. She said to the interviewer, 'Ask the old fart to give us some [voice] level.' And the Archbishop of Canterbury said, 'I think she means me.'

Told by Martyn Lewis in a speech at Cardiff (1991).

4 Journalist-turned-broadcaster William Hardcastle never really left behind the written word or, to put it another way, he was never entirely at ease as a performer. Nevertheless, his breathless delivery was redolent of the news-gathering process at its most hectic. If only one could recapture in print the full force of the occasion when he found himself completely incapable of uttering the name of the African politician 'Herbert Chitepo'. Or of the time when Hardcastle bounced on to the air and announced himself, 'This is William *Whitelaw* with *The World at One*'.

From recordings of these incidents, probably in the late 1960s.

5 Taking part in a TV interview with Patrick Garland to mark his 70th birthday, Noël Coward admitted to a lack of formal education. He said, 'I learnt all I know at Twickenham Public Lavatory ... er ... Library.'

From my diary for 7 December 1969. In *The Diaries of Kenneth Williams* (1993), the tale is recounted with the lavatories in question given as 'Battersea'. It is also suggested that Coward added, 'Oh dear! Quite a Freudian slip there, I'm afraid ...'

6 In the mid-1970s there was a kidnapper and murderer in the English Midlands

whom the popular press dubbed 'The Black Panther'. When he was eventually brought to book, a Radio 4 newsreader (who curiously continued to find employment for many years thereafter) told an astonished nation: 'At Oxford Crown Court today, the jury has been told that Donald Neilsen denied being the Pink Panther ...'

Well, he would, wouldn't he? The newsreader in question, as he later enjoyed admitting, was Edward Cole, and this must have been around 2 July 1976. Checked against a recording of the incident.

1 When I was presenting the BBC breakfast-time *Today* programme in 1976–78, I took what care I could during the preparation of the programme in the early hours of the morning not to give myself any verbal clangers to drop. I thought I had succeeded ... until several years later when I was invited to appear as a guest on a quiz about radio called *On the Air*. David Rider, the host, managed to find a clip of my more serious self on *Today* saying, apropos the then American President who had been making a series of errors, 'President Carter has made a determined effort to put his boobs behind him.'

Would it were possible to do that with one's own.

From my diary (9 June 1987).

2 A policeman had occasion to stop a car and speak to its driver. The driver did not take to being held up in this way and was rather abrupt and unhelpful to the officer. His wife, who was in the car with him, felt obliged to try and calm down the situation before her husband got himself into trouble. So she leaned over and said to the policeman: 'Please

don't pay too much heed to him. He's always like this when he's had a few ...'

Told to me by Alistair Edwards of Wilmslow (1982), who said he had heard it from the policeman himself.

3 There is the story of the man who had taken too much drink at lunch and was stopped by the police as he drove back to his office. 'The main thing,' he thought hazily to himself, 'is to be polite.' As the police officer bent down to look in the car, the driver flexed his muscles and said, 'Good consternoon, affable.'

Told in my book *Foot in Mouth* (1982).

4 Commenting on a failed assassination attempt against President Gerald Ford, former Vice-President Hubert Humphrey might have phrased his remarks a little differently. He said: 'There are too many guns in the hands of people who don't know how to use them.'

Told on BBC Radio *Quote ... Unquote* (26 January 1982).

5 Seeking re-election in 1980, President Carter addressed the Democratic Convention and was booed twice – an unprecedented reaction on such an occasion. He made fluffs and errors, which augured badly for his future. Wishing to evoke one of the great Democratic politicians who never made it to the White House, he wanted to mention the name of Hubert Horatio Humphrey. Instead, what he said was, 'Hubert Horatio Hornblower ...'

Reported in the *Daily Mail* (16 August 1980).

6 I was once being interviewed on television about graffiti, a subject on which I used to be able to speak for many

hours without notes. Suddenly, Jenni Murray, the charming interviewer, asked me in her best Robin Day manner: 'And tell me, have you ever done it in a lavatory?'

Recounted in my *The Gift of the Gab* (1985). The incident occurred at BBC Southampton on 30 September 1980. Unfortunately, Jenni realized what she had said, dissolved into a fit of giggles, and we had to start the interview again.

1 Angela Douglas, Kenneth More's wife of his later years, once stunned their friends with the news that Kennie had landed a part in 'Chekhov's *The Three Seagulls*'.

As recounted by her on BBC Radio *Quote ... Unquote* (7 September 1985).

2 The potential hazards of having to sight-read from a teleprompting device were brought home to TV presenter Anne Diamond in 1985. Following a disastrous fire that killed many people in a football ground stand at Bradford, an appeal for funds was launched. Among the fund-raising activities was a re-recording of the Gerry and the Pacemakers hit 'You'll Never Walk Alone'. One morning, Diamond managed to stop herself in time from reading what it said on the Autocue: 'You'll Never Walk Again ...'

Told to me by Anne Diamond (May 1985).

3 During the 1988 US presidential election campaign in which J. Danforth Quayle was George Bush's curious choice as running mate, Quayle said various things: 'I didn't live in this century' was one; another was, 'The government shouldn't interfere in the bondage between parent and child.'

Recalled in the *Independent* (10 November 1988). By March 1989, a British TV documentary was knee-deep in Danforthisms, the two most notable being: '[Of the Holocaust] It was an obscene period in our nation's history. No, not in our nation's but World War Two. We all lived in this century: I didn't live in this century but in this century's history' – eh? – and (as head of the Space Council) 'Space is almost infinite. As a matter of fact we think it is infinite.' Reported in the *Guardian* (8 March 1989).

In a speech to the Young Republicans National Federation in Nashville, Mr Quayle said that America was about to celebrate 'the 20th anniversary of Neil Armstrong and Buz Luken walking on the moon.' As every schoolchild knows, it was Buzz Aldrin who walked on the moon; Donald E. 'Buz' Lukens was a Republican congressman who had recently been convicted of sexual misconduct with a 16-year-old girl. Reported in the *Independent* (17 July 1989).

Forgetfulness

4 In another life, the novelist Paul Bailey was an actor playing in *Richard III* at Stratford-upon-Avon. Christopher Plummer was in the leading role and Bailey played Lovell, who, in Act III, Scene V, has to come on and say, 'Here is the head of that ignoble traitor, the dangerous and unsuspected Hastings.' One night he forgot his lines. Plummer stared at Bailey 'for what seemed like ten minutes' and then said, 'Is that the head of that ignoble traitor, the dangerous and unsuspected Hastings?' And Bailey said, '... Yes.'

Told by Paul Bailey on BBC Radio *Quote ... Unquote* (28 May 1996).

Frugality

5 A schoolteacher in New Zealand had given her class of ten-year-olds a list of words that were to be used by them,

one at a time, in writing a short passage to demonstrate their exact meaning. One word was 'frugal', which one clever boy clearly knew had something to do with saving. He wrote: 'A beautiful princess was at the top of a tall tower. She saw a handsome prince riding by. "Frugal me, frugal me!" cried the beautiful princess. So the handsome prince climbed up the tall tower and he frugalled her and they lived happily ever after.'

This story from a correspondent in Truro appeared in my *Foot in Mouth* (1982). She said the schoolteacher in question was her niece. However, the story had already appeared in *Pass the Port* (1976).

Funerals

1 Towards the end of his life, the comedian Robb Wilton, who died in 1957, was attending a funeral and loudly declared: 'There's not much point going home really, is there?'

Told on BBC Radio *Quote ... Unquote* (20 November 1990). Ned Sherrin, *Theatrical Anecdotes* (1991) has Lorenz Hart saying something similar about his Uncle Willie at his (Hart's) mother's funeral in 1943. As it happens, Hart himself died first. *Roy Hudd's Book of Music-Hall, Variety and Showbiz Anecdotes* (1993) has comedian Charlie Austin saying it to the singer Charles Coburn at the funeral of Harry Tate (which was in 1940). Frank Randle (1901–57) tells the story in a recording of his 'The Old Hiker' sketch (undated).

2 Harry Cohn, as head of Columbia studios, was greatly disliked in Hollywood, but there was a large turnout at his funeral in 1958. An observer remarked, 'It only proves what they always say – give the public something they want to see, and they'll turn up to see it.'

This version is from Oscar Levant, *The Unimportance of Being Oscar* (1968). Lillian Hellman in *Scoundrel Time* (1976) has it said by the comedian George Jessel as, 'Same old story: you give 'em what they want and they'll fill the theatre.' Also attributed to the comedian Red Skelton.

3 When Arthur Miller was asked if he would attend his ex-wife Marilyn Monroe's funeral in 1962, he replied, 'Why should I go? She won't be there.'

Miller enlarged on this remark in *The Sunday Telegraph* (11 October 1987): 'I found myself having to come about and force myself to encounter the fact that Marilyn had ended. I realized that I still, even then, expected to meet her once more, somewhere, sometime, and maybe talk sensibly about all the foolishness we had been through ... When a reporter called asking if I would be attending her funeral in California, the very idea of a burial was outlandish, and stunned as I was, I answered without thinking, "She won't be there." I could hear his astonishment, but I could only hang up.'

4 New Zealand-born Michael Miles was a somewhat overbearing TV presenter in Britain. He was 'your quiz inquisitor' on ITV's *Take Your Pick*, which ran for almost twenty years from 1955. *Take Your Pick* contestants were given the option of opening a numbered box (which might contain anything from air tickets to Ena Sharples's hairnet) or of accepting a sum of money that might turn out to be worth more – or less – than what was in the box. The studio audience would chant its advice to the contestant – usually, 'Open the box!' So when Miles died, it was said that as his coffin was brought into the church, his funeral was interrupted by the congregation shouting, 'Open the box! Open the box!'

Source unknown, but included in my book *Very Interesting ... But Stupid!* (1980).

1 The bereaved widow allowed one of her late husband's friends to say 'a few words' after the cremation service was over. He started by saying that the last time he had been at that crematorium there had been some swallows flying about. He then went on to say how he had gone on a bird-watching expedition with the deceased, and so on. He ended – the cremation took place in early January – by saying: 'Now Mr G——, and the swallows, have departed to a warmer climate.'

Told to me by the Reverend P.G. of Oxford (1982).

G

Gardening

1 A group of executives from the BBC was on a visit to Italy many years ago, and its members were invited to a grand house for lunch. They were told that the house had a very wonderful garden but, when they went outside to look at it, it turned out to be a bit of shambles. Leonard Miall commented: 'This garden rather looks as if it was laid out by Incapability Bruno.'

Told by Sir Huw Wheldon on BBC Radio *Quote ... Unquote* (10 August 1985).

Gender

2 Meeting the American playwright Edna Ferber in the Algonquin Hotel, New York, Noël Coward remarked on her trouser suit. 'You look almost like a man,' he unwisely commented. 'So do you,' she replied.

Told in Robert E. Drennan, *Wit's End* (1973).

Genius

3 Augustus John was the Welsh-born artist who more or less redefined the Bohemian life. Out swimming one day, as a young man, John dived into shallow water and cut his head on a rock. As Virginia Shankland subsequently wrote: 'He hit his head whilst diving and emerged from the water a genius!'

As noted by Michael Holroyd in Vol. 1 of his biography of John (1974), Shankland's comment appeared on the back of a Brooke Bond Tea Card as one of a series of 'Fifty Famous People' (no date available). Compare the George Melly version from BBC Radio *Quote ... Unquote* (11 May 1977): 'I understand he was a sober and pleasant young man until he fell on his head in Wales, whereupon he became the slap-dash goat of his later years.'

God

4 Somerset Maugham once asked Augustus Hare, whose practice was to read aloud to his household from the *Book of Common Prayer*, why he omitted all passages glorifying God. 'God is a gentleman,' Hare replied, 'and no gentleman cares to be praised to his face.'

Told in the *Observer* (10 November 1991). This Hare (1834–1903), biographer and writer of guide books, is often confused with his uncle, Augustus Hare (1792–1834), clergyman and writer, who does, indeed, seem more likely to have come out with this remark.

5 While reading the Bible from cover to cover in response to Evelyn Waugh's bet of £10 that he could not do so,

Randolph Churchill was heard exclaiming periodically, 'Isn't God a shit!'

Told in *The Diaries of Evelyn Waugh*, entry for 11 November 1944 (1976).

1 Field Marshal Montgomery once said, 'Consider what the Lord said to Moses – and I think he was right ...'

For a long time, I was under the impression that this was something Montgomery – that blushing violet – had actually said. Then I came across the line in a sketch called 'Salvation Army' performed by Lance Percival as an army officer (albeit with a Montgomery accent) on BBC TV's *That Was the Week That Was* (1962/63). So that must have been the start of it, though it is totally in character.

Then I discovered in *The Lyttelton Hart-Davis Letters* (Vol. 4 – relating to 1959), exactly the same joke in the form, 'Did you hear of the parson who began his sermon, "As God said – and rightly ..."?' No mention of Montgomery. Compare also a remark by Donald Coggan, Archbishop of Canterbury, on 7 June 1977, in a sermon for the Queen's Silver Jubilee service at St Paul's Cathedral: 'We listened to these words of Jesus [St Matthew 7:24] a few moments ago.' Then he exclaimed: 'How right he was!' One is reminded irresistibly of Lorenz Hart's stripper's song 'Zip' from Pal Joey (1940):

> I was reading Schopenhauer last night,
> And I think that Schopenhauer was right ...

Compare also what William Jackson, Bishop of Oxford, once preached (according to Jan Morris, *The Oxford Book of Oxford*, 1978): 'St Paul says in one of his Epistles – and I partly agree with him ...'

Goofiness

2 Although Noël Coward often recycled witticisms from his own conversation in his plays, there is one firm example of a borrowed witticism. The person he borrowed it from was David Niven. A Coward diary note for 10 December 1954 states: 'Lunched and dined with Darryl Zanuck who, David Niven wickedly said, is the only man who can eat an apple through a tennis racquet!'

This ended up as 'She could eat an apple through a tennis racquet' in Coward's play *Come Into the Garden, Maud* (1966). Compare the (American) proverbial expression, 'So buck-toothed he/she could eat a pumpkin through a picket fence', quoted in the journal *Proverbium* (1989). In fact, this would appear to be a fairly well-established American format. Somewhere between 1943 and 1946, *Transatlantic Magazine* published an article on American radio quoting this from Jack Benny's 'feud' with a fellow comedian: 'Fred Allen can eat popcorn through a tennis racquet.'

Graffiti

3 When the British 1870 Education Act became law, extending teaching to more and more young people, a Member of Parliament commented that: 'The chief effect will be that graffiti will be more numerous, better written ... and lower down.'

According to A. J. Wood of Pitsford, Northampton. Contributed to BBC Radio *Quote ... Unquote* (24 May 1978).

4 The English actor Ernest Thesiger once went to Moscow on an Old Vic theatrical tour (with Paul Scofield as Hamlet and Mary Ure as Ophelia). This was several years after the newsworthy defection to the Soviet Union of two English spies. Not wishing to leave that event unnoticed, Thesiger went into one of the public conveniences of the Soviet capital and, finding himself alone, wrote on the wall, 'Burgess loves Maclean'.

This version is from Michael Pertwee, *Name Dropping* (1974). Burgess and Maclean defected in 1951. The Old Vic tour was in 1955. Rupert Hart-Davis in *The Lyttelton Hart-Davis Letters* (for 18 March 1956) says that the tale was told to *him* by Gilbert Harding.

Gratitude

1 The following letter was received by the general manager of a motor omnibus service 'north of the Trent'. It was written from 'The Royal Infirmary':

'Dear Sir, I was prevailed upon by my husband, last Saturday, to make a journey in one of your motor omnibuses, and I am very pleased indeed that I did so, for during the journey down, a floating kidney, which has for many months resisted the best medical skill of this city, settled into its normal position and I have been free from pain ever since.

'Should you desire to communicate with me, please do so at the above address, where I am being treated for a lacerated throat due to swallowing my false teeth upon the return journey.

'Yours truly,

'A VERY GRATEFUL PASSENGER.'

Told in the *Journal of the Municipal Tramways Association* in 1924. Sent to me by Rosemary Thacker, Librarian of the National Tramways Museum in 1991.

2 After her great stage success as Eliza Doolittle in *My Fair Lady*, Julie Andrews was rejected in favour of Audrey Hepburn in the Warner Bros. film version of the musical. And this despite the fact that Hepburn's singing voice had to be dubbed. Andrews was thus available to go on and star in *Mary Poppins*, for which she duly won an Academy Award in 1964. Collect-

ing her Oscar she said, 'I'd like to thank all those who made this possible – especially Jack L. Warner ...'

Recounted in Leslie Halliwell, *The Filmgoer's Book of Quotes* (1973).

3 Laurence Olivier was given a special Oscar at the Academy Awards in 1979. His acceptance speech had some of the audience weeping into their tuxedos, the rest wondering whether perhaps he would have done better to leave his scriptwriting to Shakespeare, or someone like that. His text went: 'Mr President and governors of the Academy, committee members, fellows, my very noble and approved good masters [that bit was by Shakespeare], my friends, my fellow students ... in the great wealth, the great firmament of your nation's generosities, this particular choice may perhaps be found by future generations as a trifle eccentric but the mere fact of it, the prodigal, pure, human kindness of it must be seen as a beautiful star in that firmament which shines upon me at this moment, dazzling me a little, but filling me with warmth and the extraordinary elation, the euphoria that happens to so many of us at the first breath of the majestic glow of the new tomorrow. From the top of this moment, in the solace, in the kindly emotion that is charging my soul and my heart at this moment, I thank you for this great gift which lends me such a very splendid part in this glorious occasion. Thank you.'

From a transcript of the speech.

4 Accepting an award from the British Academy of Film and Television Arts in about 1984, the actress Julie Walters

gave a rambling acceptance speech, which can be more or less encapsulated in the words with which she ended: 'I don't know what to say.' Michael Aspel, the host, quipped, as she sat down, 'Well, you might have said "thank you".'

From my memory of the incident. It was probably when she received the Best Actress award for the film *Educating Rita*.

Hair

1 Eve Arnold, the photographer, was summoned by Marilyn Monroe to her suite at the Waldorf Hotel, New York, where the actress was also being interviewed by a journalist. Monroe opened the door wearing a diaphanous black negligée and carrying a hairbrush. In due course, she asked if those present minded if she brushed her hair. 'Of course not,' said the journalist, and Monroe proceeded to brush her pubic hair.

Recounted by Eve Arnold in the *Independent on Sunday* (24 May 1992).

2 David Hockney once told on TV of how and why he decided to bleach his hair and become the blond bombshell he is today. It was in response to a television advertisement he saw late one evening in New York City. 'Blondes have more fun,' it said. 'You've only one life. Live it as a Blonde!' He immediately jumped up, left the apartment, found an all-night hairdresser there and then, and followed the advice of the advertiser, Lady Clairol.

As recounted by a reviewer in *The Listener* (1983).

3 Shirley Williams, the estimable Labour minister and then founding member of the Social Democratic Party, was famous for (a) being a touch disorganized, getting lost on trains, arriving late and such, and (b) her hair. This was in no way reprehensible but was apt to seem dishevelled to those of a carping, satirical disposition. It had long been her Achilles heel, so to speak. It is reported that when she was a girl, Nancy Astor (the well-known outspoken first woman to take her seat in the House of Commons) said to Shirley: 'You'll never get on in politics, my dear, with that hair.'

That Lady Astor made the remark was confirmed by Shirley Williams on BBC Radio *Quote... Unquote* (9 November 1982).

Handwriting

4 Sybil Colefax, the society hostess and co-founder of the interior decorating business, Colefax and Fowler, had very bad handwriting. It was said that the only hope of deciphering her invitations was to pin them up on the wall and run past them.

Reported in *The Lyttelton Hart-Davis Letters*, for 13 November 1955 (1978).

5 A schoolmaster commented in a report on one of his pupils: 'With the dawn of legibility comes the horrendous revelation that he cannot spell.'

Source untraced. Compare what Arthur Marshall repeated on BBC Radio *Quote ... Unquote* (14 August 1980) – a school report (which he had possibly read about in the *Daily Telegraph*), 'Now that her handwriting has improved we can tell how very little she knows ...'

Happiness

1 Lunching with friends at the time of her husband's retirement, Yvonne de Gaulle was asked what she was looking forward to in the years ahead. 'A penis', she replied without hesitation. The embarrassed silence that followed was broken by the former President of France. 'My dear, I don't think the English pronounce the word like that. It is 'appiness.'

Exactly as told in Robert Morley, *Book of Bricks* (1978), but probably applied to 'Tante Yvonne' simply because she was a famous Frenchwoman. The same pronunciation is delivered as a joke in the film version of Terence Frisby's *There's A Girl in My Soup* (1970) – by a French hotel manager welcoming a honeymoon couple. In *The Diaries of Kenneth Williams* (1993), the entry for 10 April 1966 has it as told by Michael Codron and involving Lady Dorothy Macmillan. She asks Mme de Gaulle if there is any desire that she has for the future and the reply is, 'Yes – a penis.'

Headlines

2 A possibly apocryphal headline, said to have appeared in a British newspaper – presumably during the Second World War – was 'EIGHTH ARMY PUSH BOTTLES UP GERMANS'.

Recounted by Robert Lacey on BBC Radio *Quote ... Unquote* (5 February 1979). He said it came from the *News Chronicle* in 1942.

3 Dr (later Sir) Vivian Fuchs was leader of the Commonwealth Trans-Antarctic Expedition of 1957–58. For a while his surname gave a certain amount of pleasure to impish headline writers in the press. Actual examples include: 'DR FUCHS OFF TO SOUTH ICE', 'FUCHS OFF AGAIN' and 'DR FUCHS FIFTY TODAY'.

The first two of these are reproduced in Fritz Spiegl, *The Black on White Misprint Show* (1967).

4 The title of David Hockney's 1961 painting *We Two Boys Together Clinging* is from a poem by Walt Whitman. The picture shows two figures clinging together indeed, surrounded by various inscriptions including the numerals '4.2'. This is code for 'Doll Boy' – i.e. Cliff Richard. Hockney had been amused to come across a newspaper headline which stated: 'TWO BOYS CLING TO CLIFF ALL NIGHT LONG'. Although the article concerned a climbing accident and not a sexual fantasy, the reference gives an added resonance to the picture.

Described by Marco Livingstone in *David Hockney* (1981).

5 When Rupert Murdoch took over the American *San Antonio News* in the 1970s, one headline became the paradigm of his new style. Reputedly a bee with a fatal sting had been sighted in South and Central America. Hence the famous headline, 'KILLER BEES HEAD NORTH'.

Told in Michael Leapman, *Barefaced Cheek* (1983).

6 The headline 'SEX CHANGE MONK ONCE A ROYAL FOOTMAN' definitely once appeared, so I am assured, in the *Yorkshire Evening Post*.

Prior to 1979. Compare the apocryphal 'TEENAGE DOG-LOVING DOCTOR-PRIEST IN SEX-CHANGE MERCY DASH TO PALACE' mentioned in *The Lyttelton Hart-Davis Letters*, Vol. 4 (1959).

Health

1 When Irvin S. Cobb was working as a reporter on the New York *World*, he had to work under Charles E. Chapin, whom he found to be a difficult boss. Arriving at the office one day, Cobb was told that Chapin was off sick. Inquired he: 'Nothing trivial, I trust?'

Recounted in Ralph L. Marquard, *Jokes and Anecdotes* (1977). Possibly the original of an oft-told tale. Compare, from *Ego 3* by James Agate (entry for 20 November 1936): 'The week's good thing. A journalist saying that his editor was ill, Lionel Hale murmured, "Nothing trivial, I hope!"'

In the 'Gourmet Night' episode of BBC TV's *Fawlty Towers* (1975), when told that someone is ill, Basil Fawlty (John Cleese) says, 'Let's hope it's nothing trivial.' James Burke appearing on BBC Radio *Quote . . . Unquote* (19 February 1979) had this to say: 'A long time ago I was making a film in a hospital and two medics went by. One said, "I can't remember exactly what he died of – but I do recall it wasn't anything serious."' I suppose it is possible that the medic did actually repeat the old line. It is, after all, quite a reasonable thing to say, seen in a certain light.

Heckling

2 At a public meeting, a heckler demanded of the politician H. H. Asquith, 'Why did you murder those workmen at Featherstone in 1893?' He replied calmly, 'It was not 1893, it was '92.'

Told in *Geoffrey Madan's Notebooks* (ed. Gere and Sparrow, 1981). A slightly different version is given in Kenneth Rose, *Superior Person* (1969).

3 On the first night of his play *Arms and the Man* in 1894, George Bernard Shaw took a curtain call and was greeted with cheers and a solitary hiss. Shaw bowed in the direction from which the hiss came and said, 'I quite agree with you, sir, but what can two do against so many?'

Told by St John Ervine in *Bernard Shaw: His Life, Work and Friends* (1956). Oddly, the identity of the perpetrator of the hiss is known – it was R. Goulding Bright, later to become a literary agent, who was under the misapprehension that, in the play, Shaw was satirizing the British army.

4 In 1960, as British Prime Minister, Harold Macmillan was speaking about nuclear test bans before the United Nations General Assembly in New York. His speech was several times interrupted by the Soviet leader, Nikita Khrushchev, shouting out remarks and at one point angrily banging his shoe on the desk. Macmillan drolly asked if the shoe-banging could be translated.

From a recording of the incident.

5 Harold Wilson had what was considered considerable skill in dealing with hecklers. His responses were not usually humorous, but always to the point. There is a story told about a little girl who started crying while Wilson was addressing an election rally. The mother went to take her out of the hall, but Wilson said: 'Leave her where she is. It's her future we're talking about.'

Recalled in the *Herald* (Glasgow) (26 May 1995).

6 Harold Wilson was making a public speech in Kent during the 1964 General Election campaign and asked rhetorically, 'Why do I emphasize the importance of the Royal Navy?'.

A heckler called out, 'Because you're in Chatham.'

Told in A. Andrews, *Quotations for Speakers and Writers* (1969).

1 At a rally in the mid-1960s, Harold Wilson was interrupted by a cry of 'Rubbish!' from a heckler at the back of the crowd. Without missing a beat, Wilson replied: 'We'll take up your special interest in a moment, sir.'

Source untraced.

2 During one of Harold Wilson's administrations, Willie Hamilton, the MP for Fife Central, harangued him on the issue of Britain's membership of the Common Market. 'First we're in, then we're out,' cried the irate Labour MP. 'It's exactly like coitus interruptus.' The House of Commons, stunned into silence, erupted with laughter when a Conservative member shouted, 'Withdraw!'

Told on unidentified programme on BBC Radio 4 (23 October 1984).

3 A young Conservative politician was being given a hard time at a rowdy public meeting. At one point in his speech, exasperated by all the interruptions, he exclaimed, 'I can hardly hear myself speak.'
   A voice from the crowd cried, 'You're not missing much.'

Recounted by Ian Hislop on BBC Radio *Quote . . . Unquote* (27 July 1985).

4 Jack White, the comedian, was performing at Club 18 in Manhattan. Of an annoying heckler he demanded: 'Why do you heckle me? For all you know, I'm your father.'

Told to me by John O'Byrne (April 1998).

Helpful suggestions

5 Sir Herbert Beerbohm Tree was once impishly helpful to a man he saw in the street struggling under the weight of a grandfather clock. 'My poor fellow,' said Tree, 'why not carry a watch?'

Told in Hesketh Pearson, *Beerbohm Tree* (1956). Coincidentally or not, there is a cartoon in *Punch* (27 March 1907) that shows a man struggling with a large clock (the sort, however, that would fit on a mantelpiece). A bystander, characterized in the caption as 'Funny Man', says to him: 'PARDON ME, SIR, BUT WOULDN'T YOU FIND IT MORE CONVENIENT TO CARRY A WATCH?'

6 Coaching an actor, the playwright and producer Harley Granville-Barker suggested, helpfully: 'Try and look as if you had read Shelley in your youth.'

Told in Lady Cynthia Asquith, *Diaries 1915–18* (entry for 6 January 1918).

7 When Sir Anthony Eden was Prime Minister and Harold Macmillan the Chancellor of the Exchequer, both men had to come to terms with appearing on television as a tool of the politician's trade. To help him with his first ministerial broadcast, the urbane Prime Minister rather curiously sought the aid of a BBC studio manager called Johnny Day, who had a rich cockney accent and gloried in the use of rhyming slang. The reason was, a few weeks before, Day had instructed Macmillan in a Budget broadcast. 'Right, cock, over 'ere,' he had said. 'Boys, give me a piece of Duke of York.' He put a chalk mark on the blue carpet. 'Right, that's where you put your daisy roots. Now you look at the camera and go "blah, blah, blah". Then they've got a caption,

you look at it and go "blah, blah, blah" again. Right?'

Macmillan acquiesced. Thus Eden sent in a request, 'Can John Day be present when I do my broadcast?'

Recounted in Michael Cockerell, *Live from Number 10* (1988), based on a reminiscence by James Cellan-Jones.

Historical perspective

1 It is said that when a certain modern Chinese leader was asked, 'What do you think has been the effect of the French Revolution?', he replied, cautiously, 'It's too soon to tell.'

But which Chinese leader was it? The most common ascription is to Chou En-Lai (Zhou Enlai). However, the earliest citation – a review in the *Guardian* of a Barbara Tuchman book about China, *The March of Folly* – awards the palm to Chairman Mao. So no firm source for this delightful anecdote.

2 David Frost landed rather a scoop when he signed up ex-President Nixon to do a series of TV interviews. Shortly before they were transmitted, I in turn interviewed Frost for the BBC Radio *Today* programme. He was in Los Angeles and apparently suffering from jet-lag, the time difference, and possibly also from the end product of the local California vines. Anyway, at some point he said to me: 'The art of the quill has been practised since Caxton – and probably before ...'

The interview was broadcast on 5 May 1977. A number of listeners wrote and drew my attention to this interesting historical assessment but, curiously enough, I had already noticed it.

Hoaxes and practical jokes

3 Horace de Vere Cole arranged a ceremonial visit to Cambridge by 'the Sultan of Zanzibar' (impersonated by himself) and was received with great ceremony by the Mayor and councillors. In 1910, he topped this with a visit to HMS *Dreadnought*, the flagship of the Home Fleet, by 'the Emperor of Abyssinia'. Cole is also believed to have been the original person to have accosted a man in the street and asked him if he would kindly hold the end of a tape measure. He then went round the corner and found another volunteer to hold the other end. Cole then left them to get on with it.

Oral tradition.

4 On another occasion, Cole spotted a group of workmen digging up the road in Oxford. Accordingly, he went along to the police station and told the sergeant that a group of wicked undergraduates – dressed as workmen – were digging up the High Street. He then rattled down to the High Street, told the workmen that a group of wicked undergraduates dressed as policemen would shortly be arriving, and withdrew a short distance to observe the conflagration that inevitably ensued.

Oral tradition. This may be a confusion with some other hoaxer, as Cole was not an Oxford man. It may have arisen since another Cole story is that he once arrived in Piccadilly Circus in London with some friends and pretended to dig up the road. They then watched as London ground to a halt around them. (This version was mentioned in the *Independent* Magazine (2 September 1989).) Compare also the story related by Dacre Baldson in *Oxford Life* (1957) about the time when Oxford police imported plain-clothes men to deal with undergraduate brawls. One laid hands on an undergraduate and said, 'I am a plain-clothes policeman.' The undergraduate replied: 'And so, my dear sir, am I.' Then the trouble started.

1 Richard Dimbleby was notable for fronting TV current affairs programmes and for his commentaries on great state occasions. Once he introduced a film report on *Panorama* about that year's exceptionally heavy spaghetti harvest on the borders of Switzerland and Italy. The crop was shown hanging vertically from laurel bushes (having been affixed there first with Sellotape). Not everyone noticed the date on a calendar on Dimbleby's desk as he closed the programme. It was 1 April 1957.

The hoax is fully recounted in *Richard Dimbleby, Broadcaster* (1966).

Hollywood

2 In 1932, the actress Peg Entwistle, disappointed by lack of success at the studios, climbed to the top of the 50-foot-high letter H in the HOLLYWOOD sign overlooking Los Angeles, threw herself off it and died.

Recalled in the *Independent* Magazine (4 May 1991).

3 Bernardo Bertolucci, the Italian film director, appeared in person at the Academy Awards ceremony in 1988 and received an Oscar for his film, *The Last Emperor*. His use of the English language was less than award-winning, however. He said: 'If New York is the Big Apple, tonight Hollywood is the Big Nipple.' In an attempt at clarification, he added: 'It is a big suck for me.'

Reported in the *Guardian* (April 1988).

Homes

4 A tale of two department stores. When visiting a children's hospital, Queen Elizabeth (probably before she became entitled Queen Mother) asked a little boy where he lived. 'Behind 'Arrods,' came the answer. 'And where do you live?' the boy asked in turn. She replied, 'Behind Gorringes.'

Recounted by Ruth Zollschan in a letter to the *Guardian* (15 December 1986).

Homosexuality

5 Samuel Pepys, who would no doubt have wished to think himself a man of the world, did not know everything. In his diary he once wrote: 'Buggery is now almost grown as common among our gallants as in Italy, and ... the very pages of the town begin to complain of their masters for it. But blessed be God, I do not to this day know what is the meaning of the sin, nor which is the agent nor which the patient.'

Diary entry for 1 July 1663.

6 At the time of Oscar Wilde's great trouble, he was not exactly helped by his brother Willie who declared: 'Oscar was not a man of bad character: you could have trusted him with a woman anywhere.'

Told in George Bernard Shaw, *Pen Portraits and Reviews* (1932). Oscar despaired when he heard of his brother's efforts and commented: 'He tells me that he is defending me all over London. My poor dear brother could compromise a steam-engine' – quoted in Hesketh Pearson, *The Life of Oscar Wilde* (1946).

7 During the First World War, the biographer Lytton Strachey had to appear before a military tribunal to put his case as a conscientious objector. He was asked by the chairman what, in view of his beliefs, he would do if he saw a German soldier trying to violate his

sister. With an air of noble virtue, the homosexual Strachey replied, 'I would try to get between them.'

A correspondent suggests that it was much more likely that Strachey would have said something more grandiloquent – 'I would interpose my body' or some such – but the source for this anecdote is Robert Graves in *Goodbye To All That* (1929), and his version is the one given above.

1 'I once went to bed with a man to see what it was like,' is said to have been Winston Churchill's reply when asked by W. Somerset Maugham if he had ever had any homosexual affairs. Maugham then asked him who the man was. Churchill replied, 'Ivor Novello.' 'And what was it like?' asked Maugham. Replied Churchill, 'Musical.'

Told in Ted Morgan, *Somerset Maugham* (1980). The source for this story was Alan Searle, one of Maugham's acolytes. Churchill's daughter, Mary Soames, questioned it when it was included in my *Dictionary of Twentieth Century Quotations* (1987), and it is surely of dubious veracity.

2 Ivor Novello, who was very much *the* matinée idol of the 1940s and 50s, wrote musicals that he starred in himself, and always gave himself the most superb entrances. Doing *Glamorous Nights* at the Palace Theatre in London, at a matinée absolutely packed to the gills, he entered down a grand flight of stairs in a beautiful, white, shark-skin jacket with epaulets and gold braid and medals. In the silence that preceded his first line, a woman in the audience was heard to say to another: 'A homo-*what*, dear?'

Told by Anton Rogers on BBC Radio *Quote . . . Unquote* (6 June 1995).

3 Even as a schoolboy in Birmingham, Kenneth Tynan was a great ringmaster of events. In 1945, he invited James Agate, the leading drama critic of the day, to a conference at his school. Tynan went to meet the old man at the station. In the taxi, Agate put a hand on young Tynan's knee and asked, 'Are you a homosexual, my boy?' 'I'm af-f-fraid not,' stuttered Tynan. 'Ah, well,' sighed Agate, 'I thought we'd get that out of the way.'

Recounted in Kathleen Tynan, *The Life of Kenneth Tynan* (1987).

4 In the 1960s, when moves were afoot to legalize homosexual activities between consenting adults, Viscount Montgomery was fundamentally opposed to what he termed a 'Buggers' Charter'. At the committee stage of the parliamentary bill, he suggested raising the age of consent from the age of 21 to 80. He then added, disarmingly, that he would himself be reaching his four-score years at his next birthday.

Recounted in Mervyn Stockwood, *Chanctonbury Ring* (1982).

5 In 1991, Ian McKellen – just knighted – was invited to No. 10 Downing Street by the Prime Minister, John Major, to discuss gay rights. As it so happened, the next visitor due to arrive was Edith Cresson, the French Prime Minister, who had, not long before, let fall a controversial word or two about the masculinity of Englishmen.

On leaving Downing Street, McKellen said: 'I am sorry it's raining and I won't be able to linger outside to speak to Madame. But I am sure I would only confirm her worst fears.'

Told in the *Independent* (28 September 1991). Cresson's comment on homosexuality among Englishmen – 'Everyone knows it. It is in books and in history and it is a fact of civilization' – was quoted in the *Observer* (21 July 1991).

Honeymoons

1 Sir John Christie, Bart. (1882–1962) was the founder of the Glyndebourne Opera. When his wife was rushed to hospital with acute appendicitis on their honeymoon, she woke up the morning after the operation to find him in bed with her. 'I got bored,' he explained, 'so I thought I'd have my appendix out too and keep you company.'

Recalled by his son, Sir George Christie, in the *Observer* (3 May 1992).

2 When Dorothy Parker married her second husband, Alan Campbell, they both received permission to take a week off work from the film studio for a honeymoon at Lake Arrowhead. Three weeks later, they had not returned, so the studio boss's secretary rang the couple and said, 'He wants to know why you haven't come back to work.' Parker replied: 'Tell him that I've been too fucking busy and vice versa.'

Told in John Keats, *You Might As Well Live* (1971). Context from a letter by Jason Lindsey in the *Independent* (27 July 1993).

3 For a while, Orson Welles was married to Rita Hayworth. After it was all over, she said: 'Oh, Orson was clever all right ... The morning after we were married, I woke up, and I could tell by the expression on his face that he was just waiting for the applause ...'

Told in *The Kenneth Williams Diaries* (1993) – entry for 18 June 1955.

4 The 10th Duke of Marlborough (1897–1972), in his later years, on returning from one of his several honeymoons, was reported to have commented philosophically: 'I'm afraid Mr Mouse didn't come out to play.'

Reported in *Private Eye* at the time and repeated in its '300th Issue Quiz' in No. 299 (June 1983).

5 In the stormy opening weeks of the TV-am breakfast station of which he was a founder/presenter, David Frost slipped away to marry his second wife, Lady Carina Fitzalan-Howard, the daughter of the Duke of Norfolk. On his return, he quipped – possibly ad-lib – to waiting reporters, 'We have been on a working honeymoon.'

From an untraced newspaper report (March 1983).

Horsiness

6 Princess Anne (latterly the Princess Royal) is a notable horsewoman and has been a member of the British Equestrian Team. Indeed, so closely did she become identified with horses that she was quoted on one occasion as having said, 'When I appear in public people expect me to neigh, grind my teeth, paw the ground, and swish my tail.'

Told in Noël St George, *Royal Quotes* (1981).

Hospital visiting

7 Seeking to cheer up a patient in hospital, the visitor told her: 'You're lucky you're in here. It's pelting outside.'

Told by Billy Connolly in about 1985.

8 For a period in the 1980s, Margaret Thatcher appeared to specialize in arriving at the scene of disasters (fires, crashes, whatever) more speedily than

members of the Royal Family. She would congratulate rescue workers on their efforts and then descend upon the injured in hospital. Labour MP Frank Doran started offering friends cards that looked as if they were for kidney donors in the event of an accident. In fact, they bore the words, 'In the event of serious injury, not to be visited by Margaret Thatcher.'

Reported in the *Observer* (12 March 1989).

Hospitality

1 When asked to add Lady Macbeth to her repertoire, Edith Evans declined, saying it was out of the question: 'I could never impersonate a woman with such peculiar notions of hospitality!'

Related in Richard Huggett, *The Curse of Macbeth* (1981).

Hosts and guests

2 Upon what should have been a remarkable meeting of minds, quite the reverse occurred. Hans Christian Andersen once stayed in the home of Charles Dickens. Alas, the great Danish story-teller could neither speak nor understand very much English, and was described as being a 'bony bore'. After his guest's departure, Dickens stuck up a card in the guest-room mirror: 'Hans Andersen slept in this room for five weeks – which seemed to the family AGES!'

Told in Gladys Storey, *Dickens and Daughter* (1939).

3 Queen Mary – consort of King George V – was prone to what might now be termed 'hospitality abuse'. Playing upon her rank, she would virtually demand to be presented with objects that her gaze fell upon in her hosts' homes. It would be difficult to say how far the royal collections were enlarged in this way, as the rightful owners had to exert their wiles to get their possessions back. Stories are told of objects having to be spirited back to their owners when the royal predator was not looking. In *Kings, Queens and Courtiers* (1985), Kenneth Rose commented: 'Not all the anecdotes of her persistence are exaggerated. Visiting the homes of friends, acquaintances and strangers, she would stand in front of a covetable object and pronounce in measured tones: "I am caressing it with my eyes." If that evoked no impulsive gesture of generosity, the Queen would resume her tour. But on taking her leave, she would pause on the doorstep and ask: "May I go back and say good-bye to that dear little cabinet?" Should even that touching appeal fail to melt the granite heart of her host, her letter of thanks might include a request to buy the piece. Few resisted that final assault.'

Not only hosts but professionals were subjected to this behaviour. In John Pearson, *Façades* (1978) is this: 'Osbert [Sitwell] was then roped in for a trip to Bath on one of Queen Mary's collecting forays which made her the terror of the antique trade throughout the land.'

4 Sir Harold Acton, the last of the aesthetes, played host to numerous international visitors at his Renaissance villa, La Pietra, on the outskirts of Florence. One such was an internationally famous beauty and former actress. He made her welcome and took her on a tour of the house, but could not help noticing that her handbag was wide open and that she kept surreptitiously

sweeping small, though valuable, bibelots into it. When the time came for her departure, Sir Harold accepted a small kiss from her and then said, stuttering slightly, 'And now, let us go back round the house again and put back in their proper places all those pretty little things you have in your handbag.' Which they did. In silence.

This was one of Sir Harold's set-piece anecdotes and was told to me by Russell Harty on the very day he had taken lunch at La Pietra in April 1982. Sir Alec Guinness also relates it in *My Name Escapes Me* (1996), though, like me, chivalrously forbears to mention the actress's name.

Humour

1 William Wordsworth: The Joke. It must be agreed that the poet Wordsworth did not have the aspect of what we should now call a 'fun person'. He, while going along with this view of his make-up, nevertheless advanced the claim that he had been witty upon just one occasion in his life. But that was all. As he told it – and prepare for a sensational anecdote here – he had been standing at the entrance of his cottage at Rydal Mount. 'A man accosted me with the question – "Pray, sir, have you seen my wife pass by?"; whereupon I said, "Why, my good friend, I didn't know till this moment that you had a wife!!!"'

Told in Thomas Powell, *The Living Authors of England* (1849). Powell concludes: 'The company stared, and finding that the old bard had discharged his entire stock, burst into a roar of laughter, which the facetious Wordsworth, in his simplicity, accepted as a genuine compliment to the brilliancy of his wit.'

2 The question is, did Queen Victoria ever say to anyone, 'We are not amused', or if she did not, how was it that she acquired the reputation for having done so? The subject was raised in *Notebooks of a Spinster Lady* (1919) written by Miss Caroline Holland (1878–1903): '[The Queen's] remarks can freeze as well as crystallize ... there is a tale of the unfortunate equerry who ventured during dinner at Windsor to tell a story with a spice of scandal or impropriety in it. "We are not amused," said the Queen when he had finished.'

The equerry in question appears to have been the Hon. Alexander Yorke. Unfortunately, the German visitor he had told the story to laughed so loud that the Queen's attention was drawn to it. Another contender for the snub is Admiral Maxse, whom she had commanded to give his well-known imitation of her which he did by putting a handkerchief on his head and blowing out his cheeks. Interviewed in 1978, Princess Alice, Countess of Athlone, said she had once questioned her grandmother about the phrase – 'I asked her ... [but] she never said it' – and affirmed what many have held, that Queen Victoria was 'a very cheerful person'.

3 I have not heard of T. E. Lawrence (formerly of Arabia) making any other attempt at humour but this: in Cairo, a woman exclaimed, 'Ninety-two this morning, Colonel Lawrence! Ninety-two. What do you say to that?' Lawrence replied: 'Many happy returns of the day.'

This comes from Geoffrey Madan's *Notebooks* (ed. Gere and Sparrow, 1981).

4 For the amateur the funniest thing in the world is the sight of a man dressed up as an old woman rolling down a steep hill in a wheel-chair and crashing into a wall at the bottom of it. So said Groucho Marx, and added: 'But to make a pro laugh, it would have to be a real old woman.'

Distinguishing between amateur and profesional senses of humour. Told in Kenneth Tynan, 'The Crazy Gang', *Persona Grata* (1953). In J. R. Colombo, *Wit and Wisdom of the Moviemakers* (1979), this has become: 'An amateur thinks it's funny if you dress a man up as an old lady, put him in a wheelchair, and give the wheelchair a push that sends it spinning down a slope toward a stone wall. For a pro it's got to be a real old lady.'

1 A man was walking along the road with a lemon held close to his right ear. When challenged to explain this strange behaviour, he did so. 'You've heard of a hearing aid?' he asked. 'Yes,' replied the challenger. 'Well,' said the man, 'This is a lemonade.'

I would say I first heard this joke in the 1950s. John Osborne, recalling variety comedians of that era in *Almost a Gentleman* (1991), puts it in the mouth of the cockney comic, Scott Sanders, who was 'loud, brisk, seldom funny and looked as if he knew it'. He was one of the comedians Osborne drew to the attention of the company of his play *The Entertainer* (1957). These actors included Sir Laurence Olivier, who was to play the failed comedian Archie Rice with great success on stage and screen.

2 Legend has it that the comedian Max Miller was banned for a number of years from BBC radio for interpolating the following unapproved gag in his routine in the early 1940s: 'I was coming round a narrow mountain path when I suddenly found a naked young girl coming in the opposite direction. There was no room to pass and I didn't know whether to block her passage or toss myself off.' Another was: 'Our boys in the desert must be having a grand time smoking Camels and riding Egyptians – I mean, smoking Egyptians and riding camels.'

Oral tradition, probably since the 1950s. Also

wrongly attributed to Max Wall. W. Gordon McNay of Strathaven, Lanarkshire, gave me the benefit of his memories of this incident (February 1995). It has been suggested to me (in 1998) that in fact Miller would not have needed to be banned to keep him off the air: knowing his material would never work on the BBC he usually fended off all blandishments to appear.

Humourlessness

3 J. B. Morton, the immortal 'Beachcomber', sometimes complained that readers of the *Daily Express* (in which his column appeared) were unable to distinguish between his comic musings and the real news. Once he filled up space with: 'Stop Press. At 3.55 p.m. yesterday there was a heavy fall of green Chartreuse over South Croydon.' The day after publication, he received six letters from people saying they had been in South Croydon that very afternoon and not a drop of green Chartreuse had fallen.

Recounted in *The Lyttelton Hart-Davis Letters* (for 5 February 1956).

4 In 1977, when James Callaghan, the Labour Prime Minister, was compared by his son-in-law Peter Jay to Moses, Margaret Thatcher, then Leader of the Opposition, sought to make capital out of it by jesting in her speech at that year's Conservative Party Conference, 'My advice to Moses is: keep taking the tablets.'

This was, of course, a venerable jest even then. 'What Moses said to David Kossoff was "Continue taking the tablets as before"' was mentioned on BBC Radio *Quote ... Unquote* (28 march 1976). Even so, according to an account given by Alan Watkins in the *Observer* (27 May 1988), the Thatcher application of the joke very nearly misfired. When Sir Ronald Millar, Mrs Thatcher's speech-writer, presented her with the effort, she 'pronounced the joke funny but capable of improvement. Would it not be more hilarious for her to say "Keep taking the pill"?' Sir Ronald and his colleagues were appalled at this apparent lack of understanding of their little joke, and tactfully had to wean Mrs Thatcher off her version. 'Mentioning the pill would, they pretended to agree, naturally improve the joke no end. But did Margaret not think she would be taking a risk with the straiter-laced elements in the Party? Better on the whole to leave the tablets in the script.'

1 From time to time, Mrs Thatcher displayed a curious blindness to innuendo. During the 1983 General Election she said of one of her aides, 'He couldn't organize pussy' – meaning, he couldn't put a saucer of milk before a cat. The following year she appeared on Michael Aspel's TV chat show. Asked if she ever had time to relax, she replied, 'No, I am always on the job.' (She appeared mystified by the studio audience's reaction). Then during a speech at a Carlton Club dinner to mark Lord Whitelaw's retirement, she said, 'Every Prime Minister needs a Willie.'

Recalled by Michael Cockerell in the *Guardian* (8 April 1989).

2 When the publishing wing of his mighty empire moved into a London office block, it seemed perfectly natural to Robert Maxwell, the tycoon, that it should be renamed 'Maxwell House'.

It was said that he did not see anything funny about this at all.

A memory from about 1983.

Hygiene

3 It was said that Queen Elizabeth I was remarkably advanced for her time in matters of hygiene. Indeed, she was in the habit of taking a bath once a month – 'whether she need it or no'.

David Cottis wrote to me (1992): 'This sounds to me like a case of an old line becoming attached to a famous person. Certainly, the story has been told of people other than the Virgin Queen. Indeed, it is quoted as an anti-Semitic joke by no less an authority than Sigmund Freud in *Jokes and their Relation to the Unconscious* (1905)':

Two Jews were conversing about bathing. 'I take a bath once a year,' said one, 'whether I need one or not.'

David Cottis added (amusingly) that Freud explains (helpfully), 'It is clear that this boastful assurance of his cleanliness only betrays his sense of uncleanliness . . .'

Hymns

4 When an order of service was printed at one particular church it revealed this interesting sequence of musical items:

Solo: 'Death where is thy sting?'
Hymn: 'Search me, O God.'

Contributed to BBC Radio *Quote . . . Unquote* in about 1981.

I

Identification

1 Not content with having established the Old Vic theatre as a great London dramatic institution, Lilian Baylis also acquired Sadler's Wells, where she could put on opera and ballet productions. One day she fell over in the street. 'That's Lilian Baylis of the Old Vic,' said a bystander. '... and Sadler's Wells,' added the prostrate form, insistently.

Contributed to BBC Radio *Quote...Unquote* (11 May 1977).

2 There was until quite recently a small spot reserved by the River Cherwell in Oxford for dons to swim in the nude. Some young wags decided to go up the river in a punt in order to be able to see their tutors so disporting themselves. They braved the rapids and came into the quiet patch of the river where these rather corpulent dons were sitting naked on the sward. As the old gentlemen saw their pupils going past, they all – except Maurice Bowra – covered their loins with their hands. Bowra put his hands over his eyes – and explained to his colleagues, 'In Oxford I'm known by my face ...'

Told by A. N. Wilson on BBC Radio *Quote... Unquote* (20 November 1990). In his published diary for 4 February 1992,

Anthony Powell notes how he had written to the *Daily Telegraph* about another telling of this version of the story, adding: 'It was a chestnut when Maurice was born, as usual journalists missing the point, especially as they were all Balliol dons. As it was, just as the punt was disappearing, a lady was heard to say: "I think that must have been Mr Paravicini. He is the only red-haired don in Balliol."'

Identity

3 One of the first jokes I was told on arrival at New College, Oxford, in 1963, was that the late Warden Spooner (of Spoonerisms fame) had inquired of an undergraduate (in about 1918), 'Now, tell me, was it you or your brother who was killed in the war?'

Well, Frank Muir in *The Oxford Book of Humorous Prose* (1990) cites this from John Taylor's *Wit and Mirth*: 'A nobleman (as he was riding) met with a yeoman of the country, to whom he said, "My friend, I should know thee. I do remember I have often seen thee." "My good lord," said the countryman, "I am one of your honour's poor tenants, and my name is T.I." "I remember thee better now," (saith my lord). "There were two brothers but one is dead. I pray thee, which of you doth remain alive?" And the date of this version? 1630.
However, Mark English of Bradford wrote to me in 1994 to tell me of a yet earlier version of this tale: '"There were two brothers, one of whom died. On bumping into the

survivor, an egghead asked, 'Was it you who died, or your brother?'" – that comes from Barry Baldwin's 1983 translation of *The Philogelos, or Laughter-Lover,*which is an early Byzantine joke-book written between the 3rd and 10th centuries, and conventionally attributed to one Hierocles. It seems not to be dateable with certainty any more closely than that. There are many more very familiar jokes to be found there, hence the phrase "That one's as old as Hierocles", which was at one time much used by the classically educated and ill-mannered.'

1 A schoolboy once solemnly wrote: 'Homer's writings are Homer's Essays Virgil the Aeneid and Paradise Lost [*sic*] some people say that these poems were not written by Homer but by another man of the same name.'

In his essay 'English As She is Taught' in *Century* Magazine (April 1887), Mark Twain largely quotes from howlers, among which is this one, collected by Caroline B. Le Row. Later in the year, the essay appeared as the introduction to Le Row's book entitled *English as She Is Taught.* From there the observation seems to have become well-known, though not as a schoolboy howler. Compare the subsequent Aldous Huxley mention in *Those Barren Leaves,* Chap. 5 (1925): 'It's like the question of the authorship of the Iliad ... The author of that poem is either Homer, or if not Homer, somebody else of the same name.' The observation seems almost immediately to have been applied to Shakespeare: (see below).

2 Said Alphonse Allais, the French humorist (who died in 1905): 'There is no mystery about the authorship of Shakespeare's plays. They were not written by Shakespeare at all. They were all written by a total stranger, about whom all we know is that he was called Shakespeare.'

Attributed by Miles Kington (editor of *The World of Alphonse Allais*), from memory, in 1998. Jerome K. Jerome in *My Life and Times*

(1926) took up the theme: 'The Bacon stunt was in full swing about the same time, and again it was [Israel] Zangwill who discovered that Shakespeare's plays had all been written by another gentleman of the same name.'

Edwin Moore suggested that something akin to the observation was to be found in H. N. Gibson, *The Shakespeare Claimants* (1962). I'm not sure that it is. However, in outlining the Baconian theory, Gibson mentions the story that when Bacon felt his supposed authorship of *Richard II* was suspected by Queen Elizabeth I, 'to disarm her suspicions he hastily looked around for someone to use as cover. He had adopted the name "William Shakespeare" as a pseudonym for his secret works, and finding by an extraordinary coincidence an actor with a similar sounding name [Shakespere], he engaged him for the purpose.' Barking mad all this, of course, but there you are.

But if anyone can be credited with popularizing the Homer saying as adapted to Shakespeare, it may have been Robert Manson Myers in *From Beowulf to Virginia Woolf* (1954), a sort of literary *1066 And All That*: 'Until recently the so-called Shakespeare–Bacon Controversy remained a mute question, but it has finally been established, after the perusal of a rare manuscript found in a bottle, that Shakespeare never wrote Shakespeare's plays. Actually they were written by another man of the same name.'

3 The actor Sir Henry Irving did not suffer fools gladly. One day at the Garrick Club, a new member seeking to ingratiate himself told Irving of an 'extraordinary' thing that had just happened to him: 'A total stranger stopped me in the street and said: "God bless me, is that you?"' Irving replied: 'And – er – was it?'

Told by Edward Heron-Allen in Saintsbury and Palmer (eds), *We Saw Him Act* (1939).

Impersonation

4 At one time the entertainer Max Bygraves was on every impressionist's

list. His drying-the-hands gesture, his cockney drawl, his assumed conceit, were highly imitable. One impressionist, Mike Yarwood, even made a gift to Bygraves of a catch phrase, 'I wanna tell you a story', which Yarwood created. Anyway, as Bygraves used to say in his act, 'I was down at a seaside resort the other day and they were having a Max Bygraves impersonation contest, so I decided to give it a go. I came fifth.'

Told to me by Bygraves in a radio interview (1980). Compare the story about Charlie Chaplin entering a look-alike competition in Monte Carlo – he came third. (L. Lucaire, *Celebrity Trivia*, date unknown).

1 In 1977, the actor Norman Shelley claimed that he had impersonated Winston Churchill's voice on the radio during the Second World War. The BBC later confirmed that Shelley *had* recorded the Dunkirk rallying speech in 1940 (which Churchill had delivered only in the House of Commons) so that it could be broadcast in the US. The Prime Minister was too busy to do it himself but, so it was said, he had approved Shelley's impersonation and commented, 'Very good, he's even got my teeth.'

The *New Scientist* (18 May 1991) published the findings of American speech researchers who had analysed twenty recordings of Winston Churchill's speeches released by Decca on gramophone records after the war. They suggested that three of them – the Dunkirk 'on the beaches', the 'blood, toil, tears and sweat' and 'finest hour' – were not actually spoken by him. Before this, Shelley's obituary in *The Times* (30 August 1980) had mentioned his 'on the beaches' recording, 'which in 1940 the Americans believed to be delivered by Churchill himself'. In 1997, I consulted Sally Hine, the BBC's Sound Archivist, who has devoted years of her life to dealing with queries on this subject. No, she

said, there is no proof of any of it. 'People have said to me that Norman Shelley was a real "line-shooter" and that those who knew him well didn't believe a word he said. No recording has ever turned up in the US. The American speech researchers have gone very quiet.'

Importance, relative

2 When he heard a wench's chastity being praised, a stander-by who knew her to be a whore, said, 'Is she chaste? Pray, had she never a child?' Came the reply: 'Indeed, she had a child, but it was a very little one.'

Told in *Gratiae Ludentes* (1638). In Captain Frederick Marryat's novel *Mr Midshipman Easy*, Chap. 3 (1836), the exchange appeared in this form: *Woman*: 'Not a married woman and she has a child?' *Nursemaid*: 'If you please, ma'am, it was a very little one.' Then a little later came this: 'The girl who was rebuked for having borne an illegitimate child excused herself by saying, "But it is such a little one"' – Mark Twain, 'To My Missionary Critics' in *Europe and Elsewhere*, ed. James Brander (1923).

3 Judi Dench's daughter Finty looked like following in her mother's footsteps as an actress when, one Christmas, she landed the part of the innkeeper's wife in her school's nativity play. For weeks, her parents heard nothing but the lines of the innkeeper's wife repeated day in, day out. A visitor to the house asked what sort of play she was in. 'A nativity play,' explained Finty. What was it about? Finty replied: 'Well, you see, it's about this innkeeper's wife ...'

Told by Dench on BBC Radio *Quote ... Unquote* (31 July 1980). Compare, however, the story about the long-out-of-work actor who was given the part of the doctor in *A Streetcar Named Desire* by Tennessee Williams when it was revived by a theatre company in Chicago. The character only comes on at the end and has very few lines. Nevertheless, when a relative asked the actor what the play was about, he replied: 'It's about a doctor who comes to New Orleans because he's received a telephone call from a young lady whose sister is having a nervous breakdown.' As told in William Redfield, *Letters from an Actor* (1967). In the film *Shakespeare in Love* (UK/US 1999), the Nurse in the new play *Romeo and Juliet*, when asked what it is about, says, 'Well, it's about this nurse ...'

1 The actor Philip Franks was essaying the role of Hamlet for the Royal Shakespeare Company in a touring production that was almost 'in the round', and thus the audience was very close to the actors. 'I had fallen to my knees in an access of emotion,' he recalls, 'and was indeed sobbing real tears at the fate of my dead father and my fallen-from-grace mother, and I was giving it absolutely 120%. Alas, I heard two people saying on the front row, "No, no, no – it says on the sole, nine and a half."'

Told by Philip Franks on BBC Radio *Quote ... Unquote* (14 May 1996).

Imports

2 The 'international comedy dance act' of Wilson, Keppel and Betty featured two men wearing fezzes and moustaches and a scantily clad girl. They teamed up in the US in 1910 and made their first British appearance at the London Palladium in 1932. The trio performed a comic Egyptian sand dance called 'Cleopatra's Nightmare'. When they were to appear in Las Vegas they arrived at customs in New York. 'Where are you going?' they were asked. 'Las Vegas.' 'In the Nevada desert?' 'That's right.' 'What have you got in the bag?' And they said, 'Sand.' They were actually taking their own sand to Las Vegas.

As told by Ernie Wise on *Parkinson*, BBC TV, before 1975.

Improvisation

3 Edith Evans had been excluded from some improvisational exercises during a rehearsal at the Old Vic because it was thought she might not approve. In time, however, a peculiar noise emerged from where she was sitting in the auditorium. A voice inquired anxiously, 'Dame Edith, what's the matter?' She replied, 'I'm being a handbag.'

Told to me by a correspondent in 1981.

Indexers

4 Book indexers lead lives of quiet dedication, if not desperation, as they ply their trade for little reward. They do, however, have opportunities to insert subtle jokes that one day, possibly, a reader may happen to stumble across.

In the Index (Vol. XI, 1983) of the Latham and Matthews edition of *The Diary of Samuel Pepys*, there is delightfully quiet, possibly unconscious, humour to be found in the entry for one of Pepys's mistresses. Here it is, slightly abbreviated:

'BAGWELL, Mrs, wife of William: her good looks, 4/222; P plans to seduce, 4/222, 266; visits, 4/233–4; finds her virtuous, 4/234; and modest, 5/163; asks P for place for husband, 5/65–6, 163; P kisses, 5/287; she grows affectionate, 5/301–2; he caresses, 5/313; she visits him, 5/316, 339; her resistance collapses in alehouse, 5/322; amorous encounters with: at her house, 5/350–1; 6/40, 162, 189, 201, 253, 294; 7/166 ... asks for promotion for husband, 6/39–40;

P strains a finger, 6/40; has sore face, 7/191; servant dies of plague, 7/166.'

All human life is there ...

In the diary, also, Pepys several times mentions an eating house in Old Palace Yard, London, called 'Heaven' (there was also one called Hell). This enables him to write (possibly without realizing it): 'And so I returned and went to Heaven' (28 January 1660). In the Latham and Matthews edition (Vol. 1, 1970), the editors explain this reference on its first appearance and then, in a subsequent footnote, put: 'For heaven, see above.'

Inferiors

1 Some troublesome woman was being discussed and it was said, as if in mitigation, 'Anyhow she is very nice to her inferiors.' Dorothy Parker commented, 'Where does she find them?'

Told in *The Lyttelton Hart-Davis Letters,* for 22 January 1956 (1978).

Initialese

2 When people took to referring to the Prince of Wales (later Edward VIII) rather knowingly as 'the P. of W.', Lord Berners took great delight in doing the same. It was only after people wondered how on earth *his* 'P. of W.' could have been doing things most untypical of *their* 'P. of W.', that Berners explained, in all innocence, that he had, of course, been referring to the Provost of Worcester.

Source unknown.

3 Correctly speaking, there should be no full stop after the 'S' in the name of President Harry S Truman. It is not an abbreviation and is only there to provide a balancing sound between first name and surname.

The matter is somewhat complicated by the fact that Truman himself sometimes put a dot after the 'S' in his signature. The same goes for the 'O' in the name of David O. Selznick (1902–65), the American film producer. In Rudy Behlmer's *Memo from David O. Selznick* (1973), Selznick described how he took a middle initial to distinguish himself from an uncle, also called David Selznick, whom he disliked. 'I ... went through the alphabet to find [a letter] that seemed to give the best punctuation, and decided on."O".'

4 Writers who use their initials rather than a forename – D. H. Lawrence, T. S. Eliot and P. D. James, to name but three – presumably expect readers to know what sex they are. The story is told that the poet and academic D. J. Enright ('Dennis Joseph' on his birth certificate) received a fan letter from 'a male person' shortly after publishing a book of verse. 'Dear D Enright,' it began. 'Can you be the vivacious Dorothy Enright I met on a cruise to South Africa five years ago? Do you remember those nights on deck, gazing at the moon? You didn't tell me you wrote poems but I should have guessed ...'

Told in the *Independent* Saturday Magazine (11 October 1997).

Innocence

5 A Cambridge don of an earlier generation had been in the habit of speaking scornfully of some of his younger colleagues who he feared were prostituting their vocation by giving talks on the radio. One day he was astonished to be invited to broadcast himself, the invitation ending with the words, 'Fee 20 guineas'. The don sent off a telegram of acceptance, adding: 'Should I send the 20 guineas in advance?'

Told in this form in *Pass the Port* (1976).

1 Walking home from the theatre one night during the Blitz, John Gielgud happened to glance up at the moonlit barrage balloons. 'Oh dear,' he murmured to his companion, 'our poor boys must be terribly lonely up there.'

Version from John Mortimer, *In Character* (1983).

2 In a BBC *Music and Movement* programme for children (which, happily for posterity, was recorded), a woman presenter said: 'We are going to play a hiding and finding game. Imagine we've got some balls. They might be hidden. You don't know where I'm going to hide your balls. Now, are your balls high up or low down? Close your eyes a minute and dance around, and look for them. Are they high up? Or are they low down? If you have found your balls, toss them over your shoulder and play with them ...'

From a recording of the incident. Jack de Manio in *Life Begins Too Early* (1970) seems to indicate that this immortal broadcast took place in about 1950.

3 Addressing an audience of ten thousand US marines, Marilyn Monroe said, 'I hear all you guys get all excited about sweater girls. I don't know why. I mean, take away their sweaters and what have they got?'

Told by Stefan Buczacki on BBC Radio *Quote ... Unquote* (15 June 1988).

4 An elderly American visitor to an English stately home came across a sundial. When her companion explained that the sun caused a shadow to be cast from a metal blade across the face of the slab, thus allowing the time of day to be assessed, the old lady looked in-

credulous and said: 'Whatever will they think of next?'

Told to me by Mr J. Green of Rednal, Birmingham (1980). However, in David Niven, *The Moon's a Balloon*, Chap. 14 (1971), the remark is listed as a Goldwynism.

Inspiration

5 The physical appearance of Laurence Olivier's most famous interpretation on stage or screen – Shakespeare's *Richard III* – was based upon the American theatre director Jed Harris, whom Olivier also took the trouble to describe as 'the most loathsome man' he had ever encountered. The voice was based on imitations he had heard people doing of Sir Henry Irving – 'I only used three notes.'

Sources: interview with Kenneth Tynan, BBC 2 TV, *Great Acting* (26 February 1966); Laurence Olivier, *On Acting* (1986); John Mortimer, *In Character* (1983).

6 In the famous production of Sophocles' *Oedipus Rex* at the New Theatre, London, in 1945, Laurence Olivier emitted a terrible scream when the tragic, blinded hero realizes the full horror of his sins. The particular nature of the scream was derived from a method of catching ermine that he had heard about. In the Arctic, the catchers put down salt, the ermine comes to lick it, and his tongue freezes to the ice. 'I thought about that when I screamed as Oedipus,' Olivier said.

As told to John Mortimer for a newspaper interview and collected for *In Character* (1983). For a description of the cry see Kenneth Tynan's review of the production incorporated in *A View of the English Stage* (1975). John Osborne in *Almost a Gentleman*

(1991) seems to think that the ermine cry was used when Olivier was playing Shylock.

1 The bit that most people remember from Shirley Conran's novels is the scene in *Lace* (published 1982) in which a goldfish features in the sexual activities of an Arab prince and one of the book's heroines. According to Conran's ex-husband – now Sir Terence Conran, the designer – she was given the idea by him. 'I'd been to this extraordinary wild, midsummer party in Finland,' he said. 'A group of young men went into the lake and came out with nets filled with sticklebacks. They then introduced these little fish into the, er, private parts of some vodka-soaked ladies ...'

From an interview by Hunter Davies in the *Independent* (16 March 1993).

Insults

2 George Bernard Shaw sent Winston Churchill two tickets for the first night of *St Joan* (which was in 1924), with a note explaining, 'One for yourself, the other for a friend – if you have one.' Churchill sent them back, regretting he would be unable to attend the first night, but saying he would like some tickets for the second night – 'If there is one.'

I first received this anecdote in a letter from Nancy and Tony Morse of Blackley, Manchester in 1978 and I have no idea where they found it, though it is in *Pass the Port* (1976). Peter Hay in *Theatrical Anecdotes* (1987) says that it was told by his grandfather when Hay was growing up in London (1950s). I have also seen a version involving Noël Coward and Churchill. According to Michael Holroyd, *Bernard Shaw*, Vol. 3 (1991), Shaw's secretary, Blanche Patch, dismissed the story as a journalistic invention.

Insurance

3 With the approach of the third millennium, more than two dozen virgin females in Cambridgeshire took out insurance policies against the risk of immaculate conception. Each of the women, whose ages ranged from 18 to 68, paid £100 for cover against giving birth by act of God to the Messiah before the end of the year 2000. If any of them were to have an immaculate conception, confirmed by a gynaecologist, each would receive one million pounds. The potential virgin mothers were apparently concerned that the new Messiah – who might well be a woman this time round – should be brought up in a way conforming to her or his status. An insurance spokesman said, 'Normally, an act of God is an exclusion clause – in this case it is crucial.'

Reported in the *Ely Weekly News* (12 December 1996).

Integrity

4 Advertising man Raymond Rubicam's famous slogan for Squibb drug products, 'The priceless ingredient of every product is the honour and integrity of its maker', reminded David Ogilvy of his father's advice: 'When a company boasts about its integrity, or a woman about her virtue, avoid the former and cultivate the latter.'

From Ogilvy's *Confessions of an Advertising Man* (1963).

In-tray

5 During the Second World War, Winston Churchill had to announce to the House of Commons that the British had, somewhat illicitly, taken

bases in the Azores. He apparently thought he could gloss it over with a splendid speech, so he rose and said, 'I must ask the House now to come with me back over four hundred years of our eventful history ...' the Labour politician Aneurin ('Nye') Bevan interrupted: 'Good God, he's looked into his in-tray at last!'

Source untraced, but this also appears – in reference to some earlier occasion – in James Agate, *Ego 3* (1938) and *Ego 4* (1940).

Introductions

1 A frightful snob, Sir Malcolm Sargent warned the studio manager at the BBC's Maida Vale orchestral studio that he would be bringing with him a distinguished visitor, and that the visitor should be given a seat in the control room. The distinguished elderly man duly arrived and was welcomed by the studio manager. At the break, Sargent came in, shook hands with the visitor and said to the studio manager, 'I'd like you to meet my guest, the King of Sweden.' The distinguished visitor coughed quietly and corrected him: 'Norway ...'

Told by Derek Parker (who had it from Felix Aprahamian) on BBC Radio *Quote ... Unquote* (24 July 1979).

Intruders

2 Peter Ustinov recalls rehearsing with Edith Evans. He says, 'She had a very special way of suggesting that there were certain unauthorized presences in the theatre, people who shouldn't have been there. And she said to the auditorium – while wearing that jockey hat she affected – "Are we all of the family?"'

Told by him on BBC Radio *Quote ... Unquote* (18 February 1992).

3 LBC, Britain's first commercial radio station to go on the air (in 1973), had a curious design fault: none of the studio doors had a window. Thus it was not possible for anyone to look through the doors and see if it was all right to enter the studios. As always happens, the worst thing possible occurred in the midst of a very serious news bulletin. A newsreader was reporting a bomb blast at Green Park Underground station in London, when the studio door could be heard opening to reveal the sound of a studio cleaner gaily entering with vacuum cleaner at full throttle.

From a recording of the incident, about 1974.

Invitations

4 On receiving a dinner invitation at short notice from the Prince of Wales (the future Edward VII), Lord Charles Beresford telegraphed his refusal thus: 'SORRY CAN'T COME. LIE FOLLOWS BY POST.'

Reported by Ralph Nevill in *The World of Fashion 1837–1922* (1923). The same joke occurs in Marcel Proust, *Le Temps Retrouvé* (published in 1927 after his death in 1922), in the form: 'One of those telegrams of which M. de Guermantes has wittily fixed the formula: "Can't come, lie follows". [*Une de ces dépêches dont M. de Guermantes avait spirituellement fixé le modèle: "Impossible venir, mensonge suit".*]'

5 Coming across a stranger in New College quad, William Spooner, the Warden, could only remember that the man was a newcomer to the college. 'Come to tea tomorrow,' he said. 'I'm giving a little welcome do to our new mathematics Fellow.'

'But, Warden, I am the new mathematics Fellow!' the man expostulated.

'Well, never mind,' said Spooner, 'come all the same.'

A much-told tale, original source untraced. Maurice Bowra in *Memories 1898–1939* (1966) has it happening to a Fellow called Stanley Casson.

1 To a hostess who had sent an invitation stating that on a certain day she would be 'At home', George Bernard Shaw succinctly replied: 'So will G. Bernard Shaw'.

Apparently true, and recounted in Michael Holroyd, *Bernard Shaw*, Vol. 3 (1991).

2 Howard Dietz plucked up courage and invited Greta Garbo out for a dinner date, indicating that it would be 'on Monday night'. Garbo declined, saying, 'How do I know I'll be hungry on Monday night?'

Told by Benny Green on BBC Radio *Quote … Unquote* (17 October 1989).

Irishness

3 In 1970, as the Northern Ireland troubles were beginning again, a Belfast citizen was reported as saying, 'Anyone who isn't confused here doesn't really understand what's going on.'

Told in my book *Quote … Unquote* (1978). However, Walter Bryan, *The Improbable Irish* (1969) points to an earlier application: 'As Ed Murrow once said about Vietnam, anyone who isn't confused doesn't really understand the situation.'

4 Sir Huw Wheldon once recalled how he had asked an Irishman's advice at which of two restaurants to dine. He said the Irishman thought hard for a moment and then answered: 'If you go to the one, you would wish you had gone to the other.'

Told on BBC Radio *Quote … Unquote* (14 September 1985).

5 The Irish actress Brenda Fricker won an Academy Award for 'Best Supporting Actress' for her role in the film *My Left Foot*. Afterwards, she sagely commented on an apparent dual nationality that afflicts some Irish people in the world's eyes: 'When you're lying drunk at the airport, you're Irish. When you win an Oscar, you're British.'

Told in the *Observer* (8 April 1990).

J

Jargon

1 In a speech at Cardiff in 1950, Winston Churchill chose to parody official jargon, which had become all the rage under the then Labour government, and which had redesignated 'homes' as 'accommodation units'. He referred to 'Accommodation Unit Sweet Accommodation Unit'.

Recorded in Leslie Frewin, *Immortal Jester* (1973).

2 Jargon, doublespeak, non-plain English, call it what you will, this version of 'The Lord is my shepherd' was composed by an anonymous hand in the 1980s: 'The Lord and I are in a shepherd/sheep situation; and I am in a position of negative need. He prostrates me in a green-belt grazing area; He conducts me directionally parallel to non-torrential aqueous liquid. He returns to original satisfaction levels my psychological make-up; He switches me on to a positive behavioural format for maximum prestige of His identity. It should be said notwithstanding the fact that I make ambulatory progress through the umbrageous inter-hill mortality slot, terror-sensations will not be instantiated within me due to para-ethical phenomena. Your pastoral walking-aid and quadruped pick-up unit introduce me into a pleasurific mood-state. You design and produce a nutrient-bearing furniture-type structure in the context of non-co-operative elements; You act out a head-related folk ritual employing vegetable extract by beverage utensil experiences in a volume crisis. It is an ongoing deductable fact that your interrelational emphatical and non-vengeance capabilities will retain me as their target-focus for the duration of my non-death period; and I will possess tenant rights in the housing unit of the Lord on a permanently open-ended time basis.'

Published in *The Sunday Times* (14 January 1990).

3 Two occasions when judges did actually shed a little light for a change. A probation report stated that, 'He hails from a multi-delinquent family with a high incarceration index.' The judge said: 'You mean the whole lot are inside?'

Another probation report had it that, 'Inter-sibling rivalry hindered his ongoing relationships making him an isolate in a stress situation with his peers.' The judge clarified this thusly: 'You mean that he hated his brothers?'

Related by James Hunt QC in *The Sunday Times* (14 January 1990).

Jewishness

1 Otto Kahn, the banker (1867–1934),
was a convert to Christianity. One day
he was walking up Fifth Avenue in
New York with a banker who had a
hunchback. Kahn pointed to the
Temple Emmanuel Synagogue and
remarked, 'I used to be a Jew.' 'Yeah,'
said the other, 'and I used to be a
hunchback.'

Told by Larry Adler on BBC Radio
Quote . . . Unquote (22 June 1977)

2 Groucho Marx was told by the membership secretary of a beach club that he
couldn't become a member because he
was Jewish. Marx replied, 'My son's
only half Jewish. Would it be all right if
he went in the water up to his knees?'

Told in Arthur Marx, *Son of Groucho*
(1973).

3 When Marilyn Monroe was about to be
married to Arthur Miller, she paid a
visit to her prospective – Jewish –
parents-in-law and was given a meal
including matzoh balls. After picking at
them with a fork and obviously thinking very deeply about them, Monroe
turned to her loved one and asked,
'Arthur, isn't there another part of the
matzoh we could eat?'

Oral tradition. No doubt apocryphal. Gore
Vidal merely cites 'the dumb starlet [who]
would ask, What do they do with the rest of
the matzoh?' in *The New York Review of
Books* (17/31 May 1973).

4 When Laurence Olivier undertook to
play Shylock in a National Theatre production of *The Merchant of Venice* in
1970, the director was Jonathan Miller,
who had famously declared in *Beyond
the Fringe*, 'I'm not really a Jew. Only
Jew-*ish*. Not the whole hog, you know.'

Miller was disconcerted to find that
Olivier intended to give the part with
all the subtlety of Fagin as he might
have been played by Donald Wolfit.
'I do so love the Hebrew!' Olivier declared. Miller responded by suggesting
that his love might be a little more appreciated if he did not wear false teeth
and a larger-than-life false nose.

Recounted by Miller in a TV obituary for
Olivier in 1989.

Jobs

5 In the 1950s, Eamonn Andrews was
best known as the chairman of the
archetypal TV panel game *What's My
Line?* in which the panel had to guess
contestants' jobs. In the British version
of what was originally an American
show, the job still most remembered is
that of Mr R. Adams who appeared on
14 January 1952. He beat the panel
before revealing that he was a 'sagger-
makers' bottom knocker'.

A sagger is a receptacle in which china is
baked. Source: the *Television Annual*
(*c.* 1954).

6 One of band leader Ted Heath's
trumpet-players decided to move on
after 12 years with the band and told
the boss: 'Ted, I really would like to
move on.' 'You're leaving?' said Heath,
obviously annoyed. 'After only
12 years? Listen, if I'd known you were
going to be a fly-by-night, I'd never
have booked you in the first place.'

Told by Tony Brandon on BBC Radio
Where Were You in '62? (1982). Heath
(1900–69) founded (in 1944) the first
British swing band capable of comparison
with America's best.

7 When I was at Oxford, I appeared in an
undergraduate revue with Clare

Francis, who at that stage had been to the Royal Ballet School, was currently at St Clare's, a sort of Oxford finishing school, and displayed few signs of being a future intrepid lone woman yachtsperson. I took her to a ball in the spring of 1964. I think it was on that occasion I asked her what her father did – which was still the sort of question one asked girls in the early 1960s – and I think she told me he was an electrician. It was only many years later, by which time Clare had been transformed into an intrepid, lone etc., that I discovered her father had actually been Chairman of the London Electricity Board.

My memories of the incident.

1 A chauffeur was sacked on the spot by his boss because he only cleaned half the car – the side his boss got into. He regularly picked the man up at High Street Kensington station and on this day the boss was waiting for him across the other side of the road.

Told by Sydney Creamer to Kensington and Chelsea Planning Authority in 1996.

Journalism

2 When Cardinal Manning poked fun at what he called the 'Dismal Science' of Political Economy, he was lectured in its most superior manner by *The Times* on the grounds that he had mistaken cause and effect. 'That,' the Cardinal said to G. W. E. Russell, 'is the sort of criticism that an undergraduate makes, and thinks himself very clever. But I am told that in the present day, *The Times* is chiefly written by undergraduates.'

Plus ça change. Told in G. W. E. Russell, *Collections and Recollections*, Chap. 4 (1898).

3 The paradigm of 'finding the local angle' in any story by the provincial press has long been the headline said to come from a Yorkshire newspaper after a certain event in 1912: 'TITANIC SINKS – HECKMONDWIKE MAN ON BOARD.'

Probably apocryphal. However, one headline that really did appear – in the Weekly Dispatch *(London) – was* 'MANY MILLIONAIRES MISSING'. *In 1994, Mark English of Bradford – not a million miles from Heckmondwike – tried to find out whether the 'local angle' headline had ever appeared: 'This story struck me as being inherently unlikely, since Yorkshiremen don't have the narrow local chauvinism implied by this story; rather, they are citizens of the world. At all events, I took a look at some local newspapers [dated 17 April 1912] at Bradford Library. The* Bradford Daily Argus, *the* Yorkshire Evening Post *and the* Yorkshire Daily Observer *yielded nothing very close to your quote. The* Yorkshire Post *was conventional enough in its main headlines, but the sub-heads included "A Hessle Magistrate Among the Saved", "A Hull Officer On Board" and "A Dewsbury Man On Board". Now, Heckmondwike is an outlying district of Dewsbury, so perhaps more research will turn up the headline … Incidentally, I have always quoted this story as "Scotsman Dies At Sea".'*

4 Claud Cockburn claimed to have won a competition for dullness among subeditors on *The Times* in the late 1920s. The aim of the competition was to come up with the dullest headline that actually got into the following morning's newspaper. He won it only once, he said, with: 'Small earthquake in Chile. Not many dead.'

Told in his book In Time of Trouble (1956) *and incorporated in* I Claud … (1967). *At Cockburn's death it was said, however, that an exhaustive search had failed to find this particular headline in the paper. It may just have been a smoking-room story. However, the idea* lives on: it became (perhaps inevitably) the title of a book (1972) by Alastair Horne about the Allende affair (in Chile). The journalist Michael Green called a volume of memoirs *Nobody Hurt in Small Earthquake* (1990), and the cartoonist Nicholas Garland called his 'Journal of a year in Fleet Street', *Not Many Dead* (1990).

1 The absurdity of the war correspondent's job was encapsulated by a question heard during the war in the Congo in 1960. Thousands of frightened Belgian civilians were waiting for a plane to take them to safety from the newly independent ex-colony when a BBC television reporter walked among them with his camera team and posed the question, 'Has anyone here been raped and speaks English?'

The incident was reported – and used as the title of a book *Anyone Here Been Raped and Speaks English* (1978) – by the American journalist Edward Behr, who commented: 'The callous cry summed up for me the tragic, yet wildly surrealist nature of the country itself.'

2 Although the BBC Home Service/ Radio 4 *Ten O'Clock* (which later became *The World Tonight*) was an influential programme and a great training ground, it was itself a rather staid institution. It always consisted of four interviews – usually with pundits rather than the newsmakers themselves. This contrasted with the styles of other regular current-affairs programmes on the air at that time. Accordingly, I devised a little joke to characterize them. I asked, how would Radio 4 respond to the unlikely event of the Duke of Edinburgh losing his trousers in public?

Ten O'Clock, I said, would interview the editor of the Court Circular in *The Times*. The *Today* programme would send Monty Modlyn to interview a braces manufacturer in the East End of London. *Radio Newsreel* would have a report from a radio car parked outside the place where the incident had occurred. And *The World at One*? Ah – this was rather a sharp touch – *The World at One* would interview the Duke of Edinburgh ...

From my diary (16 April 1969). This story was sold to the *Guardian*'s 'Miscellany' column (for three guineas) by someone called Tim Pitt. When the joke appeared on 23 April, Jack de Manio repeated it on the *Today* programme. People seemed oddly reluctant to see the criticism in it. Humphrey Carpenter, then working for the then functioning BBC Radio Durham, added the following: 'How would Radio Durham cover the story? They'd try and find someone in Durham who had ever been to London, and interview them.'

3 When René Cutforth was a BBC radio reporter, it is said that he emerged from Broadcasting House one day and found a crowd gathered round a man who had been knocked down by a motor car. But how was Cutforth going to find out who the man was and if there was any story? He went up to the police officer who was holding back the crowd and said, 'Let me through, officer, it is my duty as an ordained minister of the church.' He then knelt, with hands clasped, by the body of the injured man, discovered that he was a diplomat from one of the embassies near by, and earned a few guineas selling the information to the news agencies.

Told in Gerald Priestland, *Something Understood* (1986).

4 In the late 1970s, Alan Towers was working for BBC TV's *Nationwide* programme as a reporter, from his base

at Pebble Mill in Birmingham. One assignment took him to Croydon where lived Herbie, a duck who had been taught to run alongside a skateboard and leap on – travelling 15 feet or more without assistance. Towers was the reporter on the consequent film, which won an award from the Royal Television Society and became part of television folklore.

In July 1993, Towers had to write to defend his place in television history when the *Independent on Sunday* wrongly ascribed the skate-boarding duck story to *News at Ten*. He was correct in thinking that this had become an archetypal example of TV news trivia. However, there are many other examples. In 1967, when I occupied the adjacent desk to Alan in the newsroom at Granada TV in Manchester, I believe the archetypal story of this type was – apart from parrots that played the piano – what I have always referred to as 'the beer-drinking cow'.

Judges

1 The celebrated barrister, F. E. Smith, was carrying out a very hostile cross-examination in court when he said to a witness: 'I suggest that on the night in question, you were as drunk as a judge.' At this point, the judge intervened and said, 'Excuse me, Mr Smith, but the normal expression is "as sober as a judge". You mean, "as drunk as a lord".' F. E. Smith instantly said, 'Yes, m'lord.'

Told by Bryan Magee on BBC Radio *Quote ... Unquote* (26 April 1994). Bertrand Russell is reported to have said once, 'I'm as drunk as a lord, but then I am one, so what does it matter?' – quoted in Ralph Schoenman (ed.), *Bertrand Russell, Philosopher of the Century* (1967).

2 At the height of Beatlemania in the early 1960s, when the papers were full of pieces about the Fab Four every day,

a High Court judge lifted the flap of his wig quizzically and inquired of counsel, 'Who *are* the Beatles?'

This is the archetypal judge's remark – often, of course, a question posed when the judge knows the answer, in order to further his reputation for fustiness and aloofness from the concerns of ordinary citizens. But did any judge ever actually ask it? I believe not. What I think happened was that an assumption was made that, when the Beatles came along, judges would ask the question – just as they had always done and still do.

In 1990, the year of the football World Cup, Mr Justice Harman actually asked, 'Who is Gazza? Isn't there an operetta called *La Gazza Ladra?*' Indeed, there is – but that has nothing to do with the footballer Paul 'Gazza' Gascoigne. A century before, in 1889, Mr Justice Stephen had asked, 'What is the Grand National?' (but he was eventually committed to a lunatic asylum). In Geoffrey Madan's *Notebooks* (ed. Gere and Sparrow, 1981 – but Madan died in 1947), Lord Hewart is credited with: 'Precedent compels me to ask: what is jazz?' In fiction, A. P. Herbert's Mr Justice Snubb asked: 'What is a crossword?' In the late 1940s a judge is supposed to have asked 'What is oomph?' In the next issue of the *News of the World* there was a cartoon of a very curvaceous young woman saying, 'What is a judge?'

I am encouraged to believe in the apocryphal nature of the Beatles remark by a report in the *Guardian* on 10 December 1963 (when Beatlemania was rampant). A QC representing the Performing Right Society at a tribunal in London in a case concerning copyright fees at pop concerts objected to a suggestion that tribunal members should attend a pop concert to see and hear what it was like. Instead, they listened to a recording of a Beatles' concert. Another QC remarked to the court: 'You will only have to suffer two or three minutes.' The *Guardian* headline over its report of all this was: '*What is a Beatle?*' which, as I say, appears to be a case of the old question being applied to a new phenomenon. But it is not an actual quotation.

1 A convicted criminal exclaimed in court, 'As God is my judge – I am innocent.' The judge replied: 'He isn't; I am; and you're not!'

Told in Matthew Parris, *Scorn* (1994). The judge's reply has been ascribed to Norman Birkett, but this is a bit unlikely, surely, except as an after-dinner speech joke.

2 Judge John Maude (1901–86) gave some advice to a hopeless drunken tramp, shaking with DTs, who appeared in court before him. The advice was that the tramp must at all costs eschew alcohol entirely forthwith. And just to reinforce the message, Judge Maude added: 'Mind now, not even a tiny glass of sherry before luncheon!'

Told in *The Times* (4 May 1998).

3 There was a judge once who had the job of sentencing two gentlemen who had been discovered in an attitude of unusual friendliness under Waterloo Bridge. Instead of just sentencing them, he said: 'You two men have done a most disgusting and immoral and depraved and terrible act. And what makes it so much worse is that you chose to do it under one of the most *beautiful* bridges in London.'

Told innumerable times by John Mortimer but, in particular, on BBC Radio *Quote . . . Unquote* (25 December 1979). *The Penguin Dictionary of Modern Quotations* (1971) ascribes the story to an 'unknown judge' and suggests that it is a traditional Bar story.

Juries

4 The colourful activities of Cynthia Payne, madam of a suburban London brothel, entertained the whole nation when a case against her was brought to court in February 1987. Payne was eventually acquitted on a charge of controlling prostitutes in the famous 'sex for Luncheon Vouchers' case. Giving the verdict, the jury foreman declared: 'M'lud, we find the defendant not guilty – but we would love to hear all the evidence again.'

Reported in *Today* (15 February 1987). Alas, when I referred to this remark in *The Sunday Times* later in the year, I received a stern rebuke from a woman who had been one of the members of the jury. In fact, I think it was probably the caption to a newspaper cartoon.

Juxtaposition

5 A BBC radio commentator in the early 1930s was describing the disembarking of the then Duke and Duchess of York from a destroyer. They were taking a long time about it, chatting to the captain on the bridge, and so on, and the commentator had to throw in every fact he could think of to keep going. Then he intimated that the couple would be coming ashore shortly as the Duchess had just left the bridge. Yet still nothing happened and the commentator unfortunately went on, 'Well, I think something really is about to happen now, as an immense amount of water is pouring from the ship's side . . . and here is the Duchess returning to the bridge . . .'

Related by Jack de Manio in *To Auntie With Love* (1967).

Kings

1   During the Second World War one of
the exiled European kings in London
was about to use the BBC's facilities
to broadcast to his people back home.
He arrived unaccompanied at the
studios and tried to cause no fuss –
hence the archetypal BBC commissionaire story he gave rise to. 'I am King
Haakon of Norway,' he told one such
commissionaire on arrival. 'Ah, yes,'
replied the commissionaire, and started
hunting for the visitor's name among
various lists in front of him. Obviously
he was having no success in finding
the distinguished visitor's name, so he
probably said, 'Half a mo', guv,' and
dialled a number, no doubt to consult
with a higher authority. 'Oh, yes,' he
said, 'got a visitor here. Can't find any
record of who's expectin' 'im. "E's the
king of . . . ' Then putting one hand
over the mouthpiece, he asked, "Scuse
me, guv, which country did you say you
was king of?'

This traditional story was told by Martin
Jarvis on BBC Radio, *Quote . . . Unquote*
(5 June 1979), in consequence of which
I received a letter from a Mr I. Thompson of
London, dated 15 April 1980. Mr Thompson
said he had been on duty at Bush House on
that very evening: 'The Norwegian King had

an appointment at B[roadcasting] H[ouse] for
recording for transmission purposes – no
doubt some very senior official was waiting to
welcome him there. The King was driven in
error to Bush House (Norwegian broadcasts
normally went out from there). There were
two reception desks at Bush, one for tenants
other than BBC ... and the other for BBC.
King Haakon approached the former first.
Someone got a little confused and the
BBC Duty Editor learned that the King of
Sweden was at reception. This piece of news
caused some alarm. However, everything
was sorted out and King Haakon duly
made his recording. So it seems that your
version has been somewhat corrupted down
the years.'

In Jack de Manio's *To Auntie With Love*
(1967), the story is related as having involved a female receptionist who mistakenly
rang up the Dutch section and said, 'Well
I've got your King here. He says he wants
to broadcast.'

Kissing

2   Some years after President Carter's
star had faded, Queen Elizabeth the
Queen Mother was reported to have
complained drolly about his behaviour:
'He is the only man, since my dear
husband died, to have the effrontery to
kiss me on the lips.'

Reported in the *Observer* (13 February
1983).

Language

1 Two literary ladies praised Dr Samuel
Johnson on the publication of his
Dictionary in 1755 for having taken
care to omit all the naughty words.
Said he: 'What, my dears! then have
you been looking for them?'

Recorded in H. D. Beste, *Personal and
Literary Memorials* (1829).

2 William Nicholson once noticed that
playwright J. M. Barrie always ordered
Brussels sprouts but invariably left
them on the side of his plate. He asked
him why. 'I cannot resist ordering
them,' Barrie replied. 'The words are
so lovely to say.'

Reported in *The Sunday Referee* (5 December
1927).

3 During filming of *The Charge of the
Light Brigade* in the mid-1930s, the
Hungarian-born director Michael
Curtiz ordered the release of a hundred
riderless steeds by shouting: 'Bring
on the empty horses!' The actors David
Niven and Errol Flynn promptly fell
about with laughter at this. Curtiz
rounded on them and said, 'You and
your stinking language! You think
I know f*** nothing. Well, let me tell
you, I know f*** all!'

Told in Leslie Halliwell, *The Filmgoer's Book*

of Quotes (1973) and in the second volume
of David Niven's autobiography, to which he
gave the title *Bring On the Empty Horses*
(1975). This would appear to be a fairly old
anecdote, much applied all round. Father
John Hagreen wrote to me (1996): 'In 1938,
a friend who had been a prisoner during the
Great War told me how their German com-
mandant got wind of an imminent escape.
He tried to deter the plotters by parading the
men and haranguing them, but ruined his
effort by ending, "You think I don't know
anything. But I tell you I know damn all!"'
A character in Nicholas Monsarrat's novel
The Cruel Sea (1951) similarly explodes:
'You English ... think we know damn
nothing *but I tell you we know damn all.*'
In record producer John Culshaw's *Putting the
Record Straight* (1981) is this: '[The conductor
Ernest Ansermet who died in 1969] prided
himself on the use of idioms, which more
often than not, went wrong. In one alterca-
tion in Kingsway Hall he announced loudly,
"You think I know fuck nothing, but you
are wrong, I know fuck all!"' One just has
to conclude that it's another eternal joke.
Inevitably, 'You think I know damn
nothing – I tell you I know damn all' is
said to have appeared as caption to a *Punch*
cartoon at some time between 1900
and 1933.

4 Traditionally, one is not supposed to
have very much sympathy with people
who run theatre box offices. They can
be off-hand in person, quite apart from
being un-get-at-able over the telephone.
Nevertheless, I did feel a smidgin of

sympathy when I had to ring up the Royal Court Theatre to book tickets for Alan Bennett's play called – and that's the problem – *Kafka's Dick*.

'Have you got two tickets for the 24th?' is what I actually said, rather than, 'Have you anything for Kafka's Dick?'

I am told that when the National Theatre announced Giraudoux's *The Trojan War Will Not Take Place*, box-office staff were often asked what they were going to put on instead.

Similarly, when the NT announced *Rosencrantz and Guildernstern are Dead*, they received many kind words of sympathy.

From my column in *Sunday Today* (29 September 1986). Compare the caption to a cartoon in *Punch* (3 August 1921): 'CAN YOU TELL ME WHAT THEY'RE PLAYING TOMORROW NIGHT?' '"YOU NEVER CAN TELL", MADAM.' 'DON'T THEY EVEN LET *YOU* KNOW?'

Language, English

1 An American visitor to England was driving through London with his English host. The host said, 'I must stop and clean the windscreen.' The American replied, 'You mean the windshield. We Americans invented the automobile, and we call it a windshield.'

To which the Englishman said, 'That's quite true. But just remember who invented the language.'

Told by Edward E. Whitacre Jr in a speech at the University of Missouri, St Louis (April 1992).

2 In 1963, Canada's Royal Commission on Bilingualism and Biculturalism criss-crossed the country to ask ordinary citizens their feelings about the possibility of French becoming the official language. Ralph Melnyk, a Saskatchewan farmer told the Commission: 'If English was good enough for Jesus Christ, it is good enough for me.'

Told in J. R. Colombo, *Colombo's All-Time Great Canadian Quotations* (1994).

3 The BBC producer and executive Richard ('Dick') Francis loved gadgets. Having organized much of the 1960s British TV coverage of US space missions, he took to wearing several wristwatches up his left arm, giving the local time in several countries. He also indulged in NASA-speak – saying 'Affirmative' instead of 'Yes', and so on. When he was organizing the BBC's coverage of the 1970 British General Election, a film editor offered him some exclusive footage of one of the polling stations. 'Negative', replied Francis, and the programme budget was charged with 400 feet of negative colour film stock.

From Leonard Miall's obituary in the *Independent* (29 June 1992), though Miall concedes that the story may be apocryphal. Still, I can recall my first meeting with Dick Francis in about 1977. He had a prominent wire coming out of one ear and it was explained to me that this dated from his time as BBC Controller in Northern Ireland when he was permanently tuned into a radio so that he would know where the latest bomb had gone off.

4 It is always risky to assume that whatever language you are speaking cannot be understood. A party of English people lunching at the desert town of Zagora in Morocco had not been impressed by the service of a particular waiter who, they considered, had a face like a horse. 'Let's not give him a

tip,' one suggested. 'Let's give him a lump of sugar.'

The waiter bowed and said in perfect English: 'I would regard that as a great honour. In my country, it is the custom for a bridegroom to give his bride sugar, which used to be a rare commodity, in recognition of her worth and beauty.'

Told in *Quentin Crewe's International Pocket Food Book* (1980).

1 Foreigners seeking to make use of English idioms are advised to do so only with caution. This exchange was overheard in a café near to Victoria Station in London. A foreign gentleman, obviously well-versed in the English use of euphemisms, asked a harassed waitress for 'the cloakroom'. She replied: 'We 'aven't got one, you'll 'ave to use the 'atstand ...'

Contributed by Mrs P.S. of Eastbourne to *Eavesdroppings* (1981).

Languages, foreign

2 When the Polish singers Jan Kiepura and Marta Eggerth opened in a New York production of *The Merry Widow* in the 1940s, an anxious Kiepura asked a fan after one performance whether he should polish up his English. 'No,' replied the fan, 'you should English up your Polish.'

Told in *The Times* (9 September 1989).

3 Master of the English language that he was, Winston Churchill was well aware that he had certain shortcomings when speaking French. In October 1940, he gave a radio address to the French people, first in French, beginning, '*Français! C'est moi, Churchill, qui vous parle!*', and then in English. In November 1958, having been decorated by de Gaulle in Paris, he gave his thanks in English: 'I have often made speeches in French but that was wartime, and I do not wish to subject you to the ordeals of darker days.'

Just after the war, in lighter mood, it is said that he began an informal speech in French, '*Prenez garde, je vais parler français ...*' (source untraced). On another occasion, about the same time, he told his (somewhat startled) audience that, looking back, he saw his career divided into two distinct and separate periods. What he actually said was: '*Quand je regarde mon derrière, je vois qu'il est divisé en deux parties.*'

The last occasion was recounted on BBC Radio *Quote ... Unquote* (29 January 1979).

4 There was an Englishman whose wife died while they were on a visit to France. Wanting a black coat to attend her funeral, the husband went into a shop and asked for a *capote noire*, explaining that his wife had died unexpectedly. Commented the shopkeeper: '*Oh, Monsieur! Quelle attention délicate!*'

Source untraced, but before 1986. (If it helps, perhaps I should explain that whereas *capote* means 'greatcoat', *capote anglaise* is French slang for a condom.)

5 Though it is sometimes told as though it were a story *about* the English theologian, priest and writer Father Ronald Knox, this is in fact only a story told by him. It is the one about the English priest who had never got beyond fourth-form French and who was asked if he would like to take confession at Notre Dame in Paris on Easter Sunday. He agreed. In due course, a little old lady from the streets

of Paris came into the confessional and started babbling about all the sins she had committed. The priest, who did not understand a word of it, was overheard mumbling, 'Ah, *vouz avez, avez-vous?*'

Based on a version told by Leslie Thomas from BBC Radio *Quote ... Unquote* (9 March 1982).

Last words

1 The last words of Alexander the Great are said to have been: ' I am dying with the help of too many physicians.'

So attributed in *The Treasury of Humorous Quotations* (ed. Esar and Bentley, 1951) and earlier, in the form, 'I die by the help of too many physicians' in *H. L. Mencken's Dictionary of Quotations* (1942), but no other evidence has been found in support. However, the idea surfaces elsewhere in the classical world. The dying Emperor Hadrian (AD 76–138) apparently came out with 'the popular saying "many physicians have slain a king"' (according to Chap. 69 of the Roman history by the Greek historian Dion Cassius). Pliny the Elder quoted an epitaph in AD 77 that goes *turba se medicorum periisse* or, in another version, *turba medicorum perii* (translated as, 'the brawling of the doctors killed me'). There is also said to be a more recent Czech proverb, 'Many doctors, death accomplished.' In addition, Molière, in the opening line of Act 2 of *L'Amour Médecin*, comes close to the sense: '*Que voulez-vous donc faire, Monsieur, de quatre médecins? N'est-ce pas assez d'un pour tuer une personne?* [What do you want with four doctors? Isn't one enough to kill someone?]'

2 When the city of Syracuse was taken by the Romans, the Greek mathematician and inventor Archimedes was ordered by a soldier to follow him. Engaged as he was on a mathematical problem by drawing figures in the sand, Archimedes said either (or both),

'Stand away, fellow, from my diagram' or 'Wait till I have finished my problem.' The soldier killed him.

Told in Barnaby Conrad, *Famous Last Words* (1961).

3 Having just been told that he was lying in the Jerusalem Chamber of Westminster Abbey, the last words of Henry IV in 1413 were, 'Lauds be given to the Father of heaven, for now I know that I shall die here in this chamber, according to the prophecy of me declared, that I should depart this life in Jerusalem.' The King had been preparing for an expedition to the Holy Land and was visiting the Abbey on the eve of his departure when taken ill.

Told in Raphael Holinshed, *The Chronicles of England, Scotland and Ireland* (1587). Shakespeare in *Henry IV, Part 2* takes this situation almost word for word from the chronicle. After the dissolution of the Abbey, the Jerusalem Chamber became the meeting place of the Dean and Chapter. Its name derives from mention of Jerusalem in inscriptions round the fireplace or on the original tapestry hangings.

4 Sir Everard Digby was hung, drawn and quartered for his part in the Gunpowder Plot of 1605. It is said that when the executioner plucked out his heart and said, 'Here is the heart of a traitor', Digby came out with the posthumous retort, 'Thou liest!'

Told in Barnaby Conrad, *Famous Last Words* (1961).

5 Dominique Bouhours, the French grammarian (1628–1702), died with these words on his lips: 'I am about to – or I am going to – die: either expression is used.'

Told in Barnaby Conrad, *Famous Last Words* (1961).

1 When an officer presented the Marquis de Fouras with his death warrant in 1790, the latter pointed out: 'You have made three spelling mistakes [*Vous avez fait, Monsieur, trois fauts d'ortho-graphie*].'

Told in my book *The 'Quote ... Unquote' Book of Love, Death and the Universe* (1980), but otherwise untraced. The Marquis (possibly de Fauras) was apparently born in 1745.

2 What were Louis XVI's last words before he was guillotined? Thomas Carlyle has it that he said: 'Frenchmen, I die innocent: it is from the scaffold and near appearing before God that I tell you so. I pardon my enemies: I desire that France ...' – and that the rest was drowned out by a roll of drums. Others complete the final sentence as: 'I hope that my blood may cement the happiness of the French people.'

The Reverend Sydney Smith commented on this question in a letter to Miss Berry (28 January 1843): 'I am studying the death of Louis XVI. Did he die heroically? or did he struggle on the scaffold? Was that struggle (for I believe there was one) for permission to speak? or from indignation at not being suffered to act for himself at the last moment, and to place himself under the axe? ... I don't believe the Abbé Edgeworth's "Son of St Louis, *montez au ciel!*" It seems necessary that great people should die with some sonorous and quotable saying. Mr Pitt said something intelligible in his last moments: G. Rose made it out to be "Save my country, Heaven!" The nurse, on being interrogated, said that he asked for barley-water.'

3 Paulette, sister of Jean-Anthelme Brillat-Savarin the celebrated French gastronome, expired in her one hundredth year during the course of a good meal, shouting: 'Quick! Serve the dessert! I think I am dying.'

Told in my book *The 'Quote ... Unquote' Book of Love, Death and the Universe* (1980), but unverified. Jean-Anthelme died in 1826.

4 John Adams, the 2nd President of the United States, though ailing, was determined to live and see the 50th anniversary of the Declaration of Independence – on 4 July 1826. This he did, though his last words, spoken in the afternoon of that day, were 'Thomas Jefferson still survives' or 'Thomas Jefferson lives.' By a remarkable accident, this was not actually true: Jefferson had died a few hours earlier. Still, it was remarkable that both former Presidents died on that significant day.

The initial report of his last words appeared in the *Columbian Centinel* (12 July 1826). *Brewer's Dictionary of Phrase and Fable* (1975) has, rather, that his dying words were 'Independence for ever.'

5 During his final illness, it was suggested to Benjamin Disraeli that he might like to receive a visit from Queen Victoria. 'No, it is better not,' he replied, 'She would only ask me to take a message to Albert.' That is a perfectly genuine quotation and is confirmed by Robert Blake in his life, *Disraeli* (1966), but they are not his last words as is sometimes suggested. The last authenticated words Disraeli uttered were: 'I had rather live, but I am not afraid to die.'

The actual last words are quoted in Wintle and Kenin, *The Dictionary of Biographical Quotation* (1978).

6 It is sometimes said that Oscar Wilde's last words in 1900 were – apropos the poor furnishings in the room where he

lay: 'This wall paper'll be the death of me – one of us'll have to go.'

This remark was indeed said by Wilde, but not *in extremis*. The jest was first recorded in R. H. Sherard, *Life of Oscar Wilde* (1906). Another version is that Wilde said to Claire de Pratz: 'My wallpaper and I are fighting a duel to the death. One or the other of us has to go' – reported in Guillot de Saix, 'Souvenirs inédits'; also in Frank Harris, *Oscar Wilde, His Life and Confessions* (1930).

1 In 1902, the author Samuel Butler, though dying, was engaged in the purchase of the freehold of a house in Hampstead. To Alfred Emery Cathie, his clerk, 'servant and friend', he said, 'Have you brought the cheque book, Alfred?' Butler then took off his spectacles and put them down on the table. 'I don't want them any more,' he said. His head fell back, and he died.

Source: Philip Henderson, *Samuel Butler: the Incarnate Bachelor* (1953).

2 The last words of the Russian playwright Anton Chekhov were, 'I've changed my mind ... I think I will have a little champagne.' One can imagine how a character in one of his plays might spend several days making up his mind about such a step.

Told by Sir Peter Ustinov on BBC Radio *Quote ... Unquote* (17 March 1992).

3 The English-born author Erskine Childers embraced the Irish Republican cause and was executed by firing squad on 24 November 1922. His last words, addressed to the firing squad, were, 'Take a step forward, lads. It will be easier that way.' Childers's nonchalance also seems apparent from the fact that he managed to get a delay of an hour in his execution time in order to see the

sunrise. He also shook hands with each of his executioners.

Told in Andrew Boyle, *The Riddle of Erskine Childers* (1976).

4 An Old Etonian and former Liberal Prime Minister, Lord Rosebery told his servant to buy him a gramophone and, when death was imminent, to play upon it the Eton Boating Song. This was actually done on 21 May 1929, 'though perhaps he did not hear it', suggested Winston Churchill. 'Thus he wished the gay memories of boyhood to be around him at his end, and thus he set Death in its proper place as a necessary and unalarming process.'

Recounted by Churchill in *Great Contemporaries* (1937). Robert Rhodes James in *Rosebery* (1963) adds: 'It is doubtful if he heard the haunting music, redolent of hot summer afternoons, the quiet laughter of friends, and the golden days of his young manhood.'

5 The family patriarch was on the way out. As he lay on his deathbed, the family gathered round. Sleepily, the old man opened his eyes and asked, 'Is Johnny here?' The eldest son quietly asserted that, yes, he was there. 'And is my good boy, Tommy, also here?' The good boy, with a lump in his throat, made it clear to his father that he, too, was there. 'And what about Henry? Is he here?' Yes, the said Henry piped up – he was there. And so on, down through the family, the roll call continued, until all the children, male and female, had been accounted for.

The patriarch still didn't look very pleased. 'If you're all here,' he finally said, very tetchily, 'Then who's minding the store?'

This punchline is found in many collections as far back as Irvin S. Cobb, *Many Laughs for*

Many Days (1925). *Who's Minding the Store?*
was used as the title of a Jerry Lewis film
in 1963.

1 Most famous for her 'Dying Swan' solo,
the Russian ballerina Anna Pavlova
(1885–1931) was touring the Nether-
lands right up to the end of her life.
Her actual last words before she died
were, 'Get my "Swan" costume ready!'

According to Barnaby Conrad, *Famous Last
Words* (1961).

2 Sir John J. (Jakie) Astor described the
last visit to his mother, Nancy Astor,
before she died in 1964. 'I sat beside
her for a bit and then she opened her
eyes and saw I was there. She looked me
straight in the face and said, "Jakie, is
it my birthday or am I dying?" – which
was quite difficult to answer. So I said,
"A bit of both, Mum."'

In John Grigg, *Nancy Astor: Portrait of a
Pioneer* (1980). Her actual last word was
'Waldorf' (the name of her husband),
uttered the day before she died.

3 On her deathbed in 1969, Baroness
Asquith's last words were, 'I feel
amphibious.'

'Isn't that wonderful – conveying that
feeling of floating off,' commented Lord
St John of Fawsley in the *Observer* Magazine
(24 January 1988). 'She never reached out
lazily for the nearest words to hand but
always perfectly judged them, even on her
deathbed.'

4 Chris Chubbock was a female news
presenter at a TV station in Sarasota,
Florida. One day she announced in a
live broadcast: 'And now, in keeping
with Channel 40's policy of always
bringing you the latest in blood and
guts, in living colour, you're about to
see another first – an attempted
suicide.' She then shot herself dead.

Told in *The Book of Quotes*, ed. Barbara
Rowes (1979).

5 When General Franco, the Spanish
dicator, died – at last – in 1975, what
he should have said was: 'Yes, we
have no mañanas.'

Suggested in my book *Quote ... Unquote*
(1978). Compare this use of the same line in
a cartoon caption from *Punch* (26 September
1923): King Alfonso of Spain – 'So you
want to start these reforms at once; not put
them off till to-morrow, which is supposed
to be our Spanish way with everything?'
President of the Directory: 'Yes, sire, we have
no mañanas to-day.' (The song 'Yes, We
Have No Bananas' had been published earlier
that year and was enormously popular.)

6 Asked on his deathbed by his son
whether, looking back on a long and
crowded life, he had any lasting regrets,
the actor Stanley Holloway replied:
'Yes – the fact that I never got the
Kipling Cake commercials.'

Related by Sheridan Morley in a *Theatreprint*
quiz, some time before 1986.

7 The actor John Le Mesurier arranged
for his own death notice to appear
in *The Times* when appropriate. It duly
appeared on 16 November 1983, in
the form: 'John Le Mesurier wishes it
to be known that he conked out on
November 15th. He sadly misses family
and friends.' His last words were, 'It's
all been rather lovely.'

From a report in the same issue of *The Times*.

8 Appearing on BBC Radio *Quote ...
Unquote* in 1984, Julian Critchley
MP told a joke based on the unfortu-
nate premise of the demise of Denis
Thatcher, husband of the then Prime
Minister. Someone who had been
present on this sad occasion was
asked whether Denis had uttered any

memorable dying words. 'No,' said the witness, 'Margaret was with him till the end.'

This was an old story grafted on to the Thatchers. 'And wot were 'is last words, Mrs Jones?' ... "E didn't 'ave no last words. Oi was with 'im till *the end*' – this appeared in *Pass the Port* (1976), also in *Pass the Port Again* (1980) as told to an Irish priest by a woman who had just lost her father.

Lateness

1 Marilyn Monroe was chronically un-punctual. In May 1962, she was due to sing 'Happy Birthday, Mr President' at a birthday party for John F. Kennedy in Madison Square Garden, New York. She kept the audience of 22,000 people waiting so long that when she did eventually arrive, Peter Lawford introduced her as 'the late Marilyn Monroe'. She died three months later.

Told in Peter Hay, *Broadway Anecdotes* (1989).

2 When Hans Keller, the slightly dotty musicologist, arrived a whole hour late for a BBC Music Division meeting, the chairman, Eric Warr, remarked: 'Ah, Mr Keller, I see you've come to prolong the meeting.' To which Hans Keller replied: 'Well, I've come too late to shorten it, haven't I?'

Told by John Rushby-Smith of Lower Soudley, Gloucestershire, and formerly with the BBC (April 1998).

3 Said Denis Thatcher, husband of Prime Minister Thatcher, on one occasion: 'I was at the 14th hole at Sandwich, looked at me watch and thought, "Bugger me, things are a bit tight." I then jumped in the car and went like a bat out of Hades up the A20. I got to Number 10, took the stairs three at

a time, did me ablutions, changed into me Sunday best, and got to the bash only two minutes late. And *still* got a bloody bollocking!'

Recounted in Peter Tory's Diary in the *Daily Star* (4 June 1985), giving the impression that he had been told the story by Thatcher himself.

Laughter, inappropriate

4 During a national fire brigade strike in 1977, Reginald Bosanquet had to read an item on ITN's *News at Ten* that told of an emergency call made to the Army. It was from an old lady whose cat was stuck up a tree. The Army fire engine duly arrived – it was a Green Goddess – and a soldier shinned up the tree and rescued the moggie. Reggie went on to report that, unfortunately, as they were backing out of the garden, they accidentally ran over the cat they had just rescued, and so killed it. Alas, he allowed the whisper of a grin to pass over his face and the switchboard was flooded with protest calls. His excuse was that he had had a lopsided grin on his face since birth.

In his autobiography *Let's Get Through Wednesday* (1980), Bosanquet denied that he had so much as moved a muscle after reading the story and added: 'It is interesting that someone in the newsroom should have found this nugget of a tailpiece in what can normally be expected to be thoroughly humourless – a Ministry handout. And I should mention that what is said to have happened afterwards is definitely not true. The firemen did not push the cat into the dear lady's letter-box with a note of apology.' Also recounted in *TV Times* (21 September 1985).

Law

5 A Yorkshire miner put in a very late claim for compensation and the case

went to court. The judge told his counsel: 'Your client is no doubt aware of *vigilantibus, et non dormientibus, jura subveniunt?* The counsel replied: 'In Barnsley, m'lud, they speak of little else.'

This much-told legal tale takes any number of forms. In *Pass the Port Again* (1980), there is a version told involving Serjeant Sullivan – 'the last serjeant of the Irish Bar to practise in the English courts'. This I take to be Alexander Martin Sullivan (1871–1959). Here, the legal tag is *'Assignatus utitur jure auctoris'* and the place where they speak of little else is Ballynattery. The legal maxims in both cases are genuine. The first means 'The laws assist the watchful, not the sleepers', and the second, 'An assignee is clothed with the right of his principal.'

Leadership

1 When Lord Hill was transferred from the chairmanship of the Independent Television Authority (ITA) to that of the BBC, he complained to David Attenborough about his cool reception at the BBC. Attenborough explained that for the BBC it was rather like inviting Rommel to take over the Eighth Army before the Battle of El Alamein. When Hill asked whether he was suggesting Rommel wasn't a good general, Attenborough replied, 'No, but we'd like to know he's fighting for the same things as us.'

A version is quoted in Lord Hill, *Behind the Screen* (1974). Sir Robert Lusty in his autobiography (*Bound To Be Read*, 1975) claimed to have made a similar analogy, though not directly to Hill himself. Leonard Miall discussed the rival claims in the *Independent* (31 July 1991).

2 When she was Prime Minister, Margaret Thatcher was dining in a

London restaurant with the Chancellor of the Exchequer and a number of other Cabinet colleagues. The PM told the waiter that she would have steak and kidney pie. 'And the vegetables?' the waiter asked. 'Oh, they'll have the same,' Mrs Thatcher said.

Given in the *Guardian* in the week preceding 24 March 1985 as an example of Mrs Thatcher's (usually not very apparent) wit. But it was an old joke even then – having been applied to football managers dining with their players and in other leaders-and-led situations.

Legs, wooden

3 To be carpingly accurate, Sarah Bernhardt never actually played Hamlet strutting about on her wooden leg. After she had her amputation, she performed sitting down. Nevertheless, that should not be allowed to spoil the story of the comment passed between two members of the audience at one of her later appearances. When there were three heavy thumps on the stage – the traditional starting signal for French tragedy – one said, 'Ah, here comes the Divine Sarah now ...'

Told by Roy Hudd on BBC Radio *Quote ... Unquote* (10 May 1978). Ned Sherrin, *Theatrical Anecdotes* (1991), has it as Jean Cocteau greeting the three knocks on the stage with, '*C'est elle!* [Here she is!]'

Letters

4 Like Winston Churchill a century and a half later, the Duke of Wellington managed to write vigorous and astonishingly detailed dispatches even at the height of battle. The Duke's withering irony over a question of priorities was notably displayed in a message,

said to have been sent to his masters in Whitehall, in August 1812: 'Gentlemen: while marching from Portugal to a position which commands the approach to Madrid and the French forces, my officers have been diligently complying with your requests which have been sent by his Majesty's ship from London to Lisbon and thence by dispatch rider to our headquarters.

'We have enumerated our saddles, bridles, tents and tent poles, and all manner of sundry items for which His Majesty's government holds me accountable. I have dispatched reports on the character, wit and spleen of every officer. Each item and every farthing has been accounted for, with two regrettable exceptions for which I beg your indulgence.

'Unfortunately the sum of one shilling and ninepence remains unaccounted for in one infantry battalion's petty cash and there has been a hideous confusion as to the number of jars of raspberry jam issued to one cavalry regiment during a sandstorm in western Spain. This reprehensible carelessness may be related to the pressure of circumstance, since we are at war with France, a fact which may come as a bit of a surprise to you gentlemen in Whitehall.

'This brings me to my present purpose, which is to request elucidation of my instructions from His Majesty's Government, so that I may better understand why I am dragging an army over these barren plains. I construe that perforce it must be one of two alternative duties, as given below. I shall pursue either one with the best of my ability but I cannot do both:

'1. To train an army of uniformed British clerks in Spain for the benefit of the accountants and copy-boys in London, or, perchance

'2. To see it that the forces of Napoleon are driven out of Spain.
'Signed,
'Your most obedient servant
'WELLINGTON.'

Letter reproduced in *TIG Brief* (May 1985). The question is, did Wellington write such a letter? Undoubtedly he was capable of the sarcasm and held the views expressed therein, but are one or two turns of phrase genuinely his, and aren't the jars of raspberry jam a little beyond even his grim-faced sense of humour?

1 A business-like exchange of notes took place in the first half of the nineteenth century between François d'Orléans, Prince de Joinville, third son of Louis-Philippe, and the actress Mlle. Rachel. He asked, '*Où? – quand? – combien?* [Where? – when? – how much?]' She answered: '*Chez toi – ce soir – pour rien.* [Your place – tonight – free.]'

Told in James Agate, *Rachel* (1928).

2 It is amazing how even the least addressed envelopes can still get to where they are intended. A letter from Italy once reached the chemist Sir Humphry Davy although it only bore the words, 'SIROMFREDEVI, LONDRA'. On another occasion, an old friend of Mark Twain's wished to send him greetings but, as he was on his travels, did not know where to address the letter. In the end, the friend put, 'MARK TWAIN, God Knows Where, Try London' on the envelope, and a few weeks later received Twain's acknowledgement: 'He did.' Further, Twain expressed himself surprised and complimented that He who was credited with knowing his whereabouts should take so much interest in him, adding: 'Had the letter been

addressed to the care of the "other party", I would naturally have expected to receive it without delay.' It is said that his correspondent tried again, and addressed the second letter, 'MARK TWAIN, The Devil Knows Where, Try London.' This found him no less promptly.

The Sir Humphry Davy story told in C. R. Weld, *A History of the Royal Society* (1848). The rest told in *Mark Twain's Speeches* (1910).

1 When T. E. Lawrence was trying to downplay his 'Lawrence of Arabia' legend and was hiding in the RAF under the name of 'Aircraftsman Shaw', he made the acquaintance of Noël Coward. Intrigued by Lawrence's affectation, Coward once wrote him a letter beginning: 'Dear 338171 (May I call you 338?)'.

Included in *Letters to T. E. Lawrence*, ed. D. Garnett (1938). The letter was dated 25 August 1930 and sent from the Adelphi Hotel, Liverpool, where Coward was staying on the tour of his play *Private Lives*. Lawrence replied on 6 September: 'It is very good to laugh: and I laughed so much, and made so many people laugh over your "May I call you 338" that I became too busy and happy to acknowledge your letter.' A pedant has pointed out to me that the really individual part of one's number in the services is at the end, so Coward should really have put: 'May I call you 171?'

2 John Peart-Binns, biographer of John Habgood, Archbishop of York, un-earthed a letter written by Habgood when he was eight years old. 'Dear God,' it began, 'If you feel lonely up in the sky would you like to come down and stay with us? You could sleep in the spare room, and you could bathe with us, and I think you would enjoy yourself. Love, John'.

Addressed to 'Our Father Which Art in Heaven' it was opened by the Post Office and marked 'Return to sender', which, as Peart-Binns commented, has fewer theological implications than 'Gone away' or 'Unknown at this address'.

Reported in the *Sunday Telegraph* (31 May 1987).

3 Gerard Hoffnung (1925–59), the German-born British cartoonist, musician and eccentric, gave a famous speech at the Oxford Union. One of the most-remembered lines con-cerns letters supposedly received from Tyrolean landladies about the desirability of their properties: 'There is a French widow in every bedroom (affording delightful prospects) …'

The speech at the Oxford Union took place on 4 December 1958. How nice to hear an old joke revisited! In the Reverend Francis Kilvert's diary (entry for 7 October 1871) he says: 'The *Hereford Times* has misprinted our report of the Clyro Harvest Festival as follows, "The widows were decorated with Latin and St Andrew's crosses and other beautiful devices in moss with dazzling flowers." This was irresistible and the schoolmaster roared with delight.'

4 'My father ran an industrial company aided, for many years, by the same secretary – so that he came to leave to her the composing and typing of replies to a whole range of letters that con-tained standard complaints or queries. The curious note he always pencilled on such letters originated with the manager of a hotel where a friend of his had stayed – and been bitten by bed bugs. His friend had then written to the manager to say that the hotel was a disgrace, that he would never stay there

again and that he would warn off all his friends.

'He received a prompt, profuse apology; such a bad thing had never happened before ... the floor maid had been sacked ... and so on. Somewhat mollified, he was just thinking, "Well, I suppose the best hotel can have the occasional lapse ... when he spotted his own letter still pinned to this reply. Across it was written in blue crayon: "WRITE THE USUAL BUG LETTER".'

Related by D.F. of Shifnal, Shropshire (May 1994). But compare the story (told earlier, for example, in *Pass the Port*, 1976) of the distinguished gentleman – an ambassador, no less – who had an unfortunate experience when travelling on the Orient Express: he was bitten by bugs. Duly complaining to the travel company, he received a fulsome letter of apology back – 'unhappily, the clerk who dealt with the complaint, by inadvertence, attached to this reply the Ambassador's original letter of complaint, across which someone had scribbled, "Usual bug letter, please".'

1 Before he became noted for his seemingly endless sentences as a columnist on *The Times*, Bernard Levin once made a very brief contribution to that paper's letters page. It consisted of but one sentence: 'Sir, I have just got a crossed line on which I heard a man getting a wrong number: is this a record?'

Told by Levin in his foreword to Kenneth Gregory, *The First Cuckoo* (1976).

2 How to go about getting a letter published in the correspondence columns of *The Times* has been the subject of some speculation. Unfortunately, this one never made it. It was written by Lt. Col. A. D. Wintle, from the Cavalry Club, on 6 February 1946: 'Sir, I have just written you a long letter. On reading it over, I have thrown it into the wastepaper basket. Hoping this will meet with your approval. I am, Sir, Your Obedient Servant ...'

The letter was not published until *The Times – Past Present and Future* (1985). Alfred Wintle (1897–1966) was a brave, idiosyncratic military hero of both World Wars about whom anecdotes cluster. Although he was the subject of TV's *This Is Your Life* and appeared on *Desert Island Discs* (12 March 1962), and although he was later portrayed by Jim Broadbent in a TV film *The Last Englishman* (1995), he has never been the subject of a biography. Nicknamed 'Mad Jack' for his daring prison escapes and solo military assaults behind enemy lines, the bemonocled Wintle once held a pistol to the head of a civil servant in the War Office who was obstructing one of his plans (for which he was sent to the Tower of London for a spell). In peacetime, he famously debagged a Brighton solicitor who had swindled Wintle's aunt. He then took photos of the solicitor wearing only underwear and a dunce's cap. This particular episode ended up in the House of Lords with the Colonel defending himself and winning ... When Prince Aly Khan appeared from Monte Carlo to pay tribute on *This Is Your Life* and said, 'I wish I could be there', Wintle barked, 'Well, why aren't you? You can afford it after all.'

3 A letter written to a teacher ran as follows: 'Dear Miss, Sorry Jimmy is late but me and my husband rather overdone it this morning.'

From a note sent to Mrs C. M. Rowntree of London SW11 when she was a teacher. Broadcast on BBC Radio *Quote ... Unquote* (7 August 1980).

4 'Dear Miss, Please excuse Mary from having a shower, being how she is. Being how you are yourself sometimes, you will understand how she is.'

Told on BBC Radio *Quote ... Unquote* (28 August 1980).

1 'Dear Miss, Please excuse Sandra being late. She was waiting for the bus at twenty to nine but came back to use the toilet and missed it.'

Told to me by Mrs. M. Rawes, married to an education welfare officer in Liverpool. Contributed to BBC Radio *Quote ... Unquote* (5 January 1982).

2 'Dear Mr Walter, Susan was away from school yesterday as I took her to the herbalist about her nose and the tops of her legs.'

Told to me by Peter J. Walter of Tiverton (1981). Contributed to BBC Radio *Quote ... Unquote* (5 January 1982).

3 'Dear Miss, Jim was off school because he caught a chill and had terrible diarrhoea through a hole in his wellies.'

Mrs J. Cowrie, letter to *Woman* (24 March 1982). In the same year I put this in my *Foot in Mouth*, after a contribution to on BBC Radio *Quote ... Unquote*: 'Dear Miss Jones, Sorry Alan was away last week but with all the wet weather he's had diarrhoea through a hole in his shoe.'

4 'Please excuse Johnny from being absent as I was having a baby – and it's not his fault.'

Contributed by Isabel Lovett of the Isle of Skye to BBC Radio *Quote ... Unquote* in August 1984.

Libels

5 When *Confidential* magazine ran a muck-raking article, going over every area of his life, Groucho Marx dashed off one of his famous letters to the editor: 'Dear Sir, If you persist in publishing libellous articles about me, I will have to cancel my subscription.'

Told in Arthur Marx, *Son of Groucho* (1973).

Libraries

6 In the tenth century, Abdul Kassem Ismael, the scholarly grand-vizier of Persia, had a library of some 117,000 volumes. On his travels as a warrior and statesman, he never parted with his beloved books. Legend has it that they were carried about wherever he went by 400 camels. Furthermore, they were trained to walk in alphabetical order.

Told by Dr Joseph Hankin, President of Westchester Community College, New York, in a speech (1998). He suspects that he may have acquired it from *Reader's Digest* in the early 1980s or from Isaac Asimov's *Book of Facts*. Unverified.

Lies

7 Bertrand Russell said that he had only once ever succeeded in making his fellow philosopher, George Moore, tell a lie – and that involved using a subterfuge. 'Moore,' he said, 'do you *always* speak the truth?' 'No,' Moore replied.

Told in Russell, *Autobiography*, Vol. 1 (1967). Jonathan Miller parodied this in 'Portrait from Memory', *Beyond the Fringe* (1961).

Life

8 On the tombstone of Mary Ann South in Ayot St Lawrence churchyard, Hertfordshire, is the inscription, 'Her Time Was Short.' She had lived in the village for seventy years, from 1825 to 1895. George Bernard Shaw, when asked why he had chosen to live in the same village, would explain that if the biblical span of three score years and ten was considered short there, it had to be a good place to live. He himself managed to live to the age of 94.

His observation is recorded in Michael Holroyd, *Bernard Shaw* Vol. 2 (1989). Hesketh Pearson, *Bernard Shaw* (1942) has the inscription as 'Jane Evesley. Born 1815 – Died 1895. Her time was short.'

1   At the height of his very public wranglings with Mia Farrow, Woody Allen was asked, 'If you had your life to live all over again, is there anything you would do differently?' Allen thought for a moment and then said: 'This time round, I wouldn't read *Moby Dick*.'

Told by Hilary Spurling on BBC Radio *Quote ... Unquote* (10 April 1998). Another version: 'If I had to live my life all over again, I would change one thing: I wouldn't read *Moby Dick*' – quoted in the *Daily Telegraph* (24 February 1994).

Likenesses

2   When Anna Pavlova made her last appearance in Edinburgh, the audience went mad with excitement at the end of the performance. They cheered, stamped, sobbed with emotion and flung flowers on the stage. Two ladies on the front row were clapping genteelly and one observed to the other: 'She's awfully like Mrs Wishart ...'

Traditional, included in my *Eavesdroppings* (1981). Eric Maschwitz in *No Chip on My Shoulder* (1957) pinpoints the originator of the tale as Walford Hyden, a conductor who accompanied Pavlova on her world tours. His version: when she gave a performance of 'The Dying Swan' in Glasgow and finally sank to the floor in her feathered costume, Hyden heard a woman in the front row observe to her companion, 'Aye, she is awfu' like Mrs Wishart.'

3   When the benign and distinguished TV newsreader Robert Dougall retired, he wrote his autobiography and then went on the promotional trail. When he was signing copies of his book in a large store at Wolverhampton, one woman in the queue, very excited at seeing the great man in the flesh, said to her friend: 'It's just like him, isn't it?'

Contributed by Margaret Bell of Cannock to BBC Radio *Quote ... Unquote* (22 December 1981).

Literary criticism

4   Like many authors, Benjamin Disraeli had to put up with would-be writers sending him their efforts for him to comment on. To one author who had sent him an unsolicited manuscript, he replied: 'Many thanks; I shall lose no time in reading it.'

Told in Wilfrid Meynell, *The Man Disraeli* (1903). G. W. E. Russell, *Collections and Recollections*, Chap. 31 (1898) had the remark earlier, but merely ascribes it to an eminent man 'on this side of the Atlantic'.

5   Many years after it was originally published clandestinely, D. H. Lawrence's infamous novel *Lady Chatterley's Lover* was issued in the United States by Grove Press. Rather oddly, this edition was reviewed in the pages of *Field and Stream*, a journal aimed at followers of outdoor pursuits. In part, the review stated: 'This fictional account of the day-by-day life of an English gamekeeper is still of interest to outdoor-minded readers, as it contains many passages on pheasant-raising, the apprehending of poachers, ways to control vermin, and other chores and duties of professional gamekeepers. Unfortunately, one is obliged to wade through many pages of extraneous material in order to discover and savour these sidelights on the management of a Midland estate, and in this reviewer's opinion,

the book cannot take the place of
J. R. Miller's *Practical Gamekeeper*.'

Told in the seventh volume of Rupert
Furneaux's *Famous Criminal Cases* (1962)
in its account of the Penguin Books/*Lady
Chatterley* trial.

1 During the 1930s, the poet and writer
Hilaire Belloc was travelling by train
when he encountered a man reading a
copy of his *History of England*, a book
he considered to be less than good, and
one of many pot-boilers he produced
in his later life. Asking the man how
much he had paid for it, and fishing
the money out of his pocket, Belloc
then proceeded to fling the book out
of the carriage window.

A. N. Wilson in *Hilaire Belloc* (1984) notes
that he had heard this story 'from many
sources, but never seen it substantiated'.

2 The actress Coral Browne appeared
as herself in Alan Bennett's TV play
An Englishman Abroad, based on her
encounter in Moscow with the exiled
spy Guy Burgess. A Hollywood writer
told her that although he had enjoyed
the play, he did not think the writing
was up to scratch. Aghast at this slight,
Browne put the American in his place
on the question of writing: 'Listen,
dear, you couldn't write "f***" on a
dusty venetian blind.'

Told by Alan Bennett in *The Sunday Times*
Magazine (18 November 1984), and the
story confirmed by Browne in a Channel 4
documentary (December 1990).

3 In 1984, Richard Cobb was chairman
of the judges of the Booker Prize for
Fiction. At the awards presentation, he
told the distinguished literary audience
about the qualities of the winning
novel: 'In an operation of this kind, one
would not go for a Proust or Joyce –

not that I would know about that,
never having read either.'

Reported in *The Times* (19 October 1984).
Cobb (1917–96), English academic with
great interest in matters French, was at
one time Professor of Modern History at
Oxford.

Litter

4 A litter lout, driving through Bury St
Edmunds, chucked a cigarette packet
out of her car window. An elderly
female resident picked up the packet
and handed it back. 'I think this
belongs to you,' she added. 'I just
threw that away,' said the litter lout.
'Finished with it. Don't want that.'
The elderly female resident said: 'And
neither does Bury St Edmunds ...'

A familiar story and set in various places.
In *The Kenneth Williams Diaries* (1993), he
has a 'Bury St Edmunds' version in his entry
for 1 January 1969. Arthur Marshall told
a version set in Cheltenham on BBC Radio
Quote ... Unquote (17 July 1979).

Logic

5 Hastings Rashdall was a moral philosopher and theologian who, from 1895
to 1917, was tutor in philosophy at
New College, Oxford. One day he was
seen by an undergraduate to be pump-
ing up the front tyre of his bicycle
although it was the back tyre that was
flat. The undergraduate said, 'But,
sir, that will do no good.' Hastings
Rashdall look surprised: 'Goodness
me,' he said, 'are they not then
connected?'

Told by Anthony Quinton on BBC Radio
Quote ... Unquote (24 April 1998).

6 It seems that William (Spoonerism)
Spooner's crazed logic could also take

physical form. Once when he spilled salt on the table, he immediately poured claret on it.

Told in a speech at a New College Commemoration of the Founder (3 July 1992).

1 Stephen Fry gave an intriguing glimpse into the lives of supermodels when he reported on an exchange he had heard at London Fashion Week. One of the organizers was apologizing for the rather poor state of affairs backstage. In particular, she pointed out that although there was a lavatory, it had no door. Asked the supermodel: 'So how do I get in?'

Told by Stephen Fry on BBC Radio *Quote . . . Unquote* (13 May 1997).

Love

2 'What is Love?' Jesting Pilate might well have asked; and still would not have stayed for an answer. Joyce McKinney thought she knew. In 1977, the former Miss Wyoming was charged in an English court with kidnapping Kirk Anderson, a Mormon missionary and her ex-lover. She allegedly abducted Mr Anderson to a remote country cottage where he was chained to the bed and forced to make love to her.

'I loved Kirk so much,' Miss McKinney declared to a stunned court, 'I would have skied down Mount Everest in the nude with a carnation up my nose.'

Reported from Epsom Magistrates' Court (6 December 1977). She was born in 1950.

Luck

3 When a young actor wished Edith Evans good luck before a radio broadcast, she reproved him, saying: 'With some of us it isn't luck.'

Related by Bryan Forbes in *Ned's Girl* (1977).

Lunch

4 After being told by a BBC executive that he was being dropped from chairing the *Any Questions* radio programme after many years on the job, David Jacobs was duly taken out to lunch. Having suffered similarly, Jack de Manio once said: 'When the BBC wants to sack you, they take you out to lunch.' What Jacobs actually said was, 'You've put the knife between my shoulder blades, but you might have spared me the fork.'

Told in my book *Say No More!* (1987).

Make-up

1 When Richard M. Nixon visited Britain as US Vice-President in 1958, he appeared on BBC TV's *Press Conference.* The production team was interested to be told in advance by an American security officer: 'If make-up is required, it will be applied by the Vice-President's Military Aide.'

Told by Leonard Miall in the *Independent* (13 May 1991).

2 Sir Robert Helpmann, the ballet dancer and choreographer, being an Australian, was devoted to taking his company on tour to some of the least accessible corners of his native continent. Once he had to dress and get made up in the changing room of a football club in the outback. He was discovered standing on a chair, holding a hand-mirror, and applying his make-up by the light of the one naked light bulb that dangled from the ceiling. Said he: 'Really, I just don't know how the footballers manage with *their* make-up.'

Told by Sally Miles on BBC Radio *Quote ... Unquote* (27 October 1984).

3 Barbara Cartland, the romantic novelist, has latterly been noted for her extremely white make-up. It has even been suggested that she uses Tipp-Ex or Snowpake, the correcting fluids. Arthur Marshall once admitted that he had described Miss Cartland as 'the animated meringue'. Far from taking offence, she sent him a telegram of thanks.

Remark recalled by Marshall on BBC Radio *Quote ... Unquote* (25 December 1979).

Malapropisms

4 Some young soldiers were being given a homily by their platoon sergeant on the subject of 'public duties' – that is, how they should behave when they were out of the barracks and moving about among civilians. Said he: 'A gentleman always gives up his seat to a lady in a public convenience.'

A correspondent in 1976 observed to me that this 'old music-hall joke' appears in Gerald Kersh's book *They Die With Their Boots Clean* (1941), a record of his experiences in the Guards.

5 Mrs Levi Zeiglerheiter, American mother-in-law of the 1st Marquess Curzon, declared on landing in New York after a stormy crossing, 'At last I am back on terracotta.'

Told in Kenneth Rose, *Superior Person* (1969).

1 Linley Sambourne, the *Punch* cartoonist, had a wonderful way of saying things that were not malapropisms or spoonerisms but were a kind of lateral *un*-thinking. Nobody knew whether his mistakes were intentional. The examples that I have most enjoyed are: 'He's so poor – he hasn't got a rag to stand on'; 'There was such a silence afterwards that you could have picked up a pin in it'; and, 'You're digging nails in your coffin with every stroke of your tongue.'

These are mentioned in literature on display at the 'Linley Sambourne House' in Kensington, which is preserved by the Victorian Society and open to visitors. Sambourne also once remarked, 'I don't care for Lady Macbeth in the street-walking scene' – quoted in R. G. C. Price, *A History of Punch* (1957).

2 A law student (in a *viva voce* examination) was asked what was necessary to render a marriage valid in Scotland. He replied: 'For a marriage to be valid in Scotland it is absolutely necessary that it should be consummated in the presence of two policemen.'

From *Samuel Butler's Notebooks* (towards the end of the period 1874–1902).

3 At a conference in 1954 in Berlin, France's foreign minister, Georges Bidault, was introduced as, 'that fine little French tiger, Georges Bidet ...'

Told in *Time* Magazine (30 March 1991).

4 It has been said that it is all too easy for radio and TV newsreaders to read whatever is put before them without allowing the material to be tasted beforehand by their brains. At lunch time one day on Radio 4, a newsreader with this failing said that someone was 'unable to revive Mr X despite giving him the kiss of death'.

Recorded in my diary on 7 July 1968. The newsreader, for whom this was an unusual lapse, was Robin Holmes.

5 A BBC foreign correspondent reporting the 1973 October War in the Middle East referred to the possibility of 'Lesbian forces moving down from the north towards Israel'.

I think I have heard a recording of this. It is one of those jokes that is just waiting to happen. In *The Kenneth Williams Diaries* (1993) – entry for 17 June 1969 – the comedian quotes his aged mother saying, 'Oh! they're opening a lesbian restaurant there!' He corrects her: 'It's Lebanese,' and notes that she went on: 'Yes ... they're all over the place now, aren't they?'

6 There was a marvellous slip by a rather po-faced newsreader belonging to the Rhodesian Broadcasting Corporation (prior, of couse, to it becoming the Zimbabwe Broadcasting Corporation). He referred to 'Aristotle Onassis, the Greek shitting tycoon'.

I heard this myself in Rhodesia and recorded it in my diary on 23 September 1977.

7 Overheard from a conversation between two women: 'She's got trouble with her eye. Doctor says it's a misplaced rectum.'

Contributed to BBC Radio *Quote ... Unquote* (29 January 1979) by Mrs Eileen Woodward of Halstead, Essex.

8 'My mother was having a cataract operation and the lady in the next bed told her that she was suffering from a "detached retinue".'

Contributed to BBC Radio *Quote ... Unquote* (26 June 1979) by Jane Baker of Thame.

1 'Received directly, face-to-face, in conversation with a friend some years ago: "Ah, poor soul, she's got something eternal, you know. She's got a cyst on her aviary."'

Contributed to BBC Radio *Quote ... Unquote* (31 July 1979) by Dorothy Mair of Brighton.

2 During the 1980 US presidential election, a newsreader on the BBC World Service told his startled audience: 'Mr Ronald Reagan has lost his head over President Carter ... er ... Mr Ronald Reagan has lost his lead over President Carter.'

The incident occurred on 20 September 1980, and I heard it.

3 A correspondent reported an overheard conversation: 'Did you see the ostriches on telly last night?' 'What ostriches?' 'The ostriches that escaped.' 'I didn't know that any ostriches had escaped.' 'Of course – you know – the American ostriches.'

This was contributed to BBC Radio *Quote ... Unquote* by Mrs S. Moore of Twickenham (1 December 1981) and followed the release of the American Embassy hostages in Tehran. However, Ned Sherrin in *Theatrical Anecdotes* (1991) pins it squarely upon Chrissie Kendall – 'singer, dancer, actress ... the champion Malapropper of the British stage' – in 1979.

4 Then there was the grandmother who was convinced, on hearing the Beatles' song 'Lucy in the Sky With Diamonds', that the 'girl with kaleidoscope eyes' was actually 'the girl with colitis goes by'.

Said to have been reported first by William Safire of *The New York Times* and known by 1981.

5 Taking part in Shakespeare's *The*

Winter's Tale for the Royal Shakespeare Company, Sheila Hancock sometimes found it rather difficult to concentrate when she returned after a long wait off-stage in the second part. One night, in the scene in which she, as Paulina, restored Hermione to the reformed Leontes, she came to the lines:

> I, an old turtle,
> Will wing me to some withered
> bough ...

Unfortunately, she had a complete black-out, and after a long, groping pause, substituted the word 'twig' for 'bough'.

As told by Hancock in *Ramblings of an Actress* (1987). 'The whole company dissolved in giggles,' she adds, 'shamefully ruining the end of the play for the bewildered audience.'

Manners and etiquette

6 Dr Samuel Johnson once shocked his dining companion by spitting out a hot potato. 'Madam,' he said, 'a fool would have swallowed that.'

Untraced and also ascribed to Winston Churchill and others. Known by 1950. Leonard Miall, the BBC's first post-war Washington correspondent, recalled (1996) attending a Dean Acheson press conference at the State Department when Acheson was asked a very cleverly loaded question. 'None of us could imagine how the Secretary of State could answer it without getting himself into trouble. Acheson stroked his guardsman's moustache for a moment and then replied, "My late law partner, Judge Covington, once attended an oyster roast on the Eastern shore of Maryland. He was given a very hot oyster which he immediately spat on to the floor, remarking, 'A bigger damn fool would have swallowed that one.'" There were no supplementaries.' So the story existed in about 1950, which probably rules out a Churchillian origin. Dr Johnson still seems the likely originator, albeit without a written source.

1 A table manners story involving Dr Johnson concerns his reaction when he was someone's guest at dinner. He objected to a large hole that was in the table cloth before him and, considering that no host should have been so unmindful of his guest, he proceeded to eat his soup through the hole.

Source untraced.

2 The Liberal Prime Minister William Gladstone was held up as an example to countless generations of children as the man who chewed his food properly. It was said that Mr Gladstone chewed each mouthful of food thirty-two times before swallowing. But it is not clear how he became a role model in this regard. Baroness Asquith recalled having had a meal with him, when she was a little girl, at which he did no such thing. Quite the reverse in fact: he bolted his food.

Told in the BBC TV programme *As I Remember* (30 April 1967). Confirmation of this deplorable fact also came in a lecture given by George Lyttelton at Hawarden (Gladstone's old home) on 24 June 1955: 'More than one lynx-eyed young spectator [has discovered] that Mr Gladstone did not chew every mouthful thirty-two times ... though I am not sure that Mr Gladstone himself might not have made some weighty and useful observations on the common and deplorable gap between principle and practice.'
   Presumably, nannies chose this towering figure as an example to their charges, simply because he was there, rather as, a little earlier, Napoleon had been selected as the figure of evil who would punish them if they misbehaved. One wonders whether Queen Victoria might not have been a more inspiring person to evoke – or, perhaps, even to contemplate her doing such a physical thing as eating was considered to be indelicate?

3 What should one call the lavatory in polite society? A young girl was at a luncheon party and half-way through the luncheon she turned to the hostess and said 'Could you tell me where the bathroom is?' And the hostess said, 'Out of the door, second on the right.' So she went along and when she got there she found that that was exactly what it was, a bathroom with a bath and a wash-hand basin. So she decided to lock herself in and use the wash-hand basin for a purpose other than for which it was intended.
   Consequently, her weight pulled the basin off the wall. She crashed to the ground, was knocked out with the basin landing on top of her, and had to be rescued fifteen minutes later by the host who was obliged to break down the door to get in.

Was the hostess deliberately being a bitch by sending the girl to the one place she'd asked for, but which is considered in some circles to be an acceptable term to describe the loo? Told to me by Una-Mary Parker in 1991 for the BBC Radio series *Best Behaviour*. She assured me that it was a true story that she had been told when she was teaching etiquette at a girls' school. The story resurfaced in the *Guardian* as one of its 'Urban Myths' series on 13 March 1993.

4 Prince Charles was making a speech in the open air to an audience of 13,500 schoolchildren in Western Australia. His theme was good manners, and he quoted a homily dating from 1897: 'Swearing is contemptible and foolish ... Ill temper can disorder the mind ...'
   A few seconds into his prepared speech, the blustery wind whipped the top sheet of paper away. 'Oh God, my bloody bit of paper,' he exclaimed.

Reported in *The Times* (9 April 1983).

Marginal comments

1 In a routine letter to the Foreign Office, the British Minister in Athens reported that the monks in some of the monasteries in northern Greece had allegedly violated their monastic vows. Unfortunately, due to a typing error, 'cows' appeared in the letter instead of 'vows'. On receiving this report, Arthur Balfour, then Foreign Secretary, pencilled a note in the margin, 'Appears to be a case for a Papal Bull.'

Contributed by Mr L. Road of Bromley, Kent, to BBC Radio *Quote ... Unquote* (5 June 1979). In Lewis Broad, *Sir Anthony Eden* (1955), the marginal comment is said to have been written by Lord Curzon.

2 A Minister making a speech in the House of Lords inadvertently read out an annotation that a civil servant had scrawled on his brief: 'This is a rotten argument but it should be enough for their Lordships on a hot summer afternoon.'

Told in Lord Home, *The Way the Wind Blows* (1976).

3 A civil servant at the Department of the Environment scribbled in the margin of a document written by a senior, 'P.O.F.' This was short for 'Pompous Old Fool'. However, when the senior noticed the initials and asked what they meant, the junior, with great presence of mind, quickly replied, 'Put On File.'

Told to me by the civil servant in question in the 1980s.

Marriages

4 Miss E. M. A. Savage wrote to Samuel Butler on the subject of Thomas and Jane Carlyle and asked, 'Are you not glad that Mr and Mrs Carlyle were married to one another, and not to other people?' Butler rose splendidly to this question and replied, 'Yes it was very good of God to let Carlyle and Mrs Carlyle marry one another and so make only two people miserable instead of four, besides being very amusing.'

Letter to Miss Savage (21 November 1884). In my very first quotation book I mistakenly attributed to Tennyson this view on the marriage of Thomas and Jane Carlyle. When it was suggested that the marriage had been a mistake – because with anyone but each other they might have been perfectly happy – I said that Tennyson had opined: 'I totally disagree with you. By any other arrangement four people would have been unhappy instead of two.' My inaccurate version was taken up by *The Faber Book of Anecdotes* (1985). However, I now know why I made the misattribution. In *The Autobiography of Margot Asquith* (1936) she recounts a meeting with Tennyson at which they discussed the Carlyles and he came out with this remark.

5 How appropriate it was that for a marriage service the minister had chosen from the Methodist Hymnal the one beginning 'Here I Raise My Ebenezer'.

Told to me by David Ashton of Pontefract, West Yorkshire (1979).

6 At the wedding of an elderly woman who had buried her first two husbands and was now marrying for the third time, a hymn was sung which had these first two lines:

> I know not what awaits me;
> God kindly veils my eyes.

Told to me by Edna Cluley of Camberley, Surrey (1992).

7 Sir Thomas Beecham's sister had a friend called Utica Wells. Out walking together one day, Beecham informed Utica, 'I don't like your Christian name. I'd like to change it.' Replied she, 'You

can't do that, but you can change my surname.' And so they were married – in 1903.

Recounted in Daphne Fielding, *Emerald and Nancy* (1976).

1 Readers of the *Sunday People* were invited to take part in a survey about their sex lives. This response was collected from a 'working class, Sunderland' man: 'They say a woman should be a cook in the kitchen and a whore in bed. Unfortunately, my wife is a whore in the kitchen and a cook in bed.'

Told in Geoffrey Gorer, *Exploring English Character* (1955).

2 At the wedding of two young people, instead of saying, 'Lawfully joined together', the priest said, 'Joyfully loined together'.

Told by Barbara Reeve of Chelmsford (1982).

Mars Bars

3 From 1967 to 1970, Marianne Faithfull was the girlfriend of Rolling Stone Mick Jagger. When he and Keith Richard appeared in court on drugs charges in June 1967, it was revealed that during the police raid a 'young lady' (Faithfull) dressed only in a fur rug had been observed. A rumour swept the country that the police had interrupted an orgy in which Jagger had been licking a Mars Bar inserted in a special part of her anatomy.

As Philip Norman noted in *The Stones* (1984), 'The Mars bar was a detail of such sheer madness as to make the story believed, then and for ever after.' In *Faithfull* (1994), the singer dismissed the myth of the Mars bar event as 'a very effective piece of demonizing that was such a malicious twisting of the facts – a cop's idea of what people do on acid.'

Meanness

4 It seems that the character actor John Le Mesurier may have been as much of a ditherer in real life as he often was on the screen. He once received news that a friend of his was in difficulties and was threatening suicide in some distant place. When asked by a fellow actor what he was doing about it, Le Mesurier replied that he was going to ring up the potential suicide – 'I'll do it after six o'clock.' 'But why wait till then?' the other actor demanded. 'He might have done it by now ...' 'Yes,' replied Le Mesurier, 'but calls are cheaper after six o'clock.'

Told to me by Kenneth Williams, in the early 1970s. A bit rich, this, as the following anecdote will reveal ...

5 The actor Kenneth Williams was mean as hell – except, that is, when he was being quietly and spontaneously generous. I remember him urging me to buy a season ticket for the deck chairs in Regent's Park – 'It'll save you 50p,' he said. He also told (with how much self-awareness, I know not) of going into Burtons, the tailors, to complain about a jacket he had bought there and which was now threadbare at the elbows ('It's a disgrace!', he added). 'How long have you had it?' they asked him. 'It must be ten years now,' he replied.

Personal recollections from the early 1970s.

6 Staying at a seaside boarding house where the portions were rather small, a woman was offered honey in a pot not much bigger than a thimble. Said she, sweetly, to the landlady: 'Ah, I see you keep a bee ...'

Contributed by Reg Capstic of Tebay, Cumbria, to BBC Radio *Quote ... Unquote*

(27 July 1985). Roy Hudd's *Book of Music-Hall, Variety and Showbiz Anecdotes* (1993) has the comment delivered by Jimmy Shand, the Scottish band-leader.

Medical matters

1 During the Second World War, budding actor Kenneth More found himself becalmed in a naval desk job at Liverpool. Wishing to see some action, he was told that the best way of bringing this about was to have his appendix out. A retired Petty Officer told him: 'Have an attack on duty. Suddenly grasp your side. Fall down in agony. Cry out with pain. You were an actor, weren't you? They'll have you off to hospital and whip your appendix out in no time. Then you'll go on sick leave. When you come back, you'll be posted somewhere else – to a ship, most likely.' More did exactly that, had his (extremely healthy) appendix taken out in a naval nursing home at Blundellsands, and in due course was posted as Watch Keeping Officer to a light cruiser, *Aurora*.

This was in May 1942. As recounted in his memoirs *Happy Go Lucky* (1959) and *More Or Less* (1978).

Memory

2 Ethel Barrymore was told that another actress had begun a new marriage by making a full confession of her past to the new husband. 'What honesty! What courage!' somebody said. Commented Ethel, 'What a memory!'

Told by Ronald Fletcher on BBC Radio *Quote ... Unquote* (14 August 1979).

Mercy

3 On one occasion John Mortimer was defending a 'lady singer' on drugs charges and heard himself going a trifle over the top in his final appeal to the Uxbridge magistrates. 'Give her justice,' he pleaded, 'for justice is what she has waited all these long weeks for – but let it be justice tempered with that mercy which is the hallmark of the Uxbridge and Hillingdon District Magistrates' Court ...'

As recounted by Mortimer on BBC Radio *Quote ... Unquote* (5 June 1979). The singer was Julie Felix.

Messages

4 In 1593, the Earl of Shrewsbury had a dispute over a weir that Sir Thomas Stanhope had built across the River Trent. The Countess of Shrewsbury sent a messenger to Sir Thomas. This was the message he carried: 'My lady hath commanded me to say thus much to you. That though you be more wretched than any creature living, and for your wickedness become more ugly in shape than the vilest toad in the world and one to whom none of reputation would vouchsafe to send any message; yet she hath thought good to send thus much to you: that she be contented you should live (and doth noways wish your death) but to this end – that all the plagues and miseries that may befall any man may light upon such a caitiff as you are; and that you should live to see all your friends forsake you and, without your great repentance (which she looketh not for, because your life hath been so bad) you will be damned perpetually in Hell Fire.'

From the introduction to Lodge, *Illustrations of British History*, Vol. 1 (1791).

1 During the American Civil War, Abraham Lincoln became concerned that General George Brinton McClellan was failing in his duties as Commander in Chief of the Army of the Potomac. And so he sent him a message, which went:

My dear McClellan:
If you don't want to use the army,
I should like to borrow it for a while.
Yours respectfully,
A. Lincoln.

In Carl Sandburg, *Abraham Lincoln,
The War Years* (1939).

2 On his seventieth birthday, Sir Thomas Beecham, the conductor, was given a dinner at which various congratulatory messages were read out. These came chiefly from great musicians all over the world. Beecham was heard to murmur: 'What, nothing from Mozart?'

In Patricia Young, *Great Performers* (1964).

3 The shortest naval signal? When the liner *Queen Elizabeth* was passing the battleship *Queen Elizabeth* in mid-Atlantic, the battleship signalled 'SNAP'.

This story is recounted by Ian Fleming in his James Bond novel *On Her Majesty's Secret Service*, Chap. 21 (1963). The commander of the battleship is named as Admiral Somerville.

Military minds

4 The ballet and theatre critic Oleg Kerensky was the grandson of Alexander Kerensky, Russian Prime Minister at the time of the October Revolution. Oleg was turned down for military service in Britain on account of his eyesight, but he loved to tell of the interview he had with a bright-eyed, moustachioed RAF officer during the selection procedure. '"Kerensky", eh? Not an English name?' he asked, perceptively. 'No', replied, Oleg, 'in fact it is Russian.' 'You were born in Russia?' asked the RAF man. 'No,' replied Oleg, 'but my father and grandfather were. They had to leave Russia, you see.' 'Ah,' wondered the RAF man, 'that wouldn't have been for any *political* reasons, by any chance?' 'Yes, in fact it was,' replied Oleg. 'You see, my grandfather was the Prime Minister.' 'Prime Minister, eh!' exclaimed the RAF man, still bright-eyed and beaming. Then after a moment's pause he added, '... Jolly good!'

Recounted by Dick Taverne at Oleg's memorial service, London (14 October 1993).

Mingling

5 A society hostess had jibbed at Fritz Kreisler's fee of $5,000 for a violin recital and added, as though in mitigation, that, after all, he would not be required to mingle with the guests. 'In that case, madam,' Kreisler answered brightly, 'the fee would only be $2,000.'

Told in Bennett A. Cerf, *Try and Stop Me* (1944). Also ascribed to Nellie Melba and other famous musicians and singers. 'Melba was engaged by a socially ambitious woman to sing at a reception. When asked her fee she said it would be five hundred guineas. The woman warned her: "I shall not expect you to mix with my guests." "Oh," said Melba with relief. "Then it will only be two hundred and fifty"' – Martin Boyd, *Day of My Delight* (1965).

It is interesting to note how, since those days, 'mix and mingle' has become a (chiefly American) term used to denote formal socializing as part of a programme, especially when a celebrity allots time to meet the public or press. For example, from *The Washington Post* (19 July 1985): '[President] Reagan will join everybody later at dinner ... Afterward, forgoing the entertainment by opera singer Grace Bumbry and the "mix and mingle" over after-dinner coffee, he will return to the family quarters.' From the same paper (13 July 1986): 'At Buckingham Palace there's the party within the party. Only those bidden to the royal tea tent actually get to mix and mingle with the royals.'

1 Jean Trumpington (graciously) says that she always assumes that nobody knows who she is. One time, she was staying with some people who were having a Christmas party and she didn't know a soul who was there. So she went up to a man and said, 'I'm mingling.' He said: 'What an extraordinary name!'

Told by Baroness Trumpington on BBC Radio *Quote ... Unquote* (15 July 1997).

Misapprehensions

2 Canvassing for her first parliamentary seat in Plymouth, Lady Astor was allotted a senior naval officer as a minder, and together they went round knocking on doors. When they approached one house, the door was opened by a small girl.

'Is your mother in, dear?' Lady Astor demanded, grandly.

'No,' the girl replied, 'but she said if a lady came with a sailor, you was to use the upstairs room and leave half a crown on the table.'

Told to me by an anonymous correspondent in about 1980.

3 When they came to ask permission of King George V to call the new Cunard liner *Queen Victoria*, they prefaced their request with an indication of their intention to honour the very greatest of British queens. 'Oh, well, May will be very pleased,' he replied. And so they had to call it *Queen Mary* instead.

Told in William Manchester, *The Last Lion* (1983).

4 The American humorist Robert Benchley came out of a night club one evening and, tapping a uniformed figure on the shoulder, said, 'Get me a cab.' The uniformed figure turned round furiously and informed him that he was not a doorman but a Rear Admiral. 'O.K.,' said Benchley, 'Get me a battleship.'

Told in the *New Yorker* (5 January 1946).

5 When it was announced that T. S. Eliot had been awarded the Nobel Prize for Literature in 1948, he was making a lecture tour of the United States. A Mid-Western reporter asked him if he had been given the prize for his great work *The Waste Land*. 'No,' replied Eliot, 'I believe I have been given it in recognition of my whole corpus.' Accordingly, the journalist wrote: 'In an interview with our airport correspondent this morning, Mr Eliot revealed that the Swedish Academy had given him the Nobel Prize not for *The Waste Land* but for his poem *My Whole Corpus*.'

Told by Philip French in the *Observer* (17 April 1994). A slightly different version – with the work entitled *The Entire Corpus* – had appeared earlier in David Wallechinsky and Irving Wallace, *The People's Almanac 2* (1978).

6 Comic actor Bernard Bresslaw's thicko remark 'I only arsked' was quite the most popular British TV catch phrase of the late 1950s. It came from Granada's *The Army Game*. A story is told of the day when the team first appreciated that they had a catch phrase on their hands. It is said that Milo Lewis, the director, was rehearsing a

scene in which the lads from Hut 29 realized that though they had been moved to a new camp, they still hadn't escaped the clutches of the sergeant-major (played by William Hartnell). 'Quite a reunion!' the sergeant-major commented. Private 'Popeye' Popplewell (the Bresslaw character) inquired, 'Can we bring girls?' 'No, you can't,' replied the sergeant-major. 'I only arsked!' said Popplewell.

At this point, Milo Lewis is said to have exclaimed enthusiastically, 'We've got a catch phrase!' The others chorused, 'You mean . . .?' 'Yes,' replied Lewis, '"Can we bring girls?"'

Told to me by Barry Cryer in about 1979.

1 Before the painter Francis Bacon became a very rich man, he was taken out to lunch by the composer Lionel Bart, who, at that particular time, was still in the money. During the meal, Bacon was aware (as who wouldn't be?) of Bart's diving under the table every so often and emerging after a while with a white powdery substance adhering to his upper lip.

At the end of the meal, Bacon saw that Bart had left behind a small bag of this white substance and decided to pick it up, reasoning that it was probably worth a good deal of money. Bacon told his friend John Edwards that this would get them into any night club in London. So indeed it did. But the doorman who had accepted the gift and had wafted them into one club soon came hurtling over to their table and ejected them.

The doorman's face, like Bart's, showed traces of white powder but his nostrils also had the appearance of being glued together. It transpired that Bacon had given him the dental fixative

that Bart had been using following an operation.

A version of this story was told by Stan Gebler Davies in the *Independent* (8 May 1993).

2 While he was Foreign Secretary, Michael Stewart was interviewed by William Hardcastle for the radio programme *The World at One*. Curiously, at the end of each answer, he was seen to smile enigmatically over the interviewer's shoulder. When the recording was completed, the producer asked Stewart the reason for his odd behaviour. 'Well, this is for television, isn't it?' he replied.

Told in *Private Eye* at the time.

3 When the troubles in Northern Ireland first blew up in the late 1960s, they were described initially as part of a 'civil rights' dispute. One morning just before the *Today* programme went on the air, Jack de Manio was recording an interview 'down the line' with a pundit in Belfast. As was then the practice, his questions had been written out for him beforehand by the producer. He faithfully read them out, but then spotting the phrase 'civil rights', he obviously wondered, 'What's this, what's this?' and actually asked, 'Is there a large coloured population in Northern Ireland?' Fortunately, it was just before the programme started so the producer was able to lop the question off.

Told to me by the producer involved, and recorded in my diary, 21 January 1969.

4 Rehearsing in Hammersmith one day, Edith Evans heard talk of some people 'who were living in Barnes'. She inquired, 'Couldn't they afford a house?'

Told by Patricia Hodge on BBC Radio *Quote ... Unquote* (10 January 1987).

1 Any Lord Chancellor in procession is an impressive figure. Bewigged and gowned, he is preceded by a mace bearer, a purse bearer (who carries the magnificently embroidered bag that used to hold the Great Seal of England), and is followed by a train bearer. There is a story that once, processing through the corridors of Westminster, Lord Hailsham spotted a friend and called out his Christian name, 'Neil!', whereupon a number of American tourists fell to their knees in reverence.

As told by John Mortimer in *Character Parts* (1986). Earlier in *Pass the Port Again* (1980).

2 When Margaret Thatcher sacked Sir Geoffrey Howe from the position of Foreign Secretary in her government, she planned to replace him with John Major. 'I am very sorry, Geoffrey,' she told him, 'but I've decided to put John Major in the Foreign Office.' 'Oh, that's all right,' replied Howe, 'I'm sure he'll be a great help to me.'

Told in the *Observer* (16 October 1994).

3 Peter Mandelson, the chief architect of New Labour in the British politics of the 1990s and – some would say – the inventor of designer-socialism, was often accused of standing aloof from Labour's working-class roots. At the 1990 Labour Party Conference, Neil Kinnock, the party leader, recalled the first time he had met Mandelson. It was during a by-election in Brecon and Radnor and, in a fish and chip shop, Mandelson had pointed to a dish of mushy peas and asked, 'Can I please have some of that avocado dip?'

In 'Peterborough', the *Daily Telegraph* (5 October 1990). The incident is sometimes said to have taken place in Mr Mandelson's Hartlepool constituency. He is also said 'furiously' to deny the story. Neil Kinnock did indeed make it up.

4 The journalist Auberon Waugh once received an invitation from a Senegalese journal to make a speech – in French – on the subject of breast-feeding. At the time, he had been writing a column in *British Medicine* and campaigning against compulsory breast-feeding in National Health hospitals – so it was not as unlikely as it might seem. He wrote the speech – in French – with considerable difficulty, only to discover, on arrival in Dakar, that his hosts were expecting a speech on press freedom.

Recounted by him in *Will This Do?* (1991).

5 When Maggie Smith was appearing in Peter Shaffer's *Lettice and Lovage* in New York, she soon found that her backstage calm was shattered when a musical show called *Queen Esther and her Gospel Singers* moved into an adjoining theatre. As it happens, both theatres were owned by the Shubert organization, so it was arranged that thick black velour curtains would be hung at the back of each building, insulating Dame Maggie from the noise. The company manager broke the news to her: 'We've hung all the blacks.' 'Well,' replied she, 'I don't think there was any need to go that far.'

Told in Michael Coveney in *Maggie Smith: A Bright Particular Star* (1992).

6 A man was driving along with a cargo of penguins when his lorry broke down. In due course, another lorry driver drew up and asked if he could be of any assistance. 'Yes,' said the first, 'I've

got this load of penguins in the back. Could you take them to the zoo?' 'Certainly,' said the second and took them away.

A few hours later, the first driver managed to get into town and saw the second driver walking in the road with the penguins strung out behind him. 'I thought I told you to take those to the zoo?' 'Sure,' said the other driver, 'I did that. Now I'm taking them to the movies.'

Told by Jessica Mitford in *The Times* (9 October 1993).

1 In New York, a prestige production of Ibsen's *Wild Duck* was under way. During the interval, a plump, well-heeled, middle-aged American couple began to discuss the play. The wife asked, 'Are you enjoying this dear?' The husband said, 'Oh, sure, honey, it's fine.' The wife persisted, 'Now, dear, I don't think you really like it, do you?' The husband gradually came out with, 'Well, honey, to be truthful, I was go-ing by the name and I thought it was going to be a leg show.'

Told to me by Barbara Spry of East Hoathly (1977).

2 Surely it can't be true, but during the immensely long run of the musical *Les Misérables* in London, any number of stoic members of the audience were said to mutter, 'And when is Les going to make an appearance?'

Recalled by Mark Steyn on BBC Radio *Quote ... Unquote* (21 November 1989).

3 The artist Francis Bacon delighted in anonymity – though his face was as recognizable as his painting style – and was happy to mingle with those who hadn't a clue who he was or of his eminence. In a Soho pub, he was offered work doing up an old house by someone who had heard he was a painter.

From the *Independent* (29 April 1992).

4 A man was making a tour of schools in order to find one suitable to send his son to. At last he found one that seemed to have a very special quality. In a classroom he came across a boy writing, very neatly, the words:

> Tomorrow, tomorrow, tomorrow.
> Sorrow, sorrow, sorrow.
> Grief, grief, grief.

When the boy was complimented on his deep insight into meaningful poetry, he replied: 'It's not poetry. It's my spelling corrections.'

Contributed by Richard A. Carsons of Prestbury, Cheshire, to BBC Radio *Quote ... Unquote* (24 May 1994).

Miscalculations

5 After comedian Charlie Drake had been given his first seven-minute slot in a BBC radio show in 1946, he wrote himself 800 fan letters. He took the tube from the Elephant and Castle, getting off at each stop to post several letters to the BBC. He thought that the BBC would be so overwhelmed that they would offer him his own show. A few days later, his mum handed him a fat parcel. It contained all the letters, unopened. It was a rule of the BBC that they never opened personal correspondence.

Reported by Russell Twisk in *Radio Times* (7 December 1967).

Misprints

1 The 1631 'Wicked Bible', through one of the most notable printer's errors in history, advised readers, 'Thou shalt commit adultery'. By missing out the word 'not', Robert Barker and Martin Lucas, the King's printers, incurred the wrath of William Laud, Bishop of London, who informed King Charles I of the error. The printers were summoned to the Star Chamber and fined the huge sum of £3,000.

Recounted in F. A. Mumby, *Publishing and Bookselling* (1930).

2 'Brigadier Bollsover, the bottle-scarred veteran, died at his home last week, aged 85.'

A famous misprint, but did it ever appear in this or any other form? In Nat J. Ferber, *I Found Out* (1939) it is related that once on the *New York Journal American* the term 'battle-scared hero' was hastily corrected in a later edition and came out reading 'bottle-scarred hero'..

3 W. H. Auden, the distinguished poet, had made a visit somewhere. The local newspaper reporting this said that Mr Auden had stepped from the train and been welcomed by 'a small but enthusiastic *crow*'.

Recounted by Nigel Barley on BBC Radio *Quote ... Unquote* (17 June 1997).

4 A very brilliant character actress had turned in an outstanding performance in one of those slippered and dressing-gowned roles. A very eminent critic said afterwards that he was going to give her an absolutely wonderful notice. But when the newspaper appeared, the actress was terribly upset to read, 'The brilliant Miss ***** was magnificently lousy in the role of ******.'

The director of the play took up the cudgels on the actress's behalf and spoke to the critic. 'Oh, I'm terribly sorry,' said he. 'I phoned the notice in, and they left the "b" off!'

Told by Peter Wood on BBC Radio *Quote ... Unquote* (25 May 1993).

5 Armand Hammer, the oil magnate, was being quoted in *The Sunday Times* on the subject of Prince Charles. His opinions came in a telephone interview from Los Angeles, but a missing letter in the printed report added extra point to his views: 'In my opinion,' Hammer said, 'he will make a great king ... He is a young man wise beyond his ears ...'

The cutting is reproduced in my book *Say No More!* (1987).

6 There was a time when the annual Notting Hill Carnival invariably ended in fisticuffs and worse between revellers, each other and the police. One year, the *Daily Star* (a newspaper) was attempting to tell its readers that towards the end of the Late Summer Bank Holiday afternoon, 'scuffles broke out in the crowd.' Unfortunately, it got one letter wrong and instead told its – somewhat bemused readers – that towards the end of the Late Summer Bank Holiday, 'souffles broke out in the crowd'. This conjured up visions of Rastafarians and other attendees, with mixing bowls and whisks, knocking up superb soufflés on the streets of Notting Hill.

Well, that's how I tell it, but the actual text of the (undated, but probably 31 August 1976) article is, in fact: 'Sid Scott made his début at a reggae concert... and stopped a riot. As "souffles" broke out in the huge crowd, he told the fans: "This is nothing to do with you or the police. It's just an unfortunate incident".'

Misreading

1 Laurence Welk, the conductor and accordionist, was a TV performer who had problems with reading the idiot boards on which his script was written up. On one occasion, he announced that he was going to play a selection of music made famous during the years 1939–45 – or, as he put it, 'During the years of World War Aye-Aye'.

Told to me by David Frost in about 1984.

2 As is well-known, the poet Sir John Betjeman was a great rejoicer in un-loved and almost neglected aspects of architecture. One evening Lord David Cecil, the literary critic, was a little surprised to see Betjeman in the audi-ence for one of his lectures, entitled 'On the pleasures of reading'. After-wards, Lord David went up to thank Betjeman for his support in coming. 'Oh no, don't thank me,' came the reply, 'I thought it was the pleasures of Reading.'

Told by Alan Bennett on the audiotape *Poetry in Motion* (1990).

Mistaken identities

3 Nell Gwyn was in Oxford during the 1681 Popish Terror and an angry crowd mistook her carriage for that of King Charles II's French Catholic mistress. To get herself out of this awkward situ-ation, she pleaded: 'Pray, good people, be civil. I am the Protestant whore.'

Told in B. Bevan, *Nell Gwyn* (1969). called in the form, 'Good people, let me pass, I am the Protestant whore.'

4 During the Second World War, Winston Churchill was mightily taken with the quality of press summaries he was receiving from the British Embassy in Washington DC and inquired who had written them. He was told simply 'I. Berlin'. This referred to Isaiah Berlin who was then a well-known Fellow of All Souls and of New College, Oxford, and on his way to becoming a philosopher of great distinction.

Some weeks later, in February 1944, the Prime Minister gave a small lunch party and duly invited Berlin along, having heard that he was in London. All went well until Churchill turned to Berlin and asked him for his views on when the war would end and on the re-election prospects of President Roosevelt. Berlin began a rather ram-bling account of his oddly ill-informed views on these topics, which were rather at odds with the sharp tone of the brilliant reports Churchill had been receiving from Washington.

Only gradually did it dawn on those present, that the 'Mr I. Berlin' they were listening to was the composer and lyricist Mr Irving Berlin who had lately arrived in Britain to entertain American troops.

This delightful mistake is recounted at greater length in 'A Tale of Two Berlins' in John Colville's *Footprints in Time* (1976) – based in turn on Colville's diary entry for 9 February 1944 which is included in Vol. 2 of his *The Fringes of Power: Downing Street Diaries* (1987). The fact that the mistake occurred had earlier been made public by Ian Mackay in *The News Chronicle* (3 January 1946): 'We are told that [Irving Berlin] kept his end up magnificently, even if it involved a bit of swift syncopation now and then.'

In an interview with Jonathan Glover for *New College News* (December 1996), Isaiah Berlin himself confirmed that Churchill had indeed once confused him with Irving Berlin: 'Yes. When I was in America I wrote reports once a week. I was a kind of foreign correspondent, save that my messages went in cipher. I was quite useful, if someone in the

State Department I knew wanted to convey they were displeased at something the Foreign Office had done but didn't want to write to them and get an official reaction. I could be used as a conduit. I got to know journalists, people in the White House, the State Department, they knew what I was doing – it was all quite open.

'I cannot think how Churchill ever heard of me. I imagine Churchill probably said to Eden, "Halifax's despatch was quite interesting." "Halifax!" said Eden, who loathed Halifax, "It's by a hack called Berlin, I'm told". So then, suddenly, in the Spring of 1944, his wife said to him, "Irving Berlin is in London, do be nice to him, because he's made quite a big contribution to one of our charitable funds." He said, "He's in London is he, I want him to come to lunch, there's something I want to ask him about." So Irving was asked to lunch. Winston said, Mr Berlin, what do you think is your most important piece you've done for us lately? He said rather hesitantly, "White Christmas." Churchill looked very cross and said, "Are you American?" Irving, with his heavy Brooklyn accent, said, "Well, yes, of course." Churchill didn't talk to him for a bit, went into a sulk. Then Mrs Churchill said, "You know we ought to be very grateful to Mr Berlin, he's been very generous." "Generous? Don't understand!" he said, and went on sulking. Then he turned to him again and asked, "Do you think Roosevelt will be re-elected this year?" "Well," said Berlin, in the past I've voted for him, but this year I'm not so sure." Finally, despairing, Churchill said, "When do you think the European war is going to end?" He said, "Prime Minister, I'll never forget this moment. When I go back to my own country, and tell my children, and my children's children, that in the Spring of 1944 the Prime Minister of Great Britain asked me when the war would end".'

1 There were two people in show business called Kenneth Horne and they were and still are frequently thought to have been the same person. During the Second World War, even more confusingly, they were both in the RAF and both wing commanders (can you believe this?) This led to a major, life-changing development for one of them, at least. Marjorie Thomas had met Horne (the playwright) at some social function and attempted to contact him by telephone at the Air Ministry. She was put through to Horne (the entertainer).

'Wing Commander Horne,' replied he.

'Oh, hallo, is that Kenneth Horne?' asked she.

'It is.'

'I hope you will remember me. We met at a party two weeks ago. Now I'm giving a little party and would love you to come.'

Horne (the entertainer), unable to resist, duly turned up and was immediately not recognized by Marjorie Thomas as the man she had met previously (i.e. Horne the playwright). He took her out to dinner and she eventually became his third wife.

Told to me (1984) by Judy Farrar, daughter of Horne (the playwright). Also described by Norman Hackforth in *Solo for Horne* (1976).

2 Groucho Marx was pottering in his yard one day when a nosey passer-by mistook him for the gardener. 'How much do they pay you?' she asked. 'Oh, I don't get paid in dollars,' replied Groucho. 'The lady of the house just lets me sleep with her.'

Told in Arthur Marx, *Son of Groucho* (1973).

3 In the long history of his radio programme *Desert Island Discs*, Roy Plomley's worst hour came when he discovered over lunch before a recording that the Alistair Maclean he was

talking to was not, as he had expected, Alistair Maclean, the world-famous author. It was Alistair Maclean, the European director of tourism for Ontario, who had been invited by mistake. Plomley ploughed on with the recording, but it was never broadcast.

The intended Maclean never made it on to the programme either. Details from the *Observer* Magazine (19 January 1992).

1 The switching of Lord Hill from the chairmanship of the Independent Television Authority (as commercial TV's regulatory body was then called) to that of the BBC in 1967 was a politically-motivated act by the then Prime Minister, Harold Wilson, who wanted Hill to set the BBC's house in order. The news was sprung upon the BBC's Acting Chairman, Robert Lusty, by the Postmaster-General, Edward Short. He was told that the new BBC Chairman was to be Charles *Smith*. Short's private secretary quickly corrected the name to Charles Hill.

Recounted by Leonard Miall in the *Independent* (24 July 1991).

2 A pregnant girl was seen to be in distress, but when the observer came close, it became clear that the girl was laughing rather than crying. The girl explained she had been on the way to the clinic and had been told to take a urine sample. The only bottle she had available was a whisky bottle and she put it in her shopping basket. On the way to the clinic she popped into a supermarket to do some shopping. When she came out, she found someone had pinched it.

Told to me by Nora Glynne-Jones. From my diary for 13 April 1968.

3 In 1976, the Queen decided to reward the man who for many years had produced Her Majesty's Christmas broadcasts. 'We must give a knighthood to that nice Mr Attenborough,' she told one of her flunkeys. Accordingly, in the next Honours List there duly appeared a knighthood for ... David's brother, Richard, the actor.

This is a story 'which is sometimes told at Buckingham Palace', according to 'The Weasel' in the *Independent* Magazine (24 July 1993). True or not, there is a telling error of detail in this version: David Attenborough did not start producing the Christmas broadcasts until later than the 1976 date would signify. He was knighted – at last – in 1985.

A similar tale of confusion – at Downing Street rather than Buckingham Palace – is sometimes told concerning the award of honours to Harry H. Corbett, the actor in *Steptoe and Son*, and Harry Corbett of 'Sooty' glove-puppet fame. It is suggested that the wrong one was given the award. However, as they were both awarded the OBE in the *same* New Year's Honours List in 1976, this is clearly not the case.

That this is not a recent problem is shown by the story of a supplier of fishing tackle called Thomas Hardy who was reputedly awarded the Order of Merit in advance of the distinguished novelist who duly received his OM in 1910.

4 Invited to open a garden fete, broadcaster Russell Harty took along as his companion the actress Madge Hindle who was appearing at the time in the TV soap *Coronation Street*. Harty became aware of people backing away from them after the vicar who was introducing Harty happened to say, 'We're very pleased to see that he's brought along with him the famous Myra Hindley ...'

Told by Russell Harty in the 1980s. Myra Hindley was one of the Moors Murderers.

1 At the end of an interview on BBC TV *Nationwide*, Liza Minelli was no doubt slightly put out when Hugh Scully, the interviewer, said, 'Thank you, Judy Garland.' But she rallied, and said, with aplomb: 'I'll tell Liza.'

Told by Ludovic Kennedy on BBC Radio *Quote ... Unquote* (3 September 1983).

Mistresses

2 King Henri IV of France was reproved by his confessor for his marital infidelities, so he ordered the priest to be fed on nothing but partridge. When the priest complained that it was *'toujours perdrix* [always partridge]', the King replied it was just the same if you had only one mistress.

Hence, the expression (in Latin, *semper perdrix*), meaning 'too much of a good thing'.

3 When King George II's wife Caroline was dying she expressed the wish to him that he would marry again. 'No,' he repied, 'I shall have mistresses [*Non, j'aurai des maîtresses*].' Said she: 'That'll be no obstacle [*Ah, mon Dieu! Cela n'empêche pas*].'

Recorded by Lord Hervey in 1737 and published in his *Memoirs of George the Second*, Vol. 2 (1848).

4 At a levee, back in the eighteenth century, a gentleman arrived escorting a lady (or woman) who, amazingly enough, had also served as mistress to both his father and grandfather. 'There's nothing new under the sun,' remarked another guest. 'Nor under the grandson,' added a third.

Told in Daniel Mannix, *The Hell-Fire Club* (1978).

5 When the future King Edward VII said to his mistress, the actress Lillie Langtry, 'I've spent enough on you to buy a battleship', she replied, 'And you've spent enough in me to float one.'

Told in Irving Wallace *et al, Intimate Sex Lives of Famous People* (1981).

6 King Leopold II of Belgium, financially crooked, sexually depraved, learnt that he must undergo a serious operation (which did indeed prove fatal). But he had a sense of humour, so sent for his principal mistress (a 25-year-old ex-prostitute whom he had made a baroness) and married her. When the ceremony was over, he said to his best man – the Prime Minister – 'Let me introduce you to my widow.'

Told to me by Margaret B. of Brussels (1979). Leopold II (1835–1909) reigned from 1865.

7 The parish priest of a village near one of King Leopold's country villas was sent by the outraged local population to remonstrate with him about his goings-on. 'Sir,' the unfortunate priest stammered, 'rumour has it that Your Majesty engages in the sin of fornication.' 'Well, well, well,' said the King, 'haven't people got vulgar minds? I was told the same story about you the other day, but I refused to believe it ...'

From the same source.

mots justes

8 Did you hear of the learned butler who, as he was falling downstairs, replied to his master's inquiry as to what was going on: "Tis I, sir, rolling rapidly.'

A learned butler, indeed, to pun in such circumstances – he was alluding to Thomas Campbell's 'Hohenlinden' (1802):

On Linden, when the sun was low,
All bloodless lay the untrodden snow,
And dark as winter was the flow
Of Iser, rolling rapidly.

W. W. Keen, the American surgeon (1837–
1932), included the anecdote in his memoirs
(1915–17). Curiously, in 1877, a writer
to the New York *World* referred to a lost letter
from John Keats to his brother George in
which Keats reported that he had heard
Charles Lamb saying the very same thing to
Thomas Campbell, having himself fallen
downstairs (*Notes and Queries*, Vol. 206).
The writer himself did not believe in the
existence of this letter, however.

1   Noël Coward, Beverly Nichols and
Godfrey Winn were all invited to
join Somerset Maugham at the Villa
Mauresque in Cap Ferrat in order
to have lunch with Edna St Vincent
Millay. As she swept on to the terrace
overlooking the blue Mediterranean,
the playwright and poet exclaimed:
'Oh, Mr Maugham, but this is
fairyland!'

Told in Ted Morgan, *Maugham* (1980).
S. N. Behrman in *Tribulations and Laughter*
(1972) has a version where the line up is
Coward, Cecil Beaton and Gerald Haxton.

2   At Lord's, a South African googly
bowler named 'Tufty' Mann was tying
a Middlesex tail-end batsman named
George Mann into such knots that the
crowd was reduced to laughter. When
it occurred for the fourth time in a
single over, John Arlott, the radio commentator, observed, 'So what we are
watching here is a clear case of Mann's
inhumanity to Mann.'

Reported in the *Daily Mail* (3 September
1980). The phrase 'Man's inhumanity to man'
appears in a poem by Robert Burns called
'Man was made to mourn', though the
thought that lies behind it is, of course, a
very old one.

Mothers-in-law

3   'Now that many years have passed since
my delightful mother-in-law was called
to that large mother-in-laws' meeting
in the sky, I am often still to be found
smiling at her remarks. She had a
wonderful habit of getting expressions
just slightly wrong. "Making money
while the hay shines" was typical. And
I remember once in church hearing her
intoning, with very serious face, the
words of the 23rd Psalm – "He maketh
me to lie down in green waters".'

Told to me by Stanley Menzies of Church
Stretton (1992). Quite when the mother-in-
law came to be regarded as a target for humorous remarks is impossible to tell, but Jerome
K. Jerome in *Three Men In a Boat* (1889) has
this in Chapter 3: 'Everything has its draw-
backs, as the man said when his mother-in-
law died, and they came down upon him for
the funeral expenses.' Irvin S. Cobb in the
foreword to *A Laugh a Day Keeps the Doctor
Away* (1923), while asserting that there was
only one mother-in-law joke in his collection,
stated: 'The mother-in-law joke could not
have originated with Adam, because Adam
had no mother-in-law, but I have not the
slightest doubt that Cain began using it
shortly after his marriage.'

Motivation

4   It is said that Talleyrand, on hearing
of the death of the Turkish ambassador
to France, wondered: 'What does he
mean by that?'

Alluded to in Ben Pimlott, *Harold Wilson*,
Chap. 29 (1992). However, another version
is that it was said rather about Talleyrand
and by King Louis Philippe in the form,
'Died, has he? Now I wonder what he
meant by that?'

5   When an actor, no doubt under the
influence of The Method, was agonizing over his 'motivation' and asked the

director, George Abbott, 'Just why do I cross the stage? Why, why?', Abbott told him: 'To pick up your pay check'.

Retold by Mark Steyn on BBC Radio *Quote ... Unquote* (11 December 1990). *The Faber Book of Anecdotes* (1985) ascribes it to Noël Coward, without offering a source. George Abbott (1887–1995), playwright, producer and director, was still at work on Broadway in his hundredth year.

1   It became public knowledge when Terry Johnson wrote his play *Cleo, Camping, Emmanuelle and Dick* (1998), that Sid James, the actor, had not been averse to getting his leg over with any passing actress during the making of the *Carry On* films. The one he had no success with, for various reasons, was Barbara Windsor. But even she finally caved in. 'I always managed to get out of it until we were in a revue and got thrown together on tour ... We came back to London [and] they asked the artists to stay in a hotel but I said no ... [Then] the publicity man comes and says, "Please, Barbara, stay. Sid's giving us shit. You have all these geezers on the go, it isn't going to hurt you. For Gawd's sake put him out of his misery." And I thought, "I like this, man. I've slept with plenty of men I don't like, so why shouldn't I sleep with him?" And that's why I went to bed with him.'

Told in the *Observer* (20 September 1998). Windsor added: 'I never mentioned it to anyone, but when I read the play, Terry had written a speech which says exactly that.'

Mottoes

2   The motto of the Order of the Garter, founded by King Edward III in about 1348, is *Honi Soit Qui Mal Y Pense*, which may be translated as, 'Evil be to

him who evil thinks.' It is traditionally said to derive from what King Edward commanded as he adjusted the Countess of Salisbury's garter when it had fallen down. Accordingly, the version given by Sellar and Yeatman in their comic history *1066 and All That* (1930) is not so wide of the mark: 'Edward III had very good manners. One day at a royal dance he noticed some men-about-court mocking a lady whose garter had come off, whereupon to put her at her ease he stopped the dance and made the memorable epitaph: "*Honi soie qui mal y pense*" ("Honey, your silk stocking's hanging down").'

The tale was current by the reign of Henry VIII and was included in Polydore Vergil's *Anglicae Historiae* (1534–55). Byron is also said to have re-translated the motto as, 'On his walk he madly puns.'

3   The favourite text of Sir James Murray was a saying of Charles Kingsley's, which hung – rather curiously – in his bedroom: 'Have thy tools ready, God will find thee work.'

Told by K. M. Elizabeth Murray in *Caught in the Web of Words* (1977). Murray (1837–1915), Scottish philologist and lexicographer, was founding editor of *The Oxford English Dictionary*. This reminds me of the overheard remark (included in my book *Eavesdroppings*, 1981): 'And, my dear, there was nothing in that room but a great double bed. And there was a framed text on the wall above it which said, "He is coming".'

Murder

4   In the days of King Idris of Libya, Elwyn Jones, the barrister, went out to Tripoli in Libya to defend a man on some charge. As soon as he arrived, the trial was postponed for a week. Elwyn Jones was worried about this because he was due to defend in a murder trial at

Cardiff Assizes the following week and he wasn't sure of the date. So he cabled his clerk, 'Please send me date of Cardiff murder trial.' The next morning, the British Ambassador in Tripoli rang up Elwyn Jones and said, 'What on earth is going on? A cable addressed to you has been opened by Security, reading: "Cable received. Murder fixed for Wednesday".'

Told by him on BBC Radio *Quote...
Unquote* (18 July 1987).

Museums

1 The comedian Wee Georgie Wood, as his name suggests, was of boyish proportions. He lived to a ripe old age. On one occasion, towards the end of his life, he hailed a taxi and said to the driver, 'Take me to the British Museum.' The driver looked alarmed at this and said, 'You're taking a bloody chance, aren't you?'

Told by Peter Jones on BBC Radio *Quote ... Unquote* (5 January 1982). Joe Ging, who was curator of the National Music Hall Museum in Sunderland told me in a letter (8 May 1984) that Wood performed his museum's opening ceremony in July 1975. During his speech, Wood said, 'I was picked up at the Post House Hotel, Washington, by a taxi-driver from Sunderland. "Where are you going to, Mr Wood?" asked the taxi-driver. "I'm going to open a museum," I replied, proudly. To which he replied, "You're taking a bloody chance, aren't you?"' Joe Ging concedes that this was too good a story for Wood only to have used on one occasion.

Musical appreciation

2 At one of the three London performances of Handel's *Messiah* in 1743, the entire audience rose to its feet as the Hallelujah Chorus began and remained standing to the end – a tradition still largely maintained by audiences in Britain. King George II was present and the cue for the move is often attributed to him.

Told in *The Oxford Dictionary of Music*, ed. Michael Kennedy (1985). Some versions state that this occurred at the first London performance on 23 March 1743. It was reported by James Beattie in a letter to the Rev. Dr Laing (1780).

Musical criticism

3 Having listened to a performance of an opera by a somewhat lesser composer, Beethoven turned to him and said: 'I like your opera – I think I will set it to music.'

Contributed to BBC Radio *Quote ... Unquote* (1984) by Mrs Kathleen Newell of Chigwell, but otherwise unverified.

4 A young composer asked Brahms if he might play him a funeral march he had composed in memory of Beethoven. Brahms replied that he might and listened intently to the young man's earnest performance. When he had finished, the young man sought Brahms's opinion. 'I will tell you,' said the great man candidly, 'I would much prefer it if you were dead and Beethoven had written the funeral march.'

A version is told in André Previn, *Music Face to Face* (1971). Some hold that Brahms had not that kind of wit to say such a thing and that the put down was administered by Rossini to someone who had written a funeral march for Meyerbeer.

5 Paderewski, the Polish pianist and politician, took out an insurance policy with Mutual Life Insurance of New York in 1921 when he was 61 years old. He was considered a good risk. The insurance agent who arranged the

policy wrote: 'I might mention that when he goes to the movies, he pays them $20 not to play the organ while he's there.

From the records of Mutual Life, quoted in the *Independent* (8 February 1994).

1 When André Previn was a very young pianist and a whizz-kid in Hollywood, there was a suggestion that he should give a performance of the Gershwin Piano Concerto with the Cleveland Symphony Orchestra conducted by the formidable Hungarian exile, George Szell. But Szell was not so sure. So Previn flew to Cleveland to convince him and was ushered into Szell's apartment. The conductor glowered at him across the table and said, 'Mr Previn would you be so kind as to play the solo part for me.' André Previn replied, 'Certainly ... but where is the piano?' Szell said, 'There is no need for the piano – just play it here on the top of the table.' So Previn set to and fingered the entire solo part of the Gershwin piano concerto on the table while Szell watched fascinated. At the end there was a pause, and Szell said: 'No, no, very sorry, long journey, waste of time, very sad, no.' André Previn paused for a moment and then said, 'I can only tell you it sounds a lot better on my table at home.'

Told by Peter Wood on BBC Radio *Quote ... Unquote* (31 March 1992).

2 In 1950, when President Truman's daughter Margaret gave a singing recital in Washington she received a bad notice from critic Paul Hume writing in *The Washington Post*. 'She is flat a good deal of the time,' he said, 'she cannot sing with anything approaching professional finish ... [and] she

communicates almost nothing of the music she presents.'

The President immediately fired off a handwritten note to Hume on White House stationery (dated 6 December 1950): 'I have just read your lousy review buried in the back pages. You sound like a frustrated old man who never made a success, an eight-ulcer man on a four-ulcer job and all four ulcers working. Westbrook Pegler, a guttersnipe, is a gentleman compared to you. You can take that as more of an insult than a reflection on your ancestry ... Some day I hope to meet you. When that happens, you'll need a new nose, a lot of beef-steak for black eyes, and perhaps a supporter below.'

Texts of the letter vary. A version was published in *Time* Magazine (18 December 1950). Subsequently, Truman asserted that he had really told Hume he would 'kick his balls in' but the published versions of the letter do not bear this out. Truman also said he worked on the assumption that 'every man in the United States that's got a daughter will be on my side' – and he was probably right.

3 Appearing on BBC Radio *Quote ... Unquote* in 1977, Kenneth Williams came up with a rather good showbiz story. He quoted what Orson Welles had reputedly said about the singing of Donny Osmond (then a popular young star): 'You have Van Gogh's ear for music.' In fact, Orson Welles did not say it, nor was it about Donny Osmond, but the reasons why the line had been reascribed and redirected are instructive. It was Billy Wilder, the film director, who made the original remark. He has a notably waspish wit but is, perhaps, not such a household name as Orson Welles. He lacks, too, Welles's

Falstaffian stature and his, largely un-
earned, reputation in the public mind
for having said witty things. And
Wilder said it about *Cliff* Osmond, an
American comedy actor who had
appeared in the film director's *Kiss Me
Stupid, The Fortune Cookie* and *The
Front Page*, but now was being considered for a singing role. As far as one
knows, he is not related to Donny
Osmond but, apparently, he had to be
replaced in the anecdote because he
lacked star status.

The correct attribution is given in Leslie
Halliwell, *The Filmgoer's Book of Quotes*
(1973). Tom Stoppard included something
very similar in *The Real Inspector Hound*
(1968): 'An uncanny ear that might [have]
belonged to a Van Gogh.'

Musicianship

1 Albert Einstein was a keen amateur
violinist. One day he was practising
sonatas at home with the pianist
Arthur Rubinstein. Someone overheard Rubinstein pointing out a late
entry on Einstein's part. 'Albert,'
he was saying, 'can't you count?'

The earliest version of this story I have
encountered is in Oscar Levant, *The
Unimportance of Being Oscar* (1968). He
places it in Princeton, New Jersey, when
Einstein was lecturing there and playing his violin in string quartets.

2 People were already telling stories about
Sir Thomas Beecham way back in the
1920s. On one ocasion, at a rehearsal, a
trombonist, who was a German, played
a single note, during a pause of the
brass instruments. Beecham, who was
conducting, tapped his desk with his
baton, and glared at the offender.
'What's that?' he growled. 'It's in de
music,' replied the trombonist. 'Let me

see,' said Beecham. As the trombonist
passed the music to his chief, he made
a strange discovery. 'Vy!' he exclaimed,
in astonishment, 'it vas a fly!' Then
he added triumphantly, 'But I blayed
him!'

As recounted in 'Stage Anecdotes' (edited by
Laddie Cliff) in *The Magazine Programme*
(24 October 1927).

3 When a famous German baritone
altered a phrase in an aria in a Bach
cantata, he justified it to the conductor,
Otto Klemperer, by claiming that Bach
had come to him in a dream and told
him he wanted the phrase changed.
The following day Klemperer turned
to the baritone and said, 'Last night
I, too, had a visit from Bach in a dream.
I told him what you said and he told
me he doesn't know you.'

Told by John Rusby-Smith of Lower
Soudley, Gloucestershire, and formerly of
the BBC (April 1998).

4 Wanda Landowska, the Polish-born
harpsichordist, once had a disagreement
with a fellow musician. She ended up
exclaiming, 'Oh, well, you play Bach
your way. I'll play him his.'

Told in Harold C. Schonberg, *The Great
Pianists* (1963).

5 Jazz trumpeter Humphrey Lyttelton's
father, George, was a master at Eton
and his later correspondence with
a distinguished former pupil, Rupert
Hart-Davis, was published in several
volumes (from 1978 onwards). In
that work, George Lyttelton recalled
receiving a report on Humphrey's
progress in the world from an examination paper that he had been marking.
The subject of the paper was 'Jazz' and
the essayist had stated: 'Humphrey

Littleton [*sic*] is the leading English trumpeter, and – like many others – plays best when he is drunk.'

From a letter dated 18 August 1960 in *The Lyttelton Hart-Davis Letters* (Vol.5, 1983).

1 Sir Adrian Boult was rehearsing an amateur orchestra before an evening concert which he had agreed to conduct. When he asked for one of the set pieces and began to conduct it, some of the members, perhaps over-awed by his presence, began to play a different one. After stopping them, he said quietly, 'I think we have time to rehearse both pieces separately.'

Told to me by Joan Hewitt of Winscombe, Avon (1992) whose mother was in the orchestra.

N

Nakedness

1 When asked if she had had anything on when being photographed for a calendar, Marilyn Monroe replied, 'Well, I had the radio on.'

Told in *Time* Magazine (11 August 1952). The incident may have occurred in 1947.

2 Just as David Niven was about to introduce Elizabeth Taylor at the Academy Awards ceremony in April 1974, a streaker appeared. Henry Mancini and the orchestra played 'Sunny Side Up' as the streaker was led off by security guards. Niven ad-libbed: 'Just think, the only laugh that man will probably ever get is for stripping and showing off his shortcomings.'

Told in F. L. Worth, *Complete Unabridged Super Trivia Encyclopedia* (1979). The streaker was Robert Opal who later reappeared in the news when he was found murdered in his San Francisco sex shop.

Name-calling

3 In 1947, Eva Perón visited Europe but was not received everywhere as she thought appropriate for the powerful wife of the ruler of Argentina. She failed to get an invitation to tea at Buckingham Palace and the papal honour she hoped for in Rome. And in northern Italy she complained to her host that a voice in the crowd had called her a 'whore'. He replied, 'Quite so. But I have not been on a ship for fifteen years and they still call me admiral.'

Cited in the article 'The Power Behind the Glory', *Penthouse* (UK)(August 1977). Tim Rice managed to squeeze the remark, just about, into his lyrics for *Evita*. It is said to have appeared first in an anecdotal notebook kept by Adlai Stevenson, where the exchange takes place, rather, with a general in Barcelona.

Name-dropping

4 A colleague remonstrated with William Clark, a one-time diplomatic correspondent and press secretary to Anthony Eden when Prime Minister: 'You are the most incorrigible namedropper I have ever met.' To which Clark replied, 'Funny you should say that, old boy. The Queen Mother was saying the same thing only last week.'

Recalled in the *Observer* (18 June 1989) and frequently put in the mouths of other folk. For example, from the *Daily Telegraph* (21 June 1979): 'Towards the end of his speech at the Museum of the Year Award lunch, Norman St John Stevas, Arts Minister, is reliably reported as saying: "But I mustn't go on singling out names … One must not be a name-dropper, as Her Majesty remarked to me yesterday".'

Names

1 He (who has tried to catch his companion's name, and wishes to find it out indirectly): 'BY THE WAY, HOW DO YOU *SPELL* YOUR NAME?' She: 'J-O-N-E-S'.

This is the caption to a cartoon in *Punch* (Vol. 122, 8 January 1902) and is presumably the forerunner of all those embarrassment anecdotes concerning name forgetting and non-recognition.

2 The rule that one should never poke fun at people's names was evidently not one adhered to by F. E. Smith (later Lord Birkenhead). He found himself seated at dinner next to a woman who introduced herself as 'Mrs Porter-Porter, with a hyphen'. Smith quickly replied that he was 'Mr Whisky-Whisky, with a syphon'.

Told in John Campbell, *F. E. Smith, First Earl of Birkenhead* (1983).

3 At Christmas 1944, Winston Churchill paid a visit to Athens. This resulted in the appointment of Archbishop Damaskinos as Regent of Greece and General Plastiras as Prime Minister. Of the latter, Churchill commented: 'Well, I hope he doesn't have feet of clay, too.'

Told in Leon Harris, *The Fine Art of Political Wit* (1966). In *Geoffrey Madan's Notebooks* (1981 – but Madan died in 1947), Churchill's remark is quoted as: 'A bewhiskered ecclesiastic, and a certain General Plastiras. I hope his feet are not of clay.'

4 During a debate in the House of Commons, a Labour MP called Paling interrupted Winston Churchill during a speech and called him a 'dirty dog'. Churchill looked over his glasses at him and said, 'And you know what dirty dogs to palings …'

Told by Jimmy Reid on *Quote … Unquote* (26 May 1982). If this is a true story, then it must have involved the Rt Hon. Wilfred Paling (1883–1971), a former colliery checkweighman who became a Labour MP and Postmaster-General (1947–50).

5 During rehearsals one day, Sir Thomas Beecham noticed a new face among the woodwinds. 'Er, Mr ——?' he began.
   'Ball,' came the reply.
   'I beg your pardon?'
   'Ball, Sir Thomas.'
   'Ball? Ah, Ball. Very singular.'

Told in Neville Cardus, *Sir Thomas Beecham* (1961).

6 Alfredo Campoli, the violinist, was known professsionally as, simply, 'Campoli'. The reason for this, as he used to say himself, was that if announced along the lines of, 'Alfredo Campoli is now going to play …', he thought people tended to hear, 'I'm afraid old Campoli is now going to play …'

An addition from Monica Parkhurst to the *Independent*'s obituary (30 March 1991).

7 The Deputy Lord Mayor of Dublin at one time was called Lorcan Burke and he had a slight vocal impediment. On the steps of the Mansion House, he was greeting Sir John Barbirolli and the Hallé Orchestra on their very first visit to the fair city. 'Now I should like to extend a hearty Irish greeting,' declared Burke, 'a *Céad Míle Fáilte*, to our very welcome guests, Sir John Barolli and his band.'

Told by Terry Wogan on BBC Radio *Quote ... Unquote* (4 June 1996). I think I have heard this told about some North Country English mayor who welcomed, rather, 'Sir John Barolli and his Hallé band'.

1 Two members of the audience of Rex Harrison's greatest success, *My Fair Lady*, were coming out of the Theatre Royal, Drury Lane, after the show. One remarked, 'Of course, Rex Harrison isn't his real name, you know.' The other person replied: 'Rex Harrison isn't whose real name?'

Told by Benny Green on BBC Radio *Quote ... Unquote* (30 October 1989). In fact, Rex Harrison was his real name. I have also heard the story told involving Laurence Olivier – but that was his own name, too. *Roy Hudd's Book of Music-Hall, Variety and Showbiz Anecdotes* (1993) has it about Jess Conrad.

2 When the film *Brighton Rock* which featured the young Richard Attenborough in a key role was being launched in America, the New York distributor wired: 'ATTENBOROUGH'S NAME TOO BIG FOR BANNERS'. The producers of the film – the Boulting Brothers – wired back: 'GET BIGGER BANNERS'.

Reported in the *Sunday Telegraph* (22 August 1965).

3 The film actress Diana Dors was born – and this will come as a mighty revelation to all those who don't know it – Diana Fluck. Her father was the railway station master, or some such, in a tiny Somerset village. Anyway, when fame and fortune descended upon her in the 1950s, the well-known star was invited back to open the village fete.

The vicar – who had to introduce her – was very conscious of the fact that he would have to mention the name by which she was still known to all in the village, and how serious it would be if by any chance he mispronounced 'Fluck'.

He worried about it, right up to the moment when he had to speak. He concluded his introduction with the words: 'And now here she is, the woman the whole world knows as "Diana Dors", but whom we will always remember as our own Diana Clunt ...'

A tale first heard by me in the late 1960s, I should think.

4 Actor Michael Caine was born in 1933 with the name Maurice Micklewhite. He was influenced in his choice of stage name by a film he'd seen called *The Caine Mutiny*.

Re-told in Elaine Galagher *et al, Candidly Caine* (1990).

5 When the stage show *Beyond the Fringe* was all the rage in the early 1960s, Dudley Moore, one of the cast, collapsed with exhaustion and had to take three weeks' holiday. He was about to fly to Italy when he bumped into Sir John Gielgud, who asked him where he was headed. When Positano was mentioned, Sir John immediately said Moore should look up his friends Rex Harrison and Lilli Palmer, and scribbled a letter of introduction. Once on board the plane, Dudley Moore looked in the letter and read: 'Darling Lilli, This will introduce you to the brilliant young pianist from Beyond the Fringe – Stanley Moon ...'

Recounted in Harry Thompson, *Peter Cook* (1997). Subsequently, Cook often referred to Moore as 'Stanley Moon', and named a character after him in the film *Bedazzled*.

1 When the American actor Chuck Connors introduced himself to Noël Coward, he said, 'I am Chuck Connors.' Coward replied, 'Of course you are, dear boy, of course you are.'

Told by Spike Milligan on BBC Radio *Quote... Unquote* (22 January 1979), though using the name 'John Wayne'. Connors is the more likely original, however.

2 When Coward was making the film *Bunny Lake Is Missing* in 1965 he encountered the American actor Keir Dullea, who said, 'Oh, Mr Coward, I am so proud to have you in my film. I am Keir Dullea.' And Coward said, 'Keir Dullea, gone tomorrow.'

Told by Sheridan Morley on BBC Radio *Quote... Unquote* (7 November 1989).

3 Many years ago, composer Michael Tippett used the fee paid to him by a television company for being interviewed by Bernard Levin to buy a washing machine. According to Levin, Tippett felt it was only right to name the device after the benefactor who was, at least, indirectly responsible for his being able to afford it. 'Hence, the odd but pleasing fact – pleasing to me, anyway – that there is washing machine in Wiltshire called Bernard Levin.'

In Levin's *Conducted Tour* (1981).

4 Few authors have been as assiduous in promoting their books as the Norwegian explorer Thor Heyerdahl. On a visit to London in the 1970s, he had a packed day of interviews with newspapers and magazines, radio and television. Towards the end of it he was due to leave the studios of Thames Television in the Euston Road and go on to do a live radio interview at the BBC's Broadcasting House. A taxi was laid on to take 'Thor Heyerdahl' the short journey, and as soon as the TV programme was over he went straight out to the taxi waiting outside.

'Sorry, guv, don't think it's for you, this one,' said the driver.

Heyerdahl, puzzled, went back to the reception, where they assured him that it must be the one. So he went back to the cab and asked the driver, 'They say you're the one to take me to the BBC.'

'Don't think so, guv. I'm waiting for four airedales.'

Story current in the late 1970s.

5 The cockney personality and broadcaster Monty Modlyn was once interviewing a doubly titled peer for TV. It was Lord De L'Isle and Dudley, the owner of Penshurst Place in Kent. Throughout the interview, Modlyn addressed him as 'Lord De L'Isle ... and Dudley' – rather as though 'Dudley' was the butler and standing just behind him ...

This must have been for Thames TV's *Today* programme in the early 1970s.

6 Under the name of 'Maureen Dufferin and Ava', the Marchioness ordered a taxi to pick her up from her home (round the back of Harrods, I believe) and take her to an important event. When the taxi arrived, the driver duly asked for 'Maureen Dufferin and Ava'. She came down and got in, but the driver – despite much urging from the Marchioness – declined to set off. Explained he: 'I'm waiting for Ava ...'

Source untraced, but told in my book *Say No More!* (1987). Marchioness of Dufferin and Ava (1907–98), English aristocrat (née Maureen Guinness), was said to be the original of 'Maudie Littlehampton' in Osbert Lancaster's cartoons.

1   The belief, firmly held by some, that the name of Sir Jack Cohen's 'Tesco' supermarkets is an acronym standing for 'The Express Supermarket Company' is incorrect. In the early days, the tea for the stores was provided by a Mr T. E. Stockwell. 'Tesco' derives from this man's initials coupled with the 'co' of 'Cohen'.

Source: Adrian Room, *Dictionary of Trade Name Origins* (1982). Cleverer wordplay on the name 'Cohen' occurs in the armorial bearings of Tesco Stores (Holdings) Ltd – a coat of arms granted in 1979. The English translation of the motto is 'May the traders be convivial together.' The Latin is: '*Mercatores Coenascent.*'

2   In the US, Alastair Cooke was known principally as the host of TV's *Masterpiece Theater*, in which he introduced (and explained) classic, quality (mostly British) TV productions. A reader wrote to *The New York Times* saying she had grown up admiring Cooke's calm erudition, but had had trouble as a small child sitting with her parents and watching *Masterpiece Theater* when the announcer said the show would be introduced by 'Alice the cook'.

A story relayed to me by Stephan Chodorov (1993).

3   The Cleese family was originally Cheese until the father of John Cleese (the actor), presumably tired of ridicule, changed it. But the new name proved difficult to convey to people over the telephone. In the 1980s, John Cleese claimed that when booking tables at restaurants he would adapt his name to suit the nationality of the res-taurant. Hence, if he was booking a table in an Italian restaurant he would say he was 'Signor Formaggio' – which is the Italian for ... Mr Cheese.

Cleese himself told me the first bit in 1973.

4   Did you hear the story about the man who put an advertisement in the paper, having lost his dog? The dog apparently had every disadvantage a beast could possibly have. It had an ear and possibly a leg missing. It was blind. It had lost its sense of smell. Probably hard pad came into it. And the dog had, of course, been doctored. According to the advertisement, it answered to the name of 'Lucky'.

You may encounter this story in all kinds of places. In 1984, I noticed it in the script of Frederic Raphael's TV series *Oxbridge Blues*. I myself had earlier twice told the story on TV – on Channel 4 a few minutes into 1 January 1984 and, before that, on ITV on 30 November 1983. I had taken it from a cutting sent to me from the Lost and Found Column of the *Westmorland Gazette*, dated 19 August 1983, which stated:

> LOST — CARTMEL AREA
> BALD ONE-EYED GINGER TOM
> Crippled in both back legs, re-cently castrated, answers to name of "Lucky".
>
> Replies to
> BOB BATEY
> PIG & WHISTLE
> CARTMEL

Was this apparently genuine ad how it had all started? I managed to track down Mr Batey in March 1987 to ask if his advertisement had really appeared and, if so, had he had any luck in recovering his poor Lucky (a cat, not a dog, you notice)? Well, no. Mr Batey, you see, was a bit of an entertainer – comedy magic was his speciality – and he'd put the ad in the paper to, well, liven things up a bit in the Cartmel area. And no, no, the joke wasn't original even in 1983, and I have no idea where he got it from.

Except that in the special edition of *Punch* published to mark the magazine's 150th anniversary (in 1991), a section was devoted to the newspaper clippings sent in by readers to the 'Country Life' column. Among the examples cited (but without date of publication given) was one from 'P. Butler' who had found this in the *Trinidad Guardian*: 'LOST – Bull Terrier, has three legs, blind in left eye, missing right ear, broken tail, recently castrated. Answers to the name of Lucky.' Back to dogs, you see. Will we ever know if this was an original advertisement?

1 John Piper, though a painter of distinction, frowned upon honours. He declined a knighthood (his letter of rejection was drafted by Sir John Betjeman), but became a Companion of Honour in 1972, apparently on the grounds (as expressed by another of his friends, Adrian Stokes) that, 'It doesn't distort the nomenclature.'

From the obituary notice by Richard Ingrams in the *Independent* (30 June 1992).

2 The critic Sheridan Morley was having lunch with an elderly American visitor and running through the London theatre scene when he happened to mention the name of the playwright Timberlake Wertenbaker. 'Timberlake Wertenbaker?' – the elderly American rolled the name round his tongue a few times and then said, 'My daughter was at school with a girl called Timberlake Wertenbaker. Any chance they might be the same person?'

Told by Sheridan Morley in *The London Magazine* (February 1993).

Nature

3 Early in the Orson Welles film *Mr Arkadin*, the eponymous character

holds a party in his castle and tells a fable: 'A scorpion, who could not swim, begged a frog to carry him to the other side. The frog complained that the scorpion would sting him. This was impossible, said the scorpion, because he would then drown with the frog. So the pair set forth. Halfway over, the scorpion stung the frog. "Is that logical?" asked the frog. "No, it's not," answered the scorpion, as they both sunk to the bottom, "but I can't help it, it's my nature."'

Told in Frank Brady, *Citizen Welles* (1989). *Mr Arkadin* (1962) was based on Welles's own novel (1956). Denis Healey recalls in *The Time of My Life* (1989) how he once 'delighted the sheikhs in the mountains surrounding Aden' with the same story. His version ended with the frog asking, 'Why did you do it? You know you'll drown.' And the scorpion replies, 'Yes, I know, but after all, this is the Middle East.' The story is also told (twice) in the film *The Crying Game* (1992).

Negotiations

4 After such films as *The Torrent* and *Flesh and the Devil*, Greta Garbo decided to exploit her box-office power and asked Louis B. Mayer for a rise – from $350 to $5,000 dollars a week. Mayer offered her $2,500. 'I tink I go home,' said Garbo. She went back to her hotel and stayed there for a full seven months until Mayer met her demands.

At one time, the phrase 'I tink I go home', spoken in a would-be Swedish accent, was as much part of the impressionist's view of Garbo as 'I want to be alone'. One version of how the line came to be spoken is told by Norman Zierold in *Moguls* (1969), as above.

Alexander Walker in *Garbo* (1980) recounts a different origin to the phrase, as told by Sven-Hugo Borg, the actress's interpreter.

Borg recalled the time in 1926 when Mauritz Stiller, who had come with her from Sweden, was fired from directing *The Temptress*. 'She was tired, terrified and lost ... as she returned to my side after a trying scene, she sank down beside me and said so low it was almost a whisper, "Borg, I think I shall go home now. It isn't worth it, is it?"'

Walker comments: 'That catch-phrase, shortened into "I think I go home", soon passed into the repertoire of a legion of Garbo-imitators and helped publicize her strong-willed temperament.'

A caricatured Garbo was shown hugging Mickey Mouse in a cartoon film in the 1930s. 'Ah tahnk ah kees you now' and 'Ah tink ah go home,' she said. This cartoon was, incidentally, the last item to be shown on British television before the transmitters were closed down on the brink of war (1 September 1939).

1 Reg Birch was a National Organizer for the Amalgamated Engineering and Electrical Trades Union. On one occasion at a tense Ford Motor Company wrangle, at which the management was spelling out in detail the new death benefits it was offering its workers, a sudden knocking was heard under the table. 'It's my dead members,' Birch explained, solemnly, 'wanting to know if it will be retrospective.'

Told to me by Raymond C. H. Morgan of Carmarthen (1998).

2 A friend of mine told me of a builder who was carrying out very extensive work for him and said, 'You know that estimate we talked about, Mr White?' (Note the careful use of 'talked about' rather than 'agreed'.)

'Yes, yes,' said my friend.

'Well, 24, I think we was talking about?'

'Yes, yes,' said my friend, '24.'

'Well, I thought I'd better warn you, what with one thing and another, that it now looks as though it will be nearer to 32 ...'

'Ah, 32, eh?' said my friend. 'I wonder if you could be a bit more specific? How much nearer will it be to 32?'

'Er, well,' replied the operative, 'Not to put too fine a point on it, and what with one thing and another, 46 ...'

Told to me by Jonathan White in about 1983.

Neighbours

3 When asked to look after their house and pets by neighbours who were going away on holiday, the Joneses readily agreed. They duly looked after the dog, but completely forgot about feeding the rabbit until one day the dog brought it in, dead and bloody. Full of remorse, the Joneses cleaned up the rabbit and put it in the cage, so that it would appear to have died a natural death. When the neighbours returned, the Joneses received a rather puzzled telephone call from them. This conveyed the information that the rabbit had died the day before they left for their holiday – 'and we buried him in the garden'.

This was told to me by Gemma O'Connor in August 1989, and it was not until some time later that I began to appreciate that it was another of those 'urban legends' that go the rounds and are always related as though they had happened to a friend – or a friend of a friend – of the teller. It also gets told as a joke. In a BBC TV documentary about Jewish humour, screened in February 1990, a joke was told of a woman wanting to take a red cocker spaniel with her on a plane going to Israel. She was told that this was not possible and that the dog would have to travel in the hold. On arrival, the baggage handlers had to find another red cocker spaniel to substitute for the one that had apparently died during the flight. But the woman had been taking her *dead* dog back to Israel to bury it.

Nevertheless

1 The ageing actor manager had just led his company to the conclusion of another performance of *Hamlet* at a small theatre in the provinces. As the somewhat desultory applause died away, he made a short speech informing the audience that on the following night the company would be giving a different play. 'I myself will be essaying the tragic role of Macbeth in the Bard's play of that name, while my lovely lady wife will be portraying Lady Macbeth.'

At this point, a voice from the gallery cried, 'Your wife's a whore!'

Barely pausing to register the remark, the actor manager continued, '... *nevertheless*, she will be playing Lady Macbeth tomorrow night.'

Told by William Franklyn on BBC Radio *Quote... Unquote* (8 August 1987). Compare this version: A university lecturer was giving a lecture on the subtleties of the English language. 'Take the word "nevertheless",' he said. Consider how many other words and expressions have a similar meaning – "however", "notwithstanding that", "moreover", "in any case" – there is a multitude of them. But "nevertheless" has a subtlety of meaning all its own, and sometimes it is the only word that will do. I will give you an example. There was a ceilidh in the Highlands of Scotland where the next performance was being announced by the Fear an Tighe. "We shall now have a song from Miss Jeannie Macleod," he said. "She's a wee whore," came a voice from the back. "Never-the-less, she will now sing ..."' (Told to me by Donald Adaway of Thurso, Caithness, in October 1994. He said he first heard it 'thirty years ago'.)

2 'I always felt very sorry for a man I heard of who, at the age of fifty, suffered a severe nervous breakdown when

he discovered that the word "hirsute" did not, as he had always believed, mean "nevertheless".'

Told by Christopher Matthew on BBC Radio *Quote... Unquote* (20 June 1995).

News

3 Martin Routh (1755–1854), the President of Magadalen College, Oxford, was a man of great composure – so much so that when an excitable Fellow rushed up to announce that a member of the college had killed himself, Routh replied: 'Pray, don't tell me who. Allow me to guess!'

Told in Dacre Balsdon, *Oxford Life* (1957).

4 The American newspaperman Horace Greeley – like another famous nineteenth-century figure (see note below) – liked to consider that the word 'news' was plural. He once sent a cable to a staff member of *The New York Tribune*, asking, 'ARE THERE ANY NEWS?' Came the reply, 'NOT A NEW.'

Told in Ralph L. Marquard, *Jokes and Anecdotes for All Occasions* (1977). Compare this letter from Queen Victoria to King Leopold (27 April 1865), reacting to the assassination of President Lincoln: 'These American *news* are most dreadful and awful! One never heard of such a thing! I only hope it will not be catching elsewhere.'

5 In these days of 'all-news' radio and TV stations broadcasting round the clock, it is salutary to be reminded that, in the early days of British radio, if the view was taken that there was no news worthy of the name, an announcer would come on and say, simply, 'There is no news tonight. We will have some piano music instead.'

Sources: the BBC's *Review of the Year 1930*, quoted in Asa Briggs, *The Golden Age of Wireless* (1965), and Ludovic Kennedy, 'The World Is Too Much With Us', The Standard Telephones and Cables Communication Lecture for 1982.

1 There was nothing particularly wrong with BBC Television News in the mid-1980s, though someone did comment on the rather severe type of woman chosen to do the job of news presenting. 'They are rather like police-women,' he said.

Told in *Sunday Today* (16 March 1986). Compare: 'It used to be said of Angela Rippon that she read the news as if it were your fault' – quoted in the *Guardian* (16 April 1995).

Nicknames

2 Each member of the Marx Brothers used a name other than the one he was born with. According to Groucho, the nicknames were acquired at a poker game in about 1918: Leonard became Chico; Adolph became Harpo (he played the harp); Julius became Groucho; Milton became Gummo (though he left the act early on); and Herbert became Zeppo (though he also left in due course). Groucho once attempted to explain the nicknames. Chico was a 'chicken-chaser', he said; Zeppo was 'after the Zeppelin' which arrived in Lakehurst, New Jersey, at the time he was born' (1901); and Gummo 'wore gum-shoes'. As for Groucho, 'I never did understand ...'

On the record album *An Evening with Groucho Marx* (1972). In *The Marx Bros. Scrapbook* (1974), Groucho gives a slightly different account – the stage names were given by a 'monologist named Art Fisher ... I think Fisher got the names from a cartoon

that was appearing in the papers. *The Monk Family* or something like that.' And as for Groucho? 'He named me because I was stern and rather serious.'

3 Mary Pickford was one of the first Hollywood stars to appreciate her worth and capitalize upon it. With Charles Charlie Chaplin and Douglas Fairbanks Sr, she founded the United Artists film company – about which it was famously said that the 'lunatics were taking over the asylum'. For her fearsome business sense she was awarded the soubriquets 'Attila of Sunnybrook Farm' and 'the Bank of America's Sweetheart'.

According to Dick Vosburgh on BBC Radio *Quote ... Unquote* (4 September 1979).

4 The nickname 'Oscar' for an Academy Award is said to derive from a comment made by Margaret Herrick when she was a secretary at the American Academy of Motion Picture Arts and Sciences. On seeing the statuette (awarded since 1928) she declared: 'Why, it looks just like my Uncle Oscar!' That is to say, one Oscar Pierce, a wheat-and-fruit grower.

Told in the *Morris Dictionary of Word and Phrase Origins* (1962, 1972).

5 We are the D-Day Dodgers, out in Italy,
Always at the vino, always on the spree.
8th Army skyvers and the Yanks,
6th Armoured Div and all their tanks.
For we are the D-Day Dodgers, the lads that D-Day dodged.

So sang British troops who had fought their way up Italy in 1943–44 only to have it pointed out that, understandably, they were not available to take part in the Normandy landings of 6 June 1944. The song they sang (and which veterans still sing) sometimes also includes the lines:

> Now Lady Astor get a load of this.
> Don't stand on a platform and talk
>   a load of piss
> … Your lovely mouth is far too
>   wide …

This refers to comments said to have been made by Nancy Astor contrasting the efforts of British forces in Italy with those taking part in the invasion of Europe. It has not proved possible to trace newspaper reports of any such remarks by her at the time. On the other hand, one theory is that a friend of the Astors wrote to them from Italy, where he was serving, and signed himself, humorously, 'D-Day Dodger'. Lady Astor replied beginning 'Dear D-Day Dodger', the letter was opened when the intended recipient was killed in action, and coinage of the unfortunate nickname was put down to her.

From correspondence with Douglas Evans of Mells, Somerset (1997).

1 The nickname of the conductor Sir Malcolm Sargent was 'Flash Harry'. It is said to have originated with a BBC announcer after Sargent had appeared on the radio *Brains Trust* and was also about to be heard in the following programme. The announcer informed listeners that they were to be taken over to a concert conducted by Sargent in Manchester. It sounded as if he had gone there straightaway, in a flash. However, the nickname also encapsulated his extremely debonair looks and manner – smoothed-back hair, buttonhole, gestures and all.

This version was given by Sargent himself in *The Sunday Times* (25 April 1965).

2 Noël Coward was known as 'The Master' throughout the theatrical profession and beyond, from the 1940s onwards. He professed not to like the nickname (perhaps because it had already been associated with Somerset Maugham) and – when asked to explain it – would reply, 'Oh, you know, Jack of all trades, master of none.'

John Mills in his autobiography *Up in the Clouds, Gentlemen, Please* (1980), puts in a bid to have first given Coward the name when they were both involved in a production of *Journey's End*. Cole Lesley, *The Life of Noël Coward* (1976) has Coward commenting: 'It started as a joke and became true.' Lesley adds: 'It seems that it did, in the 'twenties, start as a joke in his immediate circle, probably a self-defensive one made to forestall any accusations of their being yes-men, which they were not. Like most of the people who worked for him both in and out of the theatre, I called him Master.'

3 Because so many Welsh people share the same surname – Jones, Evans and so on – a tradition has grown up of distinguishing between the various ones by applying a nickname. So, for example, 'Jones the Post' was invented to distinguish him from 'Jones the Milk'. There also arose a whole range of slyly affectionate epithets such as 'Hallelujah Evans' (to mark out a man who sang loudly in chapel). Then there was a window-cleaner called Davis in South Wales who was distinguished by the nickname 'Chamois Davis Jnr'.

Vernon Noble and I included this last in our book *A Who's Who of Nicknames* (1985) believing that it was an actual example. On the other hand, I now know that Les

Dawson referred to the same nickname in BBC TV, *The Dawson Watch* (Christmas 1980), so perhaps it was no more than a joke.

1 For several years in the early 1970s, David Jason appeared regularly in BBC Radio's faintly satirical series *Week Ending*. A proper actor, who likes thorough rehearsal and direction, he was less at home in a world where he had to read scripts straight off the page. On one occasion, in some sketch about storms around the coast of Britain, he had to utter the line, 'Alert Aberdeen!' What came out of his mouth, however, was '*Albert* Aberdeen!', and this became his nickname on the programme.

From my memories of being told about the incident when I joined the programme in 1971.

2 Noël Coward is one of various authors credited with the nickname for which Edward Woodward is famous in the acting profession, and about which he is understandably modest. It is 'Fart in the Bath' – which is supposed to describe the sound made when 'Edward Woodward' is pronounced.

Conceded to me – with great reluctance – by Edward Woodward himself, in 1985.

3 The one-time Conservative MP Geoffrey Dickens (nickname 'Biffo') found himself being followed everywhere by a middle-aged woman as he toured his constituency on the Lancashire–Yorkshire border. A few days later he received a letter from this woman, apologizing for her pursuit, but explaining that she had been keen to see her MP in action. As a result, she would certainly recommend to all

her friends that they should vote for him. One small favour: could she have a signed photograph of him, please. Under her signature was the word 'Horseface'.

Dickens duly signed a photograph, put 'To Horseface with very best wishes' on it, and dropped it in the House of Commons letterbox. A few minutes later, his secretary came in and asked, 'Did you see the letter from that woman? I wrote "Horseface" at the bottom in case you had forgotten who she was.'

Recounted in *Brewer's Politics*, ed. Nicholas Comfort (1995).

Notices and signs

4 P. T. Barnum, the American showman, added Scudder's American Museum in New York to the list of his attractions in 1841. So popular did the exhibit prove and so reluctant were patrons to leave it, that Barnum resorted to a subterfuge. He put up a sign saying, 'TO THE EGRESS'. When patrons went out through this door, expecting to find some magnificent specimen of natural history, instead they found themselves out on the street.

Hugh Rawson, *A Dictionary of Euphemisms* (1981).

5 A notice outside a fried-fish shop proclaimed: 'CLEANLINESS, ECONOMY AND CIVILITY. ALWAYS HOT AND ALWAYS READY.' A passer-by remarked that this was the motto for a perfect wife.

The passer-by was possibly Edward Thomas, and the remark was recorded by E. S. P. Haynes in his *Lawyer's Notebook* (1932).

6 It is said that in 1944, the priest of a

Roman Catholic church in Putney wanted to call a statue of the Virgin Mary 'Our Lady of Putney', but his bishop demurred, saying, 'If the Germans land, they will go into the church and look at the statue and be able to tell where they are.' Accordingly, the pedestal of the statue bears the inscription: 'Our Lady of Hereabouts'.

Told to me by Iwan Williams and included in my book *Say No More!* (1987).

1 Thomas Watson was the man who founded IBM – International Business Machines. He had an exhortation: 'Read – Listen – Discuss – Observe – Think', especially the last word. By the 1940s, 'THINK' was a slogan that he had had inscribed on stationery and all over IBM offices. Not everyone subscribed to it, though. One day some rebellious wit had scribbled under a particularly large THINK display the words – 'OR THWIM'.

Recalled in Peter Hay, *Harrap's Book of Business Anecdotes* (1988).

2 It is reported that on the wall of a Foreign Legion barracks in Algeria, some well-meaning organization had stuck a poster stating that '*L'alcool tue lentement* [alcohol kills slowly].' Underneath, a legionnaire had written: '*Je ne suis pas pressé* [I'm in no hurry].'

Told to me by Michel Vercambre (November 1998). This is probably a version of the story given about Robert Benchley in Robert E. Drennan, *Wit's End* (1973): a friend told him that a particular drink he was sipping at was slow poison, to which Benchley replied, 'So who's in a hurry?'

3 Lord Berners put a sign up at his home, Faringdon House, in Oxfordshire:

'ANYONE THROWING STONES AT THIS NOTICE BOARD WILL BE PROSECUTED'.

Told in the *Independent on Sunday* (25 July 1993). Compare David Frost's narration from BBC TV's *The Frost Report* (c. 1966): 'For many of us, authority is summed up by the sign that one of the team found on the Yorkshire Moors which said simply, "It is forbidden to throw stones at this notice."' *Punch* (22 March 1939) contained a drawing of a notice which stated: 'IT IS FORBIDDEN TO THROW STONES AT THIS NOTICE BOARD'.

4 'I spent 1942–46 in Egypt. We used to go for a drink (lemonade) in the garden of the Summer Palace Hotel in Alexandria and we always giggled at the following notice in the garden: "*CONSOMMATION EST OBLIGATAIRE*".'

Contributed by Dorothy Heigham of Aldershot to *The 'Quote ... Unquote' Newsletter* (January 1995).

5 There was a battle over lavatory signs in Britain's House of Lords, following the introduction of women members in their own right in 1958. The lavatories were originally labelled 'LIFE PEERESSES ONLY'. But, as Lady Wootton pointed out, 'We are very passionate that we are not women peeresses; peeresses are the wives of peers.' Now the lavatories are marked 'PEERS' and 'WOMEN PEERS'.

Source untraced, though the story is included in my book *Foot In Mouth* (1982).

6 'There is a village near Maidstone in Kent called Loose. I do not know if the noticeboard still carries the caption outside their headquarters, but years ago it stated that it housed the "Loose Women's Institute".'

Contributed to Channel 4 *Countdown* (26 March 1990) by Audrey Thomas of London SE17. Presumably a similar fate has befallen the W.I. at Ugley, near Bishop's Stortford. As for Idle in West Yorkshire, perhaps there is a notice outside the working men's club there.

1 A notice in a New York taxi-cab refreshingly announced: 'SMOKING PERMITTED. THANK YOU FOR NOT JOGGING.'

Told by Alastair Beaton on BBC Radio *Quote ... Unquote* (11 June 1996).

Obesity

1 During the First World War, a patriotic hostess pointedly asked the more than portly G. K. Chesterton, 'Why are you not out at the Front?' He replied to her, gently: 'Madam, if you go round to the side, you will find that I am.'

An old story, recounted for example by A. N. Wilson in *Hilaire Belloc* (1984).

2 The massive Lord Castlerosse was being upbraided by Lady Astor about the size of his stomach. 'What would you say if that was on a woman?' she asked. 'Madam,' he replied politely, 'half an hour ago it was.'

Recounted by Godfrey Smith in his *Sunday Times* column during 1980. Castlerosse (1891–1943), Irish peer, later the 6th Earl of Kenmare, was the jester of Lord Beaverbrook's court. When asked on the golf course what his handicap was, he replied, 'Drink and debauchery'.

3 During the 20-minute interval of an opera performance in Florence, the 25-stone man-mountain, Luciano Pavarotti, partook of a light snack consisting of 20 meat and cheese sandwiches and three jugs of orange juice. Shortly afterwards, he explained why he takes Concorde on flights between Europe and New York: 'I cannot get in and out of aircraft toilets, but on three-and-a-half hour flights, I can hold out.'

Reported in *Today* (30 July 1987). The interestingly sized Italian tenor was once described as 'only slightly smaller than Vermont' – quoted in Norman Lebrecht, *When the Music Stops* (1996).

Obituaries

4 Sir Hereward Wake, the English soldier born in 1876, was given a generous obituary in *The Times* when he died in 1963. Shortly afterwards, there appeared in the same newspaper a tribute that paid the major-general an unusual compliment: 'He loved shooting, hunting, horses, and above all dogs. The smell of a wet dog was delicious to him, and his devoted wife never let him know that, to her, it was abominable.'

From *The Times* (7 August 1963).

5 After he had been reported dead during the Cyprus coup of 1974, Archbishop Makarios reappeared and said, 'You should have known that it was not easy for me to die – but tell me, were my obituaries good?'

Told in the *Observer* (29 December 1974).

Old age

6 On his eightieth birthday in 1921, the

former French Prime Minister Georges Clemenceau was walking down the Champs-Elysées with a friend. A pretty girl passed them by and Clemenceau exclaimed: 'Oh, to be seventy again!'

Told in James Agate, *Ego 3*, diary entry for 19 April 1938 (1938). The same remark is ascribed to Oliver Wendell Holmes Jr (1841–1935), the American jurist, on reaching his eighty-seventh year (1938) (for example, by Fadiman and van Doren in *The American Treasury*, 1955). In the film biography of Holmes, *The Magnificent Yankee* (US, 1950), this becomes, 'Do you know what I think when I see a pretty girl? ... Oh, to be eighty again.' (Perhaps this was derived from the Emmet Lavery play and the Francis Biddle book upon which the film is based). Earlier, Bernard de Fontenelle (1657–1757), the French writer and philosopher, is said in great old age to have attempted to pick up a young lady's fan, murmuring, 'Ah, if I were only eighty again!' (Pedrazzini and Gris, *Autant en apportent les mots*, 1969).

1 Towards the end of his life, Winston Churchill was sitting in the House of Commons smoking room with his fly-buttons undone. When this was pointed out to him, he said: 'Dead birds don't fall out of nests.'

Told in *The Lyttelton Hart-Davis Letters*, Vol. 2 (1979) (from a letter dated 5 January 1957, where the reply is: 'No matter. The dead bird does not leave the nest.')

2 Beryl Reid met Noël Coward at a party towards the end of his life and said to him, 'Oh, Noël, isn't it awful, we'll all be dead soon.' And Coward said, 'Oh, my darling, you mustn't worry. After we die, you must remember, little bits of you go on growing, you know. Your nails go on growing, and the hair on your chest goes on growing ...' Beryl Reid protested, 'Not the hair on *my* chest, please!' And Coward said,

'Oh, Beryl, you give up hope so easily ...'

Told by Francis Matthews on BBC Radio *Quote ... Unquote* (25 May 1993).

3 On achieving his century, Eubie Blake, the boogie-woogie pianist, ragtime composer and lyricist, said: 'If I'd known I was gonna live this long, I'd have taken better care of myself.'

Told in the *Observer* (13 February 1983). Unfortunately, five days after marking his centennial, Blake died. Even so, his felicitous remark was not original. In the *Radio Times* (17 February 1979), Benny Green had quoted Adolph Zukor, founder of Paramount Pictures, as having said on the approach to his hundredth birthday: 'If I'd known how old I was going to be I'd have taken better care of myself.' Zukor died in 1976, having been born in 1873.

4 When urging a young actress to get a move on in her scene, Edith Evans announced, rather disarmingly: 'I'm a very old lady. I may die during one of your pauses.'

Told by Denise Coffey on BBC Radio *Quote ... Unquote* (28 August 1979).

5 A 102-year-old woman was asked whether she still had any worries. 'No, I haven't,' she replied. 'Not since my youngest son went into an old folks' home.'

Contributed by Mrs V. Bedwell of Grays, Essex, to BBC Radio *Quote ... Unquote* (19 June 1980).

6 The old woman had been going on a bit, so when she asked, 'Have I ever told you about my lovely grand-children?', one of the listeners replied, 'No – and may I say how truly grateful we are that you haven't?'

Told by Rosemary Anne Sisson on BBC Radio *Quote ... Unquote* (27 August 1983).

1 The Oxford Library Club – 'for Retired Professional People and Others Interested' – was all agog to hear its guest speaker on the subject of 'Old Age, Absent-Mindedness, and Keeping Fit'. Alas, he forgot to turn up.

Told to me by a member of the club in about 1984.

One-upmanship

2 J. M. Barrie once put H. G. Wells on the spot. 'It is all very well to be able to write books,' he said, 'but can you waggle your ears?'

Told in J. A. Hammerton, *Barrie: The Story of a Genius* (1929). Wells couldn't, apparently.

3 Although the pianist Oscar Levant was the foremost exponent of George Gershwin's music, a good deal of joshing went on between them. Gershwin once said, 'Oscar, if you had to do it all over, would you fall in love with yourself again?' Levant replied, 'George, why don't you sit down and play us a medley of your hit.'

Told by Benny Green on BBC Radio *Quote ... Unquote* (3 July 1979). However, both David Ewen *The Story of George Gerhswin* (1943) and Edmund Fuller, *2500 Anecdotes for All Occasions* (1943) give Gershwin's line, rather, to Levant. Also, in the Gershwin biopic *Rhapsody in Blue* (1945), Levant (playing himself) gets to say the first line.

4 When Richard M. Nixon lost out to John F. Kennedy in the 1960 presidential election, it was said that the TV debates had been an important factor in his defeat. Nixon came over less well than Kennedy, who looked 'tanned, rested and fit', not least because Nixon visibly perspired, refused TV make-up, and allowed only minor treatment of his five o'clock shadow.

J. Leonard Reinsch, who masterminded Kennedy's success in those debates, also made things hard for Nixon by suggesting that the two candidates ought to stand during the first hourlong session. He knew that Nixon had just injured his knee on a car door.

Sources: Richard Nixon, *Memoirs* (1978); Leonard Miall in his obituary of Reinsch, the *Independent* (13 May 1991).

5 Before he became President, Lyndon Johnson was Senate Majority Leader. He was apparently very pleased with his latest toy, a car telephone, and took great delight in crowing over it to fellow Senator, Everett Dirksen. When Johnson left for home, he would see the conscientious Dirksen still at work, so he would ring him up from the car, always beginning with the query, 'Guess where I'm calling you from, Ev?' The answer was always the same: 'From my car telephone'.

Dirksen became so annoyed by this that one day he got himself a car phone, and when he saw Johnson leaving, he ran down to his own car and called up the L.B.J. car. 'Guess where I'm calling you from, Lyndon?' he asked. Johnson paused and then said, 'Hold on a minute, Ev. My other phone's ringing ...'

Original source untraced. This story has probably been told about other pairs engaged in one-upmanship.

Opera

6 In a 1936 production of Wagner's *Lohengrin* at the Metropolitan Opera in New York, the tenor Lauritz Melchior awaited the arrival of the 'swan boat'

on stage in the last act. Alas, when it came along, it departed before he had time to board. To the audience, he said: '*Wenn geht der nächste Schwann?*' – 'When does the next swan go?'

According to Hugo Vickers, *Great Operatic Disasters* (1979), Melchior was in fact quoting what Leo Slezak, the Czech-born tenor, had said on a similar occasion thirty years before. Leo's son Walter, who became an actor in Hollywood, actually entitled his 1962 memoirs, *What Time's the Next Swan?*

1 King George V went to the opera every year and the only opera he ever saw was *La Bohème*. Sir Thomas Beecham once bravely asked why this one was his particular favourite. 'Because it's much the shortest,' replied the King.

Recounted in *The Lyttelton Hart-Davis Letters* (for 4 November 1956).

2 When Stella Roman was playing Tosca in Puccini's opera, she was supposed to leap to her death from a prison parapet and land safely off-stage on a mattress. Roman, feeling insecure one night, demanded two extra mattresses to be placed to ease her fall. She leaped, and the mattresses bounced her back on stage. She had to kill herself all over again.

This version comes from Robert Merrill and Robert Saffron, *Between Acts* (1978). Hugo Vickers, *Great Operatic Disasters* (1979) claims the story originated with 'a large young American' at the City Center, New York in 1960, when a trampoline was placed instead of a mattress and the singer 'came up 15 times before the curtain fell'.

3 When invited to attend a performance of Mozart's *The Marriage of Figaro*, Queen Elizabeth II replied, 'Is that the one about the pin?'

Indeed, it is, though it is a little odd that she should have remembered this small moment. Source untraced.

Optimism

4 An example of optimism. On Christmas morning, a child finds a pile of manure in his room. His parents soon find him shovelling it away enthusiastically. As he explains to them, he is convinced, 'There must be a pony here somewhere.'

Time Magazine recorded this joke on 27 October 1986 as a particular favourite of President Reagan's. That same year it gave rise to the oddest title for a movie (albeit the TV variety) I have come across for some time, namely, *There Must Be a Pony*. This had Elizabeth Taylor as a former child star pushed back into the limelight by a major soap-opera casting after a spell in psychiatric hospital. The title is explained as an example of optimism in Robert Wagner's suicide note at the end of the film. A book (1964) by James Kirkwood (1924–89) with the title *There Must Be a Pony* has on the cover: 'With all this horse shit – there must be a pony!'

Orders, obeying

5 In the spring of 1920, Sir John Squire, the literary critic, set up an amateur cricket team called 'The Invalids'. Neville Cardus told of a match when an opposing batsman hit an easy catch high in the sky. Six of Squire's team ran to get it and jostled for position under the falling ball. Squire's voice boomed out the order, 'Leave it to Thompson!' As the ball thudded into the grass, they remembered that Thompson was not playing that week.

Recalled by Frank Muir in *The Oxford Book of Humorous Prose* (1990).

Orotundity

1 As the newly arrived US Ambassador to the Court of St James, Walter Annenberg went to present his credentials to Queen Elizabeth II in 1969. Unfortunately for him, a film crew was hovering at his elbow making the TV film *Royal Family*, so millions were able to hear the peculiarly orotund remarks he thought appropriate for the occasion. When asked by the Queen how he was enjoying his official residence, he admitted to feeling: 'Some of the discomfiture as a result of a need for, uh, elements of refurbishment and rehabilitation.'

From the soundtrack of the film.

Overheard remarks

2 Overheard remarks – or 'eavesdroppings' – bid fair to be considered a popular art form. Indeed, some writers make a point of elevating them to this plane by noting them down and using them in their works. The playwright Alan Bennett is a notable miner of this seam, especially when it is a case of ear-wigging one Yorkshirewoman talking to another. 'Who was it who painted that Sistine Chapel ceiling?' asked one. 'I don't know,' replied the other. 'It wasn't Underwoods of Bramley, was it?'

Told by Alan Bennett on BBC Radio *Quote ... Unquote* (9 March 1982).

3 A young American when he saw Manet's painting *Le Déjeuner sur l'herbe*, a picnic at which one of the participants, a woman, is without clothes, remarked: 'Yeah, you always forget something at picnics ...'

Contributed to BBC Radio *Quote ... Unquote* (26 May 1982) by Miss M.H. Browne of London W14.

4 'Hallo, Ada, have a good holiday?'
'Yes, lovely.'
'Where did you go?'
'Majorca.'
'Majorca? Where's that?'
'Don't know – we flew.'

Contributed to BBC Radio *Quote ... Unquote* (5 February 1979) by Mr G. A. Higgins of Halberton, Tiverton, Devon – one of several reports of a similar conversation at that time. Another was: 'Did you go to Portugal for your holiday?' – 'I don't know, my husband bought the tickets.'

5 Gathered from a restaurant: 'Brenda says his big toenails go off like revolvers.'

Contributed to BBC Radio *Quote ... Unquote* (17 July 1980) by Miss V. M. Smith of Croydon.

6 Overheard from one of two women sitting together on a Nottingham bus: 'Oh, yes, I've felt ever so much better since they painted my back passage spring green ...'

Contributed to BBC Radio *Quote ... Unquote* (26 May 1982) by Mrs D. Tunbridge of Yeovil.

7 Overheard on top of a Leeds tram in about 1949: 'It's all right going on your holidays, but when you get back home, your dishcloth's stiff as buckram.'

Contributed by Mrs M. Bradshaw, Leamington Spa, to BBC Radio *Quote ... Unquote* and published in *Eavesdroppings* (1981). A universal human truth, surely?

8 Two American matrons were observing and admiring the well-endowed statue of Achilles on the edge of Hyde Park in London. One was overheard saying to the other: 'No, dear – Big Ben is a clock.'

This eavesdropping was told to me by Norman Mitchell of Weybridge in 1979. What I have discovered subsequently is the long history of amusement surrounding the 20-foot-high statue in dark, naked bronze. It was unveiled in 1822 after a subscription had been raised by the 'Country-women' of the first Duke of Wellington and his comrades to commemorate the victories that had culminated in the Battle of Waterloo, seven years before. So, even while he was alive, the Iron Duke was able to look out of his windows in Apsley House, a few score yards away, and see the superb monument. In 1826, William Cobbett wrote in *Rural Rides*, with customary venom: 'The English *ladies' naked* Achilles stands, having on the base of it, the word WELLINGTON in great staring letters, while all the other letters are *very, very small*; so that base tax-eaters and fund-gamblers from the country, when they go to crouch before this image, think it is the image of the *Great Captain himself!*'

Although 'The Ladies' Trophy' – as it was originally known – was provided with a fig-leaf, the statue provoked disquiet as not being the sort of thing respectable women ought to go around putting up. Indeed, it came to be nicknamed 'The Ladies' Fancy'. Lady Holland noted in her droll fashion that the female subscribers had had to take a vote on the fig-leaf question: 'It was carried for the leaf by a majority ... The names of the *minority* have not transpired.' In fact, it seems it was the *gentlemen* co-opted to head the statue committee who had insisted on the cover-up. The fig-leaf was briefly removed by a prankster in 1961, revealing a situation which would have rendered our American tourist's remark redundant.

In his play *An Ideal Husband* (1895), Oscar Wilde has Mabel Chiltern say: 'Then he proposed to me in broad daylight this morning, in front of that dreadful statue of Achilles. Really, the things that go on in front of that work of art are quite appalling. The police should interfere.'

The actor Donald Sinden says in *A Touch of the Memoirs* (1982): 'Looking one day at the enormous nude statue of Achilles at Hyde Park Corner I heard a Londoner

say to a visitor ...' But there you go.

In any case, Claire Rayner believes the remark to have been the caption to a *Punch* cartoon in the early years of the century, but this remains untraced. In 1998, David Rees recalled giggling over this same cartoon caption in 1965. Will its origins ever be found?

1 A tourist visiting Windsor Castle was annoyed by the sound of aircraft taking off from Heathrow Airport nearby and remarked, 'What a pity they built the castle so near to the airport.'

I included this in my *Eavesdroppings* (1981) and it had whiskers on even then. Even so, it is probably a reworking of the even more traditional remark about the monks having built Tintern Abbey too close to the road.

2 Malcolm Sargent used to remark that people in concert audiences did not seem to realize that although a conductor has his back to them he can still overhear conversations in the front rows. He once heard a lady say to her friend, 'I wish my backside was as flat as his.'

Recounted in my *Eavesdroppings* (1981), having appeared earlier in Barnaby Conrad, *Fun While It Lasted* (1969).

3 A man, well past his flirt-by date, was attempting to flirt with a young slip of a thing. 'I've always wondered how old you are,' he said to her. 'My age and my bust measurement are exactly the same,' replied she. Said he, 'You can't be that young, surely? ...'

Told by Sue Limb on BBC Radio *Quote ... Unquote* (2 June 1988).

4 Two drunks were arguing in a Glasgow pub. Finally, one got the other up against the wall and started banging his head against it, interspersing with the rhythm the words: 'I'm telling you ...

there are ... FORTY-NINE ISLANDS IN THE JAPANESE ARCHIPELAGO ...!'

Told by Jimmy Reid on BBC Radio *Quote ... Unquote* (26 May 1982).

1   An old woman was in the chemist's shop and demanding of the man behind the counter if he knew of a good sweep. To much ribald laughter she said, 'I haven't had a brush up my flue for ages.'

Told to me by Nora Glynne-Jones. From my diary for 13 April 1968.

2   On one occasion, Kenneth Williams claimed to have heard two men outside a London club. One said: 'I've just been to *Evita*.' The other replied: 'You don't look very brown.'

Told by him on BBC Radio *Quote ... Unquote* (28 August 1979).

3   Wynford Vaughan-Thomas used to enjoy telling the overheard remark from the girl who had told her friend of a dreadful happening: 'He put his hand up my skirt ... you know, the Jaeger one with pleats ...'

Told on BBC Radio *Quote ... Unquote* (24 July 1980).

4   During the blackout in the Second World War, Wynford said that a voice was heard urging, 'Come on, Grandpa.' The old man explained that he could not find his teeth. To which the reply was: 'They're dropping bombs, not sandwiches.'

Told on the same programme. The joke – which was fairly traditional, after all – made an appearance in the film *Reds* (1981).

5   Peter Ustinov claims to have overheard this exchange between two charladies on the top of a London bus during the Second World War. One of them said, 'And do you know what, he said to me? – "You bitch!" But I was ready for him. I 'ad my answer prepared.' 'What did you say to 'im?' asked the other, eagerly. '"No I'm not", I said ...'

Told by Ustinov on BBC Radio *Quote ... Unquote* (11 February 1992) and, round about that time, in his show *An Evening With Peter Ustinov*.

6   The playwright and novelist John Mortimer was in the crush bar at the Royal Opera House, Covent Garden, just before a production of *Don Carlos*, conducted by Giulini, directed by Visconti, and starring Placido Domingo. In came a 'Hunting Henry' character who asked loudly of his companion: 'What are they givin' us tonight, darlin'? Singin' or dancin'?'

As told by him on BBC Radio *Quote ... Unquote* (12 February 1979).

7   A mother was travelling with her child on a bus, and for a long while did nothing as the child wiped a lolly on the fur coat of the woman sitting in front of them. Eventually, the mother spoke. 'Don't do that, dear,' she said. 'It'll get all hairy.'

Of some vintage and certainly known by the 1980s. In the *Observer* (24 September 1995), it was, probably wrongly, said to derive from one of Joyce Grenfell's nursery-school monologues.

8   A young artist saw an eminent critic and a noble lord standing in front of one of his paintings, so he crept nearer to hear what they were saying about it. The noble lord said to the critic: 'Of the two, I prefer washing up.'

I described this joke as 'traditional' in my *Eavesdroppings* (1981). It has since been pointed out to me that T. H. White discussed a comic story current just after the Second

World War in *The Age of Scandal* (1950): 'It said that there was some conference or other at Lambeth, thronged with Archbishops, Cardinals, Patriarchs, Moderators and so forth. The Archbishops of Canterbury and York were seen to be in earnest consultation in one corner of the room. Were they discussing a reunion with Rome or a revision of the Prayer Book? Thrilled with the ecclesiastical possibilities of such a meeting, one of the stripling curates managed to edge himself within earshot of these princes of the Church. They were discussing whether it was worse to wash-up or dry-up.'

1 Listening to a noisy piece of music at the Philharmonic Hall in Liverpool, Mr H. W. Simpson found himself having to give ear also to a snatch of neighbouring conversation during a sudden quiet patch. The woman in front of him was declaring in full spate: 'Well, we always fry ours in lard!'

Contributed to BBC Radio *Quote ... Unquote* (8 January 1979). Mr Simpson was not alone. In fact, this rates as a 'traditional' eavesdropping, variously reported as having been gathered in a concert audience, church congregation, or group of nuns. It appears to have been around since the nineteenth century.

2 Overheard during the First World War: 'My husband has been wounded in the Dardanelles ... and they cannot find his whereabouts.'

Contributed to BBC Radio *Quote ... Unquote* (25 August 1984) by Mrs V. Lewis of Handsworth, Birmingham, as overheard by her mother. However, in BBC TV, *The Dawson Watch* (Christmas 1980), Les Dawson spoke the line 'During the war, I was shot in the Dardanelles' – with similar implications. From Brendan Behan, *Brendan Behan's Island* (1962) – Granny Growl: 'Me tired husband, poor ould Paddins, he was shot in the Dardanelles.' Granny Grunt: 'And a most painful part of the body to be shot!' In the BBC radio show *Beyond*

Our Ken (15 July 1960) there was the line, 'The Turks pinned the Australians in the Dardanelles'.

3 Alfred Deller, the celebrated countertenor was walking behind two women when he overheard one say to the other, 'Ow's Flo? Ow's 'er feet?' The second woman replied, 'Well, of course, they're not much use to 'er now. Not as feet, that is ...'

Contributed to BBC Radio *Quote ... Unquote* (5 June 1979) by Paul Fincham of Suffolk – who heard it from Paul Jennings, who had it from Deller. Denis Norden told me (1996) that he had first heard it from the lips of Nancy Spain at a recording of *My Word* in Cambridge in that programme's early years (it began in 1956).

Ownership

4 James Gordon Bennett Jr, the eccentric American newspaper owner, spent a great deal of time in Monte Carlo. He patronized one restaurant night after night on account of the wonderful way it prepared his Southdown mutton chops. One night, however, when Bennett turned up at the restaurant unbooked, he found that his favourite table was occupied by someone else. He summoned the owner and bought the restaurant from him for the sum of $40,000. Then he asked the diners at his table to leave, even though they were only half way through their meal. At the end of Bennett's meal, he left a very large tip indeed: he made the restaurant back over to its original owner.

Told in David Frost and Michael Deakin, *Who Wants To Be A Millionaire?* (1983).

5 Lord Nuffield, the motor magnate and philanthropist, had been dining at

an Oxford college. On his departure, a porter produced his hat with great speed. Nuffield inquired, 'How d'you know it's mine?' The porter replied: 'I don't, my Lord. But it's the one you came with.'

Recounted by James Morris in *Oxford* (1965). He was told it by the 'elderly servant' who had administered the remark.

Oxford

1 There is an old Oxford story, dating from the days when there were several all-female colleges, about a girl announcing loudly in the Junior Common Room that she had just met a man. At Somerville, the other girls asked, 'What is he reading?' At Lady Margaret Hall, 'Who is his father?' At St Hugh's they asked, 'What does he play?' And at St Hilda's they asked, 'Where is he?'

If this story is taken to show that St Hilda's undergraduates once had the reputation of being the most man-hungry, be it noted that of the colleges mentioned it is now the sole remaining all-female college. The story was described as an 'old chestnut' in Dacre Balsdon's *Oxford Life* (1957). Brian A. Robinson told me (1999) of a version he encountered in Savannah, Georgia, about what *men* would say coming from different cities in that area: if meeting someone new, a man from Atlanta would ask, 'What company are you with?' A man from Macon, 'What religion are you?' From Charleston, South Carolina, 'What family are you?' And from Savannah, 'What are you drinking?'

P

Pants

1 An old Nonconformist minister chose
as his text Psalm 42 verse 1: 'As the
hart panteth after the water brooks, so
panteth my soul after thee, O God.'
His discourse, the minister said,
would be divided into three sections –
'the pants of the hart, the pants of
the Psalmist, and, finally, pants
in general'.

Source unknown. Samuel Taylor Coleridge
has caused similar amusement because of
the line from 'Kubla Khan' (1816): 'As
if this earth in fast thick pants were breathing...' C. S. Lewis evidently posed the
question whether the pants were 'woollen or
fur' (so quoted in *My Oxford*, ed. Ann
Thwaite, 1977).

Parentage

2 During the First World War, Queen
Mary was going round a hospital when
she was struck by a fair-haired mother
with a very dark baby. She commented
on this and, indeed, returned to the
woman's bedside after completing
her rounds, saying: 'His father must
have been very dark – wasn't he?' To
which the woman breezily replied:
'Sure Ma'am, I don't know – he never
took his hat off.'

From the entry for 18 August 1917 in
Lady Cynthia Asquith's Diaries (1968).

3 It is said that the artist Augustus John
automatically patted children on the
head whenever he came across them,
just in case they turned out to be his.

Source untraced.

4 Benjamin Britten, the composer, and
Peter Pears, the singer and Britten's
muse, were famously close. One day
they were walking along the windswept
beach at Aldeburgh when Britten
turned to his friend and said, 'Peter,
I don't know how to tell you this...'

   Pears turned sensitively to Britten
and replied, 'What is it, Peter? What is
it that you have to tell me?'

   But still the words would not come.
They walked a little further down
the windswept beach until Britten
finally had the courage to announce:
'Peter, I think we're going to have
another opera...'

Told in the *Daily Mail* (December 1976).

Parents and children

5 Walt, the son of Sir Walter Raleigh, was
at dinner with his father. Then, as John
Aubrey tells it, he admitted that he
had been with a whore that morning:
'"I was very eager of her, kissed and
embraced her, and went to enjoy her,
but she thrust me from her, and vowed
I should not *For your father lay with*

me but an hower ago." Sir Walt[er], being so strangely supprized and putt out of his countenance at so great a Table, gives his son a damned blow over the face; his son, as rude as he was, would not strike his father, but strikes over the face of the Gentleman that sate next to him, and sayed *Box about, 'twill come to my Father anon.* 'Tis now a common used proverb.'

Told in *Brief Lives* (*c.* 1693).

1 The American hotel owner Ernie Byfield (1889–1950) is credited in *Who's Who in American History* with popularizing tomato juice as a beverage. At one time, he used to run Chicago's famous Pump Room. When he was asked why the real caviar was so expensive, he replied: 'After all, it's a year's work for the sturgeon.' Long after this, his son Ernie Jr. was asked why he – such a young man – was running three big hotels. He replied, 'Well, I happened to run into my father in the lobby and he took a liking to me.'

Sources untraced.

Parody

2 A magazine ran a competition for the best parody of Graham Greene's style. A week after the prize-winning entry had been published, Greene wrote to say that he was delighted with the winning entry, but felt that two other competitors had deserved prizes. He had sent in all three himself. What was more, they were not parodies, but passages from some of his early novels that he had excised as not being good enough.

This is as reported in *Book-of-the-Month Club News* (October 1949). It refers to the *New Statesman* Weekend Competition No. 999 of May 1949, in which 'N. Wilkinson' [Greene] merely won second place. According, however, to Frank Muir in *The Oxford Book of Humorous Prose* (1990), Greene appears to have played the same trick more than once. In 1965, under the name 'Malcolm Collins', he entered a *New Statesman* competition for the best parody of a Graham Greene biography of his brother Hugh, then Director-General of the BBC. (Graham's parody won him honourable mention; the winner, however, was Hugh himself, writing as 'Sebastian Eleigh'.) E. O. Parrott, in *Imitations of Immortality* (1986), also finds a 'verse autobiography' written by Graham Greene under the pseudonym 'H. A. Baxter'. This appeared in the *New Statesman* on 7 April 1961.

Parsimony

3 In the 1940s, there was a brand of cigarette called De Reszke. It was promoted in advertisements featuring various movie stars and with slogans like, 'If Clark Gable Offered You A Cigarette, It Would Be A De Reszke.' Accordingly, Noël Coward is said to have remarked of the somewhat tight-fisted journalist Godfrey Winn: 'If Godfrey Winn offered you a cigarette … it would be a bloody miracle!'

Told by Jonathan Cecil on BBC Radio *Quote … Unquote* (11 June 1996).

4 As conductor of the BBC Symphony Orchestra, Sir Adrian Boult frequently ran up against official parsimony. On one occasion, when planning to conduct a piece requiring two piccolo players, he was told that only one could be afforded. He complained to his boss, Charles Carpendale, who reflected for a moment and then suggested a compromise: 'How about using one piccolo … and placing it closer to the microphone?'

Told in Andrew Boyle, *Only the Wind Will Listen: Reith of the BBC* (1972).

Partnerships

1 In the early 1950s, the character actor Peter Jones partnered Peter Ustinov in what came to be regarded as one of the classic radio comedies, *In All Directions*. Unfortunately, for ever after, all that interviewers seemed to want to talk to Jones about was the partnership with Ustinov. Jones countered with this story: 'I dreamt that I had died and, just before ascending into heaven, I floated down to Piccadilly Circus where there was a news vendor with a placard bearing, I was surprised to see, a mention of my demise. It said, 'FRIEND OF PETER USTINOV DEAD'.

Heard in the early 1970s. Barry Took, *Laughter in the Air* (1976) presents the story in a lengthier version, supposedly concocted by Peter Jones for a speech he made at a Press Association dinner. Here the placard states, 'PETER USTINOV BEREAVED'.

I wouldn't like to have to break it to Peter Jones, but in the biography circulated in 1991 by (now) Sir Peter Ustinov's press agent, it stated that *In All Directions* was 'his own show' in which Ustinov 'produced and co-starred with Peter James'.

Patriotism

2 During the First World War, Heathcote William Garrod, the classical scholar and literary critic, was stopped by a woman in the street and asked why he was not fighting to defend civilization. Replied he, 'Madam, I am the civilization they are fighting to defend.'

Told in Dacre Baldson, *Oxford Then and Now* (1970). The remark was turned into verse by Hugh MacDiarmid ('At the Cenotaph' from *Second Hymn to Lenin and Other*

Poems, 1935): 'Keep going to your wars, you fools, as of yore;/ I'm the civilization you're fighting for.'

Patronization

3 The Labour MP, Jimmy Thomas, first entered the House of Commons in January 1910. One day he happened to ask a fellow MP, F. E. Smith, the way to the lavatory. 'Down the corridor, first right, first left, and down the stairs,' Smith helpfully advised him. 'Then you'll see a door marked "Gentlemen", but don't let that deter you.'

Told in John Campbell, *F. E. Smith, First Earl of Birkenhead* (1983).

4 When Thomas complained to Smith that he "ad an 'eadache', Smith advised: 'Try taking a couple of aspirates.'

Some versions have Thomas saying he complained, rather, of 'an 'orrible 'eadache'. John Campbell (in the above book) quotes Thomas as saying, 'Ooh, Fred, I've got an 'ell of an 'eadache.'

Pay

5 BBC announcer Ronald Fletcher never threw off the urge to gamble. In his early days he had lost all the money his grandfather had left him in an unsuccessful business venture, and that is when he turned to the BBC. At one stage he was in debt to a bookmaker for several thousand pounds, and the bookmaker offered to write off the debt if Ronnie promised never to back another horse. That night he went to the dog track. On another occasion he offered a bank manager his BBC salary as collateral for a loan. When Ronnie told the manager what the salary was, he replied, 'Would a pound be all right?'

Based on the reminiscences of Eric Nicol,

as related in Bernard Braden, *The Kindness of Strangers* (1990).

Pedantry

1 Someone rather bold once said to Dr Samuel Johnson, 'You smell!' The eminent lexicographer, not taking offence, replied, 'No, you smell, I stink.'

Source untraced. Michael Grosvenor Myer had this to say (1992) about the likely provenance of the exchange: 'Surely this is merely a folk tale about a pedant insisting on precise application of words, attributed to Dr Johnson because, as a lexicographer, he would be thought fastidious about usage. Compare the somewhat similar tale of Webster (another famous lexicographer, d. 1843) discovered by his wife as he embraced one of the maidservants: "Why, Noah, I am surprised!" "No, dear, you are *astonished*; it is I who am *surprised*."'

A version of the Noah Webster version appeared in *Pass the Port* (1976). A curious sidelight when considering these two anec-dotes is that Webster actually omitted every instance of the word 'stink' when he produced his expurgated edition of the Bible – accord-ing to Allen Walker Read, *Lexical Evidence from Folk Epigraphy ... a Glossarial Study of the Low Element in the English Vocabulary* (1935).

The stink/smell distinction never goes far away. In the film *The Philadelphia Story* (US, 1940), a character says: 'Don't say "stinks", darling. If absolutely necessary, "smells" – but only if absolutely necessary.'

A yet earlier mention of Webster's alleged proclivities is in A. Hobbhouse, *Hangover Murders* (1935): 'That's what Noah Webster said to his wife when she found him in bed with the kitchen wench, "It's just a coincidence."'

2 The poet Thomas Campbell, author of *The Pleasures of Hope* and much else, once walked six miles to his printer (and back again) to make sure that a comma was changed into a semicolon.

Told to me by John O'Byrne (April 1998). William Hazlitt, in *Lectures on the English Poets* (1818), would seem to confirm Campbell's weakness on this point: 'Mr Campbell always seems to me to be thinking how his poetry will look when it comes to be hot-pressed on superfine wove paper, to have a disproportionate eye to points and commas, and dread of errors of the press.'

3 Have you ever considered the hyphen – or the lack of it – in the title of Herman Melville's novel *Moby Dick* or *Moby-Dick* (1851)? Curiously, the book was first published in Britain (just ahead of the American edition) under the title of *The Whale*. My Penguin edition (ed. Harold Beaver, 1972), whilst listing all the corrections made in what is famously a bad text, makes no mention of the silent removal of the hyphen from the name of the whale therein – but does retain it in the 'Moby-Dick' on the title page and cover ...

Discussed in *The 'Quote ... Unquote' Newsletter* (July 1997).

4 Harold Pinter is famous for the, well, 'Pinteresque' quality of his work, which usually means that the dialogue is absurd, curious and spaced out with pauses (all insisted on in the stage direc-tions for such plays as *The Caretaker* and *The Birthday Party*). The play-wright once reprimanded an actor for short-changing him over one of these pauses. 'You are playing two dots at the moment,' said Pinter, seriously, 'and I think if you check in the script you'll find it's three.'

Recounted in the *Observer* (12 September 1993). Similar attention to minutiae was shown when the text of his play *Moonlight* was published in 1993. An erratum slip drew attention to a mistake in the very first line of the play. It read 'I can't sleep. There's no moon. It's so dark, I' instead of 'I can't sleep. There's no moon. It's so dark. I'.

Perfectionism

1 David Ogilvy said that the best advertising headline he had ever written contained eighteen words: 'At Sixty Miles an Hour the Loudest Noise in the New Rolls-Royce comes from the electric clock.' He recalled that when the chief engineer at the Rolls-Royce factory read this, he shook his head sadly and said, 'It is time we did something about that damned clock.'

From Ogilvy's *Confessions of an Advertising Man* (1963). The ad first appeared in 1958.

Personality

2 The American actress Tallulah Bankhead has a rather overwhelming manner, and she could wear one out, to say the least. Howard Dietz commented: 'A day away from Tallulah is like a month in the country.'

Recalled by Dietz in his book *Dancing in the Dark* (1974).

3 When Ned Sherrin was working on the BBC TV satire shows in the mid-1960s, there was a palace revolution and one of his bosses was replaced by another (Donald Baverstock by Huw Wheldon, as Controller of Programmes, 1965). It all took place over a weekend, and when Sherrin arrived on Monday morning the new man – Wheldon – was already totally installed in his predecessor's office, except that everything representing the old man had been taken out. The office was absolutely naked and bare. Sherrin greeted Wheldon with the words, 'Oh, Huw, I see you've put your stamp on the office already.'

Told by Sherrin on BBC Radio *Quote ... Unquote* (26 June 1980), not mentioning Wheldon's name. Later, he revealed all in *Theatrical Anecdotes* (1991).

Pets

4 A taxi driver once attempted *not* to carry Mrs Patrick Campbell and a disagreeable pooch called Moonbeam in his vehicle. But she climbed in nevertheless and commanded, 'The Empire Theatre, my man, and no nonsense!' The dog decided to misbehave en route, and the taxi driver chose to point out the large damp patch on the floor of his cab. Mrs Pat was having none of it. 'Moonbeam didn't pee,' she said loudly. '*I* did!'

Bennett Cerf, *Shake Well Before Using* (1948), has an early version of this story.

Philosophical matters

5 Even Bertrand Russell, the English mathematician, philosopher and nuclear-disarmament campaigner, was at times lost for words. Apparently a taxi driver once recognized him and recalled: 'I 'ad that Bertrand Russell in the back of my cab last week. And I asked him, "What's it all about, guv?" – and, d'you know, he couldn't tell me!'

Also told involving the philosopher, A. J. Ayer. The origin lies with T. S. Eliot, whose widow, Valerie, wrote a letter to *The Times* (10 February 1970) telling a tale that Eliot himself 'loved to recount'. This version begins with the taxi-driver saying, 'You're T. S. Eliot ... I've got an eye for a celebrity. Only the other evening I picked up Bertrand Russell ...' And so on.

6 An actress rushed up to Sir Ralph Richardson at rehearsal one Monday morning and asked him if he'd had a good weekend. 'A terrible thing

happened,' he replied sadly, 'my brother and his wife were burnt to death in a fire!' 'How terrible!' exclaimed the actress. 'No, no, I hardly knew my brother, hadn't seen him for fifty years ...' 'But even so,' sympathized the actress, 'it's a terrible thing to happen'. 'Yes,' said Sir Ralph, ruminatively, 'But it won't happen again.'

Told to me by Jonathan Miller and recorded in my diary, 23 January 1976.

Photography

1   Winston Churchill had some words of advice for those in public life who attracted the attention of the press. 'Never be photographed with a glass in your hand,' he said, and added, after a pause, 'especially if it's an empty glass.'

This was said to Sir David Hunt, Churchill's Private Secretary during his second premiership, who told it to me in 1993. Evidently, Churchill went on to refer to an election in Dundee when he had been defeated by a teetotaller.

Phrases

2   There is an expresssion, chiefly in American speech, 'Katie bar the door' – meaning ' watch out for danger!', 'get ready for trouble!', 'a desperate situation is at hand', or 'all hell is about to break loose!' It is not clear whether this contains an allusion to an actual occasion when a particular Katie was invited to do her stuff. If it does, then this has been put forward as a contender: T. A. Dyer wrote to The 'Quote ... Unquote' Newsletter (October 1997): 'It is my opinion that "Katie bar the door" originated in the Royal Palace at Perth, Scotland, on the 20th February 1437 when some relatives came to assassinate King James I of Scots. The

bar to secure the door was missing and a brave young woman [Catherine Douglas] put her arms through the hasps and held it long enough for the King to escape into a secret passage. She earned the nickname Kate Barlass but it did the King no good as the passage led to the Royal tennis court and the other end had been blocked to stop balls going in, so the King was caught and killed.'

Michael Brown, James I (1994) comments that the woman's real name was Elizabeth not Catherine Douglas, and that she did not actually bar the door but fell into the passage (or drain) beside the King, and so did delay the onslaught of the attackers, but not for long.

3   'Like painting the Forth Bridge' is an expression used to describe an endless task. It is a popular belief that since it was constructed in the 1880s, the steel rail bridge over the Firth of Forth in Scotland has been continuously re-painted. That is to say, when they got to the end of it, the painters immediately started all over again. However, in 1997 it was announced that the bridge was to be given a water-repellent coating of a semi-permanent nature, removing the necessity for perpetual redecoration. Furthermore, a Railtrack project manager was quoted as saying, 'The painters have never started at one end and gone all the way to the other and then started all over again. That was always a myth.' Shame.

Reported in the Observer (25 May 1997). Is there an equivalent expression in other countries and languages? L'Abbé Raynal in his Anecdotes littéraires (1750–56) gives the response made by a translator when accused of taking too much trouble and time over a piece of work: 'A quoi il appliquait plaisamment ce qui est dit dans Martial de ce barbier *qui était si longtemps à faire une barbe qu'avant qu'il l'êut achevée, elle commençait à revenir ...* [to which he replied what it says in Martial of the barber who was so long in shaving off a beard that before he had finished, it was beginning to grow again ...].'

1   A saying that became current at the time of Watergate was, 'Once the toothpaste is out of the tube, it is awfully hard to get it back in.' This was said by H. R. Haldeman, President Nixon's aide, to another such, John Dean, on 8 April 1973. It was reported in *Hearings Before the Select Committee on Presidential Campaign Activities: Watergate and Related Activities* (Vol. 4, 1973). The remark has been wrongly attributed to his colleague, John D. Ehrlichman, and to President Nixon himself, but it is probably not an original expression in any case. Indeed, according to Lord Baden-Powell's daughter Heather, the founder of the Scout Movement would reply to those who said that Scouting was impossible for them: 'Nothing is impossible, except putting toothpaste back into the tube.'

Told in Heather King, Baden-Powell, *A Family Album* (1986).

2   Comedian Sandy Powell once told me the origins of his famous catch phrase, 'Can you hear me, mother?': 'I was doing an hour's show on the radio, live, from Broadcasting House in London. I was doing a sketch called "Sandy at the North Pole". I was supposed to be broadcasting home and wanting to speak to my mother. When I got to the line, "Can you hear me, mother?" I dropped my script on the studio floor. While I was picking up the sheets all I could do was repeat the phrase over and over. Well, that was on a Saturday

night. The following week I was appearing at the Hippodrome, Coventry, and the manager came to me at the band rehearsal with a request: "You'll say that, tonight, won't you?" I said, "What?" He said, "'Can you hear me, mother?' Everybody's saying it. Say it and see." So I did and the whole audience joined in and I've been stuck with it ever since. Even abroad – New Zealand, South Africa, Rhodesia – they've all heard it. I'm not saying it was the first radio catch phrase – they were all trying them out – but it was the first to catch on.'

From a telephone interview (1979).

Piggishness

3   An acquaintance of Lord Berners had the impertinent habit of saying to him, 'I've been sticking up for you.' He repeated this once too often and Berners replied, 'Yes, and I have been sticking up for you. Someone said you aren't fit to live with pigs and I said you were.'

This version appears in Edith Sitwell, *Taken Care Of* (1965). Compare the caption to a cartoon by A. Wallis Mills in *Punch* (28 June 1905): '*Lady A.* "HERE COMES THAT DREADFUL MAN WHO SAT NEXT TO ME AT DINNER, HE HASN'T THE MANNERS OF A PIG!" *Mrs B.* "HOW FUNNY! I THOUGHT HE *HAD*!"'

4   Winston Churchill kept a number of pigs on his farm at Chartwell. One day he said to his son-in-law, Christopher Soames, 'I am fond of pigs. Dogs look up to us. Cats look down on us. Pigs treat us as equals.'

Told in Martin Gilbert, *Never Despair* (1988). But was this perhaps a proverbial saying?

Pilgrim Fathers

1 A motion for debate that is an old stand-by of school debating societies – at least, so I recall from the 1950s – is the one proposing that instead of the Pilgrim Fathers landing on the Plymouth Rock, the Plymouth Rock should have landed on the Pilgrim Fathers.

H. L. Mencken in his *Dictionary of Quotations* (1942) has this in the form, 'How much better it would have been if the Plymouth Rock had landed on the Pilgrim Fathers' – and ascribes it to an 'Author unidentified'. Cole Porter's verse to the song 'Anything Goes' also contains the idea (1934).

Place, putting in one's

2 A journalist who had attacked Oscar Wilde in print on a number of occasions came up to him in the street one day and attempted to strike up a conversation. Wilde stared at him for a moment or two and then said: 'You will pardon me: I remember your name but I can't recall your face.'

Recounted by Max Beerbohm in one of the published *Letters to Reggie Turner* (1964).

3 A man came up to Tallulah Bankhead at a party and exclaimed, effusively, 'Tallulah! I haven't seen you for 41 years!' She replied, deadpan, 'I thought I told you to wait in the car.'

Told by Clement Freud on BBC Radio *Quote ... Unquote* (15 January 1979).

Plain speaking

4 As Prime Minister, Clement Attlee summoned a minister who, when he bounded in, was told: 'I want you to resign your job.' When the minister asked why, he was told, simply, 'You're not up to it.'

Told by Sir David Hunt on BBC Radio *Quote ... Unquote* (13 June 1995). Hunt was Attlee's Private Secretary at the time. At other times, as Kenneth Harris has observed, Attlee's use of language was very much 'prep school'. He called people by their nicknames, and used words like 'Rotten', 'Piffle' and 'Tripe'. He referred to one person as 'a good egg'. Recounted by Harris in *The Times* (15 October 1967) and also in his biography of Attlee (1982).

Playfulness

5 Lewis Carroll, the writer, was in real life the rather stuffy Oxford mathematics don, the Reverend C. L. Dodgson, who, famously, only seemed to lighten up when in the company of children (preferably girls). Sometimes his worlds collided. On one occasion, calling at the home of some of his young friends and wearing his customary clergyman's clothes, he rang the door bell, went down on all fours and started barking through the letter box. The door was eventually opened by the children's mother.

I have come to the conclusion that this favourite anecdote probably came from a booklet of reminiscences I picked up in Oxford at the time of the *Alice In Wonderland* centenary of 1965. There is nonetheless a comparable anecdote in which Carroll finds himself in the *barked at* position, given by Sir George Baden-Powell in *The Life and Letters of Lewis Carroll* (ed. Collingwood, 1898): 'Entering the house [of his tutor, Hatch] one day, and facing the dining-room, I heard mysterious noises under the table, and saw the cloth move as if someone were hiding. Children's legs revealed it as no burglar, and there was nothing for it but to crawl upon them, roaring as a lion. Bursting in upon them in their stronghold under the table, I was met by the staid but amused gaze of a reverend gentleman. Frequently afterwards did I see and hear Carroll entertaining the youngsters in his inimitable way.'

1 One day J. B. Morton (the humorist 'Beachcomber') was walking down a crowded Fleet Street with Rupert Hart-Davis, the publisher. He suddenly went up to a pillar box and shouted into the slot: 'You can come out now!'

Recounted in *The Lyttelton Hart-Davis Letters* (for 5 February 1956) where it is said to have happened '20 years ago'. (This is the vocal equivalent of the graffito 'HELP!' written on the slot as though from the inside of the pillar box.)

Playwrights

2 If Oscar Wilde had a rival as the most popular dramatist of the 1890s it was Henry Arthur Jones, whose plays treated of more serious themes. Wilde pronounced on one occasion: 'There are three rules for writing plays. The first rule is not to write like Henry Arthur Jones; the second and third rules are the same.' On another occasion, when Wilde's *A Woman of No Importance* was being rehearsed at a theatre where a Jones play was in its last week, a terrific crash was heard. Wilde spoke: 'Pray do not be alarmed ladies and gentlemen. The crash you have just heard is merely some of Mr Jones's dialogue that has fallen flat.'

Recounted in Hesketh Pearson, *The Life of Oscar Wilde* (1946).

3 During the filming of George Bernard Shaw's play *Caesar and Cleopatra* in the early 1940s, Claude Rains became so exasperated by the author's frequent interruptions that he said, 'If you're not very careful, Mr Shaw, I shall play this part as you want it.'

Told by Kenneth Williams on BBC Radio *Quote ... Unquote* (19 February 1979).

4 Agatha Christie's play *The Mousetrap* has famously become the longest continuously running stage play in the world. When it was first tried out in 1952 in Nottingham before coming to the West End, the part of Detective Sergeant Trotter was played by Richard Attenborough. He recalls that the cast was worried that the second act wouldn't work, and a good deal of agonizing over it went on. Christie, taking her leave on one occasion, remarked, 'I should stop worrying and get off to bed. I think we might get quite a nice little run out of it ...'

Told in *The Times* (22 November 1982) – but Attenborough had been telling the story long before, as on a BBC Radio *Home This Afternoon* broadcast (1966). In that, he has her say, 'Darlings, I think we might get quite a little run,' though one wonders if the 'darlings' isn't himself coming through.

5 Maggie Smith was appearing with Edward Fox in Ronald Harwood's play *Interpreters*, which was not doing terribly good business. Harwood, being a sociable cove, was nevertheless always popping in and out of the stars' dressing rooms, attempting to keep their spirits up. This did not go down well with Smith, so when she said, 'Oh, hello, and what are you doing?' to Harwood and he replied, 'Struggling with a new play, darling,' she took the opportunity to comment, 'Aren't we all?'

Michael Coveney in *Maggie Smith: A Bright Particular Star* (1992), gives the exchange as, '... Trying to finish a new play, darling' and '... Try finishing this one first.'

Plums

1 Consider the nursery rhyme:

> Little Jack Horner
> Sat in the corner,
> Eating a Christmas pie.
> He put in his thumb,
> And pulled out a plum,
> And said, What a good boy am I?

A tradition has grown up that in the sixteenth century, at the time of the dissolution of the monasteries, the Abbot of Glastonbury sent his steward Jack Horner to London. In an attempt to appease King Henry VIII, Horner was bearing a Christmas pie containing the title deeds of twelve manors. But Horner 'put in his thumb' and pulled out the other kind of 'plum' – the deeds to the Manor of Mells in Somerset – and put them to his own use. A Thomas Horner did take up residence in Mells shortly after the dissolution, and his descendants lived there until late in the twentieth century.

Source: Iona and Peter Opie, *The Oxford Dictionary of Nursery Rhymes* (1951).

Politeness

2 The Battle of Fontenoy between French and British forces in 1745 is said to have been the politest ever fought. Lord Hay, leader of the British forces, began with the words: 'My lords the French guards, please fire!' The Count of Autreroche, leading Louis XV's troops, replied: 'No, my Lords the English, you fire first!'

The English did – but still lost the battle.

Told in the *Daily Mail* (6 November 1998).

3 A formidable woman he did not admire encountered Oscar Wilde one evening at a party. 'Ah, Mr Wilde,' she said, beaming at him, 'I passed your house this afternoon.' 'Thank you so much,' he replied.

Contributed to BBC Radio *Quote ... Unquote* (1 January 1979).

Political correctness and incorrectness

4 An American broadcaster, Tex Antoine, said on air in 1975: 'With rape so predominant in the news lately, it is well to remember the words of Confucius: "If rape is inevitable, lie back and enjoy it."' ABC News suspended Antoine for his remark, then demoted him to working in the weather department and prohibited him from appearing on the air.

Told in Barbara Rowes, *The Book of Quotes* (1979). 'When rape is inevitable, lie back and enjoy it' is best described – as it is in Paul Scott's novel *The Jewel in the Crown* (1966) – as 'that old, disreputable saying'. Daphne Manners, upon whose 'rape' Scott's story hinges, adds: 'I can't say, Auntie, that I lay back and enjoyed mine.' 'A mock-Confucianism' is how Eric Partridge describes it in his *Dictionary of Slang* (1984 ed.), giving a date *c.* 1950 – and one is unlikely ever to learn when, or from whom, it first arose.

5 There is a story told of a (white) American woman TV reporter interviewing either Bishop Desmond Tutu or Nelson Mandela in South Africa. She was apparently so intent on being politically correct and on avoiding use of the word 'black' that she asked one of these gentlemen what it really felt like being an 'African-American'.

Told in my *The Politically Correct Phrasebook* (1993).

Pomposity

1 A pompous woman complained to
Lord Berners that the head waiter of a
restaurant had not shown her husband
and herself immediately to a table.
'We had to tell him who we were,' she
said. Berners, interested, inquired,
'And who were you?'

Version from Edith Sitwell, *Taken Care Of*
(1965). Also told about John Betjeman.
However, Patrick Balfour in *Society Racket*
(1933) noted: 'I discovered the other day
that [this] remark, attributed to a modern
wit (and a true wit), Lord Berners, was
in fact made by Lord Charles Beresford.' On
11 January 1933, *Punch* carried a cartoon
by Fred Pegram, with the caption: 'They had
the cheek to say there wasn't a single room
in the whole blasted place. We were simply
furious, and so we told 'em who we were.' –
'Really, and who were you?'

Possessiveness

2 After reviewing some Vietnam-bound
Marines, President Johnson moved
towards a helicopter for his return
journey to the White House. An officer
helpfully pointed out another chopper,
saying, 'That's your helicopter over
there.' 'Son,' replied L.B.J., 'they are all
my helicopters.'

Told in Hugh Sidey, *A Very Personal
Presidency* (1968).

Power

3 The name of King Canute (or Knute
or Cnut or Knut) is often evoked in a
mistaken fashion. The tale is told of his
having a throne carried down to the
water's edge, his instructing the waves
to go away from him, and his failure
thereat. The image is summoned up
when one wants to portray pointless
resistance to an idea, or clinging to an

untenable position. However, it is
wrong to paint Canute as a fool. After
all, the whole point of the story was
that Canute carried out the demonstration in order to show his courtiers
that there were limits to his power.
As he said, 'Know, all inhabitants of
earth, that vain and trivial is the power
of kings, nor is anyone worthy of the
name of king save Him whose nod
heaven and earth and sea obey under
laws eternal.'

The original anecdote, pointing the correct
moral, first appears in Henry of Huntingdon's
Historia Anglorum, a twelfth-century manuscript, from which the above quotation is
taken. Canute (*c.* 995–1035) was King of
England, Norway and Denmark.

Prayers

4 The Reverend Sydney Smith is reported
to have had alternative graces to say,
according to what was on the bill of
fare. If champagne was to be served, he
would begin, 'O, bountiful Jehovah ...'
If it was not, he would say, 'O Lord,
we thank thee for even the least of thy
benefits ...'

Told by the Reverend Roger Royle on BBC
Radio *Quote ... Unquote* (15 September
1984).

5 When King Edward VII died, Lord
Kinnoull's little daughter, who had wit-
nessed the funeral procession, refused
to say her prayers that night. 'It won't
be of any use,' she explained, 'God will
be too busy unpacking King Edward.'

Recounted in Lord Riddell, *More Pages from
My Diary 1908–14* (1934).

6 Lilian Baylis became famous for falling
to her knees and invoking divine aid
whenever it was necessary (and it was, a
lot). Once she was overheard praying,

'O God, send me some good actors – cheap.'

Told in Russell and Sybil Thorndike, *Lilian Baylis* (1938). In *The New Yorker* (16 September 1950) this became, 'O Lord, send me a good tenor – cheap.'

1 In the North Riding of Yorkshire, there was an uncle of Sir David Hunt's, who was a clergyman. His church was visited by a friendly American gentleman who was looking up his family tree and ancestors. The American had a satisfactory result, and coming away he said, 'I see you have a fund for restoring the organ and you want ten thousand and are twelve hundred pounds short of it. I will make up the shortfall.' And so he was invited to the dedication ceremony of the organ, but a slightly sour note crept into the proceedings at one point when the uncle prayed, 'We thank thee, Lord, for having heard our prayer and for having in our hour of need, sent this timely succour.'

Told by Sir David Hunt on BBC Radio *Quote ... Unquote* (13 June 1995).

2 At a village kirk in the Scottish Highlands, the minister was much given to interminable impromptu prayer, but occasionally lost his train of thought. 'Oh Lord,' he entreated, 'Thou that paintest the crocus purple ...' Here, his inspiration failing him, he rapidly concluded: '... paint us purple, too.'

Contributed by J. M. Dick-Cunyngham to BBC Radio *Quote ... Unquote* (25 August 1984).

3 Was there ever really an Anglican priest who prayed: 'Dear God, as you will undoubtedly have read in the leader column of *The Times* this morning ...'?

Recalled by Anna Ford (a clergyman's daughter) on BBC Radio *Quote ... Unquote* (29 June 1977). Richard Ingrams, *Muggeridge: The Biography* (1995) has, rather: 'A story was current at the time [1930s] of a clergyman who began an impromptu prayer with the words "Oh God, as thou wilt have read in the *Manchester Guardian* this morning ..."'

4 The comedian Ted Ray was being installed as King Rat, chief of the Water Rats, the variety performers' club. Part of his duties included saying grace before the meal – a task to which he was not accustomed and which he performed in an inaudible mumble. The toastmaster, in a typically stentorian tone, said to Ray, 'Speak up, sir, your guests can't hear you!' Quick as a flash, Ray replied, 'You mind your own business. I'm not talking to them.'

Recounted by Bernard Braden in *The Kindness of Strangers* (1990). Compare, however, this caption to a cartoon by Kenneth Beauchamp in *Punch* (11 August 1926): 'Don't mumble your prayers, Helen. I can't hear a word you say!' 'I wasn't speaking to you, Mother!'

5 Alan Melville told a story involving his Aunt Kate: 'She had a visit one tea-time from an old friend she hadn't seen for a very long time. It turned out that the old friend had "got religion" and when she came she announced to Aunt Kate that she had found Christ. Aunt Kate said the right things – that she was delighted to hear it, you know – and the old friend went on and on and on about it. Eventually, to Aunt Kate's great embarrassment this lady said, "Shall we go down on our knees and say a prayer together?" And Aunt Kate said in a panic – and she didn't mean it

to be a "funny" – "Oh, I don't think so, dear, we've just Hoovered the carpet!'"

As told by him on BBC Radio *Quote . . . Unquote* (23 July 1983).

1 The Reverend David Bradford, a journalist who took to the cloth after serving *The Scotsman* in the parliamentary lobby, was asked to say grace at the lobby's centenary lunch in 1984. He produced a nicely tailored version to bless the meeting of this semi-secret society: 'Oh God, before whom all are attributable, make us truly thankful.'

Told in *The Sunday Times* (22 January 1984).

Precocity

2 The scholar and bible-translator Ronald Knox once related how it had been alleged by a friend of the family that when Knox was a mere four years old and suffering from insomnia, he was asked how he managed to occupy his time at night. He answered, apparently, 'I lie awake and think about the past.'

In Ronald Knox, *Literary Distractions* (1941).

Presents

3 Unwanted, not to say, unwelcome Christmas presents were the subject of correspondence in *The Times* in 1988. The most disturbing tale was contained in this letter on 23 November:

Sir,
The worst passed-on present my father ever received from his eldest sister was a pair of what looked like unused bed-socks. He, in fury, gave them to me.

When I put them on I found, to my horror, a used corn plaster in one of the toe ends. My aunt, at the time, kept a small private hotel.
Yours faithfully,
J. B. Prior

Reprinted in John Julius Norwich, *A Christmas Cracker* (1991).

Press

4 President Johnson once said of the media that, if one morning he walked on top of the water across the Potomac River, the headline that afternoon would read, PRESIDENT CAN'T SWIM.

Told in *Time* Magazine (28 December 1987). This is a story beloved of politicians. Neil Kinnock, when leader of the British Labour Party, said: 'Worried about my media coverage, I consulted a fortune-teller. She told me to perform miracles, so I walked across the Thames. Next day the *Sun* headline ran: Neil Kinnock fails to swim river.' (Quoted in *Sunday Today*, 17 May 1987.) The Right Reverend Desmond Tutu, Archbishop of Cape Town, also used to tell a story about himself: 'Tutu and State President P. W. Botha are in a boat in Table Bay when a storm blows up. Tutu says: "It's all right, I'll get help" and walks across the water. The next day in the Afrikaans paper, the headline is: "Tutu Kan Nie Swem Nie" – Tutu can't swim.' (Quoted in the *Observer* Magazine, 20 March 1988.)

Pretentiousness

5 Two London taxi drivers were having a heated dispute. Said one, 'You know what you are, don't you? – pretentious!' And the other adopted a tone of hurt pride. *'Pretentious?'* he replied. *'Moi?'*

Told by Anna Ford on BBC Radio *Quote . . . Unquote* (1 January 1979). David Elias has pointed out that this story features in an episode entitled 'The Psychiatrist' in the BBC TV comedy series *Fawlty Towers*. That, too, was first broadcast in 1979. Well,

I think it must have been a joke that was in the air at the time and I don't believe that it was originated by *Fawlty Towers*. For a start, it is told as a 'joke' in the episode – and a joke that gets repeated as a 'joke'. Besides, Anna Ford recorded her version for us on 5 December 1978.

Paul Cloutman wonders whether the real begetter of this joke wasn't Miss Piggy in *The Muppet Show*, also mid- to late 1970s? Certainly she did use the word *moi*, and one can just imagine her making this response when criticized in some way by Kermit the Frog. Michael Lewis thinks it first appeared in the episode in which Miss Piggy memorably danced 'Swine Lake' with Rudolf Nureyev. If he is correct about the Nureyev show, that was transmitted in the UK on 22 January 1978 and thus the joke clearly predates the 1979 *Fawlty Towers* use.

Priests

1 Groucho Marx was going down in the lift from the sixth floor at the Hotel Danieli in Venice. At the fourth floor, four priests got in. One of them recognized Groucho and said, 'Excuse me, Mr Marx, my mother was a great fan of yours.' To which Groucho retorted: 'I didn't know you guys were allowed to have mothers.'

Told by Larry Adler (who was in the lift, too) on BBC Radio *Quote ... Unquote* (1 February 1976).

Prime ministers

2 A. J. P. Taylor, the historian, once mused upon Gladstone's reported statement that he had known eleven prime ministers and seven of them had been adulterers. Who were the seven? Taylor named Canning (with Queen Caroline when she was Princess of Wales – according to George IV, that is), Wellington (too many to count), Earl Grey of the Reform Bill (with the

Duchess of Devonshire), Melbourne (with Mrs Norton, though disputed), Disraeli (mistress traded to Lord Lyndhurst) and Palmerston (too many to count). That makes six. Who was the seventh? Did Gladstone count himself, Taylor wondered.

In *The London Review of Books* (2–29 December 1982).

3 It has become the custom for the Queen to gather her ex-prime ministers together for a spot of socializing from time to time. Harold Macmillan once mused on what the collective noun should be for such a group. He came up with: 'A *lack* of principals'.

Source untraced. However, George Lyttelton in *The Lyttelton Hart-Davis Letters* (Vol. 3, 1981) (letter of 23 January 1959) has 'a lack of principals' as the collective noun for 'heads of colleges', which is more apposite.

4 Prime Minister John Major is alleged to have said when opening his first Cabinet meeting in 1990: 'Well – who'd have thought it?'

Source untraced. Mentioned in *The 'Quote ... Unquote' Newsletter* (April 1993).

5 When John Major presided over sterling's ignominious exit from the European Exchange Rate Mechanism in 1992, he telephoned Kelvin Mackenzie, editor of the *Sun*, to ask what the newspaper was going to say about it next day. 'Let me put it like this,' Mackenzie replied, 'I've got two buckets of shit on my desk and tomorrow morning I'm going to empty both of them over your head.' There was long pause and then the Prime Minister replied, 'Oh, Kelvin you are a joker.'

Told in Andrew Marr, *Ruling Britannia* (1995).

Principles

1 George Bernard Shaw encountered a lady at a party and their conversation proceeded to the point where he asked her: 'Would you sleep with me if I gave you £10,000?' She thought about the proposition and acknowledged that, theoretically, she would. 'Good,' said Shaw, 'so would you also sleep with me for sixpence?' The lady became indignant. 'What sort of woman do you think I am?' she exploded. 'We've established what sort of woman you are,' the writer pointed out, 'we're merely haggling over the price.'

Told in Epson advertisements (May 1987) – where the figure given was £500. The origin of this exchange remains untraced. This is the earliest citation found so far, ascribing it to Shaw. Compare, from William Rushton, *Superpig* (1976): 'This is from the same stable as a Lord Curzon asking some duchess or other whether she'd bed down with him for a million pounds and saying upon her eager nod, "Having established the principle, now let's get down to the hard bargaining."'

Priorities

2 W. B. Yeats, on being told over the telephone that he had been awarded the Nobel Prize for Literature in 1923, interrupted his caller with: 'Stop babbling, man! How much?'

Told in *A Dictionary of Literary Quotations* (1990). Another version: on being told how great an honour it was for himself and for the country, he asked, 'How much is it, Smyllie, how much is it?' – attributed in *Irish Literary Portraits*, ed. W. R. Rodgers (1972).

3 Sam Goldwyn attempted to buy from George Bernard Shaw the film rights of his plays. There was a protracted haggle over what the rights would cost,

which ended in Shaw's declining to sell. 'The trouble is, Mr Goldwyn,' said Shaw, 'you are interested only in art and I am interested only in money.'

Told in Alva Johnson, *The Great Goldwyn* (1937). Bennett Cerf, *Try and Stop Me* (1947), has it that *Pygmalion* was specifically at issue.

4 The following advertisement is said to have appeared in a South African newspaper: 'Man of 38 wishes to meet woman of 30 owning a tractor. Please enclose picture of tractor ...'

According to *The Mail on Sunday* of 4 January 1987, this was an advertisement in *The Mountain Echo* of Himeville 'in Drakesburg Mountain', South Africa. (They probably meant 'Drakensberg Mountains'.) But if it did ever appear in that newspaper, it was by no means original. Compare the slightly earlier citation in a book called *Glad to Be Grey* by Peter Freedman, published in 1985: 'Young farmer with 100 acres would be pleased to hear from young lady with tractor. Please send photograph of tractor.' The source given for this was 'the personal columns of the *Evesham Admag*, 1977'.

In 1983, Ronnie Corbett or Ronnie Barker had used the same gag in one of their BBC comedy programmes (an edition featured on the video *The Best of The Two Ronnies*) – though here the context was that of a man visiting a psychiatrist and the prize was not a tractor but tickets for the Cup Final.

How far back can we take the matter beyond this? Well, Roger S. Windsor, writing to me from Arequipa, Peru, in 1988, made a confident bid for January 1963: 'I was in my final year of veterinary studies at the Royal Veterinary College in Edinburgh and we organized the Annual Conference of the Association of Veterinary Students of Great Britain and Ireland. At one of the formal lunches organized for the delegates, Arthur Smith was the after-lunch speaker. He was at the time captain of Scotland's rugby team and had recently returned from South Africa where he had captained the Lions. At the lunch he told the story of an advertisement in *The Rand Daily Mail* in which a man has advertised for a wife who had to be in possession of two tickets for the test. The advertisement ran, "Please send a photograph ... of the tickets" ...'

If nothing else, Mr Windsor's recollection takes the joke back to South Africa. Is that where it really started? And did such an ad ever appear in a paper there – or anywhere?

A curious parallel joke appeared in the obituary of Brigadier John Reed, founder of the Aldershot Military Museum, in the *Daily Telegraph* (12 March 1992). Apparently, the section of the museum devoted to the Canadian Army's connection with Aldershot displays a letter written to Vincent Massey, the Canadian High Commissioner in London (1935–46). It was from a woman who lived in the town. She wrote: 'A Canadian soldier on leave has stayed at my house and as a result both my daughter and myself are pregnant. Not that we hold that against your soldier, but the last time we saw him he took away my daughter's bicycle which she needs to go to work. Can you get him to return it?'

Privates

1 The little girl made a classic comment to the little boy when he dropped his trousers for her to have a look – 'My,' she said, 'that's a handy little gadget.'

In my book *Babes and Sucklings* (1983), I said this remark had reached me from several sources – 'One says it involved "the daughter of a friend", another says "it was told me by a friend who was a teacher about the local primary school at which he taught", and a third specifically says it concerned "our 2-year-old son".' In 1992, Miss Pera J. Bain of Brighton, having heard me allude to 'handy little gadgets' on the radio, wrote to say she had first heard it in 1941 when she was in charge of Inspection at a very small factory in Woking, staffed entirely by women. 'The Tool-Setter came from Scotland ... Relatives of hers lived in a croft on one of the outer islands. They had one small daughter, Alison,

who rarely saw another child. But they had a visit from relatives who had one small boy. Shortly after arrival this child said he needed the lavatory, so Alison was told to show him the bathroom. Which she did and presently she was heard to say, "*That's* a handy little gadget ye have there."' Indeed, I think some of the other versions I have heard were spoken with a Scots accent – even to the point of re-phrasing it, 'a handy *wee* gadget'.

2 The man in uniform dancing with the girl told her – when she asked – that he was a Gurkha officer. 'But I thought all Gurkhas were black,' exclaimed the girl. 'No,' the officer corrected her, 'only our privates are black.' Said she: 'My dear, how fantastic!'

Told in *The Kenneth Williams Diaries* (1993) – entry for 28 July 1954, where Williams says he was told it by John Schlesinger.

Promotion

3 In the days before he became a comedian, W. C. Fields was for a time a newspaper vendor in Philadelphia. As you might anticipate, he had a somewhat eccentric way of promoting his wares. 'Bronislaw Gimp,' he might say, 'Bronislaw Gimp acquires licence for two-year-old sheepdog. Details on page 26.' It is said that many citizens of Philadelphia bought copies out of simple curiosity.

Source untraced (but known by 1986).

Prompting

4 Robert Atkins's production of *Hamlet* was, on one occasion, notable for his loudly whispered stage directions to the cast. It was also clear when he himself had forgotten his lines. He would say, 'Couch me awhile and mark', shuffle down to the prompt corner for

enlightenment, and carry on until the next uncertainty brought him back there again.

Recalled by Michael York in *Travelling Player* (1991). The line 'Couch me awhile and mark' does actually occur in *Hamlet*, spoken by the Prince (V.i.222).

1 Atkins was rehearsing one of his open-air productions in Regent's Park with the cast all seated round him on the ground. When one young actress failed to pick up her cue, Atkins noted that she was sitting disconsolately with her head in her lap, and said: 'It's no good looking up your entrance, dear – you've missed it.'

Recounted by Ian McKellen on BBC Radio *Quote … Unquote* (3 July 1979).

Pronunciation

2 Sir Robert Baden-Powell's surname presented a double challenge to those wishing to pronounce it. Happily, he came to their aid with a little rhyme:

> Man, matron, maiden,
> Please call it Baden.
> Further for Powell,
> Rhyme it with Noel.

Recounted in William Hillcourt, *Baden-Powell: The Two Lives of a Hero* (1964).

3 George Bernard Shaw had a lifetime desire to rationalize English spelling. At the end of a meeting of like-minded supporters, a lady approached him and gushingly said, 'Isn't it fascinating that sugar is the only word in the English language where su is pro-nounced *sh*?' Shaw looked pityingly at the woman and said, 'Are you sure?'

Reportedly in Hesketh Pearson, *Bernard Shaw* (1942). Another version is that Liddell Hart once observed to Shaw, 'Do

you know that "sumac" and "sugar" are the only two words in the English language that begin with *su* and are pronounced *shu*?' Shaw replied, 'Sure.'

4 Dorothy Parker arrived at South-ampton aboard the *Berengaria* and was met by the press, who wanted to know what she would be doing in England. 'I came on the spur of the moment,' she answered, 'and haven't worked out a schedule [pronounced *skedule*].' When one of the reporters pointed out that in England, the pronunciation was *shedule*, Parker exclaimed, 'Oh, skit.'

Context from a letter by Jason Lindsey in the *Independent* (27 July 1993).

5 On a visit to the United States, Lady Asquith met Jean Harlow. The film actress inquired whether the name of the Countess was pronounced 'Margo' or 'Margott'. '"Margo",' replied the Countess, 'the "T" is silent – as in "Harlow".'

I have always had a lingering doubt about this story as I have never come across a reputable source. I heard it first in about 1968. It did not appear in print until T. S. Matthews's *Great Tom* in 1973. Then, in about 1983, I was given a much more convincing version of its origin. Margot *Grahame* (1911–82) was an English actress who, after stage appear-ances in Johannesburg and London, went to Hollywood in 1934. Her comparatively brief career as a film star included appearances in *The Informer*, *The Buccaneer* and *The Three Musketeer*s, in the mid-1930s.

It was when she was being built up as a rival to the likes of Harlow (who died in 1937) that Grahame herself apparently later claimed the celebrated exchange had occurred. She added that it was not intended as a put-down. She did not realize what she had said till afterwards.

Grahame seems a convincing candidate for speaker of the famous line. I believe she did say it and, when her star waned, people attributed the remark to the other, better-known and more quotable Margot.

1 On 25 December 1950, Scottish nationalists removed the Stone of Scone from under the Coronation Chair in Westminster Abbey. It is said that Lionel Marson, a senior BBC news-reader gave the news and added that, 'The stone was first brought to England in 1297 by Edward Isst.' Summoned afterwards to tell the Head of Presen-tation what on earth he had meant by saying 'Edward Isst' he is supposed to have replied lamely, 'How was I supposed to know it was Edward Iced?'

Told by Brian Matthew on BBC Radio *Quote ... Unquote* (21 August 1980). The first part is probably true, the second part probably apocryphal. Jack de Manio in *To Auntie With Love* (1967) has a version related by John Snagge, who was the Head of Presentation in question.

2 The first name of the comedienne, singer and actress, Bette Midler, is pro-nounced 'Bet' because her parents mistakenly thought that Bette Davis did likewise.

A fact.

3 Like many news broadcasters, Andrew Gardner practised hard to pronounce correctly the name of the Nigerian premier, Sir Abubakar Tafawah Balewa. 'Sir Abubakar Tafawah Balewa,' he would say, over and over again, trying to get it right. Then, just as the pro-nunciation was perfect, Sir Abubakar Tafawah Balewa was shot dead in a coup.

Related by Gardner on an edition of ITV's *It'll Be Alright On the Night* in the 1980s. Balewa died in 1966.

4 ... Time passes and little changes. TV newscasters may still find themselves faced with unpronounceable African names, though few had the aplomb of Bob Friend when dealing with a double dose once on Sky News. Two African leaders had been killed in an air crash, but the first Friend knew about it was when their unpronounceable names rolled up towards him on the Autocue. 'We'll let you know their names,' he said, 'when their next of kin have been informed.'

Recalled on *10 Years of National and International News* (Sky News, 7 February 1999).

Propaganda

5 During the Second World War, the future novelist Ian Fleming worked in 'black propaganda' with the journalist Sefton Delmer. One of their schemes – which, alas, was never put into action – was to broadcast an instruction to the German people. They would be told that, in order to allow German scientists to ensure that the war was having no deleterious effect on their digestive tracts, a mass examination of faeces was being arranged. In short, the German people was being asked to save its shit. This would then be collect-ed at various designated points. It would be suggested that the best thing for them to do was to deposit the shit in letter boxes.

Told to me by Sefton Delmer in March 1972.

Prophecies and predictions

6 Mark Twain said, the year before his death, 'I came in with Halley's comet in 1835. It is coming again next year and

I expect to go out with it. It will be the greatest disappointment of my life if I don't go out with Halley's comet. The Almighty has said, no doubt: "Now, here are these two unaccountable freaks; they came in together, they must go out together." And so it was. Twain died on 21 April 1910, the day after the comet reappeared.

Told in *The Autobiography of Mark Twain*, ed. A. B. Paine, (1912).

1 However good Thomas Edison may have been as an inventor, he did not always have a good instinct about the prospects for other peoples' inventions. In 1926, he said, 'I have determined that there is no market for talking pictures.'

Told in Stuart Berg Flexner, *Listening to America* (1982).

2 In addition, Edison seems not to have been too confident of his own inventions. He said to his assistant, Samuel Insull, on one occasion: 'The phonograph is not of any commercial value.' He had hopes that his invention would find a use in business rather than for entertainment.

Told in Robert A. Conot, *A Stroke of Luck* (1979) and Christopher Cerf, *The Experts Speak* (1984).

3 At Dirk Bogarde's Rank Organization audition, studio executive Earl St John got it all wrong. He said to him: 'Nice of you to come, but your head's too small for the camera, you are too thin, and ... I don't know what it is exactly about the neck ... but it's not right.'

Recounted by Bogarde in *Snakes and Ladders* (1978), the second volume of his autobiography.

4 A prophetic remark was attributed to French President Charles de Gaulle after attending President Kennedy's funeral in 1963. Of Jackie Kennedy he is supposed to have said: 'I can see her in about ten years from now on the yacht of a Greek petrol millionaire.' In 1968, she married Aristotle Onassis.

In *Fallen Oaks* (1972), André Malraux recalls de Gaulle as having said, rather, 'She is a star, and will end up on the yacht of some oil baron.' When later reminded that he had said this, de Gaulle told Malraux: 'Did I say that? Well, well ... Fundamentally I would rather have believed that she would marry Sartre. Or you!'
    Compare this story from *Pass the Port* (1976): Chairman Mao Tse-tung [Mao Zedong], the Chinese leader, was asked whether the world would have been any different if Nikita Khrushchev had been assassinated in 1963 instead of President Kennedy. Mao thought for a moment and then replied, 'I think there would have been one difference. I very much doubt whether Mr Aristotle Onassis would have married Mrs Khrushchev.' The origin of this version may have been a remark attributed (in *The Sunday Times*, 4 June 1989) to Gore Vidal.

Public reactions

5 Actor Peter Jones had just started to appear in the TV series *Mr Big* when he was accosted by a woman in the street: 'Oh, Mr Jones, I do so enjoy your programme. It's so *mediocre* – something in it for the whole family.'

Recounted by him on BBC Radio *Quote ... Unquote* (10 July 1979).

Publishers

6 The story has it that when John Murray, Byron's publisher, sent the poet a copy of the Bible in return for a favour, he sent it back with the words

'Now Barabbas was a robber' (John 18:40) altered to, 'Now Barabbas was a publisher ...'

Told in Kazlitt Arvine's *Cyclopedia of Anecdotes of Literature and the Fine Arts* published in Boston, Massachussetts, in 1851. In 1981, the then head of the firm, John G. (Jock) Murray, told me that those involved were in fact the poet Coleridge and *his* publishers, Longmans. But when I asked for evidence in 1988, he could only say that, 'I have satisfied myself that it was not Byron.' The copy of Byron's Bible that exists has no such comment in it. He also drew my attention to the fact that in Byron's day publishers were more usually called booksellers. *H. L. Mencken's Dictionary of Quotations* (1942), on the other hand, gives Thomas Campbell as the probable perpetrator, so does *Benham's Book of Quotations* (1948), and so did Samuel Smiles in *A Publisher and his Friends: Memoir and Correspondence of the late John Murray*, Vol. 1, Chap. 14 (1891), perhaps on account of the following anecdote.

1 Certainly, Thomas Campbell seems to have taken the required attitude. At a literary dinner he once toasted Napoleon with the words: 'We must not forget that he once shot a bookseller.'

Told in G. O. Trevelyan, *The Life and Letters of Lord Macaulay*, (1876) – diary entry for 12 December 1848. Mark Twain recalled this in one of his letters: 'How often we recall, with regret, that Napoleon once shot at a magazine editor and missed him and killed a publisher. But we remember with charity, that his intentions were good.' Details of Napoleon's achievement remain untraced.

Punctuality

2 When George Washington's secretary excused himself for being late and laid the blame on his watch, Washington simply told him: 'Then you must find another watch, or I another secretary.'

Recalled in Peter Hay, *Harrap's Book of Business Anecdotes* (1988).

3 Lord Nelson once said, 'I owe all my success in life to having been always a quarter of an hour before my time' (i.e. early). Chiefly in sea battles rather than in private life, one expects.

We have this statement by courtesy of Samuel Smiles in *Self-Help* (1859). In *The Dictionary of War Quotations* (1989) the wording is: 'I have always been a quarter of an hour before my time, and it has made a man of me.'

Punishments

4 The most famous story about Sir John Reith's reign of terror as first Director-General of the BBC concerns the youngish radio announcer who was caught *in flagrante* with a young woman. Quite what the extent of his misdemeanour was is not recorded, nor the precise location (was it at Savoy Hill – the BBC's first base – or in Broadcasting House?) Whatever the case, Reith was persuaded that the young man should not be sacked because he had never done anything like it before, and was, besides, a very good announcer. Reith only agreed to this on the understanding that, 'Never in any circumstances must he introduce the Epilogue!'

Related in Malcolm Muggeridge, *Tread Softly for You Tread on My Jokes* (1966) and Jack de Manio, *To Auntie With Love* (1967).

Puns and punning

5 When Pope Gregory came across some British captives for sale in the market-place at Rome, he inquired as to what nationality they were. 'Angles,' was the

reply. Obviously rather taken with their physical appearance, Gregory punned, '*Non Angli, sed Angeli* [Not Angles but Angels].'

In Bede's *Historia Ecclesiastica* (AD 731), Gregory's comment is given, rather, as: 'It is well, for they have the faces of angels, and such should be the co-heirs of the angels of heaven.' Rome-born Gregory I, the Great (*c.* 540–604), was Pope from 590.

1 Oliver St John Gogarty was asked for his view on the prostitutes who plied their trade under the trees down by the River Liffey in Dublin at the last turn of the century. Did he think the trees should be cut down? 'No,' he said. 'Surely the trees are more sinned against than sinning.'

Told in Ned Sherrin *In His Anecdotage* (1993).

2 One of my most treasured moments from the wireless comes from about 1980 and occurred when a foreign correspondent was referring to the Kurdish autonomy movement in Iran and Iraq. He said, 'There is a danger of civil war if the Kurds don't get their way.'

Contributed to BBC Radio *Quote ... Unquote* (28 August 1980) by Mr E. E. Harding of Bromley, Kent. This only goes to confirm one theory about the roots of humour, that people don't make up jokes, the jokes are there in the English language waiting to be let out. Ronald Pearsall in his survey of Victorian humour, *Collapse of Stout Party* (1975) relates that this joke was alive and well 'a hundred years ago ... In New College common room, Walter Thursby, don and explorer, related how he had scaled Mount Ararat. The snow was not so bad as expected, he explained, but because of marauding tribes a guard of Kurdish soldiers had been provided. Later Arthur Riding went up to him and commented: "I understand you

took some Curds with you to show the whey."' In addition, *Punch* has the punning headline 'Kurds and their ways' on 12 February 1881.

Put-downs

3 The 5th Earl of Rosebery was a lavish and hospitable host who liked to have the best wit and conversation at his dinner table that London society could supply. A frequent guest at Mentmore Towers on these occasions was an old farmer who worked on the Earl's estate. He was unlettered and of plain country speech, but with a fine head of white hair and a white beard. Lord Rosebery, who was fond of the old fellow, liked to have him present as a sort of foil to the overbred character of some of his other guests, and their hothouse talk.

One evening at such a dinner, a young aesthete was holding forth to the assembled company on the Fine Arts and matters of the intellect, and more than once turned to the farmer, who sat listening in silence, and remarked: 'You, of course, would understand nothing of this, because you are merely a Philistine.' Finally, the old man plucked up courage to protest. 'You keep telling me that I am a Philistine, but I do not even know what that means. What is a Philistine?' Rosebery, seizing the chance, came at once to the aid of his friend: 'My dear old fellow! Do you not know what a Philistine is? It is simple: *he is a man who is being annoyed by the jawbone of an ass!*

Told by Douglas J. Bolger (1998). The biblical reference is to Judges 15:16.

4 Noël Coward satirized Edith Sitwell and her two brothers, Osbert and Sacheverell, in a revue sketch with the title 'The Swiss Family Whittlebot'.

This did not go down at all well with the Sitwells, and hostilities raged between the two camps for some time. Coward summed up his opponents as 'Two wiseacres and a cow'.

Told in John Pearson, *Façades* (1978).

1 During the Second World War, Winston Churchill agreed to supply condoms to Soviet troops with the proviso that each box should be stamped with the words 'EXTRA SMALL'.

Told, for example, in the *Independent* (12 October 1998) but not sourced.

2 Gore Vidal has had a number of outstanding feuds in his life. In 1968, he had an almighty spat with William F. Buckley Jr, who, he said, 'Looks and sounds not unlike Hitler, but without the charm'. Mutual lawsuits raged for a period.

Told in the *Observer* (26 April 1981). Later, 'A power-crazed ego-maniac, a kind of Hitler without the charm' was a line used by Peter Cook about Dudley Moore in a newspaper interview of February 1979.

3 Conversing with a much-decorated Brazilian military official, Prince Philip asked him where he had won his medals. 'In the war,' said the military man. To which Prince Philip countered, with his customary tact, 'I didn't know Brazil was in the war that long?' The man replied: 'At least, Sir, I didn't get them from marrying my wife.'

Recounted in Donald Spoto, *The Decline and Fall of the House of Windsor* (1995). Another version has it that Philip asked a Brazilian admiral if he had won his medals on the artificial lake at Brasilia.

Queens

1 Not so long after Princess Margaret's wedding to the photographer Anthony Armstrong-Jones (Lord Snowdon) in 1960, the Queen was speaking to a guest at one of her garden parties. 'What is your profession?' she asked, interested as ever in the world around her. 'I'm a photographer, ma'am,' the man replied. 'Oh, how interesting,' said Her Majesty, 'I have a brother-in-law who is a photographer ...' 'Even more of a coincidence,' said the man, 'I have a brother-in-law who's a queen!'

This story comes round quite often. In *The Kenneth Williams Diaries* (1993) it is recorded on 1 May 1963 and said to be 'current at the moment'.

Questions, rhetorical

2 'Will no man rid me of this turbulent priest?' – Henry II's rhetorical question regarding the Archbishop of Canterbury Thomas Becket – which was unfortunately acted upon by the Archbishop's murderers in 1170 – is ascribed to 'oral tradition' by the *Oxford Dictionary of Quotations* (1979) in the form: 'Will no one revenge me of the injuries I have sustained from one turbulent priest?' The King, who was in Normandy, had received reports that the Archbishop was ready 'to tear the crown' from his head. 'What a pack of fools and cowards I have nourished in my house,' he cried, according to another version, 'that not one of them will avenge me of this turbulent priest!' Yet another version has, 'of this upstart clerk'. Henry would have said whatever he said in a western version of medieval French, strongly contaminated by Provençale. His native dialect was that of Maine.

An example of the phrase used allusively in conversation was played on tape at the conspiracy-to-murder trial involving Jeremy Thorpe MP in 1979. In one recording, Andrew Newton, speaking of the alleged plot, said: 'They feel a Thomas à Becket was done, you know, with Thorpe sort of raving that would nobody rid me of this man.'

Questions, unanswered

3 Beau Brummell, a dandy almost by profession, had fallen out with the Prince of Wales. He is said to have annoyed the Prince by ridiculing his mistress and also by saying once to his royal guest at dinner, 'Wales, ring the bell, will you?' When they met in London in July 1813, the Prince cut Brummell but greeted his companion, Lord Alvanley. As the Prince walked off, Brummell posed his famous

question in ringing tones: 'Tell me, Alvanley, who is your fat friend?'

Told in Capt. Jesse, *Life of George Brummell* (1844).

1 Sir John Gielgud was giving last-minute instructions to the cast of a stage production that required the men to wear tights. Having presumably seen some pretty odd sights in tights over the years, he insisted that all the males in the cast should wear jockstraps (athletic supports). A little voice popped up and inquired, 'Sir John, does that include people like me with only small parts?'

Told to me by Charles Richardson and recorded in my diary on 18 July 1966.

2 'Idiot boards' are large pieces of card held up just out of camera range to help TV performers remember their words. Mike Douglas, host of a very successful daytime talk show on American television, was once recording an interview with Kirk Douglas (no relation). The first question on the idiot board was about Kirk's latest picture – 'IS IT AN EPIC MOVIE?', it said. When they started recording, Mike peered at the idiot board and asked Kirk, in all seriousness, 'Tell me, Kirk, is it an Eric movie?'

Kirk, to give him his due, replied that, well, yes, it was an Eric movie ... if that's how Mike wanted it ...

Told to me by David Frost in about 1984.

3 I was touring Australia, giving interviews on graffiti, and was beginning to wonder whether I would ever get asked an original question on that topic. Then, one morning in an Adelaide radio station, I was. The interviewer asked me: 'And, Nigel, is there a season for graffiti?'

What did this mean? Did he suppose there was a sort of rutting season for graffiti-writers, that when the sap rose they reached for their spray-cans? I cannot, off-hand, recall my answer. This was in November 1981. Recounted in my book *Gift of the Gab* (1985).

Quoting and misquoting

4 Oscar Wilde was, for once, very taken with something witty said by another. Whatever it was that James McNeill Whistler had come out with, Wilde complimented him with, 'I wish I had said that.' Replied Whistler: 'You will, Oscar, you will.'

Told in L. C. Ingleby, *Oscar Wilde* (1907) and Douglas Sladen, *Twenty Years of My Life* (1915). Sladen says that it was of a remark made by a woman, which Wilde had rather taken a fancy to, but Hesketh Pearson, *The Life of Oscar Wilde* (1946) has it, more convincingly, that it was something said by Whistler himself that Wilde was obviously going to make his own.

In Frank Harris, *Oscar Wilde, His Life and Confessions*, Chap. 4 (1930) is this lengthier explanation: 'The art critic of *The Times*, Mr Humphry Ward, had come to see an exhibition of Whistler's pictures. Filled with an undue sense of his own importance, he buttonholed the master and pointing to one picture said: "That's good, first-rate, a lovely bit of colour; but that, you know," he went on, jerking his finger over his shoulder at another picture, "that's bad, drawing all wrong ... bad!"

'"My dear fellow," cried Whistler, "you must never say that this painting's good or that bad, never! Good and bad are not terms to be used by you; but say, I like this, and I dislike that, and you'll be within your right. And now come and have a whiskey for you're sure to like that."

'Carried away by the witty fling, Oscar cried: "I wish I had said that."

'"You will, Oscar, you will," came Whistler's lightning thrust.'

1 On the parade ground the sergeant was putting a squad of recruits through their paces. In a quiet moment, a cultured voice was heard to say, 'Come, sweet death!' The sergeant rounded on the squad, barking, 'Who said that?!', and the languid voice said from the ranks, 'Shelley, I believe it was, sergeant.'

George L. Baurley of Dessau in Germany told me this in 1992, saying, 'It dates back to wartime or postwar days, when there was still conscription.' Paul Gregson subsequently came up with another version. According to him, the quoted line was 'They also serve who only stand and wait' and the languid voice said, 'Milton', whereupon the sergeant bawled, 'Milton, one pace forward, march!'

2 When the Prince of Wales made his maiden speech in the House of Lords (13 June 1974), he began by ascribing to Oscar Wilde the quotation, 'If a thing is worth doing, it is worth doing badly.'

But this was not something said by Wilde. G. K. Chesterton had written it in 'Folly and Female Education', *What's Wrong with the World* (1910). When Frank Muir pointed out this solecism to *The Times*, he added, 'If a thing is worth quoting, it is worth quoting badly ...'

3 The CBS news correspondent Winston Burdett, involved in some matter long forgotten, became suddenly circum-spect when on the receiving end of another journalist's attention. 'I don't want to be quoted,' he declared. 'And don't quote me that I don't want to be quoted.'

Told in Barbara Rowes, *The Book of Quotes* (1979).

R

Readiness

1 Cecil B. De Mille, the famed producer of biblical epics for the cinema, was directing a battle scene that involved thousands of extras and animals and probably ended with the destruction of the entire set. Whatever the case, it would only be possible for there to be one 'take'. And so C.B. covered himself by having the scene filmed by four cameras. When the action was completed, the destruction wrought, and any chance of repeating the matter had been lost for all time, Mr De Mille checked with each cameraman that he had filmed the scene successfully. 'No, I'm afraid not,' said the first, 'the film jammed in the camera.' 'No,' said the second, 'There's a hair in the gate.' 'No,' said the third, 'the sun shone into the lens.'

In desperation, De Mille turned to the last cameraman, who said brightly, 'Ready when you are, Mr De Mille!'

Presumably this story is popular because it portrays innocence in the face of dire calamity. The punch line hangs in the air almost joyfully. *Ready When You Are, Mr McGill* became the title of a British TV play (by Jack Rosenthal, 1976) about how a TV production is ruined by an actor who can't remember his (two) lines. Here is an updated version, as told by William Franklyn on BBC Radio *Quote ... Unquote* (2 July 1996):

'During the making of *The Bridge on the River Kwai*, there is the wonderful moment when the bridge actually blows up. They had four cameras set up at different angles so they would be certain that they really got the shot. The cameras started and the bridge went up. As the dust settled, David Lean got on the walkie-talkie and said, "All right, Camera 1, how was it?" "Sorry, sir, there was a hair in the gate." "No. 2, how was it?" "The camera jammed." So he went to Camera 3 and asked, "How was it for you?" "The focus puller threw up just before we were going to turn over." By this time, Mr Lean was a little worried, and asked Camera 4. "Yes, Camera 4 here, ready when you are, Mr Lean."'

Realism

2 An American GI told Picasso that he did not like modern art because it was 'not realistic'. Picasso then looked at a snapshot that the soldier had of his girlfriend and commented, 'My, is she really as small as that?'

Told in Bill Adler, *My Favourite Funny Story* (1967).

Recognition and non-recognition

3 After bowing low to him, Theodore Hook said to an imposing gentleman, 'I beg your pardon, sir, are you anyone in particular?'

Told in W. D. Adams, *Treasury of Modern Anecdote* (1886). Theodore Hook (1788–1841) was a writer, hoaxer and joker. Compare: 'Please, are you anybody?' – caption to a cartoon by Lewis Baumer in *Punch* (16 February 1938). It showed a little girl with an autograph book approaching an impressive gentleman.

1 Edmund Gosse, the author of *Father and Son*, was travelling on an omnibus one day in the 1880s and a lady got on who was a headmistress of the local school. She sat down next to a very respectable solicitor and electrified the whole busload of passengers by saying to him, 'I can see you don't know who I am, but you are the father of one of my children.'

Re-told from her biography of Gosse by Ann Thwaite on BBC Radio *Quote ... Unquote* (6 June 1995).

2 Returning to his hotel in Manchester one night, Sir Thomas Beecham encountered a familiar-looking woman in the foyer. He thought he must know her, but could not think of her name. Recalling that the woman had a brother, he inquired politely how this brother was and whether he was still doing the same job. 'Oh yes,' the woman replied, 'He is very well – and still the King.'

Recounted in Atkins and Newman, *Beecham Stories* (1978), but without source.

3 Apparently cut by a man she knew – in the foyer of the Savoy Hotel, London – Tallulah Bankhead called out to him in a loud voice, 'Don't you recognize me with my clothes on?'

Told by Glenda Jackson on BBC Radio *Quote ... Unquote* (6 August 1983). Brendan Gill in *Tallulah* (1973) has it said to a peer. Compare this exchange from the film

Gold Diggers of 1933 (US 1933): a showgirl learns that her former Broadway producer is planning a new show, but she doesn't have anything decent to wear for auditions. 'If Barney could see me in clothes ...', she begins. A friend chips in: 'He wouldn't recognize you.'

4 A drunk lurched up to Groucho Marx and said, 'You old son-of-a-gun, you probably don't remember me.' Groucho replied: 'I never forget a face, but I'll be glad to make an exception in your case.'

Told in Leo Rosten, *People I Have Loved, Known or Admired* (1970).

5 The novelist E. M. Forster was short-sighted. When he was invited to the wedding reception of Lord Harewood, it is said that he bowed to the wedding cake, thinking it to be Queen Mary.

Told in Kenneth Rose, *Kings, Queens and Courtiers* (1986).

6 One day a charabanc turned up in a little village in Spain and a crowd of tourists piled out into the local market. Looking at various Romish artefacts and in particular the crucifixes, one of the tourists said: 'Ooh, look, this one's got a little man on it.'

Told (after John Bird) by Stephen Fry on BBC Radio *Quote ... Unquote* (17 June 1997). Even so, I think this is a pretty traditional tale. I recall excluding it from my *Eavesdroppings* on these grounds in 1981.

7 The screenwriter William Fairchild gave Daniel Massey a questionable line to speak when the actor was playing Coward in the film *Star*. An unknown woman greets Coward with the words, 'I know you, Mr Coward, but I'm sure you don't know me.' He replies: 'It's an incredible, but increasingly common phenomenon, I fear.' In real

life, Coward could be more teasing. When American matrons accosted him with, 'Oh, Mr Coward, you don't know me ...', he was inclined to answer, 'But of course I do. And how is Mabel?'

The 'Mabel' bit was told to me by Kenneth Williams in 1964. With 'Muriel', the line is in Dick Richards, *The Wit of Noël Coward* (1968). In Wallace Reyburn, *Gilbert Harding* (1978), it is back to 'Mabel'.

1 The great actress Katharine Hepburn was once observed shovelling snow outside her New York residence. 'Hey, aren't you Joan Crawford?' someone called out. 'Not any more,' was her reply.

Source untraced, but almost any famous person worth his or her salt has at some time, apparently, been asked the question, 'Hey, didn't you used to be —— ——?' Similarly, the English actor Ernest Thesiger kept on acting to a ripe old age and enjoyed telling the story of the person who had asked him, 'Excuse me, but weren't you Ernest Thesiger?' To which he replied: 'Madam, I was.' This story was told in Michael Pertwee, *Name Dropping* (1974).

2 An Irish actor recognized James Mason as he was walking along O'Connell Street in Dublin (it was in 1966 and he was there to star in the film *The Blue Max*). The fan said, with great courtesy, 'I beg your pardon, but aren't you James Mason in later life?'

Told by Hugh Leonard in a letter to *The Irish Times* (9 January 1999).

3 The Australian-born actress Coral Browne went to see the National Theatre production of Seneca's *Oedipus* in 1968. At one point the stage disclosed a huge golden phallus around which the company danced. (Irene Worth even had to embrace it and stroke it.) Browne turned to her

companion, Charles Gray, and commented reassuringly: 'Nobody we know, dear.'

Told on BBC Radio *Quote ... Unquote* (15 December 1981). The anecdote was confirmed by Coral Browne herself in a Channel 4 documentary in December 1990.

4 During the interval of a Covent Garden gala to mark the 100th birthday of Sir Robert Mayer, the musical benefactor, Lady Diana Cooper (then aged 86) was approached by 'an extremely pleasant lady' who seemed vaguely familiar. Trying to put a name to the face, Lady Diana struggled womanfully on, until the dreadful truth dawned: it was the Queen. 'I sank into a curtsey and said, "I'm terribly sorry, Ma'am, but I didn't recognize you without your crown on."'

This version from the *Daily Telegraph* (21 June 1986). Andrew Barrow in *International Gossip* (1983) dates the incident precisely to 5 June 1979, and gives the Queen's response as: 'It's Sir Robert's evening. I left it at home.' There is nothing new about this sort of error. The old, short-sighted Lord Portarlington is supposed to have told Queen Victoria, 'I know your face quite well, but dammit I cannot put a name to it!' (recalled in Robert Rhodes James, *Rosebery*, 1963).

5 Entertainer Max Bygraves was in Jersey, on his way to appear in his own show: 'When I put my glasses on and put a hat on, I can get along the street quite well without being recognized. I don't mind being stopped and asked for an autograph – I quite enjoy it – but sometimes when you want to get on, you want to get round a store ... I can really disguise myself and nobody knows who I am. Anyway, I was in this store, buying some cigars, and the girl who was serving me didn't recognize me, and a lady sidles up to me and she

says, "I recognize yer! ... 'I wanna tell you a story' ... We know who you are, Frankie!'"

In a radio interview with me (1980).

1 When he was President, George Bush paid a visit to an old people's home. After chatting to patients for a little while, he asked one of them, 'And do you know who I am?' 'No,' came the reply from one old biddie, 'but if you ask in reception I'm sure they will be able to tell you.'

Told by Derek Parker in *The Author* (Summer 1993). The story was applied to various other well-known figures in the same year.

Rejections

2 Mrs Patrick Campbell was sitting in the stalls with the director of a new play watching a new young actress rehearsing. The actress broke off and said, 'I wonder if it would be a good idea here, Mrs Campbell, if while they were talking I was arranging some flowers?' 'That's quite a good idea, my dear, do that,' came the reply, to everyone's surprise. Then later, the actress suggested, 'I was wondering if, before I said my line, I could have a coat which I took off?' 'Yes, do that, my dear.' The director turned to Mrs Pat and said, 'Clever girl, isn't she?' And Mrs Campbell said, 'Yes, *very*. What a pity she won't be with us after lunch ...'

Told by Antony Jay on BBC Radio *Quote ... Unquote* (20 November 1990).

Religiosity

3 When Winston Churchill was reproached for not going to church, he said: 'I am not a pillar of the church but a buttress – I support it from the outside.'

Recalled by Montague Browne in a speech to the International Churchill Society, London (25 September 1985). Note, however, that it was said of John Scott, Lord Eldon (1751–1838): 'He may be one of its [the Church's] buttresses, but certainly not one of its pillars, for he is never found within it.' (H. Twiss, *Public and Private Life of Eldon*, 1844). *The Oxford Dictionary of Quotations* (1992) adds that this remark was later attributed to Lord Melbourne.

4 Lady Carina Fitzalan-Howard broke it to her favourite nun, Mother Wilson, that she had met the man she wanted to marry. It was David Frost, the broadcaster. The nun asked if he was religious. 'Oh, yes,' replied the wife-to-be, 'he thinks he's God Almighty.'

Told in *The Sunday Times* (28 July 1985).

Remuneration

5 When Edmund Spenser presented some poems to Queen Elizabeth I, she ordered her Lord High Treasurer, Burleigh, to pay the poet one hundred pounds. He exclaimed, famously, 'What, all this for a song?' and Spenser continued to wait for payment. In the end, Spenser reminded the Queen of her order, in verse:

> I was promised on a time
> To have reason for my rhyme.
> From that time, unto this season,
> I received nor rhyme, nor reason.

He was duly paid.

Related by Thomas Birch in 'The Life of Mr Edmund Spenser' in an edition of *The Faerie Queene* (1751). Also in Theophilus Cibber, *The Lives of the Poets of Great Britain and Ireland ...* (1753).

Replies and ripostes

1 The 4th Earl of Sandwich said to John Wilkes: ''Pon my soul, Wilkes, I don't know whether you'll die upon the gallows or of the pox.' Wilkes replied: 'That depends, my Lord, whether I first embrace your Lordship's principles, or your Lordship's mistresses.'

A famous exchange that made an early appearance in Sir Charles Petrie, *The Four Georges* (1935), but is quite likely apocryphal. Where did Petrie get it from, and where had it been for the intervening two centuries? In *Memoirs of the Life and Writings of Percival Stockdale, Written by Himself* (1809) the exchange is given as between Sandwich and one 'Foote'.

It is frequently misapplied. George E. Allen in *Presidents Who Have Known Me* (1950) has it between Gladstone and Disraeli. It is difficult to imagine the circumstance in which either Disraeli or Gladstone could have made either of the remarks.

2 In the archaeology of humour one is never really going to know who first cracked a joke. Nevertheless, as it can be dated, why not allow W. S. Gilbert to claim credit for originating a famous exchange? On a visit to the United States with Arthur Sullivan in 1879–80, Gilbert was told by a matron at a dinner party, 'Your friend Mr Sullivan's music is really too delightful. It reminds me so much of dear Baytch [Bach]. Do tell me: what is Baytch doing just now? Is he still composing?'

'Well, no, madam,' Gilbert returned, 'just now, as a matter of fact, dear Baytch is by way of decomposing.'

This, at any rate, is how the joke appears in *Gilbert and Sullivan* by Hesketh Pearson (1947). The first appearance may have been in H. Sutherland Evans, *Personal Recollections* (1900).

3 Oscar Wilde was receiving bouquets, both spoken and floral, after the first night of one of his plays, when a would-be critic slipped in with a rotten cabbage. Wilde took it, smiled, and said: 'Thank you, my dear fellow. Every time I smell it I shall think of you.'

Source untraced. As Frank Harris described in *Oscar Wilde* (1938), Lord Queensberry did, of course, appear at the first production of *The Importance of Being Earnest* carrying a large bouquet of turnips and carrots, but was refused admission. Could these stories be linked?

4 When Judge Willis asked the lawyer and politician F. E. Smith, after a long dispute over procedure, 'What do you suppose I am on the Bench for, Mr Smith?', Smith replied, 'It is not for me, your honour, to attempt to fathom the inscrutable workings of Providence.'

Told by Winston Churchill in *Great Contemporaries* (1937).

5 Smith taunted Gordon Hewart, when Lord Chief Justice, with the size of his stomach: 'What's it to be – a boy or a girl?' Replied Hewart: 'If it's a boy I'll call him John. If it's a girl I'll call her Mary. But if, as I suspect, it's only wind, I'll call it F. E. Smith.'

I printed this anecdote in my first book *Quote ... Unquote* (1978). The story had come to me the previous year from a *Quote ... Unquote* listener who said it had been told to her brother 'by a stranger in a bus queue in Harrogate in 1923'. Smith died in 1930, Hewart in 1943.

According to Humphrey McQueen in *Social Sketches of Australia* (1978), the Antipodean version has Sir George Houstoun Reid (1845–1918) replying, in answer to the question, apropos his stomach, 'What are you going to call it, George?': 'If it's a boy, I'll call it after myself. If it's a girl, I'll call it Victoria after our Queen. But if, as I strongly suspect, it's nothing but piss and wind, I'll call it after you.'

According to *Pass the Port Again* (1981 edn) the exchange occurred between Lord Haldane and Winston Churchill, as also in John Parker, *Father of the House* (1982), in which the exchange is specifically located at the Oxford Union in 1926. *The Faber Book of Anecdotes* (1985) has the US version: President Taft (d. 1930) making the retort to Senator Chauncey Depew (d. 1929).

1 Gerald Gould, a book reviewer in *The Week-end Review*, had written something about Lord Birkenhead that his lordship objected to. The Earl wrote a letter beginning, '*A Mr Gerald Gould* has said ...' In the next issue, Gould replied, and began his letter, '*An Earl of Birkenhead* has said ...'

Told to me by Matthew Norgate (1984).

2 In his diary for 13 December 1917, Arnold Bennett records a story he had heard at dinner the previous night. It concerns an amazing encounter on the London Underground. Two working men are sitting there when into the carriage comes a man wearing very long flowing robes. He looks like an important churchman. One of the men says to the other, 'Do you think it's the Archbishop of Canterbury? Go and ask him.' So the other one goes up to the man in the robes and says, 'Excuse me, sir, are you the Archbishop of Canterbury?' And the man replies, 'What the bloody hell has that got to do with you?' So the man goes back to his friend and says, 'It's no use, mate, the old cow won't give me a straight answer either way.'

3 When Sir Edwin Lutyens, the architect, was asked a question to which he objected before a Royal Commission, he replied, euphemistically: 'The answer is in the plural and they bounce.'

Given, without source, in *The Penguin Dictionary of Modern Quotations* (1971). However, according to Robert Jackson, *The Chief* (1959), when Gordon (later Lord) Hewart was in the House of Commons, he was answering questions on behalf of David Lloyd George. For some time, one afternoon, he had given answers in the customary brief parliamentary manner – 'The answer is in the affirmative', or 'The answer is in the negative.' After one such non-commital reply, several members arose to bait Hewart with a series of rapid supplementary questions. He waited until they had all finished and then replied: 'The answer is in the plural!' Additionally, Howard Carter, the archaeologist, is said to have debunked speculation about his work on the tomb of Tutankhamun with: 'The answer is spherical, and in the plural.'

4 Responding to Peter Pan's cry of, 'Do you believe in fairies?', the actress Hermione Gingold said, 'Believe in them, darling? I know hundreds.'

Told by Clive Francis on BBC Radio *Quote ... Unquote* (22 May 1998).

5 One of comedian Tommy Trinder's catch phrases was 'Trinder's the name.' He was using it in a London night club when Orson Welles and Rita Hayworth were present. So when Trinder said it to Welles, he replied: 'Why don't you change it?' As quick as a flash, Trinder said, 'Is that a suggestion or a proposal of marriage?'

In *Before Your Very Eyes* (1975), Arthur Askey puts this just after July 1939 – a bit unlikely as Welles was not a name in London at that time. And although Askey does not mention Rita Hayworth in his version, she and Welles were not together until 1943, when they were married that September.

6 When Michael Ramsey was Archbishop

of Canterbury, a jet-setting American clergyman arrived at Lambeth Palace to see him. 'Your Grace,' he declared breathlessly, 'yesterday I saw His Holiness the Patriarch of Constantinople! This morning, I had an audience with his Holiness the Pope! And tonight I'm with you, the Archbishop of Canterbury!' To which Ramsey said: 'Prepare to meet thy God!'

Told by the Reverend Roger Royle (1984).

1 When novelists Gore Vidal and Richard Adams were appearing together on the BBC Radio show *Start the Week* (24 September 1984), Adams described Vidal's latest novel – about Abraham Lincoln – as 'meretricious'. Vidal was unfazed. 'Really?' he replied, 'Well, meretricious and a happy New Year.'

The exchange was recorded in Alan Bennett's diary (included in *Writing Home*, 1995), with the comment: 'That's the way to do it.' But, unusually for Vidal, it now appears he was quoting an old wish (a 'meretricious and a happy New Year') by Franklin Pierce Adams – so quoted in Scott Meredith, *George S. Kaufman and the Algonquin Round Table* (1977). But even Adams may not have got there first. In an episode of the Marx Brothers' NBC radio show *Flywheel, Shyster and Flywheel* broadcast on 13 March 1933, the following exchange took place between Chico and an exasperated judge who was fighting for re-election:

Judge: Ladies and gentlemen, my candidacy is being fought by a group of men who are dishonest, grafting and meretricious!
Chico: Tank you judge, and I wish you da same.
Judge: You wish me what?
Chico: A meretricious. A meretricious and a happy new year!

So, who came first – F.P.A. or the brothers M? Samuel Hopkins Adams, in *Alexander Woollcott – His Life and His World* (1945), includes among wisecracks attributed to the Algonquin Round Table, 'Frank Adams' example of a sentence embodying the word "meretricious" – Meretricious 'n Happy New Year.' No date, but as the Round Table is thought to have ceased in 1932, most likely Adams takes precedence over the Marx Brothers.

2 An example of Russell Harty's TV interviewing style: he asked a bemused Hermione Gingold whether her elderly dog could still masticate properly. Replied she: 'He does whatever nature intended, Mr Harty.'

Recounted by Compton Miller, *Who's Really Who* (1983).

3 At the Ravenscraig picket line during the British miners' strike of 1984–85, protesters were being held back by mounted police. One miner called out to a policewoman, 'Hey, love, your horse is foaming at the mouth.' She gazed down at the miner and said, 'I'm not surprised. So would you be if you'd been between my legs for the last two hours.'

Recounted in the *Observer* (20 May 1984).

Reputations

4 The eighteenth-century actress Peg Woffington was appearing in the part of 'Sir Harry' in a play. Coming to the greenroom during the course of the performance, she said: 'In my conscience, I believe half the men in the house take me for one of their own sex.' Another actress responded: 'It may be so, but in my conscience, the other half can convince them to the contrary.'

Told in W. R. Chetwood, *A General History of the Stage* (1749).

5 'Thomas Campbell LLD, author of *The Pleasures of Hope*, died June 15,

1844, aged 67' – this inscription on the coffin of the Scottish poet is ironic in the light of what is reported by William Keddie in his *Cyclopedia of Literary and Scientific Anecdote & c.* (1859): 'Campbell once explained to a friend why he did not like to be associated with his famous work, *The Pleasures of Hope.* "When I was young," he said, "I was always greeted among my friends as Mr Campbell, author of *The Pleasures of Hope.* When I married, I was married as the author of *The Pleasures of Hope,* and when I became a father, my son was the son of the author of *The Pleasures of Hope.*"'

Campbell is buried in Poets' Corner, Westminster Abbey, and there is a statue of him, bearing lines from his 'Last Man', but happily there is no mention of *The Pleasures of Hope.*

1 When Oscar Wilde was released from prison and went into exile in Dieppe, his friend Ernest Dowson, the poet, urged him to acquire 'a more whole-some taste'. Accordingly, they totted up how much money they had with them and decided there was enough to support a visit to the nearest brothel (female, that is). When the news of this got out, they were accompanied on their way by a cheering crowd. After the deed was done, Wilde confided to Dowson that it was, 'The first these ten years, and it will be the last. It was like cold mutton.' Then he added, so that the crowd could hear, 'But tell it in England, for it will entirely restore my character.'

Told by W. B. Yeats in *Autobiographies* (1926).

2 The Australian-born actor Errol Flynn was crisply summed up by David Niven: 'The great thing about Errol was that you always knew where you were with him because he always let you down.'

Told in David Niven, *Bring On the Empty Horses* (1975).

3 Tony Benn, the Labour politician, became the modern equivalent of a music-hall joke on account of his sup-posedly 'loony' policies. His brother David, a BBC producer, was made well aware of this when he had to pay a visit to someone in a mental hospital. As he was going on to stay with friends, David had a small weekend case with him and arranged in advance for a minicab to collect him from the hospi-tal and take him to the railway station.

After the visit, David emerged, clutching his case, and instructed the driver to take him to the station. To make conversation he said, 'I've just been visiting a friend of mine, you know.'

The driver merely nodded and said, 'Aye' as if to humour him. They drove on a bit further. David then added: 'I work for the BBC, you know.' The driver again nodded at this far-fetched claim and said, 'Oh aye.'

The climax came when David announced after a further pause, 'My brother is the Minister of Technology. You may have heard of him. He's Tony Benn ...'

I believe David Wedgwood Benn told this story against himself. I must have heard it in the early 1970s.

Requests

4 Sir Norman Hartnell, couturier and dress-maker to the Queen, was staying with some very horsey people. When he

admired an ornament on the mantel-piece, the daughter of the house informed him, 'Mummy won that with one of her jumpers.' Hartnell replied, 'If I sent her the wool, would she make me one?'

Told to me by T. A. Dyer (1993). I am not sure what connection, if any, this has with that most well-known of graffiti – 'My mother made me a homosexual', under which was written in another hand, 'If I got her the wool, would she make me one?' (which was in circulation by 1979).

Resignations

1 When Stanley Baldwin stepped down as Prime Minister, flushed with success over his handling of the Abdication crisis, he said to the Cabinet (28 May 1937): 'Once I leave, I leave. I am not going to speak to the man on the bridge, and I am not going to spit on the deck.' This statement was later released to the press. Earlier, on his in-auguration as Rector of Edinburgh University in 1925, Baldwin had ex-pressed a view of the limitations on the freedom of a former Prime Minister in similar terms: 'A sailor does not spit on the deck, thereby strengthening his control and saving unnecessary work for someone else; nor does he speak to the man at the wheel, thereby leaving him to devote his whole time to his task and increasing the probability of the ship arriving at or near her destination.'

When Harold Wilson resigned as Prime Minister, he quoted Baldwin's 'Once I leave ...' words in his own statement to the Cabinet (16 March 1976), and also later released them to the press.

2 Zeppo Marx recalled that his brother Groucho did not have much time for The Friars Club, a theatrical organization. Hector Arce added that Groucho had some misgivings about the quality of the members – 'doubts verified a few years later when an infamous card-cheating scandal erupted there'. So Groucho famously wrote: 'Please accept my resignation. I don't care to belong to any club that will have me as a member.'

The wording varies, but the one here is taken from Arthur Sheekman's introduction to *The Groucho Letters* (1967). The actual letter unfortunately does not survive. In *Groucho and Me* (1959), the man himself supplied the version: 'PLEASE ACCEPT MY RESIGNATION. I DON'T WANT TO BELONG TO ANY CLUB THAT WILL ACCEPT ME AS A MEMBER.' Woody Allen in *Annie Hall* (1977) appears to suggest that the joke first appeared in Freud and alludes to it in this passage: 'I would never want to belong to any club that would have someone like me for a member. That's the key joke of my adult life, in terms of my relationships with women.'

3 In March 1990, when two of Prime Minister Thatcher's ministers – Norman Fowler and Peter Walker – had withdrawn from the Cabinet, both giving as their reason for going that they wished to 'spend more time with their families', Gordon Brown, the Labour MP, suggested in the House of Commons that Nicholas Ridley might care to follow suit. But the Secretary of State for Industry was having none of it. 'The last thing I want to do,' he said, 'is spend more time with my family.'

Told in the *Independent* (14 July 1990). Ridley (1929–93) was an Old Etonian, a smoker and insensitive to the media. He was ideologically close to Margaret Thatcher and was eventually eased out after making indiscreet remarks about Germany in a *Spectator* interview a few months after the above pronouncement.

Revelations

1 When Lord Curzon happened to see some soldiers bathing during the First World War, he exclaimed: 'I never knew the lower classes had such white skins.'

Told in Kenneth Rose, *Superior Person* (1969).

2 During the Second World War, the stately Queen Mary was evacuated from London and spent the whole time staying with the Duke and Duchess of Beaufort at their home, Badminton House. Some time later, recalling this visitation, the Duchess of Beaufort told James Pope-Hennessy about Queen Mary: 'When she came here, she didn't even know what hay was – when I pointed to a hayfield and said look at our hay, she replied, studying it, "Oh, that's what hay looks like, is it? I never knew that." She was totally urban, but got used to the country.'

Pope-Hennessy reported this in his official biography *Queen Mary* (1959). It is also to be found in a memoir of the interview with the Duchess that was included in *A Lonely Business, A Self-Portrait of James Pope-Hennessy* (1981).

Rhetoric

3 Lady Astor, who was always preaching against the evils of drink, was doing this in the House of Commons one day when she said to the crowded chamber, 'Well, there's nothing I wouldn't do rather than let a glass of beer cross my lips. I'd do anything. Why, I'd even commit adultery.' A voice from the back benches said, 'And so would I!'

Told by Ludovic Kennedy on BBC Radio *Quote . . . Unquote* (30 July 1983). Walter H. Brown of Weston-super-Mare wrote to me subsequently: 'I was of the opinion that her comment of "I would rather commit adultery" was made at a public political meeting at Plymouth and immediately a reply came from the back of the hall, "Who wouldn't?"'

Pass the Port Again (1980) has the exchange involving a Cambridge academic called E. E. Genner rather than Lady Astor. In *The Lyttelton Hart-Davis Letters* (Vol. 3, 1981) in a letter dated 9 July 1958, George Lyttelton has: 'I prefer the perfectly true comment of – who was it? – who, when some teetotal ass said he would rather commit adultery than drink a glass of port, said, "So would we all, my dear L., so would we all."'

Rivalry

4 Two men who had been rivals since their schooldays eventually ended up as a bishop and an admiral. At the height of this eminence, they met at Paddington station. The bishop, not recognizing his old schoolmate but perceiving from his uniform that he was an official of some sort, addressed him with the words: 'Tell me, my man, which platform is it for Reading?' The admiral, perceiving not only who the bishop was but that he was kitted out in all his finery, replied: 'I don't know, madam – and should you be travelling in your condition?'

Told in *Pass the Port* (1976) and by Kingsley Amis on BBC Radio *Quote . . . Unquote* (12 June 1979). Could this by any chance have begun life as a *Punch* cartoon caption?

5 In April 1951, Edith Evans opened in N. C. Hunter's play *Waters of the Moon*, with Sybil Thorndike. After the play had been running for twelve months, the H.M. Tennent management announced to Evans that she would be getting a whole new wardrobe from Pierre Balmain. Said she of Thorndike,

her supposed rival: 'If I'm to have a new frock, I insist that Sybil has a new cardigan.'

Related by Sheridan Morley in *Sybil Thorndike: A Life in the Theatre* (1977). Kenneth Tynan told it slightly differently in *Woman's Journal* (1956). In his version, 'Binkie' Beaumont offered to fly Evans to Paris for a completely new wardrobe by Pierre Balmain, and Evans said, 'If I go to Paris, Sybil must have a new cardigan.'

On the subject of her relations with Thorndike, Evans is also supposed to have said: 'I don't know whether I like her [Sybil] or not, but I've named my new bicycle after her' (told by Denise Coffey on BBC Radio *Quote ... Unquote*, 1979).

1 President Reagan frequently used showbiz analogies in his political career. When asked whether he resented the popularity of Mikhail Gorbachev in 1987, he told students in Jacksonville, Florida, 'Good Lord, I co-starred with Errol Flynn once.'

Reported in *Time* Magazine (14 December 1987).

Rows

2 During rehearsals for the Broadway production of Neil Simon's *The Odd Couple*, Mike Nichols, the director, had a furious row with Walter Matthau, abusing him with every name under the sun and calling into question every possible characteristic the actor might have had. All this was played out in front of the assembled cast and stage crew. When the row finally subsided, Matthau helped break the ice by calling out, in earshot of everyone, 'Hey, Mike, can I have my balls back, please?' Nichols called out, 'Props!'

A version of this, involving the word 'prick' is told in Ned Sherrin, *Cutting Edge* (1984).

Royal jokes

3 What did Queen Elizabeth I have against tailors? When confronted by a delegation of eighteen tailors, she is reputed to have said: 'Good morrow, gentlemen both.' Was that then the reputation of tailors? Was it justified? Or was this an Elizabethan version of the modern slurs against male flight attendants, hairdressers and ballet dancers? No. In all probability, the Queen was making a royal joke by playing on the expression 'It takes nine tailors to make a man'. This is said to have come originally from the French in about 1600. The meaning of it seems to be that a man should buy his clothes from various sources.

In Frederick Chamberlin, *The Sayings of Queen Elizabeth* (1923), the sole authority given for her remark is Thomas Carlyle, *Sartor Resartus* (1836). Chamberlin notes that the ancient quip about the number of tailors it takes to make a man has 'lately been familiar in the United States through the comic opera, *Robin Hood*, by Reginald de Koven'. G. L. Apperson in his *English Proverbs and Proverbial Phrases* (1929) shows that, until the end of the seventeenth century, there was some uncertainty about the number of tailors mentioned in the expression. In *Westward Hoe* by John Webster and Thomas Dekker (1605) it appears as three.

4 A rare example of a royal joke comes from the period before King George V's death. In December 1935, it was revealed that Sir Samuel Hoare, the Foreign Secretary, had come to an arrangement with Pierre Laval, his French counterpart, whereby Abyssinia was virtually to be consigned to the Italians behind the League of Nations' back. The Hoare–Laval Pact had been concluded in Paris when Sir Samuel was

passing through on his way to a holiday in Switzerland. In the furore that followed he had to resign. The King joked: 'No more coals to Newcastle, no more Hoares to Paris.'

He may just have been repeating a remark that was current anyway, and is unlikely to have said it to Hoare himself, despite Lord Avon's recollection of what the King told him in *Facing the Dictators* (1962). Is there a link in this back to the story told about Jimmy Thomas, the Labour MP and cabinet minister around the 1920s, who was asked whether his wife would be accompanying him on an official visit to Paris? He replied: 'You don't take a ham sandwich to the Lord Mayor's Banquet, do you?' (told by Richard Toeman of London N6 in 1995)?

1 Prince Edward has tried to carve out for himself a career as a TV producer, but his first venture into paid work was as a production assistant with Andrew Lloyd Webber's Really Useful Company. Back home at Buckingham Palace after his first day, he slumped into a chair beside his mother, the Queen, and said: 'My God, I'm tired. You have no idea what a ten-hour day in the theatre is like.' The Queen replied: 'Oh, but I have. I've been to the Royal Variety Performance.'

Told by Prince Edward in an interview with Sally Jones for the *Sunday Express* (14 May 1995). His nickname at the Really Useful Company was 'Barbara', by the way.

Royalty

2 During a London season in the reign of Queen Victoria, Sarah Bernhardt essayed the role of Cleopatra in Shakespeare's *Antony and Cleopatra*. In the scene where Cleopatra receives the news of Mark Antony's defeat at the battle of Actium, she stabbed the messenger who brought her the

news, 'stormed, raved, frothed at the mouth, wrecked some of the scenery in her frenzy and finally, as the curtain fell, dropped in a shuddering convulsive heap'.

As the applause died down, an American visitor overheard a middle-aged British matron saying to her friend in the next seat, 'How different – how very different from the home life of our own dear Queen!'

So attributed by Irvin S. Cobb in *A Laugh a Day Keeps the Doctor Away...* (1921).

3 C. B. Fry, the English sportsman, was a prodigious all-rounder, but achieved fame principally as a cricketer. With Adonis-like looks, it was not long before he drifted into politics, becoming India's delegate to the League of Nations after the First World War. As if this were not surprising enough, Fry was then offered the throne of Albania. But he declined it.

Told by Fry in his memoir *Life Worth Living* (1939).

Rumours

4 Within a month of war being declared in August 1914, there was an unfounded rumour that a million Russian troops had landed at Aberdeen in Scotland and passed through England on their way to the Western Front. The detail that they were seen to have had 'snow on their boots' was supposed to add credence to the report.

Arnold Bennett was one of several people who noted the rumour at the time. In his *Journals* (for 31 August 1914), he wrote: 'The girls came home with a positive statement from the camp that 160,000 Russians were being landed in Britain, to be taken to France ... The statement was so positive that at first I almost believed it ... In the end I dismissed it, and yet could not help hoping ... The most curious embroidery on this rumour was from Mrs A.W., who told Mrs W. that the Russians were coming via us to France, where they would turn treacherous to France and join Germans in taking Paris ... This rumour I think took the cake.'

In Osbert Sitwell's *Great Morning* (1951), he records how his 'unusually wise and cautious' 16-year-old brother Sacheverell had written to tell him: 'They saw the Russians pass through the station last night ... and Miss Vasalt telephoned to Mother this afternoon and said trains in great number had passed through Grantham Station all day with the blinds down. So there must, I think, be some truth in it, don't you?'

In *Falsehood in War-Time* (1928), Arthur Ponsonby said of 'Russians with snow on their boots', that 'nothing illustrates better the credulity of the public mind in wartime and what favourable soil it becomes for the cultivation of falsehood'. Several suggestions have been made as to how this false information caught hold: that the Secret Service had intercepted a telegram to the effect that '100,000 Russians are on their way from Aberdeen to London' (without realizing that this referred to a consignment of Russian eggs); that a tall, bearded fellow had declared in a train that he came from 'Ross-shire', and so on.

In fact, the British Ambassador to Russia *had* requested the dispatch of a complete army corps, but the request was never acceded to. Ponsonby commented: 'As the rumour had undoubted military value, the authorities took no steps to deny it ... [but] an official War Office denial of the rumour was noted by the *Daily News* on September 16, 1914.' A *Punch* cartoon (23 September 1914) had the caption: *Porter:* 'Do I know if the Rooshuns has really come through England? Well, Sir, if this don't prove it, I don't know what do. A train went through here full, and when it come back I knowed there'd bin Rooshuns in it, 'cause the cushions and floors was covered with snow.'

1 Later in the First World War, a rumour spread that some Allied soldiers had received such appalling injuries that they had lost all four limbs and required transportation in baskets. This, probably, is what gave rise to the term 'basket case' to describe a mental or physical cripple, and then, by extension, any totally ruined enterprise. The rumour was, however, specifically discounted in the aftermath of the war by the *U.S. Official Bulletin* (28 March 1919): 'The Surgeon General of the Army ... denies ... that there is any foundation for the stories that have been circulated ... of the existence of "basket cases" in our hospitals.'

To complicate matters, Stuart Berg Flexner, the American word expert, describes this as being originally *British* Army slang. It has been suggested, probably misguidedly, that the association with mental disability comes from the fact that basket-weaving is an activity sometimes carried out in mental hospitals. The second meaning (a totally ruined enterprise) was established by about 1973, and is still frequently used in business journalism: 'On a continent that is full of economic basket cases, the small, landlocked nation is virtually debt free' (*Newsweek*, 11 January 1982). Here, one might guess that the original phrase has been hijacked and the implication changed. What the writer is now referring to is something that is so useless that it is fit only to be thrown into a wastepaper basket.

S

Sang-froid

1 In 1588, Queen Elizabeth I had been assured that the Spanish Armada would not be coming because it had been disabled by storms. Then, on 19 July, it was discovered approaching Lizard Point in Cornwall, at which time the captains and commanders of the English fleet – including Sir Francis Drake – were busy playing at bowls on the Hoe at Plymouth. Drake, with famous cool, declared, 'There is time to finish the game and beat the Spaniards afterwards.' Which they did.

The mention of the game of bowls occurs in William Oldys, *The life of Sir Walter Raleigh from his Birth to his death on the Scaffold* (1736), but he may have obtained it from *The Second Part of Vox Populi* (1624) by Nicholas Scott. In neither account, however, does Drake's remark appear. The original point of the story was to show that the English Fleet was very nearly caught unprepared. But nineteenth-century historians turned the game into a show of bravado and embroidered the account with Drake's remark. In the form, 'There is plenty of time to win this game, and to thrash the Spaniards too', it appears in the *Dictionary of National Biography* (1917).

2 In 1809, the Drury Lane Theatre in London was destroyed by fire. At the time, its then proprietor, the playwright and politician Sheridan, was at the House of Commons, which voted an immediate adjournment when the disastrous news arrived. Sheridan went thither, in all haste, and, whilst seeing his property in flames, sat down with his friend Barry in a coffee-house opposite, to sink a bottle of port, coolly remarking, in answer to some friendly expostulation, that 'it was hard if a man could not drink a glass of wine by his own fire'.

As told in *The Magazine Programme* (24 October 1924). An early account occurs in Thomas Moore, *Memoirs of the Life of R. B. Sheridan* (1825).

3 One of the most potent myths of the sinking of the *Titanic* in 1912 is that the band stoically kept on playing as the ship went down. But what was it playing? Was it the hymn, 'Nearer, My God, to Thee', or something else?

In the commemorative song 'Be British', written and composed by Paul Pelham and Lawrence Wright in the year the ship sank, there is a tear-jerking 'recitation after 2nd verse' enshrining the belief that it was indeed 'Nearer My God To Thee' that the band played. According to Tom Burnam, *More Misinformation* (1980), however, the band played ragtime until the ship's bridge dipped underwater, and then the bandmaster led his men in the Episcopal hymn, 'Autumn'. This version of events was based on a reported remark of Harold Bride, the surviving junior wireless operator, in *The New York Times* (19 April 1912). As opposed to this, it has been suggested that the reporter misheard Bride, who might have mentioned instead 'Aughton' – a hymn tune to which the words are more appropriately, 'And when my task on earth is done … E'en death's cold wave I will not flee.' Or he might have translated 'Songe d'Automne', the title of a waltz by Archibald Joyce, which is known to have been in the band's repertoire.

According to Walter Lord, *A Night to Remember* (1955), the 'Nearer My God To Thee' version was one of many rumours circulating within a few days of the ship sinking. It was the one the band played in the film (UK, 1958) of Lord's book.

1 A Russian prince once said that 'between the revolution and the firing squad there is always time for a bottle of champagne'.

A commonly cited remark. For example, in his address at the memorial service for Lord (Julian) Amery, Winston Churchill MP noted: 'On the day he died, Julian sent my son a case of Pol Roger. His favourite maxim was that between the revolution and the firing squad there is always time for a bottle of champagne' – quoted in the *Daily Telegraph* (4 December 1996). But which revolution was this said in? And was it necessarily said by a Russian? Could it have developed, in fact, from a passage in Claud Cockburn's auto-biography *In Time of Trouble* (1956) where the old rogue is describing Washington DC in June 1931, when President Hoover an-nounced a one-year suspension of payment of debts between governments (because of the spread of the Depression to Europe)? 'Violent wrangling' broke out over the exact terms of the moratorium between Washington and Paris, he writes. 'When "agreement in princi-ple" was finally reached, M. Paul Claudel invited a number of American officials and others to the French Embassy to celebrate the event … In the drawing-room at the Embassy M. Claudel greeted them. "Gentlemen," he said simply, "in the little moment that remains to us in between the crisis and the

catastrophe, we may as well take a glass of champagne."' (Claudel is now remembered chiefly as a poet, playwright and essayist.) Then at the time of Munich (1938), Cockburn recalls that a Russian journalist called Mikhail Koltzov quoted the Claudel story back at him (Cockburn). Could this be the original of the 'Russian prince'?

Derek Robinson commented (1999): 'I'm sure I recall a French general being quoted as saying something similar when Dien Bien Phu – which was where he was in command – was about to fall [1954]. In his case, I think it was more like: "Gentlemen, in the short time we have between the crisis and the calamity, we might as well drink a glass of champagne."'

2 On the day of one of the assassination attempts against Charles de Gaulle, his wife Yvonne had bought two chickens in aspic. She took them with her when she accompanied the President in his car. Her first question after finding out that her husband was all right was to ask if anything had happened to the chickens in aspic.

Source untraced.

3 A failed Trappist monk attempted to hijack an Aer Lingus flight on its way to Heathrow. The plane's captain, Eddie Foley, calmly announced to passengers: 'I'm sorry, ladies and gentlemen, I would like to land but there's a gentle-man here who would prefer to go to Le Touquet in France.'

From a report in the *Daily Mail* (4 May 1981).

4 Captain Moody of British Airways had to deal with an unusual problem as his 747 ran into a volcanic storm over southern Sumatra and plunged 25,000 feet. Said he, 'Ladies and gentlemen, this is your captain speaking. We have a small problem. All four engines have

stopped. We are doing our damnedest to get them working again. I trust you are not in too much distress ...'

Told in the *Sunday Express* (4 July 1982). The crew managed to restart the engines.

Scholarship

1 A bravura toast, once given at the centenary of a college, was: 'Here's to pure scholarship. May it never be of any use to anyone!'

Told by Oonagh Lahr (1993). John Julius Norwich commented that his father, Duff Cooper, used to quote this as being a toast to Higher Mathematics.

School reports

2 When he was Headmaster of Shrewsbury school, Ronald Knox is said to have divided the school reports he had to sign into two piles. On those in one pile he wrote, 'Trying', on those in the other, 'Very trying'.

Told by Dr Eric Anderson, Headmaster of Eton, on BBC Radio *Quote ... Unquote* (17 January 1987).

3 When teaching at Charterhouse school, Walter Sellar noted that one of his pupils had written at the top of his report: 'Height at beginning of term 4ft 4in. Height at the end of term 4ft 3½ ins.' He simply commented: 'Seems to be settling down nicely ...'

Told by Eric Anderson, as above. Sellar (1898–1951) was also the co-author of the humorous classic *1066 and All That*.

Self-deprecation

4 In the 1930s, a critic described the actor Robert Donat as a 'half-Greek god who had winged his way from Olympus'. Donat's response was

to sigh, 'Actually, I'm a half-Pole who's winged his way from Withington, Manchester.'

Told in Emlyn Williams in *George* (1973).

5 On being turned down when he attempted to join an exclusive golf club – the grounds given were that he was an actor – Victor Mature replied: 'I am not an actor – and I have 60 films to prove it.'

Recounted in Melvyn Bragg, *Rich: The Life of Richard Burton* (1988).

Self-effacement

6 Self-effacing off-screen, the actor David Jason tends to avoid show-business cronies and lives in the country. He has been known to take his three-legged dog for a walk round the village while himself wearing dark glasses. His neighbours think this is a less than successful attempt at disguise when you have a three-legged dog.

Told in the *Independent* (19 December 1992).

Selflessness

7 One evening Mrs Disraeli drove to Westminster with her husband, knowing that he had a very important speech to make. When Disraeli was getting out of the carriage, his wife's fingers got trapped in the door. She suffered excruciating pain but never uttered a word because she did not want to upset him and thereby spoil his speech.

Told in D. H. Elletson, *Maryannery: Mary Ann Lincoln and Mary Anne Disraeli* (1959). Selflessness seems to be a necessary quality for a Conservative Prime Minister's wife to have, as the following anecdote also illustrates.

1 I was once round at Sir Alec and Lady Douglas-Home's London flat – a curious blend of baronial and G-plan – as I was recording an interview with Sir Alec. Lady Home made herself scarce while we recorded the interview but reappeared at the end, clutching her foot. 'I dropped the kitchen table on it,' she explained, 'but I didn't like to cry out in case it spoiled the recording ...'

From my diary for 24 July 1969.

Self-opinion

2 At the end of the first night of Oscar Wilde's play *Lady Windermere's Fan* in 1892, the author was called. Wilde duly appeared before the curtain with a cigarette between his fingers to respond to the audience's cheers. 'I am so glad, ladies and gentlemen, that you like my play,' he said. 'I feel sure you estimate the merits of it almost as highly as I do myself ...'

Recalled in Frank Harris, *Oscar Wilde, His Life and Confessions*, Chap. 9 (1930). Another version of this speech (including the emphases) was taken down in shorthand by George Alexander, a member of the theatre staff. Hesketh Pearson included it in his biography of Wilde (1946): 'Ladies and Gentlemen, I have enjoyed this evening *immensely*. The actors have given us a *charming* rendering of a delightful play, and your appreciation has been *most* intelligent. I congratulate you on the *great* success of your performance, which persuades me that you think *almost* as highly of the play as I do myself.' Curiously, there was an even longer and probably more accurate transcript made of the speech for the *Boston Evening Transcript* (10 March 1892).

3 Alphonse Allais, the French humorist and playwright, was asked to deliver a lecture. He began: 'I have been asked to talk to you on the subject of the theatre, but I fear that it will make you melancholy. Shakespeare is dead, Molière is dead, Racine is dead, Marivaux is dead – and I am not feeling too well myself.'

Told in Cornelia Otis Sinner, *Elegant Wits and Grand Horizontals* (1962). Who was the first to come up with this line? Allais died in 1905, but Mark Twain had used the same idea in a speech on 'Statistics' to the Savage Club, London (9 June 1899): 'I was sorry to have my name mentioned as one of the great authors, because they have a sad habit of dying off. Chaucer is dead, Spencer is dead, so is Milton, so is Shakespeare, and I am not feeling very well myself.' (This is included in *Mark Twain's Speeches*, 1910). But, even earlier, *Punch* had had this caption by an anonymous cartoonist in Vol. 104 (6 May 1893). The cartoon is entitled 'A Lament' and shows a depressed young man ('Little Simpkins') lolling in a chair, talking to a woman friend, and saying: 'Nearly all our best men are dead! Carlyle, Tennyson, Browning, George Eliot! – I'm not feeling very well myself.'

4 David Lloyd George is reputed to have said of Winston Churchill: 'He would make a drum out of the skin of his mother the louder to sing his own praises.'

Told by Peter Kellner on BBC Radio *Quote ... Unquote* (15 August 1987). Otherwise untraced.

5 Lynn Fontanne, reporting back to Alfred Lunt on the results of the famous couple's first-ever screen test, said, 'Alfred, it was absolutely remarkable! The camera does such wonderful things. You don't seem to have any lips. But the make-up and lighting were superb, and you looked absolutely marvellous! So handsome and striking, my darling, you have an entirely new career before you. I'd be so delighted with what they've done. Whereas, I –

well, I'm absolutely appalling! Disaster! I look like some dreadful old shrew – a hag – I simply couldn't bear to look at myself another second!'

Alfred replied sadly, 'No lips, eh?'

There is a version of this in Isaac Asimov's *Treasury of Humor* (1971).

1 Having become involved in some court case, George Arliss was in the witness box and was asked by counsel, 'Would it be true to say, Mr Arliss, that you are the world's greatest actor?' Arliss replied, 'Yes', and then turned, with a smile of apology to the judge, and added: 'Forgive me, my Lord, but I am on oath.'

Told by Basil Boothroyd on BBC Radio *Quote... Unquote* (1 September 1984).

2 Of all the thousands of guests on the radio show *Desert Island Discs*, only a very few were unable to keep egotism at bay in their selection of records and books to take with them to the desert island. The entire choice of records by Moura Lympany, the pianist, was made up of eight she had recorded herself. Elizabeth Schwarzkopf came a close second with seven (plus an eighth on which she featured ...) Birgit Nilsson chose six of her own recordings, and Louis Armstrong five.

As recalled in *Desert Island Lists* by Roy Plomley (with Derek Drescher) (1984).

3 On a visit to President Lyndon Johnson's ranch in Texas, the West German Chancellor, Ludwig Erhard, said, 'I understand that you were born in a log cabin, Mr President.' 'No, Mr Chancellor,' replied Johnson, 'I was born in a manger.'

Told in Alfred Steinberg, *Sam Johnson's Boy* (1968).

Sense

4 A man was desperately searching for something beneath the light of a lamp-post. A neighbour came out to help him and asked what he was looking for. 'A $50 bill that dropped out of my pocket,' said the man. 'Do you know where you dropped it?' inquired the neighbour. 'Yes,' said the man, 'it was about ten yards up the street.' 'Then why are you looking for it here under the street lamp?' asked the neighbour. 'Because the light here is much better,' said the man.

Told by Charles G. Francis (1991) – who told me that it had been invoked by a large US oil company under pressure from state governments to reformulate its gasoline to help combat air pollution. The company felt that the answer to the problem lay elsewhere – with automobile manufacturers, not least – and so thought that, like the man in the story, the governments were looking for the right answer in the wrong place.

5 In the 1940s, Edith Evans purchased a Renoir. A woman friend, having tea with her, noticed that this new picture was hanging rather low down on a wall. They had to lift a curtain to get enough light to see it. The friend said, 'It's gorgeous, but why did you hang it down there?' Edith Evans replied, 'There was a hook.'

Told by Stephen Fry on BBC Radio *Quote... Unquote* (17 June 1997).

6 When Lady Dorothy Macmillan was chatelaine of 10 Downing Street, she found that the only time when she could turn her attention to the gardening was after dark. But how was she to see what she was doing? After all, if she was weeding, she could not hold a torch in her hand. The answer was simple. She borrowed a miner's helmet

with lamp attached, no doubt presented to her husband on some occasion, and wore it in conjunction with her petticoat.

Revealed in BBC TV series *Number 10 Downing Street* (20 September 1985).

Sermons

1 President Calvin Coolidge went to church alone one Sunday because his wife was unable to go with him. She asked him on his return what the sermon was about. 'Sin,' he replied. 'But what did he say about it?' his wife persisted. Coolidge said, 'He was against it.'

This story made an early appearance in John Hiram McKee, *Coolidge Wit and Wisdom* (1933). Mrs Coolidge said this was just the sort of thing he would have said. Coolidge himself said it would be funnier if it were true.

2 The following are actual texts from the Authorized Version of the Bible (except where stated). How many clergymen have attempted to preach sermons based on them, it is hard to say. Certainly some have been preached, if only for a dare:

'And he said unto her, Give me, I pray thee, a little water to drink; for I am thirsty. And she opened a bottle of milk.' – Judges 4:19.
'So we boiled my son, and did eat him.' – 2 Kings 6:29.
'Go not empty unto thy mother in law.' – Ruth 3:17.
'For only Og king of Bashan remained of the remnant of giants; behold, his bedstead was a bedstead of iron.' – Deuteronomy 3:11.
'He got in underneath the Elephant and thrust at it from below and

killed it. It fell to the ground on top of him, and there he died.' – 1 Maccabees 6:46 (Apocrypha).
'My God, my soul is vexed within me … one deep calleth another, because of the noise of the water-pipes.' – Psalm 42:7–9 (Book of Common Prayer version).
'And the lot fell upon Matthias.' – Acts 1:26.
'And he spake to his sons, saying, Saddle me the ass. And they saddled him.' – 1 Kings 13:27.
'Even a child is known by his doings.' – Proverbs 20:11.
'He delighteth not in the strength of the horse: he taketh not pleasure in the legs of a man.' – Psalms 146:10.
'And Isaiah said, Take a lump of figs. And they laid it on the boil, and he recovered.' – 2 Kings 20:7.
'And Adonibezak said, Three-score and ten kings, having their thumbs and their great toes cut off, gathered their meat under my table.' – Judges 1:7.
'He saith among the trumpets, Ha, Ha.' – Job 39:25.
'And I will take away my hand, and thou shalt see my back parts.' – Exodus 33:23.
'As she sat on the ass, she broke wind, and Caleb said, "What did you mean by that?" She replied, "I want to ask a favour of you."' – Judges 1:14 (New English Bible).

Servants

3 Prince Edward started his working life as a production assistant with Andrew Lloyd Webber's Really Useful Company. As such he sometimes had to perform relatively menial tasks. On one occasion, the great composer (before he actually became Lord Lloyd-Webber)

was conferring with one of his lyricists, Don Black. The door opened and in came Prince Edward bearing tea upon a tray. Black commiserated with Lloyd Webber: 'Such a job getting the right staff these days, isn't it?'

Told to me by Charles Hart (1993). When I asked about this in 1999, Don Black told me that what in fact had occurred was that he had asked for black tea – no milk, no sugar – and Prince Edward had brought him the opposite of what he had asked for, occasioning the remark: 'You just can't get the staff these days ...'

Sex

1 When the Elizabethan actor Richard Burbage played the part of Shakespeare's Richard III, a woman in the audience was so taken with him that she made an assignation. He was to meet her that night using the name 'Richard the Third'. William Shakespeare himself, getting wind of this arrangement, made sure that he arrived first at the appointed place and began to take his pleasure of the woman. When 'Richard the Third' was duly announced at the door, Shakespeare sent a message to the effect that 'William the Conqueror' had come before 'Richard the Third'.

Told in E. K. Chambers, *William Shakespeare. A Study of Facts and Problems* (1930). The story was taken from John Manningham's *Diary*, a Harleian manuscript, edited in 1868 and dating from the turn of the seventeenth/eighteenth century.

2 Sir Walter Raleigh, according to John Aubrey, 'loved a wench well; and one time getting up one of the Mayds of Honour up against a tree in a Wood ('twas his first Lady) who seemed at first boarding to be somewhat fearfull

of her Honour, and modest, she cryed, sweet Sir Walter, what doe you me ask? Will you undoe me? Nay, sweet Sir Walter! Sweet Sir Walter! Sir Walter! Sir Walter! At last, as the danger and the pleasure at the same time grew higher, she cryed in the extasey, Swisser Swatter Swisser Swatter.'

In *Brief Lives* (*c.* 1693).

3 When Queen Caroline, wife of King George IV, was investigated on the grounds of adultery and stood trial in the House of Lords in 1820, particular attention was paid to her behaviour with the dey (governor) of Algiers. The Chief Justice, Lord Norbury, merrily remarked: 'She was happy as the dey was long.'

Told in Miriam Ringo, *Nobody Said It Better* (1980).

4 A correspondent suggested to me, *en passant*, that it was Lord Curzon who had originated the saying 'She should lie back and enjoy it'. I puzzled over this for a number of years, unsure in what circumstances he might have said it and how it could ever be verified. Then I came across what he may really have said (and perhaps my correspondent may be forgiven for his confusion). According to *The Oxford Book of Political Anecdotes* (1986), when instructing his second wife on the subject of love-making, Curzon said, 'Ladies never move.'

No precise source is given, however. The book of *New Statesmen* competition winners called *Salome Dear, Not With a Porcupine* (1982 – edited by Arthur Marshall) prefers, 'A lady does not move' (and proceeds to provide the circumstances in which it *might* first have been said.) Note, however, that a completely different source for the story was found by Rupert Hart-Davis while researching Cora, Lady Strafford, a thrice-married American: 'Before one of her marriages (perhaps the second – to Lord Strafford) she thought it would be a good thing to get a little sex-instruction, so she went over to Paris and took a few lessons from a leading cocotte. On her wedding night she was beginning to turn precept into practice when her bridegroom sternly quelled her by saying: "Cora, *ladies don't move!*"' Alas, Hart-Davis does not give a source for this. (In *The Lyttelton Hart-Davis Letters*, for 19 August 1956.)

1 In answer to the question much puzzled over by Shakespearean scholars, 'Did Hamlet actually sleep with Ophelia?', an old actor-manager is said to have replied, 'In our company – always!'

Related by Sir Cedric Hardwicke in *A Victorian in Orbit* (1961). Peter Hay in *Broadway Anecdotes* (1989) identifies the actor specifically as John Barrymore. Telling this version on BBC Radio *Quote ... Unquote* (12 March 1998), Bryan Forbes had Barrymore replying: 'In New York, never ... on tour, always.'

2 It is not very difficult to understand what King Edward VIII saw in Mrs Simpson. However, a lesser-known aspect of her charms is indicated by the claim that, 'she could make a match-stick seem like a Havana cigar' – which was, perhaps, important to the man in question.

Told to me by a Royal biographer in 1981. In 1975, a journalist related how one of the rumours concerning the Duke of Windsor was that he used to enjoy watching society ladies having it off with footmen because 'his own parts were so small'. Roy Strong, *The Roy Strong Diaries 1967–1987* (1997) reports (1 January 1972) Harold Acton recalling Violet Trefusis as saying that 'Wallis Simpson ... owed her hold over the Duke of Windsor to the fact that she had learned the "Chinese clutch" in Shanghai.'

3 When the editor and academic Karl Miller was an undergraduate at Cambridge, he called on a friend whom he found *in flagrante*. So he left a note saying, 'Called to see you but you were in.'

Told in *Cosmopolitan* (UK) (*c.* 1979).

4 Tallulah Bankhead is said to have declared to a male friend, 'I'll come and make love to you at five o'clock. If I'm late, start without me.'

Told in Ted Morgan, *Somerset Maugham* (1980). In *Crying With Laughter* (1993), Bob Monkhouse claims that he invented this line for Ted Ray to say after a rousing concert performance by Diana Dors in the early 1950s: 'Thank you, Diana, you may go to my room and lie down. And if I'm not there in twenty minutes, start without me.' Monkhouse adds that this was a line that 'subsequently went all round show business to be used by comedians everywhere ... Only two years later I offered the same gag to Bob Hope. "But I know that line," he said, as if I were trying to sell him a stolen watch.' Compare the exchange between Neal (Richard Benjamin) and Brenda (Ali McGraw) as he reaches out for her in the film *Goodbye, Columbus* (1969): 'Later.' 'What if I can't wait?' 'Start without me.'

5 By the 1950s, the American-born singer and actress Frances Day was being described as a 'veteran sex symbol ... breast-waving and leggy'. She could also put on a squeaky voice. It was generally agreed that Day's off-stage activities were as energetic as her public performances. When she arrived late for rehearsal looking somewhat the worse for wear, Bud Flanagan was moved to remark: 'Little Day, you've had a busy man.'

Told in Wallace Reyburn, *Gilbert Harding* (1978).

1 Harold Macmillan liked to suggest that when he was Prime Minister and Jack Kennedy was President there was something of a father–son relationship between them. If so, the mind can merely boggle at the remark Kennedy made at their third or fourth meeting (in about 1961). He said to the world-weary (and, indeed, famously cuck-olded) older man, 'I wonder how it is with you, Harold? If I don't have a woman for three days, I get a terrible headache.'

Told in Alastair Horne, *Macmillan 1957– 1986* (1989). In a letter from Venice (3 July 1961), Nancy Mitford told her sister the Duchess of Devonshire (who was related by marriage to the President): 'They say on the beach that if [Kennedy] doesn't ... every day he has a headache.'

2 In his twilight years, Groucho Marx played the role of quiz-show host, enabling him to rough up the con-testants gently. When one of them was the mother of no less than twenty-two children, he was astonished when she offered by way of explanation: 'I love my husband.' 'I like my cigar, too,' said Groucho, 'but I take it out once in a while.'

Told in Dorothy Herrman, *With Malice Toward All* (1982).

3 Life wasn't all music-making for the American bandleader, pianist and com-poser Duke Ellington. He had other in-terests – or, rather, he had one. Indeed, a musical about his life ran into diffi-culties because originally it contained spoken introductions trying to point up the contrast between the 'public' and the 'private' Ellington. Mercer Elling-ton, his son, quietly pointed out that there was only one aspect to both: 'He spent his whole life chasing pussy.'

Told to me by a New York lawyer in April 1981. The musical that didn't result from this observation was *Sophisticated Ladies*.

4 The diminutive actor Mickey Rooney is supposed to have approached a statuesque chorus girl with the sugges-tion that they might enjoy sex together. Replied she: 'All right, but if you do and I ever get to hear about it, I'll be very, very cross indeed.'

Told by Humphrey Lyttelton on BBC Radio *Quote ... Unquote* (13 July 1988). However, I expect this may be an applica-tion of a general tall/short persons joke that had been current in Britain for some time before. the *Observer* (11 March 1984) had a version between a male and a female journalist.

5 Sir Norman Fowler was for many years Social Services Secretary in Margaret Thatcher's government. In 1986, it fell to him to spearhead the official anti-AIDS campaign and to promote 'safe sex' among the British people. Un-fortunately, as the story has it, Fowler's experience of sexual behaviour and morality dated from an earlier era. To have him masterminding a leaflet and advertising campaign that referred openly, for the first time, to condoms, anal sex and much else, meant that his civil servants had to, er, bend over backwards, to make sure he was brought up to date on such matters. In no time at all, word leaked out of Whitehall that he had actually asked a meeting of medical experts, 'What is oral sex?'

Told in *Sunday Today* (11 January 1987). A little more light was thrown on the subject when the *Observer* (3 January 1999) marked the retirement of Romola Christopherson, who had taken over as Head of Information at the DHSS at the beginning of the AIDS campaign. Referring to Fowler's inability to pronounce his R's, Christopherson recalled that he had exclaimed, rather, 'Oh cwikey!' when presented with a statistic about the number of couples who were said to practise oral sex. In the same article, Fowler was quoted as saying, 'There is a wonderful and totally untrue story that I had never heard of oral sex. Curiously enough, I had.' Christopherson did, however, make up for this disappointment by recalling that, on another occasion, when she was riding with Fowler in his chauffeur-driven ministerial car, he asked: 'Womola, what's a vibwator? What do people use it for?' She cannot remember what she replied.

1 Michael Vermeulen, publisher of *GQ* magazine, died at the age of 38 after a hectic life. Once he was in bed with a more than satisfied woman who praised his love-making to the skies. 'Don't thank me,' he replied. 'Tell your friends.'

In the *Independent* (2 September 1995).

Shakespeare

2 This is W. S. Gilbert's contribution to the debate as to whether Shakespeare or Bacon wrote Shakespeare's plays. In a letter he wrote: 'Do you know how they are going to decide the Shakespeare–Bacon dispute? They are going to dig up Shakespeare and dig up Bacon; they are going to set their coffins side by side, and they are going to get [Herbert Beerbohm] Tree to recite Hamlet to them. And the one who turns in his coffin will be the author of the play.'

Told in Hesketh Pearson, *Lives of the Wits* (1962). Alexander Woollcott wrote in *While Rome Burns* (1934) of a bad actor's performance of Hamlet: 'Scholars should have kept watch beside the graves of Shakespeare and Bacon to see which one of them turned over.'

Shopping

3 'Melly's Law' – named after the celebrated personality and jazz singer George Melly, and dating from the 1960s – was designed to help customers distinguish between male and female clothing shops. 'It's a male boutique,' Melly stated, 'if you go in to buy a tie and they measure your inside leg.'

Told by Ned Sherrin on BBC Radio *Quote . . . Unquote* (15 December 1981).

Showmanship

4 P. T. Barnum, the American showman and circus proprietor, was Sydney Bernstein's idol from an early age. So much so that in every office of the various branches of the Granada empire that Bernstein founded, there was placed a copy of a signed portrait of Barnum. This was to remind everyone – especially some of the more effete producers in Granada TV – that showmanship was or should be at the heart of the operation. In other words, whatever sort of programme you did, it was all show business. If anyone chose to remove the portrait from the wall, it would mysteriously be replaced overnight. The unstated suggestion here was that if you removed the picture, it would be replaced, and your desk and job would be thrown out instead.

Personal recollection of my time working for Granada TV in Manchester and London, 1966–67.

Silence

5 When King Archelaus was asked by a barber how he would like his hair cut, he replied: 'In silence.'

Told by W. and A. Durant in *The Story of Civilization* (1935–64). Archelaus (reigned

413–399 BC) was a Macedonian King. Possibly said, rather, by a successor, Philip II. Plutarch, however, in his *Moralia*, attributes it to Archelaus. Compare the caption to a Bernard Partridge cartoon entitled 'A DAMPER' in *Punch* (27 February 1897): *Chatty Barber:* ''Ow would you like to be shaved, sir?' *Grumpy Customer:* 'In perfect silence, please.'

1 'The soldier ... of today is ... a quiet, grave man ... perhaps like Count Moltke, "silent in seven languages".'

So wrote Walter Bagehot in 'Checks and Balances', *The English Constitution* (1867). The source of Bagehot's phrase is unknown, but it is yet another interesting description of the taciturn German, Helmuth Graf von Moltke 'The Silent' (1800–91). 'Moltke' is a name given to a taciturn, unsmiling person. Michael Wharton ('Peter Simple' columnist in the *Daily Telegraph*) described in *The Missing Will* (1984) how he was also so nicknamed, as a child, by his German grandfather after the famous general, 'who seldom spoke and was said to have smiled only twice in his life'. Geoffrey Madan's *Notebooks* (1981) recorded that these two smiling occasions were 'once when his mother-in-law died, and once when a certain fortress was declared to be impregnable'.

2 During the Australian court case in which the British government tried to prevent publication of the book *Spycatcher*, Malcolm Turnbull, appearing for the author and his publishers, told Sir Robert Armstrong, the Cabinet Secretary, 'If Lord Chancellors embody the law, you embody British secrecy.' At the same time, he let Sir Robert keep a copy of *Conspiracy of Silence* by Barrie Penrose and Simon Freeman. The following day, before the hearing started, Sir Robert presented Turnbull with a copy of *The Gift of the Gab* by Nigel Rees, and signed it with this

message: 'The only possible reply to a conspiracy of silence.'

Told in the *Independent* (27 November 1986).

Single-mindedness

3 Eric Morecambe once suffered from a bout of his recurring heart trouble while he and Ernie Wise were rehearsing a sketch for their Christmas show at Thames Television. They were deep in discussion of some difficult move when Eric succumbed. After a while spent lying on the studio floor, he was carried off by medical staff to an ambulance. Everyone turned to Ernie for his reaction. 'Well,' he said, 'I still think it would be better if I went through the door before speaking the line rather than after ...'

Told to me by Barry Cryer (who had written the show) in about 1980. Compare this story from James Agate, *Ego 3* (1938): one day in 1915 the woman partner of a bridge-fiend messed up a hand to such an extent that the old man made a considerable fuss about how the hand should have been played. A few days later, news arrived of the death of the old man's only son at the Front and naturally he did not play bridge for several weeks. When he did show up, the woman exclaimed, 'My dear Doctor F——, I am so sorry. I am so very sorry!' The old man gazed vindictively at her and said, 'That is all very well, madam, but it's too late. Had you led the King of Spades and followed it up with the Knave ...'

Situations

4 When the poet and cleric John Donne married Anne, the daughter of Sir George More, without her father's knowledge or consent, the couple were thrown out of Sir George's house and Donne lost his job. Taking refuge

in a house at Pyrford, Surrey, Donne scratched on a pane of glass:

John Donne
An Donne
Undone.

Related in Sir James Prior, *Life of Edmond Malone* ... (1860). The words were still visible at the house in 1749. However, in Izaak Walton, *The Life of Dr Donne* (1640), the lines are said to come from a letter from Donne to his wife.

Size

1 When the BBC moved to the splendid new Broadcasting House in Portland Place, London, in 1932, it commissioned Eric Gill to sculpt a statue of Prospero and Ariel to stand in a niche above the main entrance. The relevance of these two figures was not entirely clear, and Gill wondered whether Ariel was supposed to be a pun on 'aerial'. Leslie French, the actor, who was currently playing the Shakespeare character of Ariel at the Old Vic, was Gill's main model for Ariel, right down to the penis. Gill worked on the figures *in situ*, and finally the Governors of the BBC trooped along and examined them behind a tarpaulin. They requested that Ariel's genitals should be diminished.

Told in Fiona MacCarthy, *Eric Gill* (1989). Louis Marder in *His Exits and His Entrances* (1963) tells a slightly different story: Sir John Reith, the BBC Director-General, had complained of the size of Ariel's genitals, and the matter was sent to arbitration. Sir Israel Gollancz and Israel Zangwill, Shakespeare scholars, were deputed to investigate. They decided that Ariel would have been 13 years old. A medical doctor was then drawn in who decreed that the genitals as Gill had originally sculpted them were too generous. They were diminished.

2 Robert Benchley and Dorothy Parker once had to share a small office at *The New Yorker*. When asked precisely how small it was, he said, 'One cubic foot less of space and it would have constituted adultery.'

Told in R. Drennan, *Wit's End* (1973).

3 The screenwriter Harry Kurnitz had a thing about large cars. One day his own splendid limousine broke down as he was on his way to Paris, and he was forced to take a lift in a Volkswagen. When he was asked what he thought about it, he replied: 'I've been in bigger women.'

Told in Ned Sherrin, *Theatrical Anecdotes* (1991). One senses that this must have influenced Woody Allen in his line from the film *Crimes and Misdemeanors* (1989): 'The last time I was inside a woman was when I was inside the Statue of Liberty.'

4 1998 was the year in which the question of whether size does or doesn't matter became a theme of advertising slogans and yet more nudging jokes. It all began with the latest film about the sinking of the *Titanic* (the world's largest ship when it was launched in 1912). As he began to receive a slew of awards, James Cameron, the film's writer and director, commented: 'Does this prove once and for all that size does matter?' At which one might have pointed to the line of dialogue he had already given to one of his characters: 'Do you know of Dr Freud ...? His ideas about the male preoccupation with size might be of particular interest to you.' All the many allusions to the expression hinted, of course, at the age-old contention that penis size does not have any bearing on the pleasure to be had from sex.

In no time at all, a new film *Godzilla* (about the monster) was being promoted with the slogan 'Size does matter.' In the UK, the relatively small Renault Clio motor car was advertised alongside the words 'Size matters.'

1 Opera diva Jessye Norman has a big voice and body to match. In an otherwise admiring article, *Classic CD Magazine* jokingly told of the occasion when, trapped in swing doors on the way to a concert, she was advised to turn sideways and release herself. In ringing tones, Norman declared: 'Honey, I ain't got no sideways.'

Norman attempted to sue for libel on the grounds that the words conformed to a 'degrading, racist stereotype of a person of African-American heritage'. Striking out her claim, in a ruling at the Court of Appeal in London (November 1998), Lord Justice Gibson said he wished 'that Miss Norman had told the hoary old joke contained in the anecdote' as it would have shown she had a sense of humour as well as her other talents. In fact, the joke dates back to a cartoon in *Punch* (17 October 1900) by L. Raven-Hill that shows a stout countrywoman trying to board an omnibus, and the driver says, 'Try zideways, Mrs Jones, try zideways!' to which Mrs Jones replies, 'Lar' bless 'ee, John, I ain't got no zideways.'

Muriel Smith spotted another appearance of this old chestnut in Maisie Ward's *Gilbert Keith Chesterton* (1944) in an account of Chesterton's visit to the United States in 1930–31, when he gave a course of lectures at Notre Dame. The chauffeur there, Johnny Mangan, said: 'I brought him under the main building and he got stuck in the door of the car. Father O'Donnell tried to help. Mr Chesterton said it reminded him of an old Irishwoman: "Why don't you get out sideways?" "I have no sideways."'

Slogans

2 Between the First and Second World Wars, a type of fuel was on the market known as 'ethyl' (because it was derived from tetraethyl lead). For example, 'Esso Ethyl' was on sale in 1935. Despite, or because of, the less-than-exciting name, advertising copywriters were drafted in to come up with a slogan that was as dashing as the current rival, 'That's Shell – That Was!' All they could manage was, 'Flat Out – On Ethyl!' – which had to be rejected for reasons of decorum.

This was told me by Malcolm Ross-Macdonald in a letter dated 5 October 1979. Subsequently I was told by another correspondent that it had never really reached the slogan stage: it was no more than the answer to the joke question, 'What's better than 50 mph on Shell?'

3 Arriving in Los Angeles after flying on an inaugural flight over the Pole, the voluble Welsh broadcaster Wynford Vaughan-Thomas was – unusually – rendered speechless by an American broadcaster. Wynford's description of the Greenland ice-cap apparently made the American broadcaster remember his sponsors, who were makers of deodorants. Said he: 'It may be December outside, but it's always August under your armpits.'

Related in Vaughan-Thomas's *Trust to Talk* (1980). However, *News Review* (13 November 1947) reproduced from the *Evening Standard*: 'He [John Snagge] had been against commercial broadcasting ever since he heard a Toscanini radio concert in New York interrupted by the sponsor's slogan "It may be December outside, ladies, but it is always August under your armpits."' According to Miles Kington in *The Independent* (13 May 1994), when W. H. Auden was Professor of Poetry at Oxford (early 1960s), he said in a lecture: 'Never underestimate advertisers. One of the most impressive lines of poetry I have ever come across was contained in an ad for a deodorant. This was the line: "It's always August underneath your arms …"'

1 The most famous unfortunate advertising juxtaposition appears to have occurred in about 1952–53 at Charing Cross railway station, London. A bill-poster had obviously had great fun putting alongside each other an advert that had the headline 'VD' in very large letters and another advert with the slogan 'I got it at the Co-Op.'

Told in a letter from Brian Blackwood of Stevenage (23 February 1981). Others remember the second slogan as, 'You can always get it at the Co-Op.'

2 In the 1960 US presidential election, John F. Kennedy quoted 'Stand Pat with McKinley' as an example of Republican reaction, dating as it did from the days of the protectionist President McKinley. So Richard M. Nixon countered with 'America Cannot Stand Pat' – until it was politely pointed out that he was married to a woman with that name. 'America Cannot Stand Still' was rapidly substituted.

This is apocryphal but was told by William Safire in *Before the Fall* (1975).

3 When Margaret Thatcher became Leader of the Conservative Party in 1975, it wasn't long before the Young Conservatives came up with a slogan drawing attention to her sex. It was 'Put a woman on top for a change.' Originally 'Have a Woman on Top' (or 'F*** me, I'm a Tory'), it was distributed as a sticker at the Tory Party Conference in 1976. In 1979, it seems to have had some circulation as an official party slogan in the General Election that took Mrs Thatcher to Downing Street.

Information (1984) from Rob Hayward MP, who had been National Vice-Chairman of the YCs at the time. A much later re-write was: 'Get her off, she's hurting.'

4 In 1978, President Carter was due to visit West Germany and wanted to come up with a slogan as memorable as John F. Kennedy's 1963 '*Ich bin ein Berliner.*' Unfortunately, he resisted an impish suggestion allegedly made by Gerald Rafshoon, his communications adviser, that he should go instead to Frankfurt and declare, '*Ich bin ein Frankfurter*'.

Told in *Time* Magazine (24 July 1978).

5 The Mercedes-Benz company once used an interesting but ambiguous slogan to promote its cars in Britain: 'Once you've driven one, you're unlikely to drive another.' One could think of other marques that might well use the same slogan, though not in the intended sense.

Reported in *The Times* (June 1980).

6 Because the Scottish *Sunday Mail* was just about the only Sunday newspaper that was not imported from England, the Mirror Group's advertising agents came up with a slogan that they felt demonstrated the *Mail*'s ability to carry all the very latest news on its pages. The slogan was 'If it's going on, it's going in.' This served well for some months (in about 1983), but was quietly withdrawn when it was discovered that some local wits had been going round public houses applying the promotional stickers to contraceptive vending machines.

Told to me by Ken Bruce in a letter (14 March 1985).

Smells

1   When Dame Rebecca West, the writer, died, mention was made of the affair she had enjoyed seventy years before, as a young woman, with the novelist and writer H. G. Wells. One obituarist said she had been attracted to him 'because he smelt of walnuts'. He, whether it was true or not, was said to have been attracted by her 'hard mind'.

No evidence was given for the 'walnuts' assertion, but it chimes with a mention of H. G. Wells given in Ted Morgan's biography of W. Somerset Maugham. When Maugham asked Moura Budberg (another lover of H. G. Wells) what she saw in the paunchy, played-out writer, she replied, 'He smells of honey.'

Whatever Wells smelt of, it seems to have been effective, and surely ought to have been bottled and put on the market.

Discussed in the *Guardian* (16 March 1983). The honey reference is also mentioned in *The Lyttelton Hart-Davis Letters* (for 16 January 1957).

Smoking and non-smoking

2   At a certain dinner party, when a young, nervous girl lit up a cigarette after the soup, without asking permission to do so, the hostess said icily, 'We seem to have finished,' and led the party from the room. That was the end of the dinner.

I first came across this cautionary tale in Katharine Whitehorn's *Observer* column (27 July 1980), though I have subsequently found it told about a *duke* in Francis Meynell's *The Week-end Book* (1955). From

the way Meynell tells it, it was an old tale even then. I have also heard it adorned with the additional detail of the cook throwing a tantrum over the ruination of her meal, and with the moral drawn that it is an excellent illustration of the way in which manners, which are intended to put people at their ease, can be used rather to humiliate an innocent or uninitiated person. The girl who lit up is said to have run off in tears and had to leave the house next day.

3   Sir Thomas Beecham was travelling in the no-smoking carriage of a train when a woman passenger lit a cigarette with the words, 'You won't object if I smoke?' To which Beecham replied, 'Certainly not – and you won't object if I'm sick.' It was in the days when the railways were still privately owned. 'I don't think you know who I am,' the woman angrily pointed out. 'I am one of the directors' wives.' To which Beecham riposted: 'Madam, if you were the director's only wife, I should still be sick.'

Pass the Port (1976) ascribes these two barbs to Beecham, but a story about 'Harty-Tarty', the Marquess of Hartington (1833–1908) who became the 8th Duke of Devonshire, is told in Anita Leslie, *Edwardians in Love* (1972): 'When a man entering his railway carriage put the question, "Do you mind if I smoke a cigar?" Hartington serenely answered: "No, my dear sir, provided you don't mind me being sick."'

4   A Labour minister dining with King George VI at Buckingham Palace in the late 1940s was asked if he would like to have a cigar. 'Oh no, thank you,' he said, 'I only smoke on special occasions.'

I was told this story in about 1975. Theo Aronson, in *Royal Ambassadors* (1976), tells a similar story about the King's tour of Canada before the war. He remarked that a local mayor was not wearing a mayoral chain. 'Oh,' explained the mayor, 'but I only wear it on special occasions.' In Michael Pertwee, *Name Dropping* (1974), the mayor is specifically located to Montreal.

1 Robert Maxwell was against smoking in the offices of most of his companies. Getting into a lift at one of them and encountering a man puffing on a cigarette, he immediately demanded to know how much the fellow earned. 'Seventy-five pounds a week,' came the reply. Maxwell took out his wallet, handed the man £300 – to cover a month's wages – and told him, 'You're fired.'

What Maxwell hadn't realized was that the man was not an employee, but merely a visitor.

Told variously since the late 1980s. A version appears in Peter Hay, *Business Anecdotes* (1988).

Social intercourse

2 Sir Stafford Cripps flourished under Winston Churchill's leadership during the Second World War, but afterwards rejoined the Labour Party and became Chancellor of the Exchequer. As well as presiding over austere policies, he was a long, thin streak of austerity to look at, too. Having had enough of his views at a dinner party, Churchill cried: 'Who will relieve me of this Wuthering Height?'

Told in Willans and Roetter, *The Wit of Sir Winston* (1965).

3 Actor David Niven's first wife, Primmie, died tragically at Tyrone Power's house during Sardines – a game in which everyone is squashed together in a closet, or similar place, and one person has to wander about in the dark trying to find them. Alas, Primmie opened a door in the dark and fell down a flight of stone steps. As she waited for the ambulance, she murmured the thought that was obviously troubling her most, 'We'll never be invited again ...'

Recounted in Sheridan Morley, *The Other Side of the Moon* (1985).

4 Unlike some great actors one could name, Laurence Olivier was talented and circumspect on social occasions. Once when he was at a party he found himself stuck with a woman who went on and on talking to him, and he was greatly relieved when the host arrived and the woman left. Said Olivier, 'Who on earth was that woman?' The host said, 'That's my mother.' Olivier, very quickly, said, 'Isn't she marvellous!'

Told by Sir Ian McKellen on BBC Radio *Quote ... Unquote* (10 April 1998).

5 Once upon a time, Edward Heath's trademark was the heaving shoulders with which he mirthlessly greeted a joke. For a while this tended to make up for the countless tales of his abruptness. At the Conservative Party Conference in 1966, I remember him coming into a makeshift ITN studio for an interview and – noticing it was rather hot and stuffy – his saying immediately, 'Haven't you people heard of air-conditioning?'

Invited to dinner by the dons of Exeter College, Oxford, Heath retired with them to the Senior Common Room for post-prandial drinks and then, looking at his watch, declared, 'There's an organ recital at Balliol I want to hear ... come on.'

When Heath was still Leader of the Opposition, a BBC Radio producer went to interview him in his hotel room during a Conservative Party Conference. When it was over, Heath asked (to the producer's surprise), 'Would you like some tea?' (probably expecting the answer 'No'). The producer, a man of independent mind, said, 'Yes.' So Heath rang for room service and requested, 'Tea for one. And a half-bottle of champagne for me.'

Told to me by the people involved in about 1972.

Society

1 'The Tory Party is the cream of society – thick and rich and full of clots.' This comment appeared in my book *Graffiti 4* as from a wall in Cambridge. But it is not entirely original. Samuel Beckett, the playwright, once taught briefly at Campbell College in Belfast. When told he was teaching the cream of Ulster, he replied, 'Yes, rich and thick.'

Told in *The Times* Diary (21 February 1948).

2 The writer Hanif Kureishi has been described as having a 'well-advertised detachment from the usual frames of ethnic belonging'. When an Asian director challenged him with, 'Hey, Hanif, you should spend more time with your own people,' he replied, 'I do, man. I was down the Groucho Club only last night.'

Told by Kevin Loader in the *Observer* (19 February 1995). Kureishi (1954–), writer of *My Beautiful Launderette*, *The Buddha of Suburbia*, and such works, was born in Bromley, Kent, the son of Audrey Buss and Rafisuham Kureishi, an Indian Muslim civil servant who worked at the Pakistani High Commission in London.

Solidarity

3 After years of poverty, Sue Townsend, creator of 'Adrian Mole' had two books that were best sellers, she had a play on in the West End and she was wearing a new coat. But none of this seemed to count for very much when she was looking in through the window of a restaurant in St Martin's Lane, London, to see if her friends had arrived there yet. A 'bagman' came along, carrying about thirteen carrier bags, a bottle of sherry in his hand, slopping it all over the place, and stood by Townsend. She meanwhile continued peering through the restaurant window. The bagman sighed deeply and said, 'Ah, it's not for the likes of us ...'

Told by her on BBC Radio *Quote ... Unquote* (10 August 1985).

Songwriting

4 In the late nineteenth century, religious words were sometimes put to popular tunes of the day – with unusual results. This was particularly the case where the hymns had repetitive choruses in which the congregation joined, and especially so when the last line was broken up and repeated as a refrain. In one they sang:

> O catch the flee,
> O catch the flee,
> O catch the fleeing sinner, Lord.

In another, the sopranos sang,

> I want a man
> I want a man
> I want a mansion in the skies.

To which the tenors responded,

Come down Sal
Come down Sal
Come down Salvation from the skies.

And, finally, there was:

O take thy mourning pil,
O take thy mourning pil,
O take thy mourning pilgrims home.

Original letter from Peter C. Peck of
Polegate (1991). Others from the Reverend
Christine J. Hey of Mansfield, Notts., and
Florence Wilkinson of Menston, West
Yorkshire (1992).

1 One of the oddest song lyrics is that of
'The Hut-Sut Song' written by Leo V.
Killion, Ted McMichael and Jack
Owens. It was published in 1941:

Now the Rawlson is a Swedish town,
The rillerah is a stream,
The brawla is the boy and girl,
The Hut-Sut is their dream.

Hut-Sut Rawlson on the rillerah and
a brawla, brawla sooit,
Hut-Sut Rawlson on the rillerah and
a brawla sooit.

Apparently, this was one of the songs
rendered by The Merry Macs in a film
called *San Antonio Rose* (US, 1941).
Steuart Wight recalled hearing an
explanation for the origin of these
words: briefly, that they were 'based on
a very old recording by a negro singer
with a strong Southern accent (and very
few teeth)'. The chorus translates as
'Hotshot Brodie on the riverboat with
his rolling brawling sweetie.' According
to the explanation, Brodie was a well-
known riverboat captain with a
disreputable love life. The writers who
converted this into a popular song were
totally baffled by the pronunciation
and invented their own explanation in
the verse of the song.

2 On the face of it, one of the least inspired songs is a little novelty number
with the strange title, 'Ashby de la
Zouch. Castle. Abbey.' It contains such
deliriously bad lyrics as:

Where the skies are always blue,
And the cows are full of moo.

The circumstances of the song's com-
position go some way, however, to
explaining these oddities ... Written by
the respectable American team of
Al Hoffman, Milton Drake and Jerry
Livingston, and published in 1945, the
song came about because one or all of
these men had been stationed near
Ashby as GIs. They had obtained the
title from the Automobile Association's
touring-guide description of the town,
and had added 'by the sea' (which
Ashby, situated in the heart of England,
most certainly isn't) to make up the
rhyme. Another theory is that they
meant 'by the C', as Ashby was near the
'C' in 'Leicestershire' on the touring-
guide map ...

3 One of the most clichéd questions put
to songwriters is, 'Which comes first,
the words or the music?' In Richard
Strauss's opera *Capriccio* (1942), which
has lyrics by Clemens Krauss, the
eternal question is argued thus:

*Olivier: Prima le parole – dopo la
musica!* [first the words, then the
music!]
*Flamand: Prima la musica – dopo le
parole!* [first the music, then the
words!]

Most songwriters have become expert
at heading the question off. When
Sammy Cahn, the American lyricist
who died in 1993, was asked the question, he would ritually answer: 'First

comes the phone call.' Ira Gershwin is supposed to have replied: 'What usually comes first is the contract' – quoted at his death in the *Guardian* (18 August 1983). To Cole Porter is ascribed the similar view: 'All the inspiration I ever needed was a phone call from the producer.' According to the musical entertainment *Cole* (1974), however, when Porter (who wrote both music and lyrics) was asked which came first, he answered, 'Yes!'

Having designated it a cliché in my book *The Gift of the Gab* (1985), I found myself interviewing one of the breed on a television show a short while afterwards, and was dreadfully conscious of the clanger I might drop. And so I asked him, 'Which comes first, the words or the lyrics?'

The songwriter was Bill Buckley and the programme was HTV's *First Things First* (1988).

1 John Lennon, along with the other Beatles, fairly quickly lost interest in Transcendental Meditation and certainly fell out with the Maharishi Mahesh Yogi, whom he considered to be a dirty old man. Lennon wrote a song about him called 'Maharishi', but was persuaded to re-title it 'Sexy Sadie'.

Recounted in Peter Brown and Steven Gaines, *The Love You Make* (1983).

Soulfulness

2 Lady Asquith liked to tell a story about an Indian called Sir Beneval Rao who was in the jungle on a hunting expedition. After they had been out a few days, the Indian bearers laid down their burdens and refused to go a step further. Sir Beneval asked if they were tired. No, they replied, they were not in the least tired. 'But we must wait here at least twenty-four hours until our souls catch up with our bodies.'

Told on BBC TV, *As I Remember* (30 April 1967). Lady Asquith added: 'You know, I sometimes wonder whether we ought not perhaps to do the same.'

Speaking proper

3 A little girl was splashing a little boy in the swimming pool. 'I'm going to duck you,' said she. Replied he, 'No chance. You can't even say it proper.'

Told by Lord Oaksey on BBC Radio *Quote . . . Unquote* (6 December 1986).

Speech-making

4 There is an old observation about speech-making (in my early days I used to begin speeches with it: about as original as saying 'Unaccustomed as I am to public speaking . . .') to the effect that you always end up making three speeches: the one you make to the bathroom mirror before setting out, the absolute drivel you say when you stand up to speak, and the magnificent oration you convince yourself you have made, as you drive home afterwards.

I first saw this as part of an advertisement in *The Times* dating from about 1928.

5 At the first night of Noël Coward's play *Sirocco* in 1927, the leading lady – Frances Doble – was so thrown by the booing audience at the close that she launched into the only speech she had memorized. It began: 'Ladies and gentlemen, this is the happiest moment of my life . . .'

Told in Cole Lesley, *The Life of Noël Coward* (1976).

1 President Coolidge was famous for his taciturnity on all occasions, public and private. In his day, the most common method of reaching the people was to campaign by train. At one whistle-stop in a very small town, Coolidge stepped outside the railroad car to the observation platform and looked the crowd over. Then he quickly stepped back inside.

'What's the matter?' asked his campaign manager.

'This crowd,' Coolidge said, 'is too big for an anecdote and too small for an oration.'

Source untraced.

2 Gordon Hewart's most famous and shortest after-dinner speech was given in reply to a toast to 'His Majesty's Judges' at an important dinner in London. Unfortunately, there were several long-winded and unfunny speakers before him, and by the time Hewart rose to speak he was exasperated. So this is what he said: 'When I accepted the invitation to respond to this toast I was not certain at what stage of the evening I should be required to speak. So I prepared two speeches – a short one and a longer one.' With this, he looked at the clock. 'As the night is young, I propose to deliver them both. I will give you first the shorter speech – "Thank you." Now I will deliver the longer speech – "Thank you very much."' And he sat down.

Recounted in Robert Jackson, *The Chief* (1959). Gordon Hewart (Baron Hewart) (1870–1943), lawyer, politician and Lord Chief Justice of England (1922–40). He famously enunciated the principle that justice should not only be done but be seen to be done.

3 There was once a British duke who had a nightmare that he was giving an incredibly boring speech in the House of Lords. Then he woke up to discover that in fact he was giving an incredibly boring speech in the House of Lords.

Told by David Brooks in *The Wall Street Journal* (29 December 1998). He was reviewing *The Rise and Fall of Class in Britain*.

4 In John Betjeman's article on Lord Berners in *The Dictionary of National Biography*, it states: 'He never made a public speech in his life, except for the three short sentences with which he opened the Faringdon cinema.'

5 As Home Secretary, James Chuter Ede was on a visit to one of the prisons in his care. He was encouraged to make a short speech to a group of inmates. The prisoners must have been deeply reassured when he began his remarks by saying: 'I'm so glad to see you all here ...'

Told by Lord Elwyn-Jones on BBC Radio *Quote ... Unquote* (15 August 1987). Chuter Ede (later Lord Chuter-Ede) (1882–1965) was Home Secretary from 1945 to 1951 – in the days when Home Secretaries had names like Chuter Ede.

6 In the late 1940s, Oxford University awarded an honorary degree to Edward Stettinius, the former US Secretary of State. Arriving in Oxford, Stettinius asked if he was expected to make a speech of thanks. To his horror, the university officials told him they were expecting a full-scale, formal address on America's post-war international policies.

The aides travelling with Stettinius worked all night on a speech and had it typed on 3 × 5 cards just in time to hand it to him as he joined the academic procession. Unfortunately, during the procession, Stettinius dropped the cards. He placed them back in his pocket, but not necessarily in the right order.

When he stood up to speak he read from the cards well enough, but it was clear to his aides that the cards were all out of sequence. Despite this, the Oxford audience gave Stettinius a standing ovation. One of the aides asked one of the dons what he thought of the speech. 'Absolutely wonderful,' replied he. 'Statesmanlike and inspired. Churchill was never better. One of the finest speeches I have heard in my lifetime.'

'But,' said the aide, 'didn't you think the speech was organized in a very confusing manner?'

'Oh,' said the don, 'we're used to that sort of thing here at Oxford ...'

Source untraced.

1 Winston Churchill was making a speech to the Conservative Party Conference at a time when he was re-covering from a stroke (which had been hushed up). If it is true, this would have been in October 1953. His speech was awaited with great interest. It was Churchill's habit to read his speech from typed cards. As he was halfway through page 17 he sensed puzzlement from the assembly, and suddenly realized that this was not page 17 but a duplicated page 16. He continued: 'Some of you may be wondering why I am repeating myself. [Lengthy pause.] This is because the very essence of what I am trying to convey to you today is encapsulated in these last few sentences.'

John Clarke of Black Rock, Victoria, Australia claimed (1996) that this was a true anecdote. *Brewer's Politics*, ed. Nicholas Comfort (1995), tells the tale as though it were about William Whitelaw. His explana-tion, when laughed at by Labour MPs, is: 'Don't you realize that this is the most important page of my speech?'

2 Opening a Red Cross bazaar in Oxford, Noël Coward began his speech, 'Desperately accustomed as I am to public speaking ...'

Told in Dick Richards, *The Wit of Noël Coward* (1968). Sheridan Morley, *A Talent to Amuse* (1969) places this remark in 1962 when Coward was guest of honour one Sunday at a dinner given by the Gallery First-Nighters' Club.

3 A woman student at Bangor University was being courted by a man who was studying at Sheffield University. During term time, he frequently drove the two hundred miles or so to see her. Eventually they were married, and the girl's father, making the traditional speech at the wedding, proclaimed: 'It must have been true love considering he drove two hundred miles to Bangor every weekend ...'

Told to me by a correspondent, name fortunately forgotten, before 1987.

Spelling

4 When Harold Nicolson was writing the official life of George V (it was pub-lished in 1952), he had access to papers written in the King's own hand that were in the possession of the Royal Archives. From these, Nicolson was surprised to discover that the monarch had been unable to spell the word 'pre-rogative' correctly. Considering that the 'royal prerogative' of British sover-eigns – their rights not subject to

restriction – has been much discussed since the seventeenth century, this was a curious lapse in the King's English.

I forget how I heard this (in the early 1970s), though I do recall learning that Sir Harold Nicolson was rather embarrassed at having stumbled upon such a morsel.

1 J. Danforth Quayle produced a glittering garland of gaffes during his period in office as George Bush's Vice-President (1989–93). The one that may finally have scuppered any chance of his re-selection (either as Vice-President or maybe even as President) occurred in the election year of 1992. Visiting a school he corrected a schoolboy's blackboard spelling of the word 'potato'. He added an 'e'.

Reported in the *Guardian* (17 June 1992). No amount of expert explanation that 'potatoe' used to be the American spelling was able to extract Quayle from this ditch. Note, however, that *Punch* (21 December 1872) has an American spelling test featuring 'potatoe'

Spin-doctoring

2 On a visit to Chicago in 1979, Princess Margaret attended a private dinner party. A gossip columnist who talked to somebody who had sat adjacent to the Mayor of Chicago at the party published the Princess's alleged remark that 'The Irish are pigs.' In the aftermath, various explanations were offered as to what she might have said, including, 'I hate those Irish jigs.'

From various newspaper reports.

Spoonerisms

3 Spoonerisms are named after the Reverend William Spooner (1844–1930),

clergyman, academic and Warden of New College, Oxford, from 1903 to 1924. Maurice Bowra recalled Spooner's sensitivity on the matter of spoonerisms. When a High Court judge speaking at a college celebration made a heavy joke about 'New College' and 'Kew knowledge', Spooner replied by comparing himself to Homer and Shakespeare – who also had works not their own attributed to them – and said, 'If I err, I do it in very good company.'

Bowra also told of an occasion after a college 'bump supper' (following on from a rowing victory), when undergraduates stood outside Spooner's window calling for a speech. He put his head out and said, 'You don't want a speech. You only want me to say *one of those things.*'

Recounted in Maurice Bowra, *Memories 1898–1939* (1966).

4 The innkeeper, John Fothergill, was trying to off-load some pudding on to a customer, and said: 'Would you like to try some of our excellent chapel harlot?'

The customer, unpertubed, is said to have asked whether this was any relation to 'Thame Tart'. Told in *An Innkeeper's Diary* (1939). Fothergill (1876–1957) was quite well known in the 1920s and 30s, particularly as landlord of the Spread Eagle at Thame, and wrote a couple of books about his experiences.

5 Macdonald Hobley (1917–87) was a suave TV announcer of the 1940s and 50s, in the days when BBC announcers were actually seen on screen. He invariably seemed to be wearing a dinner jacket. In 1949, he was introducing a live party political broadcast (indeed, one of the first of its kind

anywhere in the world) and sat in Studio A at Alexandra Palace with one of the leading politicians of the day by his side. He said: 'Here to speak on behalf of the Labour Party is Sir Stifford Crapps ...'

Recounted by him on innumerable occasions, including BBC Radio *Where Were You in '62* (1983). The name 'Sir Stifford Crapps' had, however, already been used by a 'Chamberlainite wag' in a House of Commons circular, according to the diary of Charles Waterhouse (10 May 1940), quoted in Andrew Roberts, *Eminent Churchillians* (1994).

1 The actress Sinead Cusack made her debut at the age of eighteen as 'Everyman's First Love' in *One for the Grave* at the Abbey Theatre, Dublin. She had been warned of a potential spoonerism in one of her lines, but she was convent-educated and was playing a character who represented all that is innocent and pure in a woman, so did not worry about it. In one scene played with Everyman, she was supposed to be by a river, stare off into the middle distance, and then utter the line, 'Look at that couple in the punt.' She committed the spoonerism on the first night, the audience roared, and she was kicked out of the company three months later.

Told in the *Independent* (8 July 1998).

Sports commentators

2 BBC commentator Thomas Woodrooffe committed the most famous broadcasting boob of all on the night of 20 May 1937. He appeared on the wireless, probably drunk and repeating the famous phrase 'The Fleet's lit up'. The BBC took a kindly view of Woodrooffe's boob and, after a short suspension, it was clear that the incident had not put paid to Woodrooffe's broadcasting career. In 1938–39 he was the BBC's sole commentator for the FA Cup Final, the Grand National and the Derby. Commentating on the Cup Final, he declared in the closing minutes: 'If there's a goal scored now, I'll eat my hat.' There was, and he did.

Recounted in Asa Briggs, *History of Broadcasting in the United Kingdom* (Vol. 2, 1965). When war broke out, Woodrooffe returned to the Navy and did little broadcasting after 1939.

3 In the 1930s, Ronald Reagan's first job on graduating was as a radio sports announcer. He would give live commentaries on boxing, football and baseball, but sometimes did 'simulated' broadcasts of baseball games from the studio. He would improvise around the summaries of the progress of the game put out by Western Union telegraph. On one occasion, the ticker-tape machine went down on him and Reagan had to invent foul after foul of imaginary pitches until – six minutes later – the line came alive again and rescued him.

Recounted in *Newsweek* (21 July 1980) and *Esquire* (August 1980).

4 Commentating for the BBC on the 1949 Oxford and Cambridge University Boat Race, John Snagge allowed himself to observe at one point: 'I don't know who's ahead – it's either Oxford or Cambridge.'

How true. And he did – I have checked a recording of his commentary.

5 Introducing Harry Carpenter on some sports programme in 1973, Frank

Bough is reputed to have said: 'Harry commentator is your carpenter.'

Told by Clive James in the *Observer* (13 May 1973).

1 Brian Johnston was commentating on the Oval Test against the West Indies in 1976 with Michael Holding bowling to Peter Willey. Or as he put it: 'The bowler's Holding, the batsman's Willey.'

Recounted by Johnston on BBC Radio *Quote ... Unquote* (25 December 1980). On another occasion in the commentary box, Trevor Bailey had been singing the praises of Peter Willey when he suddenly produced the remarkable admission: 'I am, of course, a great Willey supporter.' One of Brian's other famous broadcasting moments was when, also commentating on a cricket match, he said, 'There's Neil Harvey at leg slip with his legs wide apart, waiting for a tickle.' Recounted by him on innumerable occasions.

2 During the 1978 World Cup, after several mentions of the hole in footballer Asa Hartford's heart, commentator David Coleman described him as 'a whole-hearted player'.

Told by Clive James in the *Observer* (11 June 1978). It was because of remarks like this that *Private Eye* invented the concept of 'Colemanballs' in the late 1970s. This column continues to be a repository for the inanities of TV and radio sports commentators. Coleman was BBC TV's principal sports commentator at the time. Coleman was generally supposed to have committed any number of solecisms, tautologies and what-have-you in the cause of keeping his tongue wagging. Hearers who report his sayings have often been inaccurate. It is believed, however, that he did say, among other things, 'This man could be a black horse' and 'There is only one winner in this race.'

To be fair, however, the boob that started it all has been revealed as being perpetrated by another. At the 1976 Montreal Olympics,

it was said of the athlete Alberto Juantorena, competing in the 400 metres heats, that he 'opens wide his legs and shows his class'. But it was not Coleman who said this but Ron Pickering (1930–91).

3 During the 1979 Cricket World Cup when England was playing Canada, the cricket commentator Christopher Martin-Jenkins drew attention to the inclement conditions under which the match was being played with these words: 'It is extremely cold here. The England fielders are keeping their hands in their pockets between balls.'

Recalled by him on BBC Radio *Quote ... Unquote* (23 July 1983).

Stage directions

4 J. M. Barrie was producing one of his own plays and was approached by a young actor who was having difficulty with interpreting his part. Barrie told him, 'Try and look as if you had a younger brother in Shropshire.'

Told in Lady Cynthia Asquith, *Diaries 1915–18*, entry for 6 January 1918. The story also occurs in John Aye, *Humour in the Theatre* (1932), where the advice is, 'I should like you to convey that the man you portray has a brother in Shropshire who drinks port.'

From about the same period there is said to have been a stage direction (from another dramatist): 'Sir Henry turns his back to the audience and conveys that he has a son' – quoted in Michael Holroyd, *Bernard Shaw*, Vol. 3 (1991).

5 Playing the character of Nina in Eugene O'Neill's *Strange Interlude*, Glenda Jackson was rather baffled by one of the playwright's legendarily lengthy stage directions. It went: 'She walks into the room. She stops. All the blood rushes from her face. A faint flush begins at the base of her neck, rises upward. Her

eyes dilate. Their extraordinary turquoise blue become black, then pale green.'

Recounted by her on BBC Radio *Quote...Unquote* (27 November 1990).

1 Understandably Alan Plater, the playwright and TV adapter, is also interested in the kind of stage directions that his fellow writers give to actors. One he did not write himself but which he heard of in a screenplay was the instruction to an actor: 'He thinks about whistling "Danny Boy", but decides against it.'

Recounted by him on BBC Radio *Quote ... Unquote* (27 November 1990).

Stage mishaps

2 Suzanne Lagier was a very stout actress, and in one nineteenth-century melodrama she had to be carried offstage, in a fainting fit, by the diminutive actor, Taillade. He was unable to budge her. At which point, a voice cried out from the gallery, helpfully: 'Take what you can and come back for the rest!'

From *The Era Almanack* (1876). A similar story, variously told, concerns – in one version, at least – the British melodramatic actor Tod Slaughter (1885–1956), who used to tour the provinces with plays like *Sweeney Todd* and *Maria Marten*. In the latter, he had just killed the girl, the police whistles were sounding, and he was busy asking rhetorically, 'What can I do? What shall I do with the girl?' Helpful as ever, a voice from the Gods called down, 'Shag her while she's still warm!' A politer version of this appears in Roy Hudd's *Book of Music-Hall, Variety and Showbiz Anecdotes* (1993).

3 Osgood Perkins, the American character actor, was appearing in a long-running melodrama during which he had to stab another character in the last act with a stiletto-type letter opener. One day, the props man forgot to put the knife on the table, and there was no other murder implement to hand. Instead of throttling his victim, Perkins apparently kicked him up the backside. The man fell down dead. Perkins turned to the audience and said: 'Fortunately, the toe of my boot was poisoned!'

Told to Richard Burton by Stanley Donen and recorded by Burton in his diary for 16 October 1968 (and printed in Melvyn Bragg, *Rich: The Life of Richard Burton*, 1988).

4 On tour at the Leeds Grand Theatre in the title role of Ibsen's *Hedda Gabler*, Janet Suzman was due at the very end of the play to go off into an inner room and there play the piano fantastically and wildly before shooting herself. However, the Grand did not have a piano and so it was arranged that – at this climactic point of the play – a tape recording of piano-playing would be put on. And so Suzman went behind a curtain to 'play' this wild tarantella and bring the play to its wonderful conclusion. Instead, there was a faint whirring sound and off the tape came the words: 'Ladies and gentlemen, will you please take your seats. The curtain will rise in five minutes.'

Told by her on BBC Radio *Quote...Unquote* (9 March 1982).

5 Taking part in Somerset Maugham's *The Circle* at the Haymarket Theatre in London, Martin Jarvis played the part of a husband who has summoned his wife's lover for a confrontation. As the lover entered and closed the door, Jarvis saw that the ornate door handle had

come off in his hand. The actor playing the lover was laughing and, of course, they could not look each other in the eye. As it happens, Jarvis's next line was: 'Has it struck you that you are destroying my home?'

Told by Martin on BBC Radio *Quote...Unquote* (5 June 1979).

Stardom

1 When Clark Gable was filming in Britain, he preferred to stay with the Yeatman family – it will be remembered that Julian Yeatman was co-author of the humorous classic *1066 and All That* – instead of at a hotel. Yeatman's son recalls Gable looking into a mirror, taking his false teeth out, and saying sadly, 'America's sweetheart!'

Related by Frank Muir in *The Oxford Book of Humorous Prose* (1990).

2 It has been said that the five stages of Hollywood stardom are – and here we shall use the example of Dudley Moore – (1) Who's Dudley Moore? (2) Get me Dudley Moore! (3) Get me a Dudley Moore type. (4) Get me a young Dudley Moore. (5) Who's Dudley Moore?

In the *Independent* (17 October 1995). A week later, Tommy Steele used it with reference to himself on BBC TV *Pebble Mill* (25 October 1995). The formula is ageless, however. Leslie Halliwell in *The Filmgoer's Book of Quotes* (1973) has it in the form of a casting director's view of Hugh O'Brian (1925–), the Hollywood leading man of the 1950s and 60s.

Strip, tearing off a

3 Robert Atkins once employed a young Canadian (or American) actor at the Open Air Theatre, Regent's Park,

London. The young actor went to Brighton for the day and forgot there was a matinée. When he got back to London for the evening performance, the other actors said, 'My goodness, are you for it!'

So, in fear and trembling, he presented himself in front of Atkins, who had been walking up and down a lot between the matinée and the evening performance composing this speech. He looked at the young man and said: 'You come here from a foreign shore. We instruct you in the tongue that was Shakespeare's and Milton's. We give you God's green sward to walk upon. You treat me with base ingratitude, your fellow actors with grave discourtesy, your profession with something approaching contempt. There's only one word for you, laddie – you're a shit. Those are the gates!'

Told by Siân Phillips on BBC Radio *Quote... Unquote* (18 May 1993).

Subterfuge

4 In the 1959 General Election, Norman Collins was drafted in to produce the party political broadcasts by the incumbent Prime Minister, Harold Macmillan – not the most natural of performers. The first thing Collins noted was Macmillan's guardsman-like bearing, and so suggested that he should give his final broadcast *standing up*. 'Oh, I see,' said the Prime Minister, 'but am I allowed to?'

The next thing that concerned Collins was Macmillan's stiffness and inhibition. So he told him that his voice was sounding hoarse and that a drop of port was the best medicine. Macmillan acquiesced and drank a glass. Then Collins demanded one more rehearsal to get the timing exactly right. At the end of it Macmillan said, 'I hope I shall do it better when I do it live tonight.' Replied Collins, 'Prime Minister, you have already done it and you have been recorded.' 'You are a remarkable fellow,' said Macmillan. 'This is like going to the dentist to have a tooth drawn and being told it is already drawn.'

Recounted in Michael Cockerell, *Live from Number 10* (1988) and Alastair Horne, *Macmillan 1957–1986* (1989). Macmillan did, of course, win the election.

Success

1 The speaker was very anxious to find a way of bringing home to his audience how really important dynamism and enthusiasm were in making a success of one's working life. Then, just as he was entering the lecture theatre, he noticed the word 'PUSH' written up on the door. This seemed to him the perfect slogan to draw to his audience's attention.

And so, as he reached the climax of his speech, the speaker said, 'And if there is one word which encapsulates the secret of how to get on in business, then that word is the one which is written right there on the door to this hall.'

The audience, to a man, swung its eyes to the door where – in clearly defined letters – it saw what the speaker decreed was the secret of advancement in business. It was the one word, 'PULL'.

In the days before the term 'motivational speaking' had been invented, I heard this story told in a 'careers lecture' at school, around 1960.

2 One of the first interviews I ever conducted on television was with William Mervyn, a bald, benign actor who suddenly had a great deal of success in late middle age before his rather early death. I think that in 1967, when I did the interview, he had two or three TV series running concurrently – or perhaps he had series running simultaneously on all the three channels that were then available. Anyway, already having a well-developed ear for cliché, I began by remarking, 'Well, Mr Mervyn, you seem to have struck oil.' Neatly seizing on this, he replied, 'Yes, dear boy, but I've been drilling for thirty years ...'

The 'dear boy' may be another clichéd interpolation by me. The interview was at Granada TV in Manchester on 10 April 1967.

Suicide

3 When told that some producer whom he did not admire had blown his brains out, Noël Coward commented, 'He must have been an incredibly good shot.'

Told in Dick Richards, *The Wit of Noël Coward* (1968).

4 Lenny Bruce, the satirical comedian, once leapt out of a second-storey window crying, 'I'm Superjew!' If it was a suicide bid, it was unsuccessful. He merely sustained a broken leg.

Told in the *Observer* (21 August 1966).

5 'Things that might have been expressed differently' was the title of a *Punch* series at the turn of century. Well, the editor of *The Leicester Mercury* told me of an occasion when a young man had obviously found life in Leicester too exciting and had decided to take

his own life. He had not succeeded, however, and had been found clinging by his fingernails from the window ledge of a tallish building in the city centre. The *Mercury*, on that occasion, unfortunately rushed into print and advised its readers that the young man – hanging by his fingernails – 'had declined all offers of food and drink'.

Told by Neville Stack in May 1983.

Swearing

1 At the Battle of Waterloo in 1815, General Cambronne, commander of Napoleon's Old or Imperial Guard, is *supposed* to have declined a British request for him to surrender with the words, '*La garde meurt mais ne se rend jamais/pas* [The Guards die but never/do not surrender].' However, it is quite likely that what he said, in fact, was, '*Merde! La garde meurt ...* [Shit! The Guards die ...]'

At a banquet in 1835 Cambronne specifically denied saying the more polite version. That may have been invented for him by Rougemont in a newspaper, *L'Indépendent*. In consequence of all this, *merde* is sometimes known in France as *le mot de Cambronne*, a useful euphemism when needed.

2 Norman Shelley claimed to have been the first actor to have uttered the word 'f***' on the BBC. It was in the early 1950s and in a Third Programme production of a Ben Jonson play. Unfortunately, he never encountered anyone who had heard the play, and the fact that the BBC received no complaints about it would rather suggest that no one had.

Recounted by Bernard Braden in *The Kindness of Strangers* (1990).

3 On a royal visit to New Zealand, the Queen and her husband were watching a demonstration of sheepshearing. Prince Philip, as always, had to ask a number of questions and do a lot of pointing. To the sheepshearer he said, 'How long will it take you to finish off these sheep?'

Replied the sheepshearer, 'About half a bloody hour, I reckon.'

'Come, come,' said Prince Philip, conscious of the Queen's regal presence, 'that's putting it a bit strong, isn't it?'

'Oh, all right then,' said the sheep-shearer, 'say *forty* bloody minutes.'

I probably heard this in the 1950s.

4 John 11:35 – 'Jesus wept' – is the shortest verse in the Bible (the shortest sentence would be 'Amen'). It occurs in the story of the raising of Lazarus. Jesus is moved by the plight of Mary and Martha, the sisters of Lazarus, who break down and weep when Lazarus is sick. When Jesus sees the dying man he, too, weeps.

Like it or not, the phrase has become an expletive to express exasperation. The most notable uttering was by Richard Dimbleby, the TV commentator, on 27 May 1965. He was taking part in a live broadcast from Berlin of highlights from a Royal visit there. Several times there had been technical breakdowns between Berlin and West Germany. His producer told him, 'Hold everything. We're not on the air. London isn't getting us.' Thus thinking that his words were not being broadcast, Dimbleby let slip the oath, 'Jesus wept!' This would have passed unnoticed if London had not been receiving him loud and clear.

Related by the producer, Richard Francis, in *Richard Dimbleby, Broadcaster* (1966).

A graffito from the 1970s, from the advertising agency that lost the Schweppes account, was: 'Jesus wepped.'

1 There were four motions of protest in the House of Commons. There were outraged articles in the press. There were demands that the BBC should be prosecuted for obscenity. Nothing eventually happened. Somehow or other the nation managed to survive the shock. It was the first time the word 'f***' had been said on British TV.

Kenneth Tynan said it in a discussion on theatre censorship on the TV show *BBC3* (13 November 1965).

Sympathy

2 In 1974, during the course of routine house-to-house inquiries in Belgravia, a highly placed old lady was told of the murder of Sandra Rivett, the nanny it is alleged Lord Lucan mistakenly killed instead of his wife. 'Oh dear, what a pity,' the old lady said, 'Nannies are so hard to come by these days.'

Report in *The Sunday Times Magazine* (8 June 1975).

Tabloid journalism

1 Princess Margaret has always been about the nearest the present British Royal Family has got to a Bohemian. She used to smoke visibly, is photographed holding glasses of whisky, and daringly wears dark glasses. The penalty she pays for this behaviour is not hard to find. In the early 1960s I recall seeing a headline in a French newspaper – I think it may have been *Paris Soir* – which read *'Margaret – Presque Aveugle'*. Accompanying it was a photograph of her wearing dark glasses. Hence the assumption that she was 'nearly blind'.

My memory.

Taciturnity

2 Numerous tales attest to the reticence of President Calvin Coolidge – hence his nickname 'Silent Cal'. A story about Coolidge's taciturnity was told by his wife. A woman sat down next to him at a dinner party and said, 'You must talk to me, Mr Coolidge. I made a bet with someone that I could get more than two words out of you.' Coolidge replied: 'You lose.'

This made an early appearance in Gamaliel Bradford, *The Quick and the Dead* (1931).

3 Someone also said of Coolidge: 'He

opened his mouth and a moth flew out.'

Told in Claude Fuess, *Calvin Coolidge* (1940). This would appear to be a variant on the remark often directed at mean people – that they opened their wallets and a moth flew out.

Talk

4 Tallulah Bankhead's volubility was enormous. The magician Fred Keating came away from an interview saying, 'I've just spent an hour talking to Tallulah for a few minutes.'

Told in Howard Teichmann, *Smart Aleck* (1976).

Tallness

5 Frank Swinnerton said of his fellow author Aldous Huxley that he was 'the tallest English author known to me'. Indeed, he reported that so tall (and thin) was Huxley that when he lived in Hampstead, ribald little boys were in the habit of calling out to him, 'Cold up there, guv'nor?'

Told by Swinnerton in *The Georgian Literary Scene* (1935). In this sort of contest, Alan Bennett plumped for another winner in *Forty Years On*, Act 2 (1968): 'Of all the honours that fell upon Virginia [Woolf]'s head, none, I think, pleased her more than the *Evening Standard* award for the Tallest Woman Writer of 1927, an award she took by a neck from

Elizabeth Bowen. And rightly, I think, for she was in a very real sense the tallest writer I have ever known.'

Tantrums

1 The actress Mrs Patrick Campbell was noted for her tantrums. On one occasion, W. B. Yeats involved her in his plans for the Irish drama at the Abbey Theatre in Dublin. During rehearsals, after one particular outburst, she came to the footlights and shouted at him: 'I'd give anything to know what you're thinking.' Yeats replied: 'I'm thinking of the master of a wayside Indian railway station who sent a message to his company's headquarters saying: "Tigress on the line: wire instructions."'

Told in Gabriel Fallon, *Sean O'Casey: The Man I Knew* (1965).

Tearfulness

2 Richard Attenborough's propensity for blubbing – particularly when collecting awards – was parodied by the Monty Python team as early as 1972: *'[Dickie] gets out an onion and holds it to his eyes; tears pour out ... Attenborough weeps profusely.'* *Spitting Image* later continued the lampooning, except that co-creator Roger Law stated in 1992 that Attenborough's puppet had hardly appeared at all in the two most recent series. 'He stopped being a regular character,' Law explained, 'because the overuse of his tear mechanism began rotting the puppet.'

Reported in the *Independent* (14 November 1992).

Telegrams and messages

3 The Marquess of Salisbury once sent a telegram to his heir, Viscount Cranborne, at the family seat in Dorset. It read simply: 'CRANBORNE. CRANBORNE. ARRIVING 6.30 SALISBURY. SALISBURY.'

Told in a letter to *The Times* (15 April 1985).

4 When the comedian Eddie Cantor heard that Norma Shearer, the actress wife of Irving Thalberg, had produced a son, he sent a telegram of the utmost point to the noted Jewish film producer: 'Congratulations on your latest production. Am sure it will look better after it's been cut.'

Told in Max Wilk, *The Wit and Wisdom of Hollywood* (1972).

5 Just after the Second World War, Billy Wilder's wife informed him from Paris that her accommodation did not have a bidet and would he send her one. He cabled a reply: 'UNABLE OBTAIN BIDET. SUGGEST HANDSTAND IN SHOWER.'

Originally told in Tom Wood, *The Bright Side of Billy Wilder, Primarily* (1969), where the message begins: 'Charvet ties on way but impossible to obtain bidet. Suggest ...'

6 Sir Alec Douglas-Home (later Lord Home) once received a telegram saying, 'TO HELL WITH YOU. OFFENSIVE LETTER FOLLOWS.'

Told in William Safire, *Safire's Political Dictionary* (1978).

Ten Commandments

7 When asked by a reporter what she thought of the Ten Commandments, Sarah Bernhardt replied: 'Zey are too many.'

Recalled in *The Lyttelton Hart-Davis Letters* (for 9 November 1957).

Theatrical manner

1 In 1987, during the filming of *Cry Freedom*, Richard Attenborough stood up before a crowd of 5,000 Zimbabwean extras and called them by a term of endearment they had seldom heard outside their homes: 'Darlings!' he cried, 'Look at *me*, darlings!'

Recounted in the *Independent* (14 November 1992).

Theft

2 John Dennis, the playwright and critic (1657–1734), had invented a device for making the sound of thunder in plays, and had used it in an unsuccessful play of his own at the Drury Lane Theatre, London (in about 1700). Subsequently, at the same theatre, he saw a performance of *Macbeth*, and noted that the thunder was being produced in his special way. 'See how the rascals use me!' he stormed. 'They will not let my play run and yet they steal my thunder!'

Told in William S. Walsh, *A Handy-Book of Literary Curiosities* (1893). Hence the expression 'to steal a person's thunder' meaning 'to get in first and do whatever the other wanted to make a big impression with', particularly with regard to ideas and policies. Another version of his remark is: 'That is my thunder, by God; the villains will play my thunder, but not my plays.'

3 There were a pair of brothers who became known as 'the fabulous Mizners'. They were American eccentrics. Addison Mizner was an architect and entrepreneur; Wilson Mizner was broke, but bright and very witty. The latter was walking down the street when a burglar came up to him and said, 'Can you lend me five dollars.' And

Mizner said: 'Why – has it stopped getting dark?'

Told by William Franklyn on BBC Radio *Quote ... Unquote* (24 August 1985). This story comes from Alva Johnston, *The Legendary Mizners* (1953) which relates that the burglar comes up to Mizner for a loan and is met by the riposte: 'Doesn't it get dark any more?'

4 I went for an audition as a newsreader on Capital Radio before it started in 1973. There was a long wait during which I chatted to a secretary and to a young woman who was also in for an audition. The latter told me a story of two friends of hers whose car was stolen one night but, rather oddly, returned to them the following morning. Inside the car was a note saying, very sorry, it had been needed in an emergency, and here are two tickets for The Talk of the Town on Saturday.

So, off they trotted and, of course, when they returned home from the show they found their flat had been stripped from floor to ceiling.

From my diary entry for 6 August 1973. The young woman was Tricia Ingrams. Her story was another 'urban myth'. In Tom Burnam's *More Misinformation* (1980), he calls this 'The Repentant Car Thief' story. He notes that it is well known in the US, and that the tickets have also been for 'opera, ballet, rock concert, whatever'. He also mentions that the story has been reported from Grenoble in France.

5 In November 1982, when Sir Geoffrey Howe was Chancellor of the Exchequer, he was travelling by rail on an overnight sleeper and had his trousers stolen. He merely commented, 'I have more than one pair of trousers', and it was left to an anonymous colleague – probably a fellow member of the Cabinet – to tell him, 'I am thrilled

about the loss of your trousers ... because it revealed your human face.'

This was repeated by Lady Howe in a magazine interview two years later.

Tipping

1 The eccentric newspaper owner, James Gordon Bennett Jr let slip no opportunity to spend his money. On one occasion he gave a tip of $14,000 to the guard of the Train Bleu travelling between Paris and Monte Carlo. The guard stepped off the train forthwith, resigned his job, and opened a restaurant.

Told in David Frost and Michael Deakin, *Who Wants To Be A Millionaire?* (1983).

Titanic

2 Mrs Edmund Warre was the wife of the Headmaster of Eton at the time of the sinking of the *Titanic* in 1912. She broke the news to him with remarkable understatement: 'I am sorry to hear there has been a bad boating accident.'

Recounted by George Lyttelton in *The Lyttelton Hart-Davis Letters* (for 7 December 1955). He adds, 'She came in [to say this], quivering slightly with age and dottiness ... An odd but very characteristic way of describing the sinking of the largest ship in the world and the death of some 1500 people.'

Titles

3 When she became a life peer, Jean Barker, a former Mayor of the City of Cambridge, told Garter King of Arms that she wished to take her title from Trumpington, one of the villages in those parts and also the name of the ward she had represented for many years on the council. It transpired that the title, although unused for many

centuries, belonged to somebody else. Garter King of Arms asked the formidable lady whether there was another place near Cambridge she could call herself after. 'You don't think I am going to call myself Lady Six-Mile Bottom, do you?' she replied. In due course, she emerged as Baroness Trumpington.

Told in the *Sunday Telegraph* (7 July 1996).

Tourists

4 A tourist in Vermont inquired of a native, 'Make any difference which road I take to White River?' He received the reply: 'Not to me it don't.'

Told by John O'Byrne (November 1998).

Translations

5 A favourite story of King George V – which he never tired of hearing – concerned an English-born princess paying a visit to Uppsala Cathedral in Sweden. The Archbishop was keen to show off his knowledge of English and opened a chest of drawers in the sacristy with the words, 'I will now open these trousers and reveal some ever more precious treasures to Your Royal Highness.'

Told in Kenneth Rose, *George V* (1983).

6 In the 1960s, both in the US and UK, government funding was provided for research into computerized translation and, since the Cold War was raging, the only languages the governments were interested in supporting were English and Russian. The chief groups were at MIT and at Cambridge University. The story is told that on one occasion the saying 'the spirit is willing, but the flesh is weak' was fed into the machine and translated into Russian. It was

then translated back into English as 'the vodka's all right but the meat is bad'. Similarly, 'hydraulic ram' turned into 'water goat', and 'out of sight, out of mind' was re-translated as 'invisible lunatic'.

The second example (translated as 'invisible maniac') was quoted by Arthur Calder-Marshall in *The Listener* (23 April 1964). The first is included in Margaret Boden's *Artificial Intelligence and Natural Man* (1977). Indeed, these computer 'urban myths' certainly seem to date from the 1960s/70s. T. A. Dyer clearly remembers being told the 'invisible lunatic' one at the Mathematical Laboratory at Cambridge University, where 'some very brave men were working on the problem of computer translations' in 1961.

1 Though similar in outcome, there is also a translation story told that does not involve computers. A British businessman went on a trade visit to Moscow. The high point of his visit was to be a speech he had to give at a dinner of Russian business people. He duly slaved away at his speech and paid to have it translated into Russian. He also had a phonetic transcription made so that he would be able to speak the speech himself, although he did not understand the language.

When he arrived in Moscow, however, the businessman realized that he had neglected to put the greeting 'Ladies and gentlemen' at the start of his speech. He had no idea what the Russian for this was. Then he hit upon a plan. He went down to the lavatories in the hotel where he was staying and saw men going in one door and women in the other. He took the appropriate word from over each door and put them at the start of his speech.

It went triumphantly well, and at the conclusion he was feted by the Russians

for having spoken in their language. 'Only one thing puzzled us,' explained his host. 'We weren't terribly sure why you chose to start your speech by addressing us as "water closets" and "urinals" . . .'

I remember first hearing this in about 1960.

2 On 26 June 1963, Kennedy proclaimed a stirring slogan outside the City Hall in the Western Sector of the then newly divided city of Berlin. 'All free men, wherever they may live, are citizens of Berlin, and, therefore, as a free man, I take pride in the words *Ich bin ein Berliner.*' Ben Bradlee noted in *Conversations with Kennedy* (1975) that Kennedy had to spend 'the better part of an hour' with Frederick Vreeland and his wife before he could manage to pronounce this and the other German phrases he used. In fact, *Ich bin Berliner* would have been sufficient to convey his meaning. By saying *Ich bin ein Berliner*, Kennedy unwittingly drew attention to the fact that in Berlin, *ein Berliner* is the name given to a type of sponge cake. So it was rather as if the proud boast of free men everywhere was 'I am a doughnut.'

I first drew attention to this matter on Channel 4 TV *Countdown* in November 1984. I can't recall who put me up to it.

3 In 1965, prior to a reception for Queen Elizabeth II outside Bonn, President Lübke of West Germany attempted an English translation of '*Gleich geht es los*' ('It will soon begin'). He came out with, 'Equal goes it loose.'

Three years earlier, Lübke had greeted the President of India at an airport by asking – instead of 'How are you?' – 'Who are you?' (To which his guest naturally replied, 'I am the President of India.')

Told in *Time* (30 March 1981).

1 On his first visit to a Soviet-bloc country – Poland – President Carter wanted to make a good impression. In his prepared remarks, he told the Poles, 'I have come to learn your opinions and understand your desires for the future.' However, the official American interpreter translated these phrases, somewhat surprisingly, as, 'I desire the Poles carnally.'

Reported in the *Daily Mail* (29 December 1978). The interpreter was duly sacked.

2 The worldwide spread of the soft drinks Coca-Cola and Pepsi Cola has given rise to some difficulties in translating their slogans. It is said that 'Come alive with Pepsi' became, in German, 'Come alive out of the grave,' and, in Chinese, 'Pepsi brings your ancestors back from the dead.'

When Coca-Cola started advertising in Peking, 'Put a Smile on Your Face' came out as 'Let Your Teeth Rejoice'. Odder still, the famous slogan 'It's the Real Thing' came out as 'The Elephant Bites the Wax Duck.'

Sources: J. C. Louis and Harvey Yazijian, *The Cola Wars* (1980), and *Time* Magazine (30 March 1981).

3 An Englishwoman found the bed in her French hotel extremely uncomfortable, and put this down to the fact that the mattress was next to useless. Complaining at the reception desk, she unfortunately chose the word *matelot* for mattress. When this failed to produce the desired effect, she got very hot under the collar and shouted, *'Je demande un matelot sur mon lit!'*

When the hotel proprietor was told of this somewhat bizarre demand, she commented, *'Ah, les anglais! Quelle nation maritime!'*

Told by Eleanor Bron on BBC Radio *Quote ... Unquote* (13 December 1986). I had earlier encountered a version told about an Afrikaans-speaking South African couple on their honeymoon in Amsterdam ...

4 The English-language version of a car-rental firm's brochure in Tokyo exhorted hirers thus: 'When passenger of foot heave in sight, tootle the horn. Trumpet him melodiously at first, but if he still obstacles your passage, then tootle him with vigour.'

Told in the *Independent* (12 August 1993).

5 A story is told by British members of the European Parliament about the day when a pompous French politician stood up and held forth at great length about *'la sagesse normande* [the sagacity of the French]'. Unfortunately, the simultaneous translation for the benefit of non-French speakers rendered the pompous phrase as 'Norman Wisdom.' The more the British laughed at the idea, the more irate the Frenchman became, repeating the line again and again.

Told by Antony Jay on BBC Radio *Quote ... Unquote* (8 May 1998).

Travellers

6 *Eothen* is an account of A. W. King-lake's travels in the Middle East when he was about twenty-six years old in the early nineteenth century. One of the most extraordinary encounters he describes is in the Sinai Desert with a British army officer returning from India to England. They were both

riding camels. Not having been introduced, the two gentlemen were not minded to speak, but their servants did chat to each other. Kinglake takes up the anecdote: 'The masters, therefore, had no sooner passed each other, than their respective servants quietly stopped, and entered into conversation. As soon as my camel found that her companions were not following her, she caught the social feeling and refused to go on. I felt the absurdity of the situation, and determined to accost the stranger, if only to avoid the awkwardness of remaining stuck fast in the Desert, whilst our servants were amusing themselves.'

The other master had similar thoughts, and the two turned their camels and rode back toward each other: 'He was the first to speak; too courteous to address me as if he admitted the possibility of my wishing to accost him from any feeling of mere sociability, or civilian-like love of vain talk; he at once attributed my advances to a laudable wish of acquiring statistical information, and, accordingly, when we got within speaking distance, he said, "I dare say, you wish to know how the Plague is going on at Cairo?"'

From A.W. Kinglake, *Eothen*, Chap. 17, 'The Desert' (1844).

1 After somewhat improbable rumours had been circulating that he was to marry Violet Trefusis, the 'friend' of Virginia Woolf and Vita Sackville-West, Lord Berners put a notice of his travels in the newspapers, as was then the custom. It read, 'Lord Berners has left Lesbos for the Isle of Man.'

Told in the *Sunday Telegraph* (11 September 1983).

2 In the 1930s and 40s, the Questors Theatre in the London suburb of Ealing established a reputation for outstanding (what would now be called) fringe theatre. Ralph Macdonald Hastings, playwright and critic, was one critic who rather resented being dragged away from the traditional beat of Shaftesbury Avenue and the West End. In a memo to the editor of the *Daily Express*, he wrote: 'Sir, I respectfully submit that I am your dramatic critic for London, not Asia Minor.'

Recounted by Adam Benedick in the *Independent* (4 March 1991). Compare the story told about A. B. Walkley of *The Times*: according to *The Lyttelton Hart-Davis Letters* (for 19 February 1956), he was sent tickets for a play at Richmond, and returned them to the editor with a note saying, 'I was engaged as *The Times* dramatic critic for central London, not for Asia Minor.' And James Agate's version (from *Ego 4*, for 25 July 1938): 'Richmond Theatre. This is what Basil [sic] Macdonald Hastings called being the dramatic critic for Asia Minor.' Basil (1881–1928) was presumably the father of Ralph, and also combined precariously the two professions of playwright and critic.

Trends

3 At lunch in the New York restaurant, La Grenouille, matters were not helped by the fact that Liza Minelli apparently mistook her host, Diana Vreeland, the editor of *Vogue*, for the PR woman of the Plaza Hotel. Accordingly, at the end of the meal, Minelli bade Vreeland farewell with the words, 'Please say hello to Ed, the piano player, for me' – the 'Ed' in question being featured in the Oak Room Bar of the Plaza Hotel. Vreeland was mystified by this but couldn't bring herself to accept that Minelli had failed to recognize her. So

she went back to the *Vogue* office and upbraided her staff for not keeping her abreast of the latest slang. 'Say hello to Ed the piano player' subsequently appeared in several editions of *Vogue* as a trendy way to say 'goodbye'.

Recounted in the *Independent* Magazine (2 September 1989) as having taken place 'about 20 years ago . . .'

Truth

1 Probably the most famous anecdote about absolutely anybody is the one about George Washington and the cherry tree. When, as a boy, he was asked how a certain cherry tree had come to be cut down, he looked 'at his father with the sweet face of youth brightened with the inexpressible charm of all-conquering truth, [and] he bravely cried out: "I can't tell a lie. I did cut it with my hatchet."'

As told by Mason Locke Weems, Washington's first popular biographer, in *The Life of George Washington: With Curious Anecdotes Equally Honorable to Himself and Exemplary to His Young Countrymen* (1800). Sometimes the admission is remembered as, 'Father, I cannot tell a lie. I did it with my little axe.' A tale almost certainly invented by Weems.

2 On 18 November 1986, Sir Robert Armstrong, then the British Cabinet Secretary, was being cross-examined in the Supreme Court of New South Wales. The British government was attempting to prevent publication in Australia of the book *Spycatcher* about MI5, the British secret service. Defence counsel Malcolm Turnbull asked Sir Robert about the contents of a letter he had written that had been intended to convey a misleading impression.

'What's a "misleading impression"?' inquired Turnbull. 'A sort of bent un-truth?' Sir Robert replied: 'It is perhaps being economical with the truth.'

This explanation was greeted with derision not only in the court but in the world beyond, and it looked as if a new euphemism for lying had been coined. In fact, Sir Robert had prefaced his remark with: 'As one person said . . .' and, when the court apparently found cause for laughter in what he said, added: 'It is not very original, I'm afraid.'

Indeed not. The Earl of Dalkeith MP had referred to Harold Wilson's 1967 post-devaluation broadcast in a House of Commons question (4 July 1968): 'Would he openly admit that he either made a gross miscalculation, misled the people, or at least had been over-economical with the truth?' Dr E. H. H. Green, writing to the *Guardian* on 4 February 1987, said he had found a note penned by Sir William Strang, later to become head of the Foreign Office, in February 1942. Describing the character of the exiled Czech President Beneš, Strang had written: 'Dr Beneš's methods are exasperating; he is a master of representation and . . . he is apt to be economical with the truth.'

The notion thus appears to have been a familiar one in the British Civil Service for a very long time. Samuel Pepys apparently used the precise phrase in his evidence before the Brooke House Committee in its examination of the Navy Board in 1669–70.

Mark Twain wrote, 'Truth is the most valuable thing we have. Let us economize it.' – *Following the Equator* (1897).

In March 1988, Armstrong said in a TV interview that he had no regrets about having used the phrase. And he said again, it was not his own, indeed, but Edmund Burke's. The reference was to Burke's *Two Letters on Proposals for Peace* (1796): 'Falsehood and delusion are allowed in no case whatsoever. But, as in the exercise of all the virtues, there is an economy of truth.'

Twerps

1 A man called T. W. Earp matriculated at Exeter College, Oxford, in 1911 and became President of the Oxford Union after the First World War. He was, so it seems, the very opposite of a rugby-playing 'hearty'. Roy Campbell (in Portugal, 1957) spoke of Earp kindling 'Goering-like wrath ... in the hearts of the rugger-playing stalwarts of Oxford ... by being the last, most charming, and wittiest of the "decadents".'

Romilly John in *The Seventh Child* (1932) provides a description of Earp as a soft-spoken, gently humorous man, his hair close-cropped, his head shaped like a vegetable, 'who had taken his lack of ambition to the extreme of becoming an art critic' – or, at least, this is how the information appears in Vol. 2 of *Augustus John* (1975) by Michael Holroyd.

Anthony Powell in *Messengers of Day* (1978) adds that Earp had a 'thin, trembling voice'. As he had been ineligible for military service in the First World War, he had remained at Oxford and become secretary and almost sole member of every conceivable Oxford club.

I don't know whether any of the foregoing is relevant but *The Oxford English Dictionary* (Second Edition) produces a couple of citations (one, be it noted, from J. R. R. Tolkien) to demonstrate that this man gave rise to the use of the word *twerp* to mean a 'foolish fellow'. It is still not totally clear what Mr Earp really did to make his unfortunate gift to nomenclature.

If indeed he did – it is not proven. The Speaker of the House of Commons added the word 'twerp' to the list of unparliamentary expressions in May 1987.

U

Underestimation

1 On arriving in Hollywood, Fred Astaire had to undergo the usual screen test. The verdict? 'Can't act. Slightly bald. Can dance a little.'

Told in David Niven, *Bring On the Empty Horses* (1975). Ned Sherrin's *Theatrical Anecdotes* (1991) has the additional information that the test was for RKO in 1933 and that the test report also stated: 'Enormous ears and bad chin-line [but] his charm is tremendous.'

2 When Bill Fraser was waiting to be demobbed at the end of the Second World War, he formed a touring company to keep the troops entertained. By the time he got back to camp, he found he'd been demobbed two weeks previously. 'Well, Fraser,' his CO said, 'What are you going to do in civvy street?' 'The theatre,' Fraser replied. 'Oh dear, dear. They've blown up all the piers, haven't they?'

Fraser's own version appeared in the *Radio Times* (24 January 1974).

3 When the British disc jockey Chris Evans decided to pull out of his popular breakfast-time slot on BBC Radio 1, he did so in controversial circumstances. Matthew Bannister, the BBC chief who had first brought him to the station, sought to pour oil on the troubled waters. Whether the statement he issued helped in this task, is another matter. It stated of Evans that 'his contribution cannot be underestimated'.

Told in the *Independent* (22 January 1997).

Undertakers

4 One day the comedian and writer Spike Milligan walked into an undertakers' shop in Camden Town, lay down on the floor and cried, 'Shop!'

Recounted by Jimmy Grafton in *The Goon Show Companion* (1976).

Vice-Presidency

1 Vice-President John Nance Garner was walking down the halls of the Capitol at a time when the circus was in Washington DC. A fellow came up to him and introduced himself. 'I am the head clown in the circus,' he said. Very solemnly, Garner replied, 'And I am the Vice-President of the United States. You'd better stick around here a while. You might pick up some new ideas.'

Theo Lippman Jr in *The San Francisco Chronicle* (25 December 1992) provided this story. Garner (1868–1967) was Vice-President from 1933 to 1941 during F. D. Roosevelt's first two terms. He famously said of his job that it wasn't 'worth a pitcher of warm piss' – though this was quickly bowdlerized to 'warm spit'.

Visitors

2 As a young man, Denton Welch paid a visit to the painter Walter Sickert, and later wrote a description of the oddities he had encountered. The great man persecuted and terrified him and, during tea, danced in front of him wearing boots 'such as deep sea divers wear ... to see how Denton would react to the experience' (in Edith Sitwell's phrase). As Welch left the house, Sickert said to him, 'Come again when you can't stay so long.'

Denton Welch's 'Sickert at St Peter's' appeared in *Horizon*, Vol. vi, No. 32 (1942). In *Taken Care of* (1965), Edith Sitwell commented on the article but gave the tag as, 'Come again – when you have a little less time.' Either way, this farewell was not originated by Sickert. Indeed, Welch ends his article by saying, 'And at these words a strange pang went through me, for it was what my father had always said as he closed the book, when I had finished my bread and butter and milk, and it was time for bed.'

3 After a dull weekend, Mrs Patrick Campbell took pen in hand and wrote in the hostess's elaborate visitor's book, 'Quoth the raven ...'

Told in Bennett Cerf, *Shake Well Before Using* (1948). But often attributed to other performers, especially John Barrymore.

4 Comedians Morecambe and Wise were often faced with the difficult task of what to write in the visitors' books that theatrical landladies traditionally asked their guests to sign. If they did not like the digs, Morecambe and Wise would settle for the wonderfully equivocal: 'We shall certainly tell our friends.'

Recounted by Norman Vaughan on BBC Radio *Where Were You in '62?* (2 August 1983).

Voices

1 On a tour of Australia with Katharine Hepburn, Robert Helpmann began to tire of Hepburn's incessant chatter, not to mention her characteristic accent. Seeking to get away from her, Helpmann went off to the beach and was really enjoying himself when suddenly he heard her calling him, 'Barb! Barb!' He told himself he mustn't look. 'Barb! Barb!' came the cry again. Helpmann thought this was just too much. He opened his eyes and saw – 'Barb! Barb!' – that it was a kookaburra.

Told by Victor Spinetti on BBC Radio *Quote . . . Unquote* (20 November 1990).

2 The pot calling the kettle black, etc.: when it was suggested to Edith Evans that Kenneth Williams should be cast in a play with her, she told the impresario that she viewed this with great apprehension. 'Why him?' she asked. 'Well, he's right for the role.' 'But he's got such a peculiar vooooiiiiicccce!'

Told to me by Kenneth Williams on 29 October 1964, when I was interviewing him for an Oxford undergraduate publication. In *The Kenneth Williams Diaries* (1993), he reports it a year earlier on 24 October 1963 as 'a story going round'. In that version the impresario is named as Binkie Beaumont. Williams adds: 'It's only funny when the impersonation of her is good.'

3 The newspaper columnist Jean Rook once memorably described Barry Manilow's voice as sounding like 'a bluebottle caught in the curtains'.

Told in Lynn Barber, *Mostly Men* (1991).

Votes

4 On 18 March 1931, Stanley Baldwin attacked the press lords during a by-election campaign in London. He said: 'The papers conducted by Lord Rothermere and Lord Beaverbrook are not newspapers in the ordinary acceptance of the term. They are engines of propaganda, for the constantly changing policies, desires, personal wishes, personal likes and dislikes of two men . . . What the proprietorship of these papers is aiming at is power, and power without responsibility – the prerogative of the harlot throughout the ages.'

Harold Macmillan, who had been sitting on the platform for the meeting, recalled how his father-in-law, the Duke of Devonshire, exclaimed at this point in Baldwin's speech: 'Good God, that's done it, he's lost us the tarts' vote.'

Baldwin's cousin, Rudyard Kipling, had originated the 'harlot' criticism many years previously. He had also already used it in argument with Beaverbrook. Source for the Devonshire story mislaid.

Vows

5 A young nun enters an order that operates a strict vow of silence. She is told that the vow can only be broken once every three years, and then only by the use of two words. So, after the first three years, the girl goes to the Mother Superior and says: 'Uncomfortable beds'. The Mother Superior replies, 'Right, my child, you have had your say and now must return to your duties.'

Three more years pass and again the nun has the opportunity to say two words to the Mother Superior.

'Bad food,' she says. 'Right,' says the Mother Superior, 'you may return to your work.'

Another three years pass and the no-longer young nun returns again to the Mother Superior and announces – in more than two words – 'I wish to go home.'

'Thank goodness,' replies the Mother Superior, 'you've done nothing but bitch since you got here ...'

This story is told as an example of a joke in John Osborne's play *Hotel in Amsterdam* (1968). In a version about a monastery, it is told by Lord Delfont in *Pass the Port* (1976).

Waiters

1 A classic eavesdropping was collected
by Gilbert Harding when, having
arrived at a restaurant well after last
orders had been taken, he persuaded
the staff to find him something to
eat. Just as he was digesting the last
morsel, he overheard one waiter say to
another, incredulously, 'He's eaten it!'

Told by Spike Milligan on BBC Radio
Quote ... Unquote (1 January 1979) – giving
the impression that he had been told the
tale by Harding himself concerning an
incident when food was in short supply after
the Second World War. The same story was
told by Brigadier Sir Otho Prior-Palmer in
Pass the Port (1976), without mention of
Harding. In Michael Pertwee, *Name
Dropping* (1974), there is this: 'I vividly
recall one story [Compton Mackenzie] told.
He was sitting in the Café Royal, dining
alone. Near him, leaning against a pillar,
was a waiter. A second waiter approached
the first waiter, looked surreptitiously all
round, then whispered confidentially:
'Well ... He's eaten it.'

One more spotting: Robin Ray wrote to
The Sunday Times (10 September 1995):
'A friend of mine was seated in a busy
restaurant at the worst table, next to the
door leading to the kitchen. None the less
he was in a favourable position to overhear
the following exchange between two waiters,
one embarking with full plates, the other
returning with empty ones. In obvious
reference to a difficult customer, the waiter
with the empty plates raised a smile from
his colleague by muttering just three words:
"He's eaten it!"'

My response appeared in the paper the
following week: 'If Robin Ray is who I
think he is, then he would appear to have
inherited his father [the comedian] Ted
Ray's incomparable memory for old jokes.
The story he attributes to "a friend" was
ascribed by Spike Milligan to Gilbert
Harding on my radio show in 1979.
However, the real origin probably lies in a
Punch cartoon by G. L. Stampa that
appeared on 16 May 1934. "He's eaten it!"
was the caption below a picture of two
waiters and a diner.'

Wales and Welshness

2 In 1837, William Day, an assistant
poor-law commissioner, was looking
into poor-law provision in the Bala area
of Wales. He wrote back to his office:
'Half Welsh though I am myself, yet
I confess that if those whom I have
lately met are samples of the ancient
Britons, I can but think it a great pity
that the Danes did not destroy the
whole race. Mrs Day says they have
only so far removed from the savage
state as to have lost the only virtue of
savages – hospitality.'

From correspondence in the Public Record
Office (Ref. MH 32/14). Quoted in
Anthony Brundage, *The Making of the
New Poor Law 1832–39* (1978).

1 Where did Welshmen get their names
from? And why do so many end up
with the same few ones? An anonymous
nineteenth-century comic verse tells of
a judge sorting out a crowd of people
in his court and coming to a sensible
conclusion:

> Then strove the judge with main
> and might
> The sounding consonants to write.
> But when the day was almost gone
> He found his work not nearly done,
> His ears assailed most woefully
> With names like Rhys ap Griffith
> Ddu,
> Aneirin, Iorwerth, Ieuan Goch
> And Llywarch Hen o Abersoch,
> Taliesin ap Llewelyn Fawr
> And Llun ap Arthur bach y Cawr.
> Until at length, in sheer despair,
> He doffed his wig and tore his hair
> And said he would no longer stand
> The surnames of our native land.
> Take ten, he said, and call them
> Rice;
> Take other ten and call them Price;
> Take fifty others call them Pughs,
> A hundred more I'll dub them
> Hughes;
> Now Roberts name some hundred
> score
> And Williams name a legion more.
> And call, he moaned in languid
> tone
> Call all the other thousands –
> Jones.

Told in Trevor Fishlock, *Wales and the Welsh*
(1972).

2 According to a newspaper report, the
poet Dylan Thomas was once asked
what his thoughts were on the subject
of Welsh nationalism. Evidently,
Thomas 'replied with three words, two

of which were Welsh nationalism'.

Told by Charles Causley on BBC Radio
Quote ... Unquote (19 January 1982).

War

3 A somewhat effete Englishman was
asked what it had been like to be in the
midst of battle. Replied he: 'Oh, my
dear fellow, the noise ... and the
people!'

According to the *Oxford Dictionary of
Quotations* (1979), quoting the *Hudson
Review* (Winter, 1951), a certain Captain
Strahan said this after the Battle of Bastogne
in 1944. Various correspondents have
suggested it was earlier in the war than that,
however. Roy T. Kendall wrote (1986):
'I heard this phrase used, in a humorous
manner, during the early part of 1942. It
was related to me as having been said by a
young Guards officer, newly returned from
Dunkirk, who on being asked what it was
like used the expression: the inference
being, a blasé attitude to the dangers and
a disdain of the common soldiery he was
forced to mix with.' Tony Bagnall Smith
added that the Guards officer was still
properly dressed and equipped when
he said it, and that his reply was: 'My
dear, the noise and the people – how they
smelt!'
    The *ODQ* (1992 edition) appears to have
come round to the earlier use regarding
Dunkirk. It finds it in the form 'The noise,
my dear! And the people!' already being
quoted in Anthony Rhodes, *Sword of Bone*,
Chap. 22 (1942).
    Another originator of the remark is said
to be Lord Sefton, a Guards officer at
Dunkirk (suggested in correspondence in
The London Review of Books beginning
29 October 1998). In the same correspondence, an assertion reappeared that it had
been something said by the actor Ernest
Thesiger at a dinner party in 1919 regarding
his experiences as a soldier in the battle of
the Somme ...

Weather

1 A few hours before a devastating storm broke over southeastern England in October 1987, Michael Fish reassured BBC TV viewers: 'A woman rang to say she'd heard there was a hurricane on the way. Well, don't worry. There isn't.' Technically he was right – it wasn't a hurricane – but few noticed the difference.

Told in the *Observer* (19 October 1987).

2 Another legendary TV weather forecaster – not Fish – was distracted by a letter falling off the map, in the days when weather maps were actually in front of the camera rather than electronically generated. The first letter of the word 'FOG' had disappeared, and the forecaster duly apologized for the 'F in Fog'.

Oral tradition.

Whereabouts

3 After producing the play *The Faithful Shepherdess* by John Fletcher (1579–1625), Sir Thomas Beecham received a letter from the Inland Revenue seeking information of regarding Fletcher's whereabouts for the purposes of taxation. 'I was able to reply that to the best of my knowledge his present residence was the South Aisle of Southwark Cathedral, and I went on to venture the opinion that he might find some difficulty in changing it.'

Told in *Beecham Stories* (ed. Atkins and Newman, 1978). Beecham arranged music for several productions of Fletcher's plays, and gave the Oxford Romanes Lecture on the playwright in 1956. His grave bears an inscription from another of Fletcher's plays.

Wigs

4 An anxious actor rushed up to Noël Coward after a dress rehearsal and demanded, 'Could you see my wig-join?' Replied Coward, 'Perfectly, dear boy, perfectly.'

Source untraced.

5 When Brendan Bracken became Minister of Information in the Second World War, a journalist told him, 'I don't believe a word you say, Brendan. Everything about you is phoney. Even your hair, which looks like a wig, isn't.'

Told in Charles Edward Lysaght, *Brendan Bracken* (1979). This may possibly be based on what the journalist Claud Cockburn wrote in *Crossing the Line* (1958): 'A wartime Minister of Information is compelled, in the national interest, to such continuous acts of duplicity that even his natural hair must grow to resemble a wig.' Brendan Bracken (1st Viscount Bracken) (1901–58), Irish journalist and Conservative politician, was a close associate of Winston Churchill who, on this account, some held must have been his father.

6 The popular journalist Godfrey Winn went to interview Bernard Braden and his wife, Barbara Kelly, in the early 1950s. He arrived bearing pencil and pad, and a square cardboard box, which the Bradens' children suspected might contain something for them. They were to be disappointed. When the interview was over, Winn summoned a photographer and a make-up girl. The latter did her stuff and then opened the cardboard box, lifting out a toupee that she then placed on Winn's head.

Related by Bernard Braden in *The Kindness of Strangers* (1990). I can vouch for the likelihood of this story. In 1967, as researcher on a Granada TV programme called

X Plus Ten, I entered a TV make-up room just as Winn's portable hairpiece (merely a quiff at the front by this time) was being delicately lowered into position.

1 Once, when filming in Africa, the TV journalist Reginald Bosanquet had to stoop to enter a mud hut. The cameraman who was following him – possibly Cyril Page – suddenly became aware of a fearsome hairy beast on the floor and stamped heavily upon it. Reggie complained vociferously that his hairpiece was ruined and he wouldn't be able to wear it before the camera.

Told at ITN in about 1967. And, no, I'm not going to repeat the story about the nude photographs taken of Reggie when he was swimming in Loch Ness while making a report on the monster.

Wills

2 Documentary evidence of William Shakespeare's life is slight. One of the very few items that would seem to prove that somebody of that name existed is his will dated 1616, the year he died. The best remembered clause in the will is: 'Item I give unto my wife my second best bed with the furniture.'

But what is the implication, if any? 'Second best' here means 'next in quality to the first' and need not necessarily suggest that Shakespeare was snubbing his wife with the bequest. Peter Levi, *The Life and Times of William Shakespeare* (1988) has this comment: 'Much crazy speculation has been raised on this small foundation. It is true that most wills provide for widows and this does not, but the reason is obvious. John Hall and Susanna [son-in-law and daughter] were to move into New Place [the Stratford-upon-Avon home] and look after Anne Shakespeare as they were uniquely fitted to do. The "second best bed" was William and Anne's old marriage bed. The grander New

Place bed in the best bedroom must go to John Hall and Susanna, but William remembered at the last moment to reserve his wife's bed, in which she no doubt habitually slept, for her own.' Garry O'Connor, *William Shakespeare* (1991) adds: 'Anne had asked for this, which otherwise would have gone to Susanna. A correspondent in *The Times* in 1977 suggests that this is roughly similar to a modern testator who, having disposed of the bulk of his estate, turns to his solicitor and says, "And don't forget to leave Anne the mini."'

Windbags

3 At Ascot one year, Lady Astor told the Duke of Roxburghe, 'You are really becoming too grand for words ... never leaving the royal stand. You might just as well be the court dentist.' To which Roxburghe retorted, 'If ever I do have to pull out the King's teeth, I shall certainly come to you for the gas.'

Told by Kenneth Rose in *King George V* (1984).

4 A hostess dealt with a maddeningly garrulous guest by sharply saying to him: 'While you've got your mouth open, would you ask the maid to serve dinner?'

Told to me by Miss V. Ruth Bennett of Swindon (1980).

5 A patrician lady in her country house invited an extremely boring and loquacious gentleman to come and pay her a visit. He ended up trapping her in a corner and talking and talking and talking to her. After a while, she said, 'How very interesting, my dear. Why don't you go away and write it all down?'

Told by Dr John Rae on BBC Radio *Quote ... Unquote* (30 July 1983).

Word-counts

1 I once saw in a book of 'amazing facts' a report to the effect that although the American Bill of Rights contains 463 words, the Ten Commandments 297 words, and Lincoln's Gettysburg Address a mere 266, an EEC directive on butter contained no less than 26,911 words ...

At once, I knew this to be untrue. Not that I checked whether there was any such EEC directive. It is simply that this 'fact' is merely a colourful jibe at bureaucracy in general and has been around for a very long time. Max Hall in 'The Great Cabbage Hoax: A Case Study' (*Journal of Personality and Social Psychology*, 1965, Vol. 2, No. 4) made a thorough survey of its origins. This was a follow-up to his original 1954 study. The origins seemed to lie with the US Office of Price Administration during the Second World War, though the joke really only began to spread wildly in 1951, during US involvement in the Korean War. Numerous examples were found in press and broadcasting of the rumour that the then Office of Price Stabilization had a 26,911-word cabbage order. This was compared with the brevity of the Gettysburg Address, the Ten Commandments and the Declaration of Independence. In another version, the cabbage order became a 12,962-word regulation on manually operated foghorns.

As with rumours of a more inflammatory kind, is it not amazing that such a story can keep on turning up – even when the true facts have been established? There was never any cabbage order of any kind from the OPA or the OPS.

Writers and writing

2 Edward Gibbon presented a copy of the first volume of his *Decline and Fall of the Roman Empire* to the 1st Duke of Gloucester. When the second volume came out, Gibbon did likewise. The Duke appeared to be pleased by the presentation, but commented: 'Another damned, thick, square book! Always scribble, scribble, scribble! Eh! Mr Gibbon?'

Told in Henry Beste, *Personal and Literary Memorials* (1829). Also ascribed to King George III and to a Duke of Cumberland.

3 There are those who insist that *The Case-Book of Sherlock Holmes* (1927) shows a marked falling off in the standard of Conan Doyle's story-telling. Some would say that the rot had set in even earlier. Howard Haycraft in *Murder for Pleasure: the Life and Times of the Detective Story* (1942) comments: '*The Return of Sherlock Holmes* was purchasable on both sides of the Atlantic in 1905. The reading public was properly grateful and would not for any known worlds have had matters otherwise. And yet – the reception of the new tales was not entirely unmixed. Doyle enjoyed relating a homely incident that expressed the state of the popular mind neatly, "I think, sir," he quoted a Cornish boatman as saying to him, "when Holmes fell over that cliff he may not have killed himself, but he was never quite the same man afterwards."'

4 An as-yet untraced example of screenwriter's fatuousness was quoted by Chris Langham on BBC Radio *Quote ... Unquote* (5 June 1998), though in fact he reported the line of dialogue as lip-read from an actor in a silent epic: 'Men of the Middle Ages, tomorrow sees the beginning of the Hundred Years' War.'

Probably apocryphal – indeed, it may be no more than a development of a joke ending for a play, as told by Max Beerbohm to his actor brother Herbert Beerbohm Tree and recorded in Hesketh Pearson, *Lives of the Wits* (1962): 'Herbert ... howled with laughter when Max suggested an effective line to bring the curtain down on a play, "Where are you going?" asks the sorrowful heroine. "I am going to the Thirty Years' War," answers the distraught hero.'

1 The Marx Brothers were famous for taking liberties with the scripts of the stage shows they performed, often working up the material for transfer to their films. At a rehearsal of the film *Animal Crackers* for which he wrote the script, George S. Kaufman suddenly erupted with: 'Excuse me for interrupting, but I actually thought I heard a line I wrote.'

Told in Scott Meredith, *George S. Kaufman and the Algonquin Round Table* (1974). In fact, the remark probably dates from the days of the stage version of *The Cocoanuts* (also subsequently filmed). In *Harpo Speaks* (1961), the silent one recalls: 'We were a hit ... But we still didn't know George well enough. He came backstage with his chin on his chest and said that Act One seemed to be all right, but Act Two needed another cut. Somewhere in the middle of Act Two – he wasn't exactly sure where – he could have sworn he heard one of his original lines.' In Arthur Marx, *Son of Groucho* (1973), Kaufman turns to Alexander Woollcott at a stage performance of the show and says, 'Be quiet a minute, Alex – I think I just heard one of the original lines.'

2 In 1960, Dirk Bogarde played the title role in the Hollywood biopic *Liszt*. As he tells it, one of the lines that some screenwriter had toiled over for the script was: 'Hiya, Chopin, this is my friend George Sand. She's a great friend of Beethoven's.' However, Bogarde seems to have been successful in mocking the line, as it does not appear in the finished film.

Recounted by Bogarde in *Snakes and Ladders* (1978), the second volume of his autobiography.

3 Told that Nancy Mitford was staying at a friend's house in order to finish a book, Edith Evans remarked, 'Oh, really? What exactly is she reading?'

I put this in my book *Quote ... Unquote* (1978), source forgotten. Alexander Walker, in a letter to me (dated 23 September 1985), claimed to have overheard Evans saying it to Katharine Hepburn during the filming of *The Madwoman of Chaillot* (in about 1968).

4 When Harold Pinter received the David Cohen Literature Prize in 1995, he made a speech in which he said: 'In a career attended by a great deal of dramatic criticism one of the most interesting – and indeed acute – critical questions I've ever heard was when I was introduced to a young woman and her six-year-old son. The woman looked down at her son and said: "This man is a very good writer." The little boy looked at me and then at his mother and said: "Can he do a 'W'?"'

Recounted in *The Author* (Summer 1997). John Lahr told the tale on BBC Radio *Quote ... Unquote* (24 July 1980).

5 The Australian entertainer Barry Humphries in his persona of 'Dame Edna Everage' is able to make sharp points that perhaps – and only perhaps – he might not make directly to people if speaking as himself. To Melvyn Bragg, when no one in the audience admitted to having read any of his novels, he/she said: 'You're going to have to slow down. We can't keep up with you!'

On the TV show *An Audience With Dame Edna Everage* (in about 1981). Michael Coveney in an article on Humphries in the *Observer* Magazine (16 March 1997) gave the line as: 'Why do you do it, Melvyn, why go to all that bother for so little recognition?' Coveney added: 'Bragg had no choice but to crease his face in signs of hysterical laughter, along with everyone else. He might have been weeping inside.'

Yes-persons

1 To impresario Lew Grade is ascribed the remark: 'I can't stand the suspense of waiting for someone to say yes.'

Told in the *Guardian* (23 April 1995).

Zoology

2 David Attenborough tells a lovely story of the time when he had made a TV natural-history programme that involved the re-creation of a pterodactyl. A radio-controlled model of this long-extinct prehistoric bird was made and then filmed apparently flying over the cliffs in Dorset. At the end of the day, Attenborough was due back in London to attend a charity event in aid of some conservation body. Greeted by one of the organizers ('who might have been a duchess, or if she wasn't she certainly looked like one'), he was asked what wonderful things from the natural world he had recently been filming. 'By golly, I'm going to shake her,' thought Attenborough, and proceeded to tell the putative duchess that, earlier in the day, he had actually been filming a pterodactyl flying above the cliffs of Dorset. Was she impressed? 'Oh yes,' she said, 'they are so lovely, aren't they?'

Told on BBC Radio *Quote… Unquote* (11 May 1993). I am including this Attenborough story as a way of saluting the man I consider to be the best anecdotalist I have ever encountered. Perhaps unsuspected by viewers of his mighty natural-history TV programmes, Attenborough has a wonderful ability to tell a story like this and, indeed, to re-tell it on demand. I first discovered his anecdotal skill when he came to speak to an undergraduate society at Oxford in November 1965. Over dinner he told a story about the early days of television, involving a woman TV announcer, a studio manager and a programme on the artificial insemination of cows. Unfortunately, as it involves a certain visual gesture, it defies representation here, but David Attenborough repeated it with just as much effect when we moved on from dinner to the undergraduate meeting he was addressing. He has a rare skill.

Index

This index is to prominent names occurring in the anecdotes and in the background notes. It also provides a general guide to subjects and themes within the anecdotes. '55:7' indicates that the relevant anecdote is number 7 on page 55.